*The Variety of
American Evangelicalism*

The Variety of American Evangelicalism

Edited by Donald W. Dayton
and Robert K. Johnston

The University of Tennessee Press
KNOXVILLE

Library of Congress Cataloging in Publication Data

The Variety of American evangelicalism / edited by
    Donald W. Dayton and Robert K. Johnston. — 1st ed.
        p.   cm.
    Includes bibliographical references and index.
    ISBN 0-87049-659-x (cloth: alk. paper)
        1. Evangelicalism—United States.   2. United States—Church
history.   I. Dayton, Donald W.   II. Johnston, Robert K., 1945–
BR1642.U5V38   1991
277.3'082—dc20   90-36516   CIP

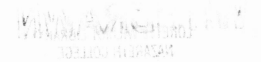

Contents

1. Introduction
   Robert K. Johnston and Donald W. Dayton   1

2. Premillennialism and the Branches of Evangelicalism
   Timothy P. Weber   5

3. Fundamentalism and American Evangelicalism
   George M. Marsden   22

4. The Limits of Evangelicalism: The Pentecostal Tradition
   Donald W. Dayton   36

5. Adventism
   Russell L. Staples   57

6. The Theological Identity of the North American
   Holiness Movement
   Paul Merritt Bassett   72

7. Are Restorationists Evangelicals?
   Richard T. Hughes   109

8. Black Religion and the Question of Evangelical Identity
   Milton G. Sernett   135

9. Baptists and Evangelicals
   Eric H. Ohlmann   148

10. Pietism: Theology in Service of Living Toward God
    C. John Weborg   161

11. Evangelicalism: A Mennonite Critique
    C. Norman Kraus   184

12. Evangelicals and the Self-Consciously Reformed
    Mark A. Noll and Cassandra Niemczyk   204

13. Lutheranism
Mark Ellingsen   222

14. Some Doubts about the Usefulness of the Category "Evangelical"
Donald W. Dayton   245

15. American Evangelicalism: An Extended Family
Robert K. Johnston   252

Contributors   273

Index   279

The Variety of
American Evangelicalism

CHAPTER I

Introduction

Robert K. Johnston and Donald W. Dayton

In his essay, "'No Offense: I Am an Evangelical': A Search for Self-Definition," David Wells describes an idealized American evangelicalism of thirty
years ago.[1] He portrays a united front, rallying behind the Billy Graham
Crusades, working together under the aegis of the National Association
of Evangelicals, and finding intellectual coherence in *Christianity Today*
and its first editor, Carl F.H. Henry. Wells bemoans the fact that today
evangelicalism seems but a sprawling empire, frequently at odds with itself, its cohesion and intellectual coherence in jeopardy. But, as Thomas
Askew remarked in his reply to Wells, at the very conference where the
essay was presented:

> Wells' assertion probably applies only to a particular brand of evangelicals,
> those primarily associated with Calvinistic Presbyterian and Baptist networks,
> and especially those found in the North and West. I see the evangelical faith
> and motif as a much broader tradition or current in American church history,
> one with a dozen substreams and marked by great diversity. Fundamentalism
> is merely one exclusivistic subculture within that stream.[2]

In the chapters that follow, essayist after essayist will show that Wells' sprawling empire never has been as united or as clearly defined as Wells might desire.
Instead, what one discovers is the variety of American evangelicalism.

What's in a name—or, in this case, a title? The difficulty we have had
in finding a title for this volume reflects the complexity of the subject itself. "The Variety of American Evangelicalism." "Varieties of American
Evangelicalism." "Charting the Uncharted." "The Limits of Evangelicalism." "American Evangelicalism?" As Timothy Weber suggests in his essay
in this volume, "Defining evangelicalism has become one of the biggest
problems in American religious historiography." Anyone who has wan-
dered into this intellectual thicket, intentionally or not, cannot but agree
with such a sentiment.

Yet the increasing importance of a range of movements and currents
outside the patterns of the so-called "mainstream" of American religious
life is one of the significant religious facts of our time. It is imperative
both that we seek to let these minority Christian traditions define them-

selves apart from broader categories and that we develop a conceptual framework with which to analyze and discuss them vis-à-vis the larger evangelical phenomenon. What is necessary, in other words, is a critical approach that will do justice both to the diversity (such as there is) and to the unity (such as there is) of American evangelicalism.

This book had its origins in very concrete decisions. Its fundamental question is: Should we speak of the variety of American evangelicalism, the varieties of American evangelicalism, the varieties of American evangelicalisms, or even of American evangelicalism as a coherent category at all? That question had been a matter for discussion and even disagreement between the two editors of this volume, as we attempted to function as co-chairs of the Evangelical Theology Group of the American Academy of Religion (AAR). Dayton saw more incoherence; Johnston, more coherence. The matter came to a head when a group of scholars petitioned the executive committee of the AAR for a "consultation" on pentecostalism, hoping to found a "pentecostalism" group that would parallel our group on "evangelicalism." The leadership of the AAR suggested that "pentecostalism" was a subcategory of "evangelicalism" and instructed us to consider incorporating such themes within our work.

The logic of this decision was obvious to some members of our steering committee (e.g., Johnston) and not at all obvious to others (e.g., Dayton). The vigor of the ensuing debate and the need to come to some practical resolution of the issues suggested that we should confront the topic head-on, while at the same time broadening the discussion beyond the pentecostal tradition to include other traditions sometimes grouped under the rubric "American evangelicalism." This led to a session at the 1986 AAR meeting, entitled "The Limits of Evangelicalism," in which three of the chapters in this volume first were presented (Dayton on pentecostalism, Ohlmann on the baptists, and Bassett on the holiness movement). Interest in the subject led to an expanded discussion in 1987 on "The Varieties of Evangelicalism" (Sernett on black Christianity, Weber on premillennialism, and Hughes on restorationism) and eventually to this book.

The editors identified a dozen traditions, or currents, that seemed typically to be grouped under the umbrella of American evangelicalism. They enlisted contributors who were known from earlier writings to be leading interpreters of particular traditions and who in some sense stood at the intersection of the traditions in question and evangelicalism. In all but three cases (Marsden on fundamentalism, Dayton on pentecostalism, and Sernett on black Christianity), the essayists also were chosen because they stood within the traditions they interpret.

After the first year, we provided the contributors with Dayton's essay on pentecostalism as a model (hence the occasional references to this essay

by other conributors) and gave them a threefold assignment. Each contributor was requested (1) to offer a careful interpretation of the theological understanding of the movement in question, (2) to root that reading
of the movement in its sources, and (3) to compare and contrast this "logic"
or "self-understanding" with what the author and/or movement understood "evangelicalism" to be. Contributors were told that the editors would
then use the essays as data for two concluding essays that would attempt,
by synthesis and analysis, to advance the discussion.

The assignment was left open, so as not to foreclose too quickly any
of the basic questions or perspectives that need exploration. The results
are illuminating. The essays differ in genre and orientation in ways that
reflect not only the perspectives of the authors themselves but also the
movements in question. The essays on pietism and Lutheranism, for example, are theologically oriented and look back to European sources more
than the essays on American-born movements. The essay on anabaptism
is more "oppositive" in character, reflecting the tendency of that tradition,
ever since the sixteenth century, to define itself over against dominant or
established traditions. Similarly, there is no imposed understanding of
evangelicalism — and the essays differ widely in their assumptions. Guided
in part by the histories and dynamics of their respective traditions, the
essayists differ in the period, form, and descriptors that they take to be
normative for evangelicalism.

As readers of this volume move through the essays, they should keep
in mind the titles individual essayists have chosen. They are suggestive of
the ease, or dis-ease, with which their respective traditions have found a
home within American evangelicalism. Thus, Marsden, Weber, Ohlmann,
and Noll and Niemczyk have had little trouble linking their traditions to
evangelicalism: "Fundamentalism *and* American Evangelicalism," "Baptists
and Evangelicals," and so on. Others have seen the relationship of their
traditions with American evangelicalism as more problematical. Hughes
has wondered, "Are Restorationists Evangelicals?" Sernett explores "Black
Religion and *the Question* of Evangelical Identity." Kraus offers "Evangelicalism: A Mennonite Critique," and Dayton, "The Limits of Evangelicalism: The Pentecostal Tradition." There is yet a third group of titles reflecting a still greater level of discomfort at identifying a particular tradition
with American evangelicalism. It is not accidental or insignificant that the
chapter titles for the essays on the holiness churches, Adventism, pietism,
and Lutheranism make no mention at all of evangelicalism. Their essayists
see a fundamental disparity between their respective traditions and evangelicalism that is not easily reconciled.

The editors have kept several goals in mind while working on this project. From one angle, we hoped to "chart" more fully certain largely un-

charted contours of the American religious landscape, by displaying more publicly and more carefully the range of traditions that are often lumped under the single label "evangelical." We hope that this volume will be a useful reference for those who need a map of this territory. But beyond this task of description and introduction, we hope to contribute, especially in our concluding essays, to refining the conceptual frameworks by which this territory may be understood and interpreted.

The task of editing this volume has been both satisfying and difficult. In addition to the usual problems of coordinating the schedules of a dozen busy contributors, there have been the complexities of the subject itself. As the final essays demonstrate, the editors have not always agreed in their orientation to the basic issues involved or the most useful approach to them. Moreover, such differences in perspective have not proven reconcilable simply by additional information or superior argument. Thus, it seemed best to lift these differences into the central problematic of the book and invite the reader to join a larger discussion that seems in no imminent danger of resolution: How are we to understand the variety of American evangelicalism?

NOTES

1. David F. Wells, "'No Offense: I Am an Evangelical': A Search for Self-Definition," in *A Time to Speak Out: The Evangelical-Jewish Encounter*, ed. A. James Rudin and Marvin R. Wilson (Grand Rapids, Mich.: Eerdmans, 1987), 37.

2. Thomas A. Askew, "A Response to David F. Wells," in *A Time to Speak Out*, ed. Rudin and Wilson, 43.

CHAPTER 2

Premillennialism and the Branches of Evangelicalism

Timothy P. Weber

To paraphrase H.L. Mencken's old and rather unsanitary observation, it would be hard to spit into a crowd of American evangelicals these days without hitting a premillennialist. They seem to be everywhere. They get more headlines, buy more television time, and sell more books than anyone else around. Nearly all celebrities of the electronic church preach premillennialism.[1] And since 1970, no author, evangelical or otherwise, has sold more books than Hal Lindsey, whose *Late Great Planet Earth* spread the premillennial gospel to the largest audience ever. There was even a premillennialist in the White House, and some of Ronald Reagan's critics have suggested that he might have formulated his foreign policy with one eye on his prophetic charts.[2]

Premillennialism's popular support is enormous. It is almost impossible to find a fundamentalist who is not also a premillennialist, and only slightly less difficult to find a pentecostal who is not. Scores of evangelical denominations, missions societies, Bible institutes, colleges, seminaries, and publishing houses are "officially premillennial" in their by-laws, statements of faith, or traditional practice. In thousands of evangelical congregations, nonpremillennialists are excluded from membership. Family cars and pickup trucks cruise America's highways with bumper stickers that read, "In Case of Rapture, This Car Will Be Driverless" or "Beam Me Up, Jesus." One might be tempted to conclude that premillennialism has leavened the whole evangelical lump.

But that is not quite the case. Today parts of American evangelicalism want nothing to do with premillennialism; and some premillennialists stay out of the evangelical "mainstream" and avoid any connection with it. Although the two movements overlap in significant ways, premillennialism and evangelicalism are far from synonymous. In fact, the relationship between the two has been rather complicated.

Defining Premillennialism

Naturally, any discussion of premillennialism's relationship to evangelicalism depends on what we mean by each term. Though premillennialism occasionally has served as the centerpiece of an elaborate theological system, its basic teachings are quite simple and can fit into a variety of religious frameworks. In fact, to qualify as a premillennialist, all one has to believe is that there will be an earthly reign of Christ which will be preceded by his Second Coming.

Premillennialism is not so much a theology as it is a particular view of history. Premillennialists reject popular notions of human progress and believe that history is a game that the righteous cannot win. For them, the historical process is a never-ending battle between good and evil, whose course God has already conceded to the Devil. People may be redeemed in history; but history itself is doomed. History's only hope lies in its own destruction. While premillennialists have differed widely in their views of the sequence of events, these days most of them believe something like the following: At the end of the present age, the forces of evil will be marshaled by Satan's emissary, the Antichrist, who will attempt to destroy God's people and thwart God's purposes. After an intense period of tribulation, Christ will return to earth, resurrect the righteous dead, defeat Antichrist and his legions at Armageddon, bind Satan, and establish his millennial reign. Thus the coming Golden Age will not be a part of history at all: the millennium will be discontinuous with all that preceded it and will arrive only with the supernatural suspension of the present. Despite major differences in how premillennialists use them, a rather literalistic reading of a few key biblical passages — Daniel 7–11; Ezekiel 37–39; Matthew 24; I Thessalonians 4; II Thessalonians 2; and Revelation, especially chapter 20, which is the only text that explicitly mentions a future millennium — forms the basis of most premillennialist teachings.

Premillennialists were present in earliest Christianity;[3] and, in America, they were there from the beginning of European settlement. Most Puritans who settled New England were premillennialist in one way or another. Cotton Mather, the quintessential Puritan pastor of the early eighteenth century, liked to speculate about the Second Coming and the approaching millennium; and historians have noted the Puritans' ability to translate their experience into millennial terms.[4] But the Puritans were not particularly picky about prophetic details. Thanks to the interpretive insights of Daniel Whitby and Moses Lowman and his own experience in the Great Awakening, Jonathan Edwards concluded that the millennium will come before the return of Christ and will probably begin in America.[5] Unlike Mather, Edwards believed that history would be redeemed and that God intended to "Christianize" the world before Christ's coming. In the early nineteenth century, this more optimistic *postmillennialism* quickly became the eschatological view most popular among evangelicals.

But there were exceptions. As Charles Finney observed, Americans in his day were "drunk on the millennium," and their inebriation took many forms. Millenarian groups grew like Topsy in the first few decades of the nineteenth century. The Shakers believed that the Second Coming already had occurred, in the person of their founder, Mother Ann Lee (c. 1736–84), who had set up outposts of the coming millennium in the Shaker communities.[6] Joseph Smith (1805–1844) and the Mormons expected the returning Christ to establish his millennial headquarters near Independence, Missouri. Smith claimed that God had revealed to him a plan for the New Jerusalem and its temple; but the Mormons were driven from Missouri before they could build their Zion.[7] John Humphrey Noyes (1811–86) built his communal experiment at Oneida on the twin pillars of perfectionism and premillennialism, though at times his eschatology is difficult to decipher.[8]

For the most part, American evangelicals rejected these movements for noneschatological reasons. Among other things, the Shakers were mystics who spiritualized the Bible and required celibacy to enter the millennium; the Mormons claimed access to continuing revelation through their prophets and practiced polygamy; and the followers of Noyes promoted sinless perfection at the same time they had sex with each others' spouses.[9] Such activities were sufficient to disqualify them as evangelical millenarian movements.

Much more acceptable, from the evangelical perspective, were the Millerites, who were the American version of a more traditional millenarian revival which began in Britain at the end of the eighteenth century.[10] Events surrounding the French Revolution seemed to confirm the theory held by many evangelicals that the Bible's prophecies of the "last days" actually were an overview of the entire church age. Using a "historicist" hermeneutic, these premillennialists tinkered with Scripture and historical events until they were certain that they had cracked the prophetic code and could predict the Second Coming of Christ. Unlike other premillennialists who appealed to mysticism or new revelation, these "millenarians" remained slavishly tied to the biblical text. In their careful and exacting hands, apocalypticism nearly wrapped itself in Enlightenment robes. For them, the Bible was not a prompter of visions or flights of fancy; it was a complicated and precise handbook of past, present, and future events.[11]

Like many evangelicals of his time, William Miller (1792–1849) believed in common sense and the role of reason in religion. In fact, he started his journey to Christian orthodoxy as a skeptical deist who ridiculed the Bible on rational grounds. After the study of history proved disillusioning, however, Miller commenced an inductive study of the Scriptures. In time he became a stickler for literal interpretation and concluded that the Bible could stand up to the most intense scrutiny. He was especially fascinated with the study of prophecy. By means of "millennial arithmetic," he calculated Christ's Second Coming in about 1843. Thanks to the genius of promoter Joshua Himes, Millerism quickly grew into a sizable movement that cut across denominational lines.

Recent studies have shown that Millerism drew almost exclusively from the evangelical mainstream. Miller stayed orthodox theologically, condemned sectarianism, and adhered to traditional mores. He refused to wear the prophet's mantle: he claimed that his conclusions were available to anyone who applied common sense and the accepted principles of biblical interpretation.[12] Nevertheless, most evangelicals still considered Millerism a scandal. Under pressure from his supporters, Miller set a specific date for Christ's coming, 22 October 1844, which produced some fanaticism and primed the movement for its Great Disappointment. But Millerism's sin was more serious than date setting. He was fundamentally out of step with the evangelical ethos of his day. Millerite premillennialism denied the premise of the evangelical empire: that the evangelical united front for revival and reform was God's way of turning history into the millennium. Most evangelicals believed that God had committed himself to the success of their enterprises and had guaranteed the redemption of time and space through the ordinary means of grace; but the Millerites rejected such notions. History was finished; do-gooding evangelicals would be better off spreading the news of Christ's return. Thus Millerism's denial of human instrumentality and its "hyper-supernaturalism" doomed it to failure long before Christ's nonappearance in 1844. In short, Millerite premillennialism was the sworn enemy of evangelical progress.[13]

Consequently, it is nothing short of astounding that, within four decades after the Great Disappointment, a different variety of premillennialism became popular in evangelical circles. It succeeded because it was able to distance itself from Millerism and because the optimism of the evangelical empire was in serious disarray.[14] This new premillennialism was dispensationalism, the brainchild of John Nelson Darby (1800–1882), a leading teacher in the British Plymouth Brethren. Darby divided biblical and subsequent history into eras, or dispensations, during which God tested people concerning some specific aspect of his will. According to C.I. Scofield, one of Darby's American followers, "these periods are marked off in Scripture by some change in God's method of dealing with mankind, in respect to two questions: of sin, and of man's responsibility. Each of the dispensations may be regarded as a new test of the natural man, and each ends in judgment — making his utter failure in every dispensation."[15]

What really made Darby's dispensationalism distinctive was its "futurism" and the way it viewed Israel and the church.[16] Unlike the earlier historicist premillennialism, futurism held that "last days" prophecies will be fulfilled just before Christ's return. In addition, Darby taught that God has two completely different plans operating in history, one for an earthly people (Israel) and one for a heavenly people (the church), and that he operates only one plan at a time.[17] Thus, "to rightly divide the word of truth" meant keeping the two programs and their respective prophecies straight, and separate.

In essence, dispensationalism made God's prophetic dealings with Israel the baseline of its entire hermeneutic. God's plans for the Jews were revealed in a series of covenants with Abraham, Moses, and David: God promised to make the Hebrews his special people and eventually to set Messiah on David's throne forever.[18] Furthermore, dispensationalists believed, the prophet Daniel had spelled out in precise detail how and when Messiah will come (Daniel 7–9). Writing during a period of Gentile domination over the Jews, Daniel saw the "times of the Gentiles" extending through four successive Gentile world powers (Daniel 7). Along the way, a powerful Gentile ruler would issue a decree to rebuild the fallen city of Jerusalem; and seventy weeks later the Messianic kingdom would be established (Dan. 9:24–27). More specifically, in the first seven weeks, the city would be rebuilt; and sixty-two weeks later Messiah would arrive but be "cut off" or rejected. During the seventieth week, which dispensationalists equated with the "great tribulation" (Matthew 24, II Thessalonians 2, and most of Revelation), an evil ruler would try to destroy the Jews but would be stopped by the returning Messiah, who would vindicate God's people and restore David's throne.

In order for the prophecy to make sense, dispensationalists translated Daniel's seventy weeks to seventy weeks *of years* (490 years), thereby showing, after some strenuous arithmetic, that Jesus Christ's crucifixion ("cutting off") happened at the end of the sixty-ninth week, right on schedule. But, then, why did Christ not return seven years later to establish his kingdom? To resolve this problem, dispensationalists devised a "postponement theory." When the Jews rejected Jesus as their Messiah, God postponed Christ's scheduled return and unexpectedly turned his attention to the Gentiles. Thus God suspended the prophetic timetable at the end of Daniel's sixty-ninth week, then formed a new and more heavenly people, the church.[19] In other words, the church had no prophecies of its own and occupied a kind of prophetic time warp or "great parenthesis." Because God worked only with one people at a time, dispensationalists believed that the church had to be removed from the earth before God could resume his dealings with Israel in Daniel's seventieth week.

That conviction produced dispensationalism's most controversial and distinctive doctrine: the pretribulational rapture of the church. Though scholars still debate where he got it, by about 1830 Darby was teaching that the church will escape the tribulation by being removed or "raptured" from the earth to meet Christ in the air (I Thess. 4:16-17). Thus there will be two phases to the Second Coming: first, before the tribulation, Christ will come *for* his saints; then, after the tribulation, he will come *with* his saints to defeat Antichrist and establish the kingdom. Because the church found itself in suspended prophetic time, no prophesied event stood between the present and the rapture. Thus it may occur at any moment. As far as we can tell, no premillennialist — historicist or futurist — had ever taught the doctrine before; but something like it was almost demanded by the system that Darby had developed.[20]

Historically speaking, dispensationalism came to America at the right time. The evangelical empire was under siege after the Civil War, and conservative evangelicals were ready to overlook minor differences to protect the old gospel. Higher criticism of the Bible, comparative religion studies, and evolutionary teaching undercut many traditional evangelical convictions. Industrialization, the flood of immigrants, and the growth of the cities challenged the hegemony of evangelicals in society. More liberal evangelicals believed that adjustments were necessary and took steps to bring evangelical theology up to date,[21] but more conservative evangelicals resisted such changes by forming a defensive alliance broad enough to include premillennialists.

Dispensationalism's acceptance still did not come easily. For a long time, the new premillennialists worked hard to establish their evangelical credentials. It was relatively simple to show that dispensationalism differed from the earlier Millerism: its futurism, total separation of the church and Israel, postponement theory, and anticipation of a pretribulational rapture of the church set it apart. And its notion of suspended prophetic time relieved it, at least theoretically, of date setting.[22]

The real challenge, however, was showing that its eschatology did not undercut any other accepted evangelical doctrine. Not surprisingly, dispensationalists never doubted their own orthodoxy: "If you accept the second coming, you are under bonds logically to accept the doctrines with which it is so indissolubly bound up. The second coming is so woven into these basic doctrines of the Christian faith . . . that you cannot deny the one without denying the other."[23] At times they claimed even more, that a grasp of dispensational truth was the only sure antidote to liberalism and a host of other heresies.[24] Many evangelicals found that assertion ludicrous, but they were willing to grant dispensationalists associate status in the fight against liberalism anyway.

Including them in the conservative alliance was not all that difficult, because dispensationalism shared most of evangelicalism's basic assumptions. Both operated within the same philosophical and scientific framework. As George Marsden and others have shown, the nineteenth-century evangelical world view was anchored in the Common Sense Realism of the Scottish Enlightenment and in a Baconian view of science.[25] Evangelical "scholastics" at Princeton, for example, believed that their approach to theology was identical to the most popular scientific method of their day: it was inductive, logical, and committed to a rigorous use of reason. Dispensationalists claimed the same,[26] though not all evangelicals agreed with their assessment.

Despite their minority status, dispensationalists quickly learned how to gain credibility and make converts. This facility can be seen in the way they nearly commandeered the so-called Bible conference movement of the 1870s and 1880s. The Niagara Bible Conference was founded in 1875 and became a prototype for hundreds of others. For two weeks each summer, in some resort setting, evangelicals gathered to hear the old doctrines defended. Dispensationalist went to Niagara in large numbers, and some of them even got to preach. When they did, they worked hard at building bridges and making premillennialism sound like one of the doctrines that needed to be saved from the liberal onslaught. It worked. By 1878, the "Niagara Creed" included a premillennialist plank.[27] When some conferees objected to the heavy prophetic emphasis at Niagara and other Bible conferences, premillennialists organized their own prophetic conferences instead.[28]

After the success of the Bible and prophetic conferences, dispensationalists never doubted their ability to attract evangelicals and employed a variety of means to do so. They became fierce promoters of the Bible institutes, which were founded by the score after the mid-1880s. Eager laypeople and would-be pastors came for practical training in Christian work and afterward carried premillennialism to churches, missions agencies, and other evangelical enterprises. Dispensationalists became masters of the print media and spread their views through magazines, journals,[29] and a number of enormously popular books, including the *Scofield Reference Bible* (1909), whose notes set the text of Scripture within a proper dispensational framework.[30] In the controversy with liberals, dispensationalists always sided with conservatives, maintaining traditional evangelicalism's high view of Scripture, its commitment to evangelism and foreign missions, and its belief that Christianity was rooted in the supernatural. In the Protestant holy wars of the late nineteenth century, no-one ever doubted where the new premillennialists stood.

But none of those things would have won over large numbers of evangelicals, had not optimism and the belief in progress declined. As dispensationalists loved to point out, postmillennialism had not delivered on its promise of an imminent millennium. Despite massive evangelical efforts, the Golden Age seemed farther away than ever. Dispensationalists believed that the world was getting worse, not better; and even those evangelicals who did not share their eschatology found it hard to argue otherwise.[31] Many people said that they became dispensationalists after they concluded that the world was not turning to Christ as they had expected it would.[32] In other words, the same world view that had undercut its credibility before the Civil War brought premillennialism a better hearing in the years around World War I. In a world that most evangelicals believed was falling apart, premillennialism increasingly made sense. But not all evangelicals felt that way. Premillennialism's rather uneven appeal in American evangelicalism was due to the fact that not all evangelicals were alike.

Defining Evangelicalism

Defining evangelicalism has become one of the biggest problems in American religious historiography. At best, "evangelicalism" is a diverse movement which at times seems to have more dividing it than uniting it. In fact, some observers find it nearly impossible to speak of evangelicalism as a single entity and prefer to see it in terms of its constituent parts.[33] Timothy Smith speaks for many scholars when he calls evangelicalism a mosaic or even a kaleidoscope.[34]

It would be foolhardy to deny or downplay evangelical diversity. American evangelicalism is no monolith and never has been. But nothing is gained by ignoring its underlying unity. Evangelicals have argued, competed, and even condemned each other; and most have insisted that their brand of evangelicalism is far superior to all others. But even in their worst moments, most evangelicals have recognized that the evangelical house has many rooms and that the similarities that bind evangelicals together are stronger than the differences that pull them apart.[35] I like to compare evangelicalism to a large extended family, some of whose members feel close and others estranged from time to time. I see four main branches in the family tree: classical, pietistic, fundamentalist, and, for lack of a better term, progressive.[36]

Classical evangelicals are loyal primarily to the doctrines of the Protestant Reformation: the ultimate authority of the Bible, justification by faith, an Augustinian anthropology, and usually a substitutionary view of the atonement. They tend to be "creedalists" who downplay the role of religious experience in "doing theology." In this category, I place the continental churches (Lutheran and Reformed) and, in the nineteenth century, Old School Presbyterianism. *Pietistic evangelicals* stand in the Reformation tradition, too, but they seek to complete it by incorporating the experiential emphases of pietism, Puritanism, and the evangelical awakenings of the eighteenth century. They can fight over theology; but they are basically religious pragmatists who stress conversions and holy living, and promote revivals, social reform, and "higher life" movements. In this category belongs most of the "evangelical establishment" of the nineteenth century: Methodists, baptists, Oberlin Perfectionists, New School Presbyterians, holiness groups, and, later on, pentecostals. *Fundamentalist evangelicals* are shaped by the debates of the fundamentalist-modernist controversy. They embraced many of the characteristics of classical and pietistic evangelicalism, but focused on a few "fundamentals," in opposition to liberal, critical, and evolutionary teaching. In this category are found not only the fundamentalists, but also their "neo-evangelical" offspring who emerged after World War II. Though the latter departed from fundamentalism in significant ways, they still maintained many of its "anticritical" concerns. *Progressive evangelicals* incorporate elements from the other branches but do so with a conscious sense of "modernity." As I see it, progressive evangelicalism comes from two rather different sources: the "new evangelical" attempt to reform fundamentalism by making it more responsive to the needs of a secular and increasingly "post-Christian" and pluralistic age, and the large conservative element in the "mainline churches" that maintained its ecumenical orientation during the modernist-fundamentalist controversy and never accepted fundamentalist separatism. Although its parameters still are not firmly fixed, progressive evangelicalism maintains its hold on traditional orthodoxy, with, however, a somewhat lighter touch, especially in the area of biblical inerrancy, the use of biblical criticism, and certain behavorial mores.[37]

What do these four branches have in common? What is there about them that justifies our speaking of evangelicalism, rather than evangelicalisms? These are not easy questions to answer. The temptation is to define evangelicalism in either theological or existential/spiritual terms. Some want to force a kind of theological uniformity on evangelicalism which historically it never had, while others want to speak almost exclusively of an evangelical spirit, without specifying any theological boundaries. As is often the case, the truth lies somewhere in between these two extremes. From my perspective, evangelicalism is both a set of theological convictions and an ethos. Theologically, the evangelicalism of the four branches is hedged in by a commitment to more or less historical Christian orthodoxy, as interpreted through the Protestant Reformation: the Scriptures are divinely inspired and therefore true, the ultimate source for believing and living; Jesus Christ is the incarnate Son of God, whose ministry was characterized by supernatural power and authority; personal salvation is rooted in the grace of God, not in human works, and is mediated to sinners through their faith in Jesus Christ alone; and Christian conversion implies a life committed to holiness and to Christ's ongoing mission in the world. Naturally, it would be easy to show that evangelical theology has included more than this; but I do not believe it ever included less. Yet that core of basic Christian orthodoxy does not become "evangelical" until it is joined to a spirit of renewal and conversion—of individuals, churches, and, at least to some extent, the world. Evangelicalism is more than a point on the theological spectrum; it is a driving force, a dynamic bent on personal and corporate revival. In short, I see evangelicalism as a movement of spiritual renewal which is grounded in certain theological convictions. All four branches of American evangelicalism share those things, though each possesses its own emphases and characteristics.

Premillennialism and Its Place in Evangelicalism

With these distinctions in mind, we may see how evangelicalism and premillennialism have related to each other. In a nutshell, premillennialism, especially as expressed in dispensational form, found relatively little acceptance among classical evangelicals, made significant inroads among pietistic evangelicals, came nearly to dominate fundamentalist evangelicals, and appears to have only marginal support among progessives.

With few exceptions, classical evangelicals reject premillennialism, though they have often cooperated with premillennialists. Advocates of the old Princeton theology illustrate this ambivalence. A.A. Hodge called the pretribulation rapture "an unscriptural and unprofitable theory." Francis Patton worked with premillennialists but said confidentially, "I am not foolish enough to be one of them."[38] B.B. Warfield criticized dispensationalism's proof-texting approach to theology;[39] and J. Gresham Machen accepted premillennialists as allies against liberalism but expressed serious concern about their "false method in interpreting Scripture which in the long run will be productive of harm."[40] Likewise, Lutheran and Reformed churches were mainly hostile; their historic creeds rejected premillennialism by equating it with radicalism and social revolution.[41]

The first converts to dispensational premillennialism after the Civil War were pietistic evangelicals who were attracted to its biblicism, its concern for evangelism and missions, and its view of history, which seemed more realistic than that of the prevailing postmillennialism. Most of the new premillennialists came from baptist, New School Presbyterian, and Congregationalist ranks, which gave the movement a definite Reformed flavor.[42] Wesleyan evangelicals who opposed premillennialism used this apparent connection to Calvinism to discredit it among Methodists and holiness people.[43] But in time, dispensationalism had its devotees within the Wesleyan tradition as well. More radical holiness groups resonated with its prediction of declining orthodoxy and piety in the churches; and pentecostals found in it a place for the outpouring of the Spirit in a "latter-day rain" before the Second Coming.[44]

Dispensationalism's greatest sucess, however, was among fundamentalist evangelicals, especially those who became militant and separatist in the late 1920s and 1930s. Premillennialism gave such fundamentalists a clear framework for understanding their place in the churches and the world. Dispensationalism taught that shortly before the Second Coming there will be a great apostasy, which fundamentalists equated with the rise of modernism. In 1925, Arno Gaebelein declared that the "modernistic cancer is too far gone" and advised the faithful to leave the churches.[45] Many of them did. To be sure, not all those who fled the churches did so for eschatological reasons; but for many, premillennialism probably made leaving a little easier.[46]

Thus, in the long run, premillennialism's strongest support came from the new fundamentalist organizations that emerged in the 1930s and 1940s. In those years, one almost had to be a dispensationalist to participate in militant fundamentalism.[47] Many Bible institutes, seminaries, missions agencies, and local churches made dispensationalism a nonnegotiable of fundamentalist orthodoxy[48] and essentially erected a sign over the doors of their organizations: "Nondispensationalists need not apply." The gospel-song parody was meant in jest, but it had the ring of truth: "Our hope is built on nothing less/Than Scofield's notes and Moody Press."

There were some exceptions to this dispensationalist hegemony. Early on, dispensationalism competed with "historic premillennialism," as it came to be called, which shared dispensationalism's futurism but did not separate Israel and the church so strictly or teach the pretribulation rapture. By World War I, dispensationalism essentially had overcome its rival.[49] After World War II, historic premillennialism had a modest revival in the new evangelical movement. The main catalyst in its resurgence was George Ladd of Fuller Seminary, whose *Crucial Questions About the Kingdom of God* (1952) and *The Blessed Hope* (1956) showed how one could retain an evangelical and premillennialist perspective while using the latest methods of biblical scholarship.[50] It remains an option for those who want to stay premillennialists but cannot accept a dispensationalist hermeneutic. In fact, some form of Ladd's approach is about the only kind of premillennialism that exists among progressive evangelicals.

In the 1980s, dispensationalism itself underwent some significant adjustments. Under pressure from the advocates of historic premillennialism and the increasing sophistication of their own exegetical methods, many dispensationalists grappled with their system and were willing to modify it at a number of crucial points, including the postponement theory, the absolute distinction between Israel and the church, and the viability of dispensationalism as the organizing principle for systematic theology. A lively debate has ensued within dispensational circles over the essence of their eschatological system and the limits of doctrinal development.[51] As a result, the lines separating dispensationalism and other kinds of premillennialism are starting to blur.

Conclusion

All this leads us to the most important question of all: How has premillennialism affected evangelicalism as we have defined it? Study of the last century shows that the two movements can be quite compatible theologically. While some premillennialists have forsaken evangelical orthodoxy, dispensationalists and historic premillennialists have maintained it, sometimes with a vengeance. Even when dispensationalists make premillennialism the hub of their entire theological system, standard evangelical doctrines manage to survive.[52] Classical evangelicals, who are premillennialists' most dedicated detractors, in the end grudgingly admit that they share theological essentials.

But what about the relationship between premillennialism and the evangelical ethos? At first glance, their compatibility seems rather obvious. Pietistic evangelicals were attracted to the new premillennialism in part because it lent such strong support to their enterprises. Premillennialists conducted revivals, threw themselves into foreign missions, founded schools, and built churches. But because they operate from such a radically different perspective, premillennialists ended up changing the ethos in subtle but substantial ways.

For example, premillennialists always have supported revivals, but for reasons different from those of earlier evangelicals. Charles Finney saw the revival as a way of bringing in the earthly kingdom of God, while D.L. Moody viewed it in terms of rescuing a few souls before history's rendezvous with the Antichrist: "I look upon this world as a wrecked vessel. God has given me a lifeboat and said to me, 'Moody, save all you can.'" Similarly, premillennialists gave money and blood to foreign missions, but not because they expected the world to turn to Christ. Rather, they did so because they believed that Christ will not return until the gospel is preached as a witness throughout the world. Some premillennialists kept up the traditional evangelical support for social reform, but not because society could be permanently changed. Reform might slow, but never stop, the social order's slide toward Armageddon. Thus premillennialists were willing to conduct a kind of rear-guard harassing action until Jesus arrives to change things for good.[53] Premillennialism even made a difference in the evangelical quest for personal holiness. While Wesleyan and Oberlin perfectionism elicited strenuous effort and exercise of the will, premillennialists preferred the Keswick movement's version of holiness, which taught that the "victorious Christian life" consisted of "letting go and letting God." Keswick perfectionism was based on a personal surrender of the self and the will, so that Christ, not the individual, bore full responsibility for one's holiness.[54]

In my view, such subtle and not-so-subtle changes add up to a reordering and redefining of the evangelical ethos. One might be tempted to say that this reorientation grew out of a failure of nerve, a giving up on the world before God does, or out of an attempt to regain order and control in a world gone wrong.[55] But that might be going too far. I prefer to see premillennialism as a kind of midcourse correction during times of declining evangelical expectations. Premillennialism was a haven for those who had given up on history; but, as premillennialists like to point out, it also guaranteed that the perfect world was on the way. Christ himself will establish it at his coming, and nothing can stop it. In other words, in order to save the evangelical ethos during such terrible times, premillennialists *had* to change it.

It is important to remember that premillennialism did not create the crises of the last century; it simply capitalized on them. In a world out of control, the premillennialist view of the future provided both a blessed hope and a way of understanding why things were going so badly. There is an ironic comfort in knowing that centuries ago, the Bible predicted the current mess. As Pat Robertson has observed, "We are not to weep as the people of the world weep when there are certain tragedies or breakups of the government or systems of the world. We are not to wring our hands and say, 'Isn't it awful?' That isn't awful at all. It's good. That is a token, an evident token of our salvation, of where God is going to take us."[56] The rise of liberalism, the secularization of society, the widespread denial of traditional values, and the privatization of religion to the point where it touches nothing of importance in modern life—these are part of God's plan after all. Let nations rage, wars increase, and society disintegrate; premillennialists are confident that by and by they will ride with Christ on the clouds of heaven and make everything right. In a world such as ours, many evangelicals believe that that is good news—maybe the best news around.

NOTES

1. Jerry Falwell, Jimmy Swaggert, Oral Roberts, Rex Humbard, Kenneth Copeland, and Richard DeHaan proclaim it, as did Jim Bakker and Pat Robertson, before they left their television ministries for other work.

2. Ronnie Dugger, "Does Reagan Expect a Nuclear Armageddon?" *Washington Post* 8 Apr. 1984; *Time*, 5 Nov. 1984; *Newsweek*, 5 Nov. 1984; Timothy P. Weber, *Living in the Shadow of the Second Coming: American Premillenialism, 1875–1982* (Chicago: Univ. of Chicago Press, 1987), vii–xi.

3. For historical overviews, see Shirley Jackson Case, *The Millennial Hope* (Chicago: Univ. of Chicago Press, 1918), and D. H. Kromminga, *The Millennium in the Church* (Grand Rapids, Mich.: Eerdmans, 1945).

4. E.L. Tuveson, *Redeemer Nation: The Idea of America's Millennial Role* (Chicago: Univ. of Chicago Press, 1968); H.R. Niebuhr, *The Kingdom of God in America* (New York: Harper and Row, 1937); C. Cherry, ed., *God's New Israel* (Englewood Cliffs, N.J.: Prentice-Hall, 1971), 25–109.

5. Jonathan Edwards, *Works*, v. 1, Worcester ed., (Boston: Leavitt and Allen, 1843); C.C. Goen, "Jonathan Edwards: A New Departure in Eschatology," *Church History* 27 (Mar. 1959): 25–40.

6. For Shaker eschatological views, see Lawrence Foster, "Had Prophecy Failed? Contrasting Perspectives of the Millerites and Shakers," in *The Disappointed: Millerism and Millenarianism in the Nineteenth Century*, ed. Ronald Numbers and Jonathan Butler (Bloomington, Ind.: Indiana Univ. Press, 1987), 173–88.

7. On early Mormon millenarianism, see Jan Shipps, *Mormons* (Urbana: Univ. of Illinois Press, 1985), 131–49.

8. Michael Barkun, "'The Wind Sweeping Over the Country': John Humphrey Noyes and the Rise of Millerism," in *The Disappointed*, ed. Numbers and Butler, 153–72.

9. For an interesting study of these millenarian groups, see Catherine Albanese, *America: Religions and Religion* (Belmont, Calif.: Wadsworth, 1981), 141–49.

10. For a good summary of this millenarian revival, see Ernest R. Sandeen, *The Roots of Fundamentalism: British and American Millenarianism, 1800–1930* (Chicago: Univ. of Chicago Press, 1979), 1–7.

11. Nathan O. Hatch, "Millennialism and Popular Religion in the Early Republic," in *The Evangelical Tradition in America*, ed. Leonard I. Sweet (Macon, Ga.: Mercer Univ. Press, 1984), 113.

12. Wayne Judd, "William Miller: Disappointed Prophet," in *The Disappointed*, ed. Numbers and Butler, 17–35. For Millerism's relationship to evangelicalism, see David Rowe, *Thunder and Trumpets* (Chico, Calif.: Scholars Press, 1985), and Ruth A. Doan, *The Miller Heresy, Millennialism, and American Culture* (Philadelphia: Temple Univ. Press, 1987); Jonathan Butler, "The Making of a New Order: Millerism and the Origins of Seventh-day Adventism," in *The Disappointed*, ed. Numbers and Butler, 189–208.

13. For a more extended argument, see Ruth A. Doan, "Millerism and Evangelical Culture," in *The Disappointed* ed. Numbers and Butler, 118–38.

14. C. Norman Kraus, *Dispensationalism in America: Its Rise and Development* (Richmond, Va.: John Knox Press, 1958); Sandeen, *Roots of Fundamentalism*, 59–80.

15. C.I. Scofield, *Rightly Dividing the Word of Truth* (Oakland, Calif.: Western Book and Tract Company, n.d.), 18.

16. Weber, *Living in the Shadow*, 16–23.

17. C.C. Ryrie, *Dispensationalism Today* (Chicago: Moody Press, 1965), 66–78.

18. J.M. Darby, "The Covenants," *Collected Works,* ed. William Kelley (London: G. Morrish, 1967), 3:75; James H. Brookes, *Israel and the Church* (St. Louis, Mo.: Gospel Book and Tract Depository, n.d.), 42–43.

19. For a discussion of the counting of the sixty-nine weeks, see Weber, *Living in the Shadow,* 18–19 and 247–48, n. For a classic description of the postponement theory, see C.H. Mackintosh, *Papers on the Lord's Coming* (Chicago: Bible Institute Colportage Association, n.d.), 101–102.

20. For typical presentations of this view, see I.M. Haldeman, *The Coming of Christ* (Los Angeles: Bible House of Los Angeles, 1906), 297–325; John Walvoord, *The Rapture Question* (Findlay, Ohio: Dunham Publishing, 1957). For a spirited but not altogether convincing theory of the origins of the pretribulation rapture position, see Dave McPherson, *The Incredible Cover-Up: The True Story of the Pre-trib Rapture* (Plainfield, N.J.: Logos International, 1975).

21. William Hutchison, *The Modernist Impulse in American Protestantism* (Cambridge: Harvard Univ. Press, 1976).

22. Sometimes premillennialists yield to the date-setting temptation. Hal Lindsey predicted that the rapture will occur within a generation (40 years) of the founding of the state of Israel in 1948. Lindsey, *Late Great Planet Earth*, 53–58.

23. I.M. Haldeman, *Professor Shailer Mathews' Burlesque on the Second Coming* (New York: Privately printed, 1918), 23.

24. R.A. Torrey, *The Return of the Lord* (Los Angeles: Bible Institute of Los Angeles, 1913), 8; W.B. Riley, *The Evolution of the Kingdom* (New York: Charles C. Cook, 1913), 5.

25. George Marsden, *Fundamentalism and American Culture* (New York: Oxford Univ. Press, 1980), 14–16, 55–62; Theodore Dwight Bozeman, *Protestants in an Age of Science: The Baconian Ideal and Antebellum American Religious Thought* (Chapel Hill: Univ. of North Carolina Press, 1977); S.A. Grave, *The Scottish Philosophy of Common Sense* (Westport, Conn.: Greenwood, 1973).

26. E.g., R.A. Torrey, *What the Bible Teaches* (New York: Revell, 1898), 1.

27. Sandeen, *Roots of Fundamentalism,* 132–61, 273–77.

28. Weber, *Living in the Shadow,* 26–28.

29. James H. Brookes' *The Truth,* A.J. Gordon's *Watchword,* A.C. Gaebelein's *Our Hope,* and Moody Bible Institute's *Christian Workers Magazine,* to name only the leading ones.

30. William E. Blackstone, *Jesus Is Coming* (New York: Revell, 1908) was the *Late Great Planet Earth* of its time.

31. The optimism associated with postmillennialism died hard in some circles. World War I shattered the optimism of most but not all believers in progress. Compare Shailer Mathews, *New Faith for Old* (New York: Macmillan, 1936), 196–97, and James Snowden, *Is the World Growing Better?* (New York: Macmillan, 1919). For a study of the widespread view of crisis during this period, see F.C. Jaher, *Doubters and Dissenters: Cataclysmic Thought in America, 1885–1918* (New York: Free Press of Glencoe, 1964).

32. Weber, *Living in the Shadow,* 41–42.

33. In *The Young Evangelicals* (New York: Harper and Row, 1974), Richard Quebedeaux lists five evangelical subgroups; Cullen Murphy, "Protestantism and the Evangelicals," *Wilson Quarterly* 5 Aug. 1981): 105–116, lists twelve; and Robert Webber, *Common Roots* (Grand Rapids, Mich.: Zondervan, 1976), 25–35, lists eighteen.

34. See Leonard I. Sweet, "The Evangelical Tradition in America," in *The Evangelical Tradition in America,* ed. Leonard I. Sweet (Macon, Ga.: Mercer Univ. Press, 1984), 83–86, for a helpful summary of various positions.

35. Marsden forcefully argues that despite the diversity, it is possible to speak of an "evangelical denomination." George Marsden, "The Evangelical Denomination," in *Evangelicalism and Modern America*, ed. George Marsden (Grand Rapids, Mich.: Eerdmans, 1984), vii–xvi.

36. These categories follow closely those developed in Max L. Stackhouse, "Religious Right: New? Right?" *Commonweal* 29 (Jan. 1982): 52–56. His categories were puritan Evangelicalism, pietistic Evangelicalism, and fundamentalist Evangelicalism.

37. See George Marsden, *Reforming Fundamentalism: Fuller Seminary and the New Evangelicalism* (Grand Rapids, Mich.: Eerdmans, 1987); James D. Hunter, *Evangelicalism: The Coming Generation* (Chicago: Univ. of Chicago Press, 1987).

38. Both quotes are from James H. Brookes, *The Truth* 12 (1886): 109–111 and 20 (1894):518.

39. The comment was made in B.B. Warfield's review of Torrey, *What the Bible Teaches*, in *Presbyterian and Reformed Review* 39 (July 1898); 562–64. See also his "The Gospel and the Second Coming," *The Bible Magazine* 3 (1915): 300–309.

40. J. Gresham Machen, *Christianity and Liberalism* (New York: Macmillan, 1926), 49–50.

41. Classical evangelicals still reject premillennialism. See Oswald T. Allis, *Prophecy and the Church* (Philadelphia: Presbyterian and Reformed, 1945); Anthony Hoekema, *The Bible and the Future* (Grand Rapids, Mich.: Eerdmans, 1979; Robert Clouse, ed., *The Meaning of the Millennium: Four Views* (Downers Grove, Ill.: InterVarsity Press, 1977), esp. 155–88.

42. Douglas Frank, *Less Than Conquerors: How Evangelicals Entered the Twentieth Century* (Grand Rapids, Mich.: Eerdmans, 1986), 85.

43. Joseph Agar Beet, *The Last Things* (New York: Methodist Book Concern, 1897); Daniel Steele, *A Substitute for Holiness; or Antinomianism Revived; or, The Theology of the So-Called Plymouth Brethren Examined and Refuted,* 2d ed. (Boston and Chicago: Christian Witness, 1899); George W. Wilson, *The Signs of Thy Coming; or Premillennialism, Unscriptural and Unreasonable* (Boston: Christian Witness, 1899); Harris Franklin Rall, *Modern Premillennialism and the Christian Hope* (New York: Abingdon, 1920, 111–19, 250–53.

44. For holiness premillennialism, see W.B. Godbey, *An Appeal to Postmillennialists* (Nashville, Tenn.: Pentecostal Mission Publishing, n.d.); George D. Watson, *Steps to the Throne* (Cincinnati, Ohio: God's Revivalist, [1891]); W.B. Godbey and Seth Vook Rees, *The Return of Jesus* (Cincinnati, Ohio: God's Revivalist, n.d.). See also Robert Mapes Anderson, *Vision of the Disinherited* (New York: Oxford Univ. Press, 1979), 83–89; Donald W. Dayton, *Theological Roots of Pentecostalism* (Grand Rapids, Mich.: Zondervan, 1987), 143–71; Gerald T. Sheppard, "Pentecostals and the Hermeneutics of Dispensationalism: The Anatomy of an Uneasy Relationship," *Pneuma* 6 (Fall 1984):5–33.

45. A.C. Gaebelein, *Our Hope* 31 (Jan. 1925):426.

46. On the role of premillennialism in the splitting of the Northern Baptist and Presbyterian churches, see Weber, *Living in the Shadow*, 158–76, and George Dollar, *A History of Fundamentalism in America* (Greenville, S.C.: Bob Jones Univ., 1973), 145–83.

47. Dollar, *A History of Fundamentalism*, passim. This view is somewhat modified in David O. Beale, *In Pursuit of Purity: American Fundamentalism Since 1850* (Greenville, S.C.: Unusual Publications, 1986).

48. See Timothy P. Weber, "The Two Edged Sword: The Fundamentalist Use of the Bible," in *The Bible in America: Essays in Cultural History*, ed. Nathan Hatch and Mark Noll (New York: Oxford Univ. Press, 1982), 101–120.

49. For the conflict between "historic premillennialists and dispensationalists," see Sandeen, *Roots of Fundamentalism,* 208-232.

50. Ladd's evangelical but critical biblical scholarship has had enormous influence in evangelical academic circles. See Mark Noll, *Between Faith and Criticism* (New York: Harper and Row, 1987).

51. Robert Saucy, "Contemporary Dispensational Thought," *TSF Bulletin* 7 (Mar.-Apr. 1984):10-11; Elliott E. Johnson, "Hermeneutics and Dispensationalism," in *Walvoord, A Tribute,* ed. D.K. Campbell (Chicago: Moody Press, 1982), 239-55. See also Craig Blaising, "Developing Dispensationalism" (unpublished paper delivered at the Dispensational Theology Pre-meeting at the Evangelical Theological Society, Atlanta, Ga., 20 Nov. 1986). I would like to thank Prof. Ronald Clutter of Grace Theological Seminary for providing a copy of Blaising's paper. Up to this point, most dispensationalists have been unwilling to reexamine the doctrine of the pretribulation rapture.

52. The classical example is Lewis Sperry Chafer, *Systematic Theology,* 8 vols. (Dallas, Tex.: Dallas Seminary Press, 1948).

53. See Weber, *Living in the Shadow,* for an extended discussion of these themes.

54. See Frank, *Less Than Conquerers,* 103-166, for a fascinating analysis of the Keswick view of holiness.

55. This is essetially Frank's argument, ibid., 60-102.

56. Quoted in William Martin, "Waiting for the End," *Atlantic* 249 (June 1982): 34.

CHAPTER 3

Fundamentalism and American Evangelicalism
George M. Marsden

John R. Rice was perhaps the prototypical fundamentalist leader. A pro-tégé of one of the founders of the movement, controversial Texas evangelist J. Frank Norris, Rice was a mentor of Billy Graham in Graham's fundamentalist days and later of Jerry Falwell. He participated in the organization of the National Association of Evangelicals in 1942, when the fundamentalists who founded that organization were seeking allies; but in the 1950s, along with his good friend, Bob Jones, Sr., he took the lead in separating strict fundamentalists from Graham and his neo-evangelical cohorts. Most importantly, Rice's weekly newspaper, *The Sword of the Lord*, which reached a circulation of some 250,000, and his more than a hundred books did as much as anything between the 1930s and the 1980s to shape a consensus among the oft-fragmented fundamentalists. At one time or another, virtually all the major leaders of fundamentalism attended Rice's "Sword of the Lord," conferences and looked to his leadership.[1]

Rice's definition of fundamentalism is, therefore, a good place to start in looking for fundamentalist understandings of themselves. In 1975 Rice wrote, in *I Am a Fundamentalist*: "So as we define fundamentalism it means a vigorous defense of the faith, active soul winning, great New Testament–type local churches going abroad to save multitudes, having fervent love for all of God's people and earnestly avoiding compromise in doctrine or yoking up with unbelievers." Rice went on to observe that fundamentalism originally "simply meant you believed the Bible and the historic Christian faith." Although lines had not been drawn clearly in the earliest years, all true fundamentalists today, he said, affirm the inerrancy of the Bible and the premillennial return of Christ, and deny all biological evolution. Rice also pointed out that he was not simply a conservative,

---

I have borrowed a few of the paragraphs from this essay to use in "Defining Fundamentalism," to be published in *The Fundamentalist Phenomenon: A View from Within: a Response from Without*, Norman J. Cohen, ed. (Grand Rapids: Wm. B. Eerdmans, forthcoming).

but also a soul winner, and that he was not a "New Evangelical," which was neither new nor evangelical. A true fundamentalist, he further insisted, should follow a strict moral code, including modest dress; must be a good citizen; and must resist the heresy of modern speaking in tongues.[2]

Rice's account encompasses most of the issues essential to modern fundamentalist self-understanding. He assumes that most of fundamentalist doctrine is conservative Protestant (he goes so far as to define it specifically as baptist), and that its two most prominent distinguishing features are militant defense of the faith and soul winning. A true fundamentalist adds to these two qualities an adherence to the other doctrines and practices he mentions as defining fundamentalist boundaries. These include, of course, the specifics of the traditional "fundamentals." As Rice put it:

> It is generally understood that the fundamentals of the Christian faith include the inspiration and thus the divine authority of the Bible: the deity, virgin birth, blood atonement, bodily resurrection, personal second coming of Christ; the fallen, lost condition of all mankind; salvation by repentance and faith; grace without works; eternal doom in Hell of the unconverted and eternal blessedness of the saved in Heaven.[3]

Taking Rice as a paradigmatic definer of fundamentalism, however, also points to the difficulties in offering a firm definition of fundamentalism or of its relationships to other movements. The main difficulty is that fundamentalism has been constantly changing. Moreover, these changes have had to do primarily with a series of splits that have kept fundamentalists' relationships to other movements in flux.

As Rice observes, fundamentalism at first was a broad coalition of evangelical defenders of the faith. Most of these were within mainline denominations. They were conservative evangelicals, dedicated to soul winning and conscious of a need for militancy in defending the faith. The relationship of evangelicalism to this movement must be understood in context; almost all nineteenth-century American Protestants had been evangelical, that is, part of a coalition reflecting a merger of pietist and Reformed heritages and growing out of the eighteenth- and nineteenth-century awakenings in America. Typically, all sorts of subtraditions within this evangelical movement emphasized revivalism and the accompanying doctrines of Christ's atonement, the necessity of regeneration, the sole authority of the Bible, and a separated life of holiness marked by avoidance of notorious bar-room vices. All fundamentalists wanted to preserve this nineteenth-century heritage, and so all fundamentalists were evangelicals. But in the early twentieth century, by no means all evangelicals were fundamentalists. Not all traditional evangelicals were militant. More-

over, many who still called themselves evangelicals were liberals or modernists who had abandoned most of the distinctive emphases of the awakenings; so the term *evangelical* had lost its usefulness. Fundamentalists
nonetheless thought of themselves simply as preserving the evangelical
heritage.

Though preserving the central elements of the evangelical heritage
was a large part of what they were doing, they were also establishing
another subtradition with some distinctive features. Recognizing that these
two enterprises — supporting evangelicalism as a whole and supporting or
establishing one of its subtraditions — are not mutually exclusive is the key
to unlocking a puzzle that is often, as in this volume, posed: Is there one
evangelicalism or many? The anwer, of course, is both. This means that
no one part can be equated with the whole. On the other hand, it affirms
that there *is* a whole, even if sometimes it is difficult to define precisely.
Within evangelicalism, various subgroups pay more or less attention to
the movement as a whole. Many submovements are content to remain
relatively isolated in their own tradition. Others, such as fundamentalists
and their neo-evangelical heirs, have been much concerned with the whole
of evangelicalism, which they hoped to reform and control. Nonetheless,
they were at the same time building subtraditions.

Fundamentalist George W. Dollar's definition in *A History of Fundamentalism in America* helps us go a step further than Rice, by more
systematically defining the outstanding features of the subtradition. Dollar writes, "Historic fundamentalism is the literal exposition of all the
affirmations and attitudes of the Bible and the militant exposure of all
non-Biblical affirmations and attitudes."[4] In Dollar's definition, as in Rice's,
we see that militancy is one of the leading features that distinguishes fundamentalism from other types of revivalist evangelicalism. A fundamentalist is ready to stand up and fight for the faith. Militancy, of course, is
not a sufficient condition for distinguishing fundamentalists from other
evangelicals (the Sojourners community has been militant), but it is a necessary condition. Central to being a fundamentalist is perceiving oneself
to be in the midst of religious war. The universe is divided between the
forces of light and darkness. Spiritually enlightened Christians can tell
who the enemy is. In such war, there can be no compromise.

As Dollar's formula suggests, fundamentalists universally see the war
as primarily a war over the Bible. To this extent, they would agree with
outside observers who claim that fundamentalism is, in its distinctive
aspects, a modern movement. Though fundamentalists see this battle for
the Bible as recent, they insist that their inerrancy doctrine is the historic
position of the church. To a large degree, fundamentalism is a militant
reaction to modern higher criticism of the Bible and the displacement of

the Bible as a central culture-forming force in American life.[5] Fundamentalists see this war as started by the modernists and secularists who attacked the Bible. As Dollar writes, "It was more deadly than military warfare, for it swept away the spiritual foundations of our churches, our nation, and our heritage."[6]

For fundamentalists, the battle for the Bible almost always has two fronts. They are fighting against modern interpretations of the Bible that they see as destroying most American denominations. At the same time, they are fighting to save American civilization, which they see as founded on the Bible.

Dollar's formula suggests, in addition, that the battle for the Bible is over a particular type of interpretation of the Bible — what Dollar describes as "the literal exposition of all the affirmations and attitudes of the Bible." Fundamentalists equate this literal interpretation of the Bible with belief in the Bible itself. They see people who claim to believe the Bible, but who interpret it in other ways, as actually denying the truth of the Bible and putting their own standards of interpretation above the Bible. The way of getting at this point that has become virtually universal for fundamentalists is to assert that the Bible is "inerrant." For fundamentalists, this means that the Bible not only is an infallible authority in matters of faith and practice, but also is accurate in all its historical and scientific assertions. Of course, fundamentalists do not hold that everything in the Bible is to be interpreted literally (the mountains do not literally clap their hands). Rather, "literal where possible" is their interpretive rule. Whatever in the Bible can reasonably be given a literal reference should be interpreted as literal and accurate.

Once we draw the above bounds (positively in the aggressive soul-saving tradition of American evangelical revivalism, negatively militant in defense of literal interpretations of the Bible), we see more clearly the difficulty of precisely pinpointing fundamentalism among the evangelical submovements. These attitudes are not ones that would be confined to just one, or even to just a few, of the submovements of American evangelicalism during the past century. Rather, such stances can be found, to greater or lesser extents, in all sorts of revivalist evangelical groups — even among many who would not call themselves fundamentalist. Many holiness and pentecostal groups, for instance, and revivalists white and black share many of these traits and hence reasonably might be called fundamentalist in a broad sense. Certainly they would properly have been called fundamentalists during the early formative stage of fundamentalism, during the 1920s, before fundamentalism had as precise a meaning as it has today. So fundamentalism, which cuts across much of evangelicalism, is, like evangelicalism itself, a broad coalition. The confusing feature is that fundamentalism in this broad sense can refer to any who take a militant fundamentalist stance in favor of soul saving and in defense of a literally interpreted Bible. At the same time, however, the term has been used by only some of these groups as a primary self-designation. These latter, who use the self-designation, might be called *card-carrying fundamentalists.*

The nature of this terminological problem becomes clearest if we look at fundamentalism in the American South. Fundamentalism, as a self-conscious, more or less organized coalition of militants, developed first in the North, and the word "fundamentalism" was invented in 1920 by a baptist editor to describe his conservative party in the Northern Baptist Convention. Soon the term spread to similar groups fighting modernism. In the South, however, fundamentalism, as an organized movement, was redundant. The vast majority of southern evangelicals already both were committed to soul saving and were firm Bible-believers, assuming literal interpretations. Moreover, many white southerners were militant in defense of their biblical faith, which since the Civil War they had contrasted with northern liberal Protestantism. Blacks remained firm Bible-believers, but, even more than southern whites, they were kept isolated from liberalism, from wider cultural influence, and hence from antiliberal campaigns. In any case, with traditional evangelical attitudes so dominant in southern culture, there was little reason to organize as fundamentalists. Southern affinities to organized fundamentalism, however, soon became apparent, during the anti-evolution crusades of the 1920s. White southerners quickly adopted the anti-evolution cause and promoted legislation banning the teaching of biological evolution in public schools. Evolution, southern majorities agreed, conflicted with the Bible, literally interpreted. They viewed the preservation of the literally-interpreted Bible in the public schools as essential to saving American civilization. In this sense, vast numbers of southerners could properly be designated fundamentalists.

Fundamentalism thus can be traced on two tracks, one a broad militancy for soul-saving, Bible-believing evangelicalism, and the other a more explicitly organized coalition of such militants.

Keeping this ambiguity in mind, we can focus primarily on the development of the more explicitly organized fundamentalists. Ernest Sandeen, in *The Roots of Fundamentalism: British and American Millenarianism, 1800–1930,*[7] has shown that the most successful organizers of fundamentalism were dispensationalist premillennialists. Sandeen goes so far as to equate the fundamentalist movement with this millenarianism (as he calls it). That thesis is plausible, since these dispensationalists have been so immensely influential among organized fundamentalists. Sandeen's thesis creates some interpretive problems, however. First, it eliminates most uses of the term *fundamentalism* in the broad sense. This exclusion could be seen as a warranted sacrifice of the broad use of the word in the interest of gaining precision. But, second, Sandeen's strict usage also eliminates a good number of people who thought of themselves as fundamentalists. This would be especially true for the era of the 1920s through the 1940s, when fundamentalism usually was seen as a broad coalition of militant conservative evangelicals, including many nondispensationalists. The same problem occurs today with respect to the numerous Southern Baptist fundamentalists, for whom dispensationalism is not a test of affiliation. Sandeen solves such problems by introducing the distinction between the *fundamentalist movement*, which he sees as millenarianism by another name, and the *fundamentalist controversies*, which he views as not definitive of the organized movement. The controversies, he argues, temporarily allied millenarians with other militants and introduced some extraneous issues, such as anti-evolution. But with this interpretive move, much of the precision of Sandeen's approach seems lost in a new distinction between two types of fundamentalists, those in the movement and those involved in the controversies.[8]

Nonetheless, we should keep in mind the very extensive overlap of dispensationalism and fundamentalism. Dispensationalists have always been central to shaping fundamentalism. We can see something of the connection by looking at the leading organizer of early fundamentalism, William B. Riley (1861–1947) of Minneapolis, founder of the World's Christian Fundamentals Association (WCFA) in 1919. Riley's account of early fundamentalism is very close to what we find later in Rice or Dollar. The battle, Riley emphasized, was over the Bible, and the first point of the creed of the WCFA asserts the inerrancy of Scripture. The other fundamental doctrines it emphasizes are the Trinity, the virgin birth, the fall of humans, the substitutionary atonement, the bodily resurrection and ascension of Christ, the premillennial return of Christ, salvation by faith, and the final resurrection and last judgment. Only two of these points would separate fundamentalists from most traditional Protestantism. Specifying inerrancy of Scripture as a test of faith was rare before the late nineteenth century, though most earlier Protestants assumed something like it. A more substantial wedge was the premillennial plank in the WCFA creed: "We believe in 'that blessed hope,' the personal, premillennial, and imminent return of our Lord and Savior Jesus Christ." Riley recognized that this premillennial plank would exclude some potential allies. Nonetheless, he affirmed that "fundamentalism insists upon the plain intent of scripture-speech" and that premillennialism was the only interpretation logically consistent with that intent.[9]

Partly because of the insistence on premillennialism and the dispensationalism that almost always went with it, not all who called themselves fundamentalists in the 1920s were allied with the WCFA. Nonetheless, there was a considerable coalition of cobelligerents. The largest battles took place in the Northern Baptist Convention and the (northern) Presbyterian Church in the U.S.A. In both cases, militant denominational conservatives, with some dispensationalist aid (especially among the baptists), built fundamentalist campaigns. Presbyterian conservatives, who had their own confessional agenda, accepted the fundamentalist designation only with some reluctance. In the early 1920s, these parties sometimes could enlist majorities of the representatives of their denomination and seemed to have prospects for limiting the spread of liberal theological views. After 1925, however, the strength of these fundamentalist parties declined within these denominations.[10]

During the next two decades fundamentalism was both reorganizing and growing.[11] The chief problem faced by fundamentalists, with their influence sharply curtailed in all major northern denominations, was: How could their movement gain institutional strength? On this point the fundamentalist coalition brought together groups with opposed tendencies. Many who regarded themselves as fundamentalists thought that they should simply continue to champion their cause within the major denominations, building individual fundamentalist congregations that could resist liberal influences of denominational leadership. Other fundamentalists increasingly concluded that the submovement should form its own separate institutions, which could be freed from corrupting entanglements with the major denominations. Dispensationalists especially were inclined in this separatist direction, since one of the dispensationalist teachings was that the major churches of this age would become apostate. Many, though not all, dispensationalists carried this teaching to the conclusion that Christians must separate themselves from any such apostasy. Typically such separatism led to the formation of independent local congregations, almost always baptistic, that might be loosely associated in fundamentalist associations or connected in small denominations.

Through the 1940s, however, separatism still was not necessarily a test of fundamentalist faith. William B. Riley, for instance, did not separate from the Northern Baptist Convention until 1947, the year of his death. In the meantime, fundamentalism, whether of the separatist or nonseparatist variety, was growing through evangelistic agencies independent of any denominational affiliation (they avoided the separatist question, since in practice they were largely independent anyway). During World War II, fundamentalists promoted successful revivalism, marked especially by the organization of Youth for Christ in 1945. Billy Graham got his start as the first full-time evangelist for Youth for Christ and as the successor Riley hand-picked to head his schools in Minneapolis.[12] Card-carrying fundamentalism thus was growing through networks of interrelated agencies. Often Bible institutes served as virtual headquarters for various fundamentalist subgroups.[13] The quip of Daniel Stevick that fundamentalism may be defined as "all those churches or persons in communion with Moody Bible Institute," while overstated, suggests a method that works almost as well as any to identify card-carrying fundamentalists of this era.[14]

In this context, the explicitly organized parts of fundamentalism began a process that eventually led to some major splits. An early sign of the impending crisis was the formation of two competing organizations in the early 1940s. The most important of these was the National Association of Evangelicals (NAE), founded under the leadership of Harold John Ockenga and others in 1942. Some months earlier, in 1941, Carl McIntire had established the American Council of Christian Churches (ACCC). The major difference between the two was that McIntire's organization demanded that member denominations be strictly separatist and have no connection with the Federal Council of Churches. The NAE, on the other hand, allowed individual members who belonged to denominations associated with the Federal Council. Ockenga himself, for instance, held ordination in the Presbyterian Church in the U.S.A. at the time of the founding. The NAE also was a more truly evangelical, rather than strictly fundamentalist, group, in that it was open to a variety of evangelical traditions. Its membership included denominations that were pentecostal, holiness, baptist, Mennonite, Friends, Methodist, and Reformed. All the member denominations were small; the total constituency represented by 1956 totaled only about one and a half million. Larger evangelical or conservative groups, such as the Southern Baptist Convention, the Missouri Synod Lutherans, and the major black churches, stayed out. The creed of the NAE also was broader, asserting fundamental doctrines that Protestant biblicists could agree on but not specifying either inerrancy of Scripture or premillennialism. The considerably smaller membership of the ACCC, by contrast, was strictly fundamentalist and retained the fundamentalist submovement's traditional opposition to pentecostalism.[15]

The early leadership of the NAE, as well as of much of the para-church revival of the 1940s, was still, like Billy Graham and Ockenga at this time, essentially fundamentalist. Those who were at the center of organized transdenominational fundamentalism came predominantly from the more Reformed traditions, especially baptist and Presbyterian. Fundamentalist beliefs and attitudes, however, had carried over into other traditions, such as those that joined the NAE. The Wesleyan Methodists at Houghton College in the 1940s were, despite their holiness traditions, just as fundamentalistic as any of the Reformed groups. The various submovements of revivalist evangelicalism had so many common traditions and so much influence on each other that it was difficult to draw clear lines among them. Card-carrying fundamentalists, for instance, often adopted Keswick holiness doctrines, which were a Reformed variation of nineteenth-century holiness teachings. Some pentecostals held similar views, while others' teachings were closer to Wesleyan holiness doctrines. Most pentecostals were dispensationalists and denominational separatists. Virtually all of the groups were very conservative politically, though they covered the spectrum from political activism to almost total noninvolvement. Virtually all insisted on literal interpretations of the Bible and adamantly opposed modernism and higher criticism. "Revivalist evangelical" is the term that might best describe these interrelated subgroups as a whole, although, in the 1940s, "fundamentalist" would have been a more common designation.[16]

By the end of the 1950s, a major realignment had taken place that brought about a redefinition of fundamentalism. Essentially, a breakup occurred within the more or less Reformed coalition of card-carrying fundamentalists, who long had exerted disproportionate influence in shaping the transdenominational movement. The central event in this realignment was Billy Graham's New York crusade in 1957.[17] Rather than conduct his crusade with the sponsorship only of other fundamentalists, Graham accepted the sponsorship of the city's council of churches. That meant that some of his converts would be guided to liberal churches and denominations. This was the last straw for many stricter fundamentalists, most influentially John R. Rice, who had supported Graham up to that point. Associated with Graham were a group of leaders, including Carl F.H. Henry, the founding editor (in 1956) of *Christianity Today*, and Ockenga, both of whom already sometimes had been using the terms "new evangelical" or "evangelical" to distance themselves from fundamentalist extremes. These neo-evangelicals were softened fundamentalists who wanted to preserve the essentials of the tradition but not its extremes. They retained the basic fundamentalist biblicism and opposition to liberal theologies, but they did not demand separatism; and they deemphasized some of the strictest prohibitions of the fundamentalist moral code. Although they usually remained premillennial, they dropped dispensationalism.

The question of biblical inerrancy soon split neo-evangelicals themselves into two major camps. Progressives thought inerrancy too narrow a way to define biblical authority; more fundamentalistic neo-evangelicals insisted on inerrancy as a test of faith. Fuller Theological Seminary, the leading neo-evangelical educational center, split over this question and fell into the hands of progressives.[18] More fundamentalistic neo-evangelicals, usually supported by Graham and *Christianity Today*, took the lead in promoting the inerrancy test for as much of evangelicalism as possible. Most influential in these campaigns was Harold Lindsell, editor of *Christianity Today* from 1968 to 1978, whose *Battle for the Bible*, published in 1976, was the *Uncle Tom's Cabin* of the inerrancy movement. Although few of the heirs to neo-evangelicalism and related submovements still designated themselves fundamentalists, fundamentalist influences remained strong. By 1979, Lindsell had concluded that "the term *evangelical* has been so debased that it has lost its usefulness" and that it might be better to accept the designation *fundamentalist*.[19]

In the meantime, *evangelical* had become the popular term for almost any theologically conservative Protestant who affirmed the necessity of regeneration, and the movement clearly included so many subgroups that no one group could claim to speak for the whole.[20]

All these developments cleared the way for a more precise use of the term *fundamentalist*. Now, in its narrow sense as a self-designation, it referred primarily to separatist, dispensationalist baptists and members of independent Bible churches. The one major exception was the "conservative" or "fundamentalist" party, which, under the banner of the inerrancy of Scripture, successfully gained a majority voice in the Southern Baptist Convention during the 1970s and 1980s.[21] These Southern Baptist fundamentalists were more like those of the first stage of the northern movement through the 1940s, when the term *fundamentalism* most often designated militantly biblicist denominational conservatives.

With this large exception, fundamentalism could be used to refer almost exclusively to noncharismatic (including nonpentecostal) dispensationalists. These, too, however, like the neo-evangelicals, split into two camps. Fundamentalist scholar George W. Dollar, a strict separatist himself, designates these as *militant fundamentalists* and *moderate fundamentalists*.[22] The militants not only strictly insist on separation from denominations that tolerate theological liberalism, but also refuse fellowship even with fundamentalist individuals in such denominations. This principle is known as "second-degree separatism." For instance, during the late 1970s, Bob Jones III split with John R. Rice, because Rice was consorting with fundamentalist leaders in the Southern Baptist Convention, such as W.A. Criswell or Robert G. Lee. Jones considered these men corrupted, because they still belonged to a "backslidden, apostate" denomination.[23]

Within moderate fundamentalism may be included some very influential networks associated with leading dispensationalist schools, such as Moody Bible Institute, Dallas Theological Seminary, Talbot Theological Seminary, and Grace Theological Seminary. These schools in practice are separate from major denominations but do not insist on strict separatism. Because of their greater openness, moderate fundamentalists have been more influential within them than the strict militants.

Both these types of fundamentalists typically distinguished them-selves sharply from evangelicals and neo-evangelicals, who were targets of some of their fiercest fire. Robert Lightner's *Neo-Evangelicalism*[24] was perhaps the most widely circulated of many fundamentalist polemics dur-ing the 1950s and 1960s. George W. Dollar called neo-evangelicals (or *modified fundamentalists*) "an enemy from within."[25]

The situation changed once again in the late 1970s, with the emer-gence of large-scale political activism among moderate fundamentalists. Jerry Falwell's Moral Majority assumed the leadership in this movement. One of the earliest neo-evangelical critiques of fundamentalism had been that it lacked a social program. This charge was not entirely true, since some fundamentalists, such as Carl McIntire and Billy James Hargis, were for many years militantly conservative political crusaders. Other funda-mentalists, however, associated any political program with a "social gos-pel" and proudly eschewed political involvements.

Falwell's coalition in some ways replicated and went beyond the ear-lier neo-evangelical program. In order to build a large following and na-tional influence, the Moral Majority was open to alliances with all sorts of groups, including conservative Catholics and Mormons, traditional ob-jects of fundamentalist attack. The leadership of the Moral Majority pro-fessed itself fundamentalist, however, and hence had to insist on separa-tism. Falwell resolved this difficulty by making a strict distinction between his eccelesiastical affiliations, which he kept separatist, and his political activities, which could involve broad alliances. In order to make such alliances and to expand his influence, he found it necessary in many situa-tions to tone down fundamentalist militancy. Nonetheless, in ecclesias-tical situations Falwell still insisted on such fundamentalist distinctives as inerrancy, dispensationalism, and opposition to the pentecostal and charis-matic movements.

Though Falwell and other moderate fundamentalists had much in common with the more conservative neo-evangelical leadership, funda-mentalists were so used to defining themselves in contrast to evangelicals (or neo-evangelicals) that such bridges were especially difficult to build. Falwell, however, made some efforts. *The Fundamentalist Phenomenon: The Resurgence of Conservative Christianity*, written largely by two of Falwell's lieutenants, Ed Dobson and Ed Hindson, and appearing under Falwell's editorship in 1981, not only offered the standard warning that neo-evangelicalism would lead to liberalism, but also castigated "hyper-fundamentalists."[26] Their equation (in their subtitle) of "conservative Christianity" with fundamentalism suggested an effort to broaden the tra-dition slightly. *The Fundamentalist Journal*, largely under the editorship of Dobson, during the mid-1980s also cautiously suggested toning down fundamentalist abrasiveness and extremism in doctrinal and behavioral demands. In *In Search of Unity: An Appeal to Fundamentalists and Evangelicals* (1985), Dobson once again looked for common ground between the two. He listed as fundamentalist strengths "Militancy, Truth, Preaching, Evangelism, Pastors," and as evangelical strengths "Moderation, Love, Teaching, Worship, Scholars." Fundamentalist weaknesses were "Intolerance, Absolutism, Pride of accomplishment, Worry over labels, and Split to the right." Evangelical weaknesses were "Overtolerance, Relativism, Pride of Intellect, Worry over credibility, Drift to the left."[27]

The Falwell group was trying to keep one foot in each camp, adopting some neo-evangelical programs and attitudes while at the same time retaining fundamentalist identity. Bob Jones III and his allies predictably designated Falwell a "pseudo neo-fundamentalist."[28] The "pseudo" appellation probably was inappropriate, since Falwell probably was not faking his stance; but "neo-fundamentalist" might accurately suggest the degree to which Falwell's movement parallels the earlier neo-evangelical effort. Nonetheless, as with most who called themselves fundamentalist in the 1980s, the designation "evangelical" is still anathema.

Fundamentalism today can be classed as one of the subtypes of evangelicalism, if we use *evangelical* in the broad sense, as referring to the now-classical tradition arising out of the eighteenth-century awakenings. Historically, fundamentalists belong to one of the branches growing out of that movement. Doctrinally, they would agree with most other evangelicals on 95 percent of the issues. Nevertheless, the term *evangelical* (like *fundamentalist*) has both a broad and a narrow meaning. In the post-World War II era, *evangelical* was a term used by one subgroup, the neo-evangelical reformers of fundamentalism. Fundamentalists (narrowly defined as separatists, etc.) and such evangelicals (narrowly defined as neo-evangelicals) sharply dissociated themselves from each other. Nonetheless, if we look at the broader picture since the eighteenth century, these are two very closely related subtypes within the larger evangelical movement. The wars between them have been so fierce precisely because they are particularly close relatives within an extended family.

NOTES

1. George W. Dollar, *A History of Fundamentalism in America* (Greenville, S.C.: Bob Jones Univ., 1973), 355; John R. Rice, *I Am a Fundamentalist* (Murfreesboro, Tenn.: Sword of the Lord, 1975), 15; Jerry Falwell, "Let's Promote, Upgrade, Increase Fundamentalism," *Sword of the Lord*:2 (12 Jan. 1979):1.

2. Rice, *I Am a Fundamentalist*, 7–12, 151–218.

3. Ibid., 9.

4. Dollar, *History of Fundamentalism*, xv.

5. On the cultural role of the Bible and fundamentalist reactions, see Nathan O. Hatch and Mark A. Noll, eds., *The Bible in America* (New York: Oxford Univ. Press, 1982).

6. Dollar, *History of Fundamentalism*, 1.

7. Ernest R. Sandeen, *The Roots of Fundamentalism: British and American Millernarianism, 1800–1930* (Chicago: Univ. of Chicago Press, 1970).

8. See also George M. Marsden, "Defining Fundamentalism," *Christian Scholar's Review* 1 (Winter 1971):141–51, and Ernest R. Sandeen's reply in *Christian Scholar's Review* 1 (Spring 1971):227–32. The editors of the present volume have implicitly rejected Sandeen's approach, by including separate chapters on premillennialism and fundamentalism.

9. William Bell Riley, "The Faith of the Fundamentalists," *Current History* 26 (June 1927):434–46, reprinted in *Controversy in the Twenties, Fundamentalism, Modernism, and Evolution*, ed. Willard B. Gatewood, Jr. (Nashville, Tenn.: Vanderbilt Univ. Press, 1969), 74–76.

10. For a fuller discussion of fundamentalism up to this point, see George M. Marsden, *Fundamentalism and American Culture: The Shaping of American Evangelicalism, 1870–1925* (New York: Oxford Univ. Press, 1980). The subtitle of this volume is confusing. The fundamentalist controversies reshaped much, but not all, of American evangelicalism in the broad sense. It shaped later neo-evangelicalism (sometimes confusingly called just evangelism), as well as later fundamentalism (see discussion below).

11. Joel A. Carpenter, "Fundamentalist Institutions and the Rise of Evangelical Protestantism, 1929–1942," *Church History* 49 (Mar. 1980):62–75.

12. Carpenter, "From Fundamentalism to the New Evangelical Coalition," in *Evangelicalism and Modern America*, ed. George M. Marsden (Grand Rapids, Mich.: Eerdmans, 1984), 3–16, and "Youth for Christ and the New Evangelicals' Place in the Life of the Nation," in *American Recoveries: Religion in the Life of the Nation*, ed. Rowland A. Sherrill (Urbana: Univ. of Illinois Press, 1988).

13. See William Vance Trollinger, Jr., "One Response to Modernity: Northwestern Bible School and the Fundamentalist Empire of William Bell Riley" (Ph.D. diss., Univ. of Wisconsin, Madison, 1984). Also see Virginia Lieson Brereton, "Protestant Fundamentalist Bible Schools, 1882–1940" (Ph.D. diss., Columbia Univ., 1981).

14. Daniel B. Stevick, *Beyond Fundamentalism* (Richmond, Va.: John Knox Press, 1964), 45. My thanks to Joel A. Carpenter for reading a draft of the present essay and for suggesting the importance of this point.

15. Louis Gasper, *The Fundamentalist Movement* (The Hague: Mouton, 1953), 28–29, and Carpenter, "The Fundamentalist Leaven and the Rise of an Evangelical United Front," in *The Evangelical Tradition in America*, ed. Leonard I. Sweet (Macon, Ga.: Mercer Univ. Press, 1984), 257–88.

16. Carl F.H. Henry recalled in retrospect, "In the 1930s we were all fundamentalists. . . . The term 'evangelical' became a significant option when the NAE was organized (1942). . . . In the context of the debate with modernism, fundamentalist was an appropriate alternative; in other contexts [of the debate within the fundamentalist movement], the term evangelical was preferable." He also writes, "Nobody wanted the term 'evangelical' when NAE was formed in 1942; in social context and in ecumenical context it implied what was religiously passe." Henry to Marsden, 2 Feb. 1986.

17. Butler Farley Porter, Jr., "Billy Graham and the End of Evangelical Unity" (Ph.D. diss., Univ. of Florida, 1976).

18. For further discussion of these developments, see George M. Marsden, *Reforming Fundamentalism: Fuller Seminary and the New Evangelicalism* (Grand Rapids, Mich.: Eerdmans, 1987).

19. Harold Lindsell, *The Bible in the Balance* (Grand Rapids, Mich.: Zondervan, 1979), 319–20.

20. For a discussion of the various ways the term *evangelical* can legitimately be used, see George M. Marsden, "The Evangelical Denomination," in *Evangelicalism and Modern America*, ed. Marsden, vii–xix.

21. For an exposition of the fundamentalist or conservative viewpoint, see James Carl Hefley, *The Truth in Crisis: The Controversy in the Southern Baptist Convention* (Dallas, Tex.: Criterion Publications, 1986). See also David O. Beale, *S.B.C.: House of Sand?* (Greenville, S.C.: Unusual Publications, 1985).

22. George W. Dollar, "Facts for Fundamentalist" (pamphlet), rev. ed. (Nov. 1983), and Dollar, *History of Fundamentalism*, 282–89. In both these places, Dollar lists fundamentalist organizations in each of the camps.

23. Bob Jones III, "Facts John R. Rice Will Not Face" (pamphlet) (Greenville, S.C.: Bob Jones Univ., 1977), 17 and 19. Rice responds to Jones in "Here is Historic Fundamentalism," *Sword of the Lord* 44 (22 Sept. 1978):1, 7. I am most grateful to Steve Doan and Henry Fernandez, who collected these and many other valuable fundamentalist materials during the 1970s and furnished me with them.

24. Robert P. Lightner, *Neo-Evangelicalism* (Des Plaines, Ill.: Regular Baptist Press, 1959, and several subsequent editions).

25. Dollar, *History of Fundamentalism*, 203–211.

26. Jerry Falwell with Ed Dobson and Ed Hindson, eds., *The Fundamentalist Phenomenon: The Resurgence of Conservative Christianity* (Garden City, N.Y.: Doubleday, 1981), 143–85.

27. Edward Dobson, *In Search of Unity: An Appeal to Fundamentalists and Evangelicals* (Nashville, Tenn.: Thomas Nelson, 1985), 66–72.

28. Falwell with Dobson and Hindson, *Fundamentalist Phenomenon*, 160–61.

CHAPTER 4

The Limits of Evangelicalism: The Pentecostal Tradition

Donald W. Dayton

Does pentecostalism have a distinct theology? If so, in what ways may it be said to differ from other forms of Christian theology, especially those labeled "evangelical"? These questions are not easy to answer, and their very appropriateness is a matter of dispute. Certainly it has not been characteristic of pentecostalism to be as productive of dogmatic or formal theology as other traditions. Is this, as some have suggested, because its particular gift is to offer a nondogmatic and experiential form of Christianity — and thus to challenge the very shape and logic of, for example, the classical Reformation traditions? Or is the lack of such theological articulations to be related to the relative youth of the movement — so that we may yet see a flowering of pentecostal theology? Both of these suggestions have elements of truth, but I am more inclined toward the latter position and expect that we shall see emerge a more formal articulation of pentecostal theologies.

Meanwhile, it is still possible to pursue the question of whether pentecostalism has a distinct theological self-understanding, one that can be compared to the self-understandings of other traditions to which it bears some sort of family relationship. We are often misled by the classical Christian traditions to understand "theology" only in the sense of "academic theology," in which Christian truth is systematically and philosophically explicated according to the dominant intellectual ethos. But there are other modes of theological articulation, especially among more populist and dissenting movements such as pentecostalism. These movements often eventually produce full systematic articulations in the academic sense — as I am convinced pentecostalism will do — but in the meantime they may not be dismissed condescendingly as "atheological" or "pretheological." They carry, even in their popular and nonsystematic articulations, a theological

Large parts of this chapter have already appeared in Donald W. Dayton *Theological Roots of Pentecostalism* (Scarecrow Press and Francis Asbury Press, 1987).

vision whose elements form a distinct "gestalt," the features of which can be discerned and whose logic can be described. I believe that pentecostalism can be described theologically in this sense. This paper is my effort to describe the theological vision of pentecostalism and to compare it with that of evangelicalism.

The pentecostal movement has often been interpreted — naturally enough, it must be admitted — primarily in terms of its most characteristic feature: glossolalia, or "speaking in tongues." This has been true both within and without the movement. Carl Brumbeck's classic *apologia* for pentecostalism, *What Meaneth This?*, is basically a defense of glossolalia.[1] Similarly, the critical literature has tended to denounce pentecostalism with the epithet, "the modern tongues movement."[2] Even the apparently broader study of more recent developments, authored by Roman Catholic Kilian McDonnell, *Charismatic Renewal and the Churches*, is essentially a survey of the psychological and sociological research on glossolalia.[3]

Though not without its value, of course, such an approach to pentecostalism has several limitations. In the first place, glossolalia fails to define the movement adequately in such a way as to distinguish it fully from other religious movements. Until the recent appearance of the "charismatic movement" or "neopentecostalism" within the traditional churches, such a definition served reasonably well to distinguish the pentecostal churches from other Christian churches. "Pentecostal" churches were those whose members "spoke in tongues." But the practice of "glossolalia is actually a common religious phenomenon,"[4] occurring in a great variety of contexts. In America, for example, glossolalia appeared in such nineteenth-century groups as the Shakers and Mormons.[5] In spite of some common features, such movements are only very indirectly related to pentecostalism. Glossolalia by itself, therefore, cannot serve to define pentecostalism or to distinguish it fully from other religious movements.

Second, concentration on glossolalia by interpreters of pentecostalism encourages the claims of some pentecostal advocates that pentecostalism emerged totally *de novo*, without historical antecedent, either about 1900 in a small Bible college near Topeka, Kansas, under the leadership of "holiness" evangelist Charles F. Parham, *or* half a dozen years later in a black mission in Azusa Street, Los Angeles, depending on the set of claims to which one gives most credence.[6] Both critics and, to a lesser extent, apologists have been inclined to center their attacks or defenses on attempts to discount or establish a historical line of those advocating and practicing this "gift of the Spirit" within the Christian tradition. In particular, such an orientation to glossolalia has discouraged careful theological and historical analysis of developments in the late nineteenth century and has encouraged an immediate jump to such earlier antecedent movements as the British "Irvingites" of the 1830s, who adopted many pentecostal-like practices and theological claims.[7]

Third, the attention given to the practice of glossolalia has diverted interpreters from theological categories of analysis. Sociological and psychological categories have been employed more regularly.[8] Until the recent appearance of glossolalia in the cultural and ecclesiastical mainstream, the phenomenon has been understood largely as an abnormal response to some form of "deprivation," whether sociological or psychological.

Even when theological analysis has been attempted, the concentration on glossolalia has foreshortened the theological analysis by restricting the type of questions considered. The result has been that typical theological analysis of pentecostalism has centered almost exclusively on questions of pneumatology, especially the doctrine of the "baptism in the Holy Spirit" and the "gifts of the Spirit."[9] While such an understanding is a decided advance over those interpretations of pentecostalism which see only glossolalia, it still fails, as we shall see, to grasp the logic of the more complicated gestalt of theological themes that constituted original pentecostalism at least. Such reductionism in the treatment of pentecostal theology not only prevents the fullest understanding of the movement, but also precludes critical evaluation of its most distinctive claims.

These limitations, inherent in efforts to interpret pentecostalism primarily in terms of glossolalia, raise the question of whether an alternative analysis might penetrate beneath the practice of "speaking in tongues" to a fuller understanding of the theological claims supporting that practice — and do this in such a way as to enable the interpreter to understand the precise historical and theological relationships of pentecostalism to antecedent and related theological and ecclesiastical traditions. At first blush, any effort to reduce the bewildering variety of pentecostal traditions to a common theological pattern seems doomed to failure. Fortunately, however, much of the variety within pentecostalism is derived from cultural factors, such as divisions along racial lines or allegiance to a founder whose charismatic leadership has produced a given faction perpetuating her or his own idioscyncratic practices and convictions.[10] For our theological purposes, these factors may be largely ignored.

But even the formalized statements of belief and doctrine within pentecostalism reflect an amazing variety, containing not only the classical and common doctrines of the Christian church (usually amplified by various additions on pentecostal distinctives — tongues, baptism in the Spirit, and so forth) but also "articles of faith" on such topics as foot washing, church property, the usefulness of camp meetings, and membership in secret societies or labor unions.[11] In the search for a characteristic theological understanding of pentecostalism, such statements are not always to be trusted. Often they are appropriated from other ecclesiastical and theological traditions and then expanded in pentecostal directions, often in an apparent effort to assert "orthodoxy" and historical continuity with more classical Christian traditions. The 1948 "Statement of Truth" of the Pentecostal Fellowship of North America, for example, was taken *verbatim* from the "Statement of Faith" promulgated five years earlier by the National Association of Evangelicals—with the exception of article 5: "We believe that the full gospel includes holiness of heart and life, healing for the body and baptism in the Holy Spirit with the initial evidence of speaking in other tongues as the Spirit gives utterance."[12]

This statement does provide some clues in the search for a "gestalt" of characteristically pentecostal claims, especially when amplified by an emerging consensus in the effort to develop a typology of pentecostal groups. David W. Faupel, elaborating the work of such predecessors as Klaude Kendrick and Everett Moore, divides pentecostal churches and movements into three groups, according to their distinctive theological themes: (1) those teaching a doctrine of sanctification in the Wesleyan, holiness tradition (these are the so-called "three-works-of-grace" pentecostals, who maintain that Christian experience normally finds expression in a pattern of: conversion, "entire sanctification" as a distinct subsequent experience, and a further "baptism in the Holy Spirit" that empowers the believer for witness and service, as evidenced by "speaking in tongues"); (2) those reducing this pattern to "two works of grace" by collapsing the first two works into one "finished work," supplemented by a process of gradual sanctification (thus advocating a pattern focusing on conversion and a subsequent "baptism in the Holy Spirit" as just defined); and (3) those holding a "oneness" or "Jesus only" view of the Godhead (thus proclaiming an "evangelical unitarianism" of the second person of the Trinity).[13]

While the third of these types is in many ways the most novel and deserves sympathetic analysis in its own right,[14] for our purposes it is primarily a subgroup of the second type, evoked by a subsidiary problem. The "oneness" movement is a variation within pentecostalism produced by a literalistic effort to harmonize the trinitarian baptismal formula in Matt. 28:19 with the more common pattern in Acts (especially Acts 2:38), of baptism in the name of the "Lord Jesus" or "Jesus Christ." This branch of pentecostalism resolves this difficulty by affirming the pattern in Acts 2:38 and related passages and arguing that Jesus is the full manifestation of the Godhead in this dispensation. Though touching on broader issues, such as a dispensational understanding of the trinitarian involvement of God in human history and the larger pentecostal problem of relating the work of the Spirit to the work of Christ, this cluster of ideas expresses nothing universally characteristic of pentecostalism. The "Jesus Only" movement derives, both theologically and historically, from the second or "two works of grace" branch of pentecostalism.

Our problem, then, is to develop a theological analysis of pentecostalism that is characteristic of both major types of the movement and that, if possible, helps explain why pentecostalism separated into these two strands. But to focus too quickly on the tension between the "two works of grace" and the "three works of grace" would produce a soteriological reductionism not unlike the reductionism produced by too early a concentration on glossolalia. The article above, taken from the "Statement of Truth" of the Pentecostal Fellowship of North America, uses the expression "full gospel" and draws attention to "healing for the body" as well as "holiness" and the "baptism in the Holy Spirit." The term "full gospel" is characteristically used within pentecostalism and describes a constellation of themes partially submerged in the larger PFNA doctrinal statement.

These themes of the "full" or "whole gospel" are spelled out as follows in an early statement:

> During the Reformation God used Martin Luther and others to restore to the world the doctrine of justification by faith. Rom. 5:1. Later on the Lord used the Wesleys and others in the great holiness movement to restore the gospel of sanctification by faith. Acts 26:18. Later still he used various ones to restore the gospel of Divine healing by faith (Jas. 5:14, 15) and the gospel of Jesus's second coming. Acts 1:11. Now the Lord is using many witnesses in the great Pentecostal movement to restore the gospel of the baptism with the Holy Ghost and fire (Luke 3:16; Acts 1:5) with signs following. Mark 16:17, 18; Acts 2:4, 10:44–46; 19:6; 1:1–28:31. Thank God, we now have preachers of the whole gospel.[15]

This passage suggests the five themes included in the "whole gospel"—the three of the "three works of grace" strand of pentecostalism, plus two more, "divine healing by faith" and "Jesus's second coming." These two extra themes may be added to the teachings of either branch of pentecostalism and regularly occur in passages listing the distinctive themes of pentecostalism. This constellation of motifs recurs throughout the whole pentecostal tradition.

The pattern appeared, for example, at the very beginning, when students at Bethel Bible College were straining toward the final link in the chain of pentecostal teachings. As their teacher Charles F. Parham reported:

> In December of 1900 we had our examination upon the subject of repentance, conversion, consecration, sanctification, healing and the soon coming of the Lord. We had reached in our studies a problem. What about the second chapter of Acts? . . . I set the students at work studying out diligently what was the Bible evidence of the baptism of the Holy Ghost.[16]

This assignment raised the question that a few days later resulted in the emergence of pentecostal theology, when student Agnes N. Ozman "receive[d] the Holy spirit" and purportedly spoke in the Chinese language.[17]

A similar pattern appears in the black denomination, the Fire Baptized Holiness Church of God of the Americas, formed by merger in 1926 but tracing its roots back to 1898. The basis of union contained the following doctrinal themes, among the denominational commitments: repentance, regeneration, justification, sanctification, pentecostal baptism, speaking with other tongues as the Spirit gives utterance, divine healing of the body, and the premillennial Second Coming of Christ.[18] Likewise, the pattern may be found in the Apostolic Faith Mission, one of the oldest pentecostal bodies, tracing its origin directly to the Azusa Street Revival that launched pentecostalism into worldwide notice and notoriety:

> This church . . . places special emphasis on the need of having three definite, separate, spiritual experiences wrought out in the heart and life: JUSTIFICA-TION, SANCTIFICATION, THE BAPTISM OF THE HOLY GHOST . . . These doctrines concerning spiritual experience, together with the teachings on Divine Healing, the Imminent Second Coming of Jesus — premillennial . . . provide the solid, scriptural foundation on which the church stands.[19]

This pattern is, if anything, clearer in the other main branch of pentecostalism, where the second theme of sanctification drops out, to leave an emphasis on the "full gospel" as a "fourfold gospel." Modern Asemblies of God theologian Stanley Horton organizes his denominational training manual, *Into All Truth*, around "four fundamental teachings — salvation, healing, the baptism in the Holy Spirit, and the second coming of Christ" because "these four teachings have received special emphasis and illumination by the Holy Spirit during the present-day pentecostal revival."[20] This pattern, however, finds even clearer expression in the work of Aimee Semple McPherson, the controversial founder of the International Church of the Foursquare Gospel, whose basic message she summarized as follows: "Jesus saves us according to John 3:16. He baptizes us with the Holy Spirit according to Acts 2:4. He heals our bodies according to James 5:14–15. And Jesus is coming again to receive us unto Himself according to I Thessalonians 4:16–17."[21]

We shall take this latter fourfold pattern as the basis of our theological and historical analysis. Though the fivefold pattern was prior historically and thus has a certain claim on our attention, the fourfold pattern expresses more clearly and cleanly the logic of pentecostal theology. It is, moreover, contained within the more complex pattern, and thus may be veiwed as prior, logically if not historically, to the fivefold pattern. These four themes are well-nigh universal within the movement, appearing, as we have been arguing, in all branches and varieties of pentecostalism,[22] while the theme of entire sanctification finally is characteristic of only the holiness branch. To opt for the more streamlined fourfold pattern is not to ignore the holiness branch. The theological and historical reasons for its existence will be revealed as we work with the more universal pattern.

It must be admitted immediately that all of the elements of this four-fold pattern occur separately or in various combinations in other Christian traditions. Even the fourfold pattern itself is to some degree antici-pated in, for example, the "fourfold gospel" of A.B. Simpson, founder of the late-nineteenth-century Christian and Missionary Alliance, who spoke of Christ as our "Saviour, Sanctifier, Healer and Coming King."[23] But the emergence of this pattern, in fact, was the last step in the complex process of development that culminated in pentecostalism. It is nonetheless possi-ble to argue that this fourfold pattern is sufficiently characteristic of the movement as a whole to be used as the basis of historical and theological analysis. While other analyses might well be offered, the value of this one is demonstrated empirically, as we have been arguing, by the fact that it appears so widely in the literature of pentecostalism; theologically, as we will indicate momentarily, by the way in which it permits the logic of pente-costal thought to be explicated; and historically, as I have argued in *Theo-logical Roots of Pentecostalism* (1987), by the fact that tracing the emer-gence of these four themes reveals, perhaps for the first time with full clarity, the roots of pentecostal theology.

The discreet elements of the "foursquare gospel," of course, are pre-sent in many traditions, but within pentecostalism they are linked to-gether in a distinctive constellation that expresses the inner logic of the movement. These four themes coinhere within pentecostalism in such a way as to reinforce one another. The characteristic logic of this linkage can be seen most easily by exploring three early names given to the move-ment: the "pentecostal movement," the "apostolic faith," and the "latter rain movement." All three of these expressions occur in the title given by Charles F. Parham to his first report of the new phenomenon, "The Latter Rain: The Story of the Origin of the Original Apostolic or Pentecostal Movements."[24]

Exploring the title "pentecostal movement" reveals how the first two elements of the fourfold gospel — salvation/justification, and baptism in the Holy Spirit — are linked together. This pattern is grounded in a distinct hermeneutic, a distinctively pentecostal manner of appropriating the Scrip-tures. In contrast to magisterial Protestantism, which tends to read the New Testament through Pauline eyes, pentecostalism reads the rest of the New Testament through Lukan eyes, especially using lenses provided by the Book of Acts. As W.J. Hollenweger comments, "The Pentecostals and their predecessors based their views almost exclusively on the Gospel of Luke and the Acts of the Apostles."[25]

But to turn from the Pauline texts to the Lukan ones is to shift from one genre of literature to another, from didactic to narrative material.[26] Narrative texts are notoriously difficult to interpret theologically.[27] Pentecostalism reads the accounts of Pentecost in Acts and insists that the general pattern of the early church's reception of the Spirit, especially as it is in some sense separated in time from the church's experience of Jesus, must be replicated in the life of each individual believer. In making this claim, pentecostalism stands in a long tradition of a "subjectivizing hermeneutic." Claude Welch, for example, indicates that an integral part of pietism's turn toward subjective experience was its insistence that "the drama of the race—of Creation, Fall and Redemption—is to be reenacted in each life." Within pietism, "the true birth of Christ is his birth in our hearts, his true death is in that dying within us, his true resurrection is in the triumph of our faith."[28] The "higher life" antecedents to pentecostalism in the nineteenth century used a similar approach to Scripture, appropriating elements of the Old Testamant *Heilsgeschichte* devotionally. The exodus from Egypt, the wilderness wanderings, and crossing the Jordan River into the Promised Land all became stages in the normative pattern of the spiritual pilgrimage from conversion into the "second blessing" ("Beulah Land").[29]

Thus Assemblies of God historian William Menzies suggests:

> The Pentecostal Movement is that group of sects within the Christian Church which is characterized by the belief that the occurrence mentioned in Acts 2 on the Day of Pentecost not only signaled the birth of the church, but described an experience available to believers in all ages. The experience of an enduement with power, called the "baptism in the Holy Spirit" is believed to be evidenced by the accompanying sign of "speaking with other tongues as the Spirit gives utterance."[30]

This captures the key claim of pentecostalism and indicates why it carries the name that it does. The movement's distinctive way of reading the New Testament leads it to the conclusion that, like the early church, the modern believer becomes a disciple of Jesus Christ and receives the fullness of the Spirit's baptism in separate events or "experiences." In this manner, the first two elements of the "foursquare gospel" are tied together by a distinctive hermeneutic.

But to raise the question of the availability of the experience of Pentecost to every generation is implicitly to raise the question of the permanent validity of phenomena apparently reported in the New Testament — not only the so-called "charismata" such as glossolalia, but also the still more difficult question of "divine healing," also designated in the New Testament as a "gift of Spirit." Pentecostalism affirms the integral place in the ministry of Jesus of literal miracles of healing and insists that, because these were part of the post-Pentecost experience of the early church, as reported in the book of Acts, they are to be experienced in our own time as well. These miracles of healing not only are part of the salvation and relief brought to humanity in the gospel, but also are a sign of reassurance to the believer and of witness to the unbeliever. As Charles F. Parham put it in 1902:

> Christ did not leave his believing children without signs of distinction to follow them that the world might know who were Christians and who were not. Neither did he send forth his servants to preach vague speculative theories of a world to come, but with mighty power for the relief of suffering humanity; feeding the hungry, clothing the naked; healing the sick; casting out devils; speaking with tongues; confirming the word of inward benefit — wrought in Jesus Christ — by these outward visible signs.[31]

In this quotation a key word is "power." As one of the prepentecostal "higher life" teachers, Andrew Murray, put it: "Wherever the Spirit acts with power, there He works divine healings. . . . If divine healing is seen but rarely in our day, we can attribute it to no other cause but that the Spirit does not act with power."[32] If, then, the pentecostal "enduement with power" is available to all generations, then the power of the Spirit will manifest itself in our own day in miracles of divine healing, at least in the lives of those who truly have experienced the pentecostal baptism and know to look for such blessings.

In making this claim, pentecostalism reveals a "restorationist" motif that flies directly in the face of the tendency of classical Protestantism to argue that the "charismata" and "supernatural gifts of the Spirit" ceased with the close of the apostolic era. Illustrative of this way of handling the supernatural element in the New Testament are the words of Benjamin B. Warfield, an advocate of the old "Princeton Theology" who used the doctrine to refute the prepentecostal healing movements of the late nineteenth century. While granting to the pentecostals that the "Apostolic Church was characteristically a miracle-working church," Warfield insisted that this state of affairs was

> the characterizing peculiarity of specifically the Apostolic Church, and it belonged therefore exclusively to the Apostolic age. . . . these gifts . . . were part of the credentials of the apostles as the authoritative agents of God in founding the church. Their function thus confined them to distinctively the Apostolic Church, and they necessarily passed away with it.[33]

Pentecostalism, however, argues from the unchangeableness of God[34] that the nature of the apostolic church in this respect is normative for all time. In claiming to restore the supernatural elements of the apostolic era, the pentecostal movement claimed to be in effect the "apostolic faith"—a name frequently used by early adherents and applied by them to a large number of early journalistic efforts and institutions. As an early advocate put it, in a book entitled *The Apostolic Faith Restored*:

> There is, in the religious world of today, a great activity of the Lord's Spirit known as the Pentecostal or Apostolic Faith Movement. . . . the honest-hearted thinking men and women of this great movement have made it their endeavor to return to the faith and practice of our brethren who served God prior to the apostasy. They have made the New Testament their rule of life. . . . The Pentecostal Movement . . . leaps the intervening years crying "*Back to Pentecost.*" . . . this work of God is immediately connected with the work of God in New Testament days. Built by the same hand, upon the same foundation of the apostles and prophets, after the same pattern, according to the same covenant . . . they do not recognize a doctrine or custom as authoritative unless it can be traced to that primal source of church instruction, the Lord and his apostles.[35]

This assertion of direct access to the experience of Pentecost, then, leads quickly to a claim of having restored the "apostolic faith" and all the supernatural elements reported in the New Testament. Among these is "divine healing," which becomes not only a gift of God to his people in suffering, but also a sign of the Spirit's presence to the believer and a form of witness to the unbeliever in the work of evangelism.

But such a claim to have restored the "apostolic faith" raises severe apologetic questions for pentecostalism. How can something apparently so rare in the history of the church claim to be an essential manifestation of Christian faith and practice? Pentecostalism had two answers to this question. Some adherents—usually pressing the evidence beyond its limits— claimed that it was possible to "establish a fellowship of faith and practice[36] by unearthing in most ages of the church persons and movements that experiencd "speaking in tongues" and other "gifts of the Spirit." But there was another response to this question, one truer to the logic of at least early pentecostalism. This answer was bound up in the doctrine of the "latter rain," a teaching that illustrates how the expectation of the imminent return of Christ is linked in pentecostal thought to the other elements of the "foursquare gospel."

In early years, pentecostalism often took the name "latter rain movement."[37] The classic expression of this doctrine is found in *The Latter Rain Covenant*, by D. Wesley Myland.[38] The account of Pentecost in the second chapter of Acts quotes the prophecy from the book of Joel that in the "latter days" the Spirit will be poured out on all humanity. Pentecostals, therefore, were immediately attracted to the book of Joel[39] and to hints there, in James 4:7–8, and elsewhere in Scripture of an "early" and a "latter" rain. Physical rainfall in Palestine comes in two main seasons, one accompanying the spring planting, and the other in the fall, ripening the crops for harvest. This literal rainfall pattern provides the image by which pentecostalism understands its own relationship to the apostolic church and to the imminent end of the age. The original Pentecost of the New Testament was the "early rain," the outpouring of the Spirit that accompanied the "planting" of the church. Modern pentecostalism is the "latter rain," the special outpouring of the Spirit that restores the gifts in the last days, as part of the preparation for the "harvest," the return of Christ in glory. Myland insisted, "Now we are in the Gentile Pentecost, the first Pentecost started the church, the body of Christ, and this, the second Pentecost, *unites* and *perfects* the church into the coming of the Lord."[40] Myland went so far as to plot the physical rainfall in Palestine as part of a related argument that an increasing amount of rain in the late nineteenth century paralleled the spiritual emergence of pentecostalism, confirmed its validity, and indicated that the end was imminent.[41]

Though the specific parallels with Palestinian rainfall lost their value, the broader "latter rain" doctrine provided a key premise missing in the logic of pentecostalism. It gave the movement a key role in the approaching climax of history, as the means by which God was preparing the "bride" (the church) to meet her Lord. Mary B. Woodworth-Etter, a somewhat neglected figure in the history of pentecostalism, in these words described her "special call for this work" in a vision:

> To give the Household of Faith their Meat in due season; to give the Last Call to the Gentile sinners, the Last Call to the Marriage Supper of the Lamb, for His wife is about to enter the marriage relationship . . . ; and to get those who have been called to be established, to be faithful and true, that they may be anointed with the Holy Ghost and with power, and sealed with the proper knowledge of His coming.[42]

Beyond indicating the special task to be performed in the "last days" by the rise of pentecostalism, the "latter rain" doctrine explained why the gifts and miracles should have reappeared after such a long "drought." As Woodworth-Etter explained: "God says before Jesus comes, these same 'signs and wonders' shall come to pass; the sick shall be healed, devils cast out, people shall speak with tongues — just before he comes."[43] Not only do these "signs and wonders" tie the eschatological themes into the whole complex of the "foursquare gospel," but also the "latter-rain" framework makes the great apologetic problem of pentecostalism into a major apologetic asset.[44] The long drought from post apostolic times to the present is seen to be a part of God's dispensational plan for the ages. What seemed to make the movement most illegitimate—its discontinuity with classical forms of Christianity—has become its greatest legitimation.

Such, then, is the logic by which the elements of the fourfold gospel of pentecostalism cohere. The fact that this logic does exist and can be explicated confirms, to a certain extent, the appropriateness of a theological analysis emphasizing this distinctive pattern of four themes. In my book, *Theological Roots of Pentecostalism*, I have used this analysis to trace the development and interplay of these themes in the historical and theological genesis of pentecostalism. But here the question is how to relate this analysis to evangelicalism. The survey above already has hinted at answers to this question, but the hints lack consistency and so reveal that the question is more difficult than it may appear at first. On the one hand, John Nichol has classified pentecostalism as a subcategory of fundamentalism or evangelicalism, on the basis of the fact that the pentecostals—at least those (primarily white) bodies that have come together in the Pentecostal Fellowship of North American (PFNA)—use in slightly expanded form the National Association of Evangelicals (NAE) statement of faith. Similarly, I have quoted Maltby above to illustrate the lineage that pentecostals usually claim for themselves, one that traces their roots through the Reformation (the first theme); usually through the Wesleyan revival and its developments, such as the holiness movement (for sources of the emphasis on Spirit baptism); and often through the rise of the prophecy and healing movements (the other two themes). On the other hand, some of the distinctiveness of pentecostal claims has been seen in contrasts with the classical forms of Protestantism, as illustrated by B.B. Warfield.

The question is further complicated by the difficulty of arriving at a univocal definition of evangelicalism and the fact that often the self-understanding of evangelicalism has little relationship with the actual historical lineage that produced the institutions of evangelicalism. The concept "evangelical" in many ways is, to use an expression from the British analytical philosophical tradition, an "essentially contested concept" whose core meaning is in dispute. My own efforts to bring order to this discussion have centered on an analysis that suggests that the English word *evangelical* covers three diverse meanings that are kept distinct in languages such as German. The first of these, the one associated with the continental Reformation, has less relevance to the Anglo-American scene, where the other two meanings predominate. This first meaning, represented by the German adjective *evangelisch*, refers basically to the Reformation themes, especially in the Lutheran tradition as over against Catholicism, and is usually expressed in the tradition of an Augustinian anthropology and the

Reformation doctrines of divine initiation and sovereignty and their correlated doctrine of election. While most pentecostals on some level would identify themselves with classical Protestantism, even when they do, questions remain about the identification. When Aimee Semple McPherson speaks of Jesus as "savior," she really has in mind more the conversionist orientation of revivalism than the classical Reformation doctrine of justification. And her other three themes lead her even further away from the themes and concerns of the classical Reformation.

In the Anglo-Saxon world, there are two basic claimants to the label "evangelical." The first of these is the cluster of movements the Germans would call *Pietismus, Erweckungsbewegung,* or *Neupietismus*, or what I would call "classical evangelicalism," intending to encompass the roots of "convertive piety" in pietism and Puritanism, its flowering in the evangelical revival and the awakening traditions of the eighteenth century, and its more ambiguous expression in the revivalism that dominated in the nineteenth century. In this convertive tradition, there is a sort of theological "soteriological reductionism" that emphasizes conversion, mission, and evangelism; social concern; and a cluster of related themes. Over against this reductionism is the fundamentalist experience, with its associated "neo-evangelical" party that has emerged since World War II, and for which the Germans have been forced to coin the neologism *evangelikal*. This meaning of evangelical is difficult to define theologically but represents something of a coalition of groups that wish to affirm their basic "orthodoxy" or "conservativism," in contrast to the "acids of modernity" and the rise of "liberalism," especially as the latter has found expression in the wake of the Enlightenment. Many of the other themes from the two earlier movements find expression in various aspects of this coalition, but they cannot serve as defining because of the diversity of ecclesiastical traditions involved. The fundamentalists and neo-evangelicals, as represented in the Evangelical Theological Society, for example, have found the common element primarily in a doctrine of Scripture, especially in its inerrancy, although that strategy works less and less well in the contemporary scene.

John Nichol suggests that pentecostals are in some sense a subcategory of fundamentalism and evangelicalism. There is an obvious affinity here, and some pentecostals have moved in that direction, especially white pentecostal churches such as the Assemblies of God, which have been inclined more and more to articulate their theology in the fundamentalist/ evangelical mode. But this tendency is not as prominent in other white groups and even less so among the black and ethnic pentecostals. There is also the complicated question of the "unorthodox" tradition of Oneness Pentecostalism, and the subsidiary question of whether this tradition represents a minor "heresy" or a central thrust within pentecostalism. On a broader level, there is the complicated question of the difference between the largely "precritical" perspective of earlier pentecostalism and the largely tutored "anticritical" perspective of the fundamentalist tradition. It is not clear that pentecostalism, as it continues to mature theologically, will find its identity in such an "anticritical" tradition — especially as it continues to interact with the "neopentecostalism" of the charismatic movement, where the intellectual traditions are different and do not require the same precritical or anticritical methodology. One also could pursue the complicated question of whether the pentecostal emphasis on the continuing gift of "prophecy" in the church constitutes a perspective on revelation that is not easily assimilated into either the classical Protestant or modern fundamentalist theological tradition. It is at least clear that pentecostalism stands in a tradition that is not easily assimilated into the inerrancy tradition, with its distinctive logic and answers to basic questions.

Something of what is at issue in all of this may be seen in Bernard Ramm's *The Evangelical Heritage*, an effort to describe "evangelicalism" theologically in a historical and geographical mode. While I am convinced that Ramm's understanding of the situation is incorrect, it represents the dominant self-understanding of most self-identified evangelicals. Ramm argues that, theologically, evangelicalism is part of the Christian West rather than the East, that it is part of the Reformation rather than the Catholic tradition. After the Reformation, Ramm traces "evangelicalism" through Protestant orthodoxy until the rise of the Enlightenment, during which time he identifies evangelicalism with efforts to preserve the structure of orthodoxy against erosion. The line that he traces runs through the Old School Calvinism of nineteenth-century Princeton Theology, as represented by Charles Hodge and B.B. Warfield, and into the twentieth century, via J. Gresham Machen and fundamentalism. Implicitly Ramm represents the theological self-understanding of the neo-evangelical party that emerged from fundamentalism after World War II. I am convinced that something like this position is assumed by most who claim the label "evangelical" today.

The problem with this position is that it is historically accurate only for a very small percentage of those inclined to use the label "evangelical," including, especially, pentecostals and their near neighbors historically. If, as I argue in *Theological Roots of Pentecostalism* and as Vinson Synan argues in *The Holiness Pentecostal Movement in the United States*, pentecostalism is to be understood as a radical wing of the Wesleyan/holiness movement of the late nineteenth century, then Ramm's explication takes the wrong turn at nearly every point. It is becoming increasingly clear that many of Wesley's distinctive ideas, especially the cluster of themes about perfection, were rooted in Eastern rather than Western Christianity. And his basic thought patterns were (through his reliance on the Catholic and Anglican traditions of piety, in his doctrines of grace, etc.) as much Catholic as Protestant, especially when one has in mind the continental Reformation, to which Wesley and Methodism are related only tangentially. In the post-Reformation period, Wesley was a product of Puritanism and pietism rather than orthodoxy. With regard to the orthodoxy, it is important to notice that pietism shared with the Enlightenment many points in a critique of orthodoxy, in many ways seeing itself as an *alternative* way of "completing" the Reformation. Nor has this pietist tradition been inclined to defend the structures of Protestant orthodox theology. It has largely rejected the continental Reformation's doctrine of election, been critical of its anthropology, and drawn its alternative theories of the atonement from Grotius and the traditions of moral government rather than from the penal substitutionary tradition of orthodoxy. In the nineteenth century, these traditions would have identified with the "New School" Arminianized Calvinism and interdenominational revivalism that Princeton fought against. It was these traditions that Warfield so polemicized against in his essays on "perfectionism," his writings against the "counterfeit miracles" of the healing movement, and so forth. These traditions characteristically did not express their doctrine of Scripture in the language of Protestant orthodoxy and its doctrine of the "inerrancy of Scripture" until they fell under the influence of fundamentalism and neo-evangelicalism in the mid-twentieth century.

Ramm's book actually is a rather strange phenomenon in many ways. One wonders how a "baptist" came to write it. The anabaptist tradition finds its way only into one footnote. Except for the fact that the baptist tradition has its roots in a general way in Calvinism, the book ignores the currents that most shaped the baptists. Intellectually, it represents the world view of the fundamentalist Presbyterian tradition of Machen and the split at Princeton that produced Westminster Theological Seminary. Historically, the volume is a sort of "Presbyterian" paradigm for understanding the nature of evangelicalism, one that accurately describes only a small wing of the evangelical traditions (as represented, for example, in the NAE) but also one that, for a variety of reasons, has been accepted widely as the appropriate paradigm for understanding what it means to be evangelical. To the extent that this paragraph reigns as the dominant way to understand the nature of evangelicalism, it is difficult to see pentecostalism as a subcategory of fundamentalism or of evangelicalism.

The problem with this conclusion, of course, is that Ramm's book works historically to explain very little of evangelicalism. Against the "Presbyterian" paradigm of Ramm, one might pose the "pentecostal" para-

digm and ask to what extent the categories appropriate in describing pentecostalism apply to the broader evangelical currents that now are typically
understood according to the "Presbyterian" paradigm. According to this
perspective, one would notice the roots of the Wheaton College tradition
in the "New School" of Presbyterianism and in its affinity with the "Oberlin Perfectionism" that marked the convergence of Presbyterian and Congregational revivalism with Methodism. On would notice the prevalence
of near-pentecostal themes in the late-nineteenth-century revivalism of
Dwight L. Moody and his associates (their development of a doctrine of
"baptism with the Holy Spirit," etc.) One would note within the baptist
tradition the prevalence of a "Keswick" higher or "victorious Christian
life" piety, with its roots in the holiness revival and its real affinity to
pentecostalism—as well as the parallel phenomenon among Anglican evangelicals often oriented to the Keswick Conventions. Within Presbyterianism, one would notice that what have come to be "evangelical" churches
and institutions often are rooted in the Finney traditions of New York's
Third Presbytery or in phenomena such as the emergence of A.B. Simpson
and the Christian and Missionary Alliance. The Alliance with its emphasis on the "fourfold gospel" of Simpson, was probably the clearest antecedent to pentecostalism, lacking only the latter's emphasis on tongues and
the baptism of the Holy Spirit. One would notice the themes of A.J. Gordon in New England and his advocacy of the healing movement, premillennialism, and higher-life doctrines of the Spirit. Very similar would be the
currents around the Evangelical Free Church and the work of persons like
Fredrik Fransen, with his pentecostal-like advocacy of the ministry of
women and related styles of ministry and church life. One might be inclined to place even Fuller Theological Seminary and the "Old-Fashioned
Revival Hour" of Charles Fuller in this tradition. I could go on, but I hope
that the point has been made. Much of what constitutes evangelicalism
today is, historically and theologically, illuminated more by the "pentecostal" paradigm than by the "Presbyterian" paradigm.

If we shift paradigms, we become able to understand again the relationship of pentecostalism and evangelicalism. If, but only if, we understand "evangelicalism" in terms of my middle or "classical" paradigm,
pentecostalism becomes a subcategory of evangelicalism. Then it becomes
a variation within the revivalist tradition—one that actually is much closer
to the heart of that tradition than is usually imagined. But if we maintain
the "Presbyterian" paradigm, then pentecostalism is best understood as
a major alternative to evangelicalism, with a distinctive logic all its own
that cuts across the distinctive claims of Protestant orthodoxy.

NOTES

1. Carl Brumbeck, *What Meaneth This?: A Pentecostal Answer to a Pentecostal Question* (Springfield, Mo.: Gospel Publishing House, 1946).
2. See the survey of this literature in Horace S. Ward, Jr., "The Anti-Pentecostal Argument," in *Aspects of Pentecostal-Charismatic Origins*, ed. H. Vinson Synan (Plainfield, N.J.: Logos International, 1975), 99–122. The equation of pentecostalism and glossolalia is seen, for example, in an early Lutheran critique of the movement by H.J. Stolee, *Pentecostalism* (Minneapolis: Augsburg Publishing House, 1936); rptd. as *Speaking in Tongues*, 1963).
3. Kilian McDonnell, *Charismatic Renewal and the Churches* (New York: Seabury, 1976).
4. John T. Bunn, "Glossolalia in Historical Perspective," in *Speaking in Tongues: Let's Talk About It*, ed. Watson E. Mills (Waco, Tex. Word Books, 1973), 46.
5. Edith Waldvogel and George H. Williams, "A History of Speaking in Tongues and Related Gifts" in *The Charismatic Movement*, ed. Michael Hamilton (Grand Rapids, Mich.: Eerdmans, 1975), 81–89.
6. This disputed issue depends in part on whether the white or black origins of pentecostalism are stressed and in part on whether the first statement of the full pentecostal theology or the beginnings of its worldwide impact are sought. Present theological concerns here dictate a focus on the former event. For the issues involved, see Leonard Lovett, "Black Origins of the Pentecostal Movement," in *Aspects of Pentecostal-Charismatic Origins*, ed. Synan, 123–41.
7. See this tendency in chap. 2, "Antecedents of Modern Pentecostalism," of John Thomas Nichol, *Pentecostalism* (New York: Harper and Row, 1966; reissued in 1971 by Logos International as *The Pentecostals*), 18–24, a standard historical treatment of the movement. More recent efforts treat late-19th-century developments in more detail. See esp. Frederick Dale Bruner, *A Theology of the Holy Spirit* (Grand Rapids, Mich.: Eerdmans, 1971); and Waldvogel, and Williams, "A History of Speaking in Tongues," already containing intimations of Edith Waldvogel, "The Overcoming Life: A Study in the Reformed Evangelical Origins of Pentecostalism" (PhD. diss., Harvard Divinity School, 1977). Literature emphasizing the Irvingite antecedent includes Andrew Landale Drummond, *Edward Irving and His Circle, Including Some Considerations of the 'Tongues Movement' in the Light of Modern Psychology* (London: James Clarke, 1937); Larry Christenson, "Pentecostalism's Forgotten Forerunner," in *Aspects of Pentecostal-Charismatic Origins,* ed. Synan, 15–35, perhaps summarizing his *A Message to the Charismatic Movement* (East Weymouth, Mass.: Dimension, 1972); and Charles Gordon Strachan, *The Pentecostal Theology of Edward Irving* (London: Darton, Longman and Todd, 1973).
8. The literature is surveyed by McDonnell, *Charismatic Renewal and the Churches*, in an effort to refute the "deprivation" theories of the emergence of pentecostalism.
9. This tendency is evident, e.g., in the best theological interpretation of pentecostalism to date, Frederick Dale Bruner, *A Theology of the Holy Spirit* (doctoral diss., Univ. of Hamburg, Germany, 1963), which consists almost entirely of an extended exegesis of the relevant texts in Acts and the Corinthian epistles. See also James D.G. Dunn, *Baptism in the Holy Spirit* (London: SCM Press, 1970; Naperville, Ill.: Allenson, 1970, and Philadelphia: Westminister, 1977).
10. These factors are indicated in the standard surveys of pentecostalism, perhaps most helpfully in Vinson Synan, *The Holiness-Pentecostal Movement in the United States* (Grand Rapids, Mich.: Eerdmans, 1971).

11. The fullest collection of this material is in W. J. Hollenweger, *Handbuch der Pfingstbewegung* (Geneva: Privately published, 1965-67). This 10-volume Zurich dissertation has been deposited by the author in major libraries around the world and is available from the Board of Microtext of the American Theological Library Association. Extracts have been published in various languages (English, French, German, and Spanish) with differing contents. The English edition is published as *The Pentecostals* (London: SCM Press and Minneapolis: Augsburg Publishing House, 1972).

12. The full statement is in Nichol, *Pentecostalism*, 4-5. Nichol uses this fact to classify pentecostalism as a subgroup of American fundamentalism or evangelicalism.

13. David W. Faupel, *The American Pentecostal Movement: A Bibliographical Essay*, Occasional Bibliographic Papers of the B.L. Fisher Library, no.2 (Wilmore, Ky.: B.L. Fisher Library, Asbury Theological Seminary, 1972), builds on earlier work of Everett L. Moore, "Handbook of Pentecostal Denominations in the United States" (M.A. thesis, Pasadena College, 1954), and Klaude Kendrick, *The Promise Fulfilled: A History of the Modern Pentecostal Movement* (Springfield, Mo.: Gospel Publishing House, 1961).

14. This analysis is provided by David Reed, "Aspects of the Origins of Oneness Pentecostalism," in *Aspects of Pentecostal-Charismatic Origins*, ed. Synan, 143-68, an advance report on "Origins and Development of the Theology of Oneness Pentecostalism in the United States" (Ph.D. diss., Boston Univ., 1978). Dayton is editing (with Jeff Gill) a volume of the proceedings of the Harvard Symposium on Oneness Pentecostalism.

15. H.S. Maltby, *The Reasonableness of Hell* (Santa Cruz, Calif.: n.p., 1913), 82-83.

16. Charles F. Parham, "The Latter Rain," reprinted in Sarah E. Parham, *The Life of Charles F. Parham, Founder of the Apostolic Faith Movement* (Joplin, Mo.: Tri State Printing, 1930; rptd. Joplin, Mo.: Hunter Printing, 1969), 51-52. See the same pattern in her own preaching, in a sermon, "Earnestly Contend for the Faith Once Delivered to the Saints," in Robert L. Parham, comp., *Selected Sermons of the late Charles F. Parham, Sarah E. Parham, Co Founders of the Original Apostolic Faith Movement* (n.p.: 1941), 9-22. Both of these volumes have been reprinted under the editorship of Donald W. Dayton, in a facsimile reprint series, "The Higher Christian Life," Garland Publishing, 1985.

17. This is reported in Charles F. Parham, "The Latter Rain," and more fully in Agnes N. Ozman LaBerge, *What God Hath Wrought* (Chicago: Herald Publishing, n.d.), rptd. in "The Higher Christian Life" series, Garland Publishing.

18. This staement is reported in Bureau of the Census, *Census of Religious Bodies: 1936*, vol. 2 pt. 1 (Washington, D.C.: U.S. Government Printing Office, 1941), 696. See the more elaborate statement of faith, similar but lacking a clause on the Second Coming, in the first issue of *Apostolic Faith* (Sept. 1906), the organ of the Azusa Street Mission and its black leader W.J. Seymour. The early issues of *Apostolic Faith* have been reprinted by Fred T. Corum in *Like As of Fire (Wilmington, Mass.: n.p., 1981)*. The text of the statement is available in an appendix to Hollenweger, *The Pentecostals*, 513.

19. *A Historical Account of the Apostolic Faith, Trinitarian-Fundamental Evangelistic Organization* (Portland, Oreg.: Apostolic Faith Mission Headquarters, 1965, 20-21, delineating its "doctrinal foundation." Elsewhere (31-32) the "doctrines of Christ, as spoken by Him," are listed with proof-texts as justification and salvation, sanctification, the baptism of the Holy Ghost, divine healing, and his Second Coming.

20. Stanley Horton, *Into All Truth: A Survey of the Course and Content of Divine Revelation* (Springfield, Mo.: Gospel Publishing House, 1955), 13.

21. Raymond L. Cox has compiled the writings of Aimee Semple McPherson around this pattern, *The Four-Square Gospel* (Los Angeles: Foursquare Publications, 1969), 9. See the similar way of expressing pentecostal doctrine in Britain, in the work

of the founder of the Elim Foursquare Gospel Alliance, George Jeffreys, whose teachings are expressed in *The Miraculous Foursquare Gospel—Doctrinal*, vol. I (London: Elim Publishing, 1929), especially chap. 1, 1–11. Similarly, D. Wesley Myland reports, in *The Latter Rain Covenant* (Springfield, Mo.: Temple Press, 1973), being accosted in camp meeting with the greeting, "What are you doing? Still preaching the fourfold gospel?", 119.

22. This pattern also could be traced outside classical pentecostalism, in the "charismatic movement" and perhaps even in Third World manifestations such as certain of the African Independent churches. The belief in divine healing is pervasive and may well be more characteristic of these movements than glossolalia itself. Joseph H. Fichter's sociological study of the Catholic charismatic movement not only indicates the prominence of belief in "healing" but also finds among elements of "heterodoxy" in the revewal prayer groups that a majority of participants agree that "accepting Jesus as my personal Savior means that I am already saved" and that "the Second Coming of Christ is imminent." See Fichter, *Catholic Cult of the Paraclete* (New York: Sheed and Ward, 1975), ch. 3, esp. p. 44. The doctrine of "the baptism of the Holy Spirit" also has been carried into the traditional churches, but at this point, esp. in Catholicism, there has been an effort to critique this doctrine exegetically and substitute such expresions as "release of the Spirit." On this see, e.g., Simon Tugwell, O.P., *Did You Receive the Spirit?* (New York: Paulist Pres, 1972; and London: Darton, Longman and Todd, 1972.

23. A.B. Simpson, *The Four Fold Gospel* (New York: Gospel Alliance Publishing, 1925). A preface traces the theme back 40 years earlier. Other late 19th-century figures fascinated with these four themes include R.A. Torrey, Andrew Murray, and A.J. Gordon, though always without glossolalia.

24. Charles F. Parham, "The Latter Rain: The Story of the Origin of the Original Apostolic or Pentecostal Movements," ch. 7, in Sarah E. Parham, *Life of Charles F. Parham*.

25. Nichols, *The Pentecostals*, 336.

26. Critics of pentecostalism, esp. from classically Protestant traditions, have on occasion identified this as the major flaw of pentecostal exegesis and hermeneutics—that it starts with narrative rather than didactic texts within the Scriptures. See, e.g., John R.W. Stott, *Baptism and Fullness: The Work of the Holy Spirit Today* (Downers Grove, Ill.: InterVarsity Press, 1976), 15.

27. One of the few efforts to approach pentecostal claims in terms of this issue is Gordon D. Fee, "Hermeneutics and Historical Precedent—A Major Problem in Pentecostal Hermeneutics," in *Perspectives on the New Pentecostalism*, ed. Russell P. Spittler (Grand Rapids, Mich.: Baker Book House, 1976), 118–32.

28. Claude Welch, *Protestant Thought in the Nineteenth Century*, Vol. 1: 1799–1870 (New Haven, Conn.: Yale Univ. Press, 1972), 28.

29. This common pattern is perhaps epitomized in Martin Wells Knapp, *Out of Egypt into Canaan; Or, Lessons in Spiriual Geography* (Boston: McDonald, Gill and Co., 1889).

30. William Menzies proposes this definition in *Anointed to Serve* (Springfield, Mo.: Gospel Publishing House, 1971), 9, the most recent history of the dominant white American pentecostal denomination. This definition is also adopted by Faupel, *American Pentecostal Movement*, 9.

31. Charles F. Parham, *A Voice Crying in the Wilderness*, 4th ed. (Joplin, Mo.: Joplin Printing Co. for Robert L. Parham, 1944), 44–45. This book was first published in 1902.

32. Andrew Murray, *Divine Healing* (New York: Christian Alliance Publishing, 1900), 26.

33. Benjamin B. Warfield, *Counterfeit Miracles* (New York: Charles Scribner's Sons, 1918; rptd. London: Banner of Truth Trust, 1972), 5–6. This book also has been issued as *Miracles: Yesterday and Today, True and False* (Grand Rapids, Mich.: Eerdmans, 1953).

34. This appeal is regularly explicit. See for example, Maltby, *Reasonableness of Hell*, 84; Robert L. Parham, *Selected Sermons of the Late Charles F. Parham, Sarah E. Parham* 18; B.F. Lawrence, *The Apostolic Faith Restored* (St. Louis, Mo.: Gospel Publishing House, 1916), 13–14; Mrs. M.B. Woodworth Etter, *Signs and Wonders* (Indianapolis: Privately published, 1916), 192–93.

35. Lawrence, *Apostolic Faith Restored*, 11–12. This volume has also been reprinted in the facsimile series, "The Higher Christian Life," Garland Publishing.

36. Ibid., 12. Lawrence apparently was one of the first adherents to develop such a lineage, the validity of such attempts soon becoming the major focus of pentecostal apologetics and critique.

37. See Lilian Thistlethwaite, "Wonderful Hisory of the Latter Rain," an early report of the events that transpired at Charles F. Parham's Bethel Bible College, ch. 8, Sarah E. Parham, *Life of Charles F. Parham*, 57–68. *The Latter Rain Evangel* was a journal published from 1908 in Chicago. See also the early exposition of pentecostalism by T.B. Barratt, *In the Days of the Latter Rain* (London: Simpkin, Marshall, Hamilton, Kent & Co., 1909; rptd. in "The Higher Christian Life" series, Garland Publishing.

38. D. Wesley Myland, *The Latter Rain Covenant and Pentecostal Power with Testimonies of Healings and Baptism* (Chicago: Evangel Publishing House, 1910), rptd. with pagination changed by A.N. Trotter of Billings, Missouri (Springfield, Mo.: Temple Press, 1973); facsimile rpt. in "The Higher Christian Life" series, Garland Publishing.

39. See, e.g., Aimee Semple McPheson, *Lost and Restored* (Los Angeles: Foursquare Bookshop, n.d.), an elaborate interpretation of church history and the process by which the "apostolic faith" is "lost and restored," in terms of the prophetic imagery of the Book of Joel, esp. the passages surrounding the second chapter of Acts.

40. Myland, *Latter Rain Covenant*, 101.

41. Argued by means of a rainfall chart appended to the original edition, indicating that "forty three percent more rain fell between the years 1890 and 1900 than fell from 1860 to 1870." Ibid., 95.

42. Woodworth Etter, *Signs and Wonders*, 189–90.

43. Ibid., 535.

44. Despite this demonstration of the necessity of eschatology and the doctrine of the latter rain to the inherent logic of pentecostalism, there remain some questions at this point. There is, as mentioned above, no article of eschatology in the first *Apostolic Faith* statement of 1906 (see n. 18, above). And the "latter rain doctrine did tend to drop out of pentecostalism (only to reappear, however, in the radical Latter Rain revitalization movement of the 1940s), though broader eschatological themes remained. Such developments may indicate that the eschatological element is not as integral to pentecostal logic as the other elements. Nils Bloch Hoell, e.g., says that the theme is vibrant but not crucial, in *The Pentecostal Movement* (Oslo: Universitetsforlaget, 1964), 154–56. More likely is the fact that such an apocalyptic orientation is the first element to yield to the forces of institutionalization in such movements. Robert Mapes Anderson argues that eschatology is in fact the central element in the pentecostal message, in *Vision of the Disinherited: The Making of American Pentecostalism* (New York:

Oxford Univ. Press, 1979), ch. 5. David W. Faupel has argued in "The Everlasting Gospel: The Significance of Eschatology in the Development of Pentecostal Thought" (Ph.D. diss., University of Birmingham, England, 1989) that the "latter rain" theme is the key to understanding pentecostalism. I am arguing here that eschatology is *a* crucial element, but not *the* central theme of pentecostalism.

CHAPTER 5

Adventism

Russell L. Staples

The Seventh-day Adventist movement cannot be understood apart from its history. Of course, the theological positions on which the movement is grounded can be spelled out; but even though these may be explicated in terms of mutually accepted principles of interpretation and theological argument, only part of the meaning of the movement is thus revealed. And what is revealed may fail to explain its inner consciousness or its ordering of priorities. Some such matters lie beneath the surface and may be better accounted for by historical experience than by exposition of belief. This may be truer of the Adventist church than of some others, on two counts. First, it grew out of the Millerite movement, and the events and meaning of that experience have been indelibly engraved on its corporate memory and serve as one of the beacons lighting its course. Second, the function of the inner Adventist conviction that it was accorded supernatural guidance in the ministry of Ellen White must be seen in historical perspective in order to be understood. Therefore, it seems necessary to lay some historical groundwork before embarking upon the more explicitly theological concerns of this essay.

The Millerite Experience

Millenialism almost always has been a characteristic feature of American evangelicalism, and millennial ideology has given shape to numerous ideas and movements, including: an understanding of history which accords the American nation a special place in the divine purpose; experiments in perfectionism, such as Oneida, the Shakers, and the Mormons; the Christianization of society; ideals of liberty and health; and the relationships between church and state.

Recent studies have served to locate the Millerite movement in closer proximity to the religious outlook of American evangelicalism than was previously thought to be the case.[1] It now appears that the Millerites are better understood as comprising a normal cross-section of society than as a group of fanatics and eccentrics and their leaders as men of reason, driven by what was to them inexorable logic, rather than as fanatical prophets appealing to the emotions of the unstable and disinherited.

The process of change accompanying the restructuring of social and political life in the early years of the Republic was seemingly without historical precedent, and persons who believed in the divine ordering of history were motivated to study the prophecies to discover the meaning of what was happening. All the churches to some extent taught the second advent of Jesus Christ, the end of the world, final judgment, the lake of fire, and a coming millennial reign of peace. Thus, when William Miller began to preach about the soon coming of Christ, it was not an altogether strange message. He used familiar language and appealed to the accepted authority of Scripture. True, the predominant doctrine at that time was a postmillennial reign of peace, which was to be brought about, in part at least, by human agency, but it was becoming increasingly difficult to argue the case for the inauguration of a perfect society. Manifestations of evil seemed to be on the increase, and the times seemed to be growing less auspicious for the ushering in of the reign of peace. Miller therefore could undergird his case for premillennialism by appealing to the state of society.

Reason was accorded high priority in Miller's epistemology, and this was in keeping with the spirit of the age. It was on the basis of reason that he had become a deist, and it was as a rationalist that he returned to traditional Christianity. After two years' intensive study of Scripture, he wrote, "The Bible was now to me a new book. It was indeed a feast of reason."[2] Even more revealingly, "I felt that to believe in . . . a Savior without evidence would be visionary in the extreme."[3] Hatch describes Miller's use of reason in the study of prophecy: "Miller was confident that by his inductive investigation a clear and simple system of truth was evident in the Bible. . . . Miller became a stickler for literal interpretation. . . . Upon applying mathematical science to Scriptural prophecy, thus eliminating theory and speculation, a precise formula emerged that pointed with awesome moment to the year 1843."[4]

Miller painstakingly demonstrated how every person could understand the prophecies for himself. Just as he sought to avoid speculation, so also he eschewed any form of inner enlightenment or appeal to subjective mysticism. Accused of fanaticism and religious excesses, the Millerites responded: "We have sought to spread the truth, not by fanatical prophecies arising out of our own hearts, but by the light of the Scriptures, history, and by sober argument. We appeal only to the Bible, and give you our rules of interpretation."[5]

Millerism was a mass movement, distributed across the Northeast and Midwest of the United States from Maine to Michigan, and its preachers came from many of the churches. Of the 174 preachers with identifiable religious affiliation, 44 percent were Methodist, 27 percent Baptist, 9 percent Congregational, 8 percent Christianite,[6] and 7 percent Presbyterian, with smaller numbers of Dutch Reformed, Episcopalians, Lutherans, and Quakers.[7] The movement, in its early stage, was antiseparatist. Millerite prayer circles and study fellowship meetings were promoted, but followers were encouraged to remain in their churches. And a wide variety of theological opinion was tolerated — one critic reported, "Here we find annihilationists who unite with universalists . . .; Arians, Socinians . . . and yet united on this one point [Millerism] they are all brethren, hale fellows well met."[8]

The prophetic basis of the movement was Daniel 8:14 and 9:23–27. Simply put, Miller calculated the 2,300 years (on the day-for-a-year principle) until the "cleansing of the sanctuary" (8:14) from the decree of 457 B.C. "to restore and rebuild Jerusalem" (9:25). By simple arithmetic, this period was calculated to terminate about 1843–44. This basic formula was bolstered by a network of parallel prophetic calculations. The sanctuary to be cleansed was understood to represent the earth; the cleansing event, the Second Coming of Christ. This was so, it was reasoned, because only Christ has the power to cleanse the world of sin and bring the millennium. Almost all the events of the last days were understood to occur at this time: separation of the righteous from the wicked, resurrection of the righteous dead, destruction of the earth, creation of the new heavens and new earth, and the commencement of the millennium.

The second stage of the movement commenced in 1844. By then it was realized that 2,300 years commencing in 457 B.C. would end in A.D. 1844, not 1843. The "cleansing of the sanctuary" was now coupled with the Day of Atonement — the day of the annual cleansing of the temple in the ancient Hebrew cultic year (Leviticus 16). The Day of Atonement thus was seen to be a prototype of the cleansing of the earth at the Second Coming of Christ. This day, it was calculated, would fall on 22 October in the year of 1844.

Excitement ran high as this message was preached and rose higher as the day drew nearer. As enthusiasm rose, the movement became more volatile and overran many of its more moderate leaders. Some of the churches became alarmed at the excitement generated by Millerites within their communities and responded by disfellowshipping some of them; some churches expelled ministers who were active in the movement. In place of the earlier antiseparatist stance, there now arose in some quarters of the movement a vigorous cry, in the name of the angel of Rev. 18:1–4, to "come out" of the churches that were refusing to prepare for the coming of the Lord. Several of the leaders took Millerite condemnation of the churches to its logical conclusion. Denominations were the Antichrist, were prophetic Babylon; and all saints must now "come out of Babylon" lest they partake of the destruction to fall on the wicked. "If you are a Christian, *come out of Babylon.* If you intend to be found a Christian when Christ appears, *come out of Babylon*, and come out *now*"[9] (Italics in original.)

There thus arose, among some Millerites, a rather sharp sense of particularism.

Beginnings of the Adventist Church

The movement was shattered by the delay of the parousia — subsequently called the Great Disappointment. Some rejected the movement altogether. Perhaps the majority response of those who still affirmed the movement was to continue expectantly awaiting the Advent, on the grounds that there quite easily could have been an error of a few years in the calculations. They experienced a difficulty, however, in that, because of prevailing anti-Millerite sentiment, there seemed to be no church home to which they could comfortably turn. The Advent Christian Church eventually arose out of this stranded group. Other Millerites argued that Christ's Second Coming actually *had* occurred in a spiritual sense, and some such joined the Shakers.

The Seventh-day Adventist Church arose out of one of the smaller segments of the Millerites; however, it was comprised of a broad spectrum of evangelical Protestants, among whom Methodists and Christianites seem to have exerted a dominant influence. Reaffirmation of the validity of the Millerite[10] message provided positive incentive to remain separate from the churches. Several developments contributed to the coalescence of this cohort of disheartened Millerites into a committed core group. Perhaps the first development was a reaffirmation of the divine origin of the Millerite movement, accompanied by an elongation of the timetable of the awaited parousia. The instrumentality of these affirmations was a vision received by Ellen Harmon in late 1844 and subsequently communicated to the group. This message gave the members both the incentive and the sense of time necessary for the formation of an organization.[11]

The second key factor was the reinterpretation of the meaning of the "cleansing of the sanctuary" (Daniel 8:14). Continued study of the Israelite sanctuary services and comparison of the earthly type with the heavenly antitype led to the conviction that, instead of leaving heaven to come to earth, Christ had entered the most holy place of the heavenly sanctuary to commence a new phase of his priestly ministry.

The third facilitating event was acceptance of prophetic guidance in the ministry of Ellen Harmon (later White). There had been several in the Millerite movement who claimed to have visions and revelations.[12] The Millerite leaders responded negatively to these manifestations: "We have no confidence whatever in any visions, dreams or private revelations. . . . We repudiate all fanaticism."[13] But the Adventist church, in the process of formation, did accept one such; and the results were both immediate and far-reaching. The idea of prophetic guidance was not necessarily strange to the Millerites. They lived close to the Scriptures, derived their models from the early church, believed they had seen the hand of God in recent events in human history, and were open to a progressive unfolding of revelation. Besides, these early Adventists identified themselves with the "remnant" of Rev. 12:17, which "have the testimony of Jesus Christ"; and they understood this phrase to mean the "spirit of prophecy" on the basis of Rev. 19:10.

Two other doctrines which came to be distinctive of the Seventh-day Adventist Church had surfaced in the Millerite movement: the seventh-day Sabbath[14] and "soul sleep."[15] A logical concomitant of the latter is the rejection of an ever-burning hell. Interest in the doctrine appears to have arisen from immediate existential concern regarding the fate of the wicked at the Second Coming, and revolved about the theodicy problem rather than from a rethinking of Platonic dualism.

The process by which the scattered Millerites were drawn together and concensus was achieved centered on a series of conferences conducted in New England and New York for "friends of the Sabbath," which commenced in 1848 and ran for several years. The sense of distinctiveness inherited from the Millerites was reified in the process of establishing corporate and doctrinal identity. It was further reinforced as the members came to identify in their studies with the remnant of Rev. 12:17 and felt called to proclaim the messages of the three angels of Revelation 14. A church was established in 1861, when the members in Michigan signed an agreement associating themselves together "as a church, taking the name of Seventh-day Adventist, covenanting to keep the commandments of God and the faith of Jesus Christ."[16]

Themes in Adventist Theology

Having briefly traced some aspects of the historical origin and doctrinal orientation of the coalescing Adventist church, we are now in a position to give consideration to the theological issues relevant to this study. What follows is not an exhaustive survey of the Adventist doctrinal system, nor an apologetic defense. The concern is more to place Adventist thought in perspective and describe some of its functions. The discussion is organized into two sections. In the first, the underlying matrix and basic features of Adventist belief vis-à-vis the larger Christian tradition are described. The second section is more heuristic and seeks to explore what might be regarded as the central organizing and motivating theme of Adventism, along with some of its more distinctive doctrinal features. There is also an attempt to account for the particularistic tendency that has tended to keep the movement apart from the wider evangelical community.

The Adventist corpus of belief, broadly speaking, is a set of biblically-endorsed doctrines and is perhaps better thought of as a coordinated system of fundamental beliefs than as a theological system formulated about a central organizing principle.[17] In this it is consistent with its Millerite origins and the anticreedal stance of the Christianite members of the founding group. For years the movement seems to have had the consciousness of a pilgrim band pressing on the upward way, with a lively concern for obedience to the truth as revealed in Scripture, but with more pressing matters to attend to than the discussion of moot tenets of theology. In addition, there has been an openness to the use of reason and therefore also to natural theology and to continuing revelation. This openness stemmed partly from the movement's Arminian base but was also a function of its eschatological focus, which freed it somewhat from a philosophical orientation. A negative attitude was maintained toward the formalization of a creed, inasmuch as the latter was seen to constitute a potential obstacle to the acceptance of advancing truth and light.

Adventists always have held a high view of the Bible. It is regarded as divinely inspired: the authoritative revelation of God's will, the source of doctrine, and a practical guide to the Christian life. Futhermore, the Bible is interpreted in a direct and fairly literal manner. This understanding of the Bible antedates the modernist/fundamentalist controversy and the formulation of the doctrine of verbal inerrancy, an affirmation the group stopped short of accepting. Along with Adventism's literalism, it has maintained a dynamic view of inspiration: "The Infinite One by His Holy Spirit has shed light into the minds and hearts of His servants. . . . And those to whom the truth was thus revealed have themselves embodied the thought in human language."[18] Several Adventists were involved in the modernist/fundamentalist controversy as protagonists on the conservative side, but the church was not torn by internal conflict over such matters.[19]

It has been noted that there is a fairly direct relationship between premillennial dispensationalism on the one hand, and the literal interpretation of Scripture, infallibility, and inerrancy on the other. Those who study the prophecies with an interest in eschatological timetables and the correlation of prophetic description with historical event must presuppose a high degree of verbal reliability in the Scriptures. This approach also predisposes toward literalism in biblical interpretation. These tendencies have functioned to maintain the centrality of the Bible and also a degree of biblical literalism in Adventist thought.

In the early days of Adventism, several of its leaders, who formerly had been Christianites, held mildly antitrinitarian and semi-Arian views, which derived from an earlier Socinian influence. Apart from these early deviant views, Adventists have held orthodox views regarding the God-head and what are generally considered to be the cardinal doctrines of the Christian faith. The cluster of doctrines relating to the Fall and sin and salvation constitute a thoroughgoing evangelical Arminianism. Universal atonement is affirmed, while determinism is rejected. A degree of free will is endorsed, but without the subtlety of the Wesleyan doctrine of prevenient grace. Sin and its results are viewed with utter seriousness. A doctrine of human nature is maintained that is more optimistic, however, than is found in British Methodism; and in this its anthropology is at some remove from the Augustinian doctrine of the Reformers.

The balance maintained between divine sovereignty and human effort is Wesleyan. And it is a balance that endeavors to safeguard the divine initiative in salvation without undercutting human responsibility. As in Wesleyan theology, salvation is thought of in two consecutive moments. Primary is the divine conferral of grace in justification; there follows the lifelong process of sanctification, which is thought of ontologically as healing and making righteous. Sanctification is regarded as being as much a work of grace as is justification. It is in connection with the doctrine of sanctification and growing in grace that the optimism of Adventism is most obvious. Most Adventists have grown up with expressions such as the following ringing in their ears:

> Every human being, created in the image of God, is endowed with a power akin to that of the Creator — individuality, power to think and to do. . . . Higher than the highest human thought can reach is God's ideal for His children. Godliness — God-likeness — is the goal to be reached. . . . He will advance as fast and as far as possible in every branch of true knowledge.[20]

Perhaps the noted Adventist upward-mobility syndrome is in part an expression of this optimism of grace.

Both sides of Christology are well developed in Adventist thought and experience. Theologically, emphasis is placed on the divine Christ, in whom was life underived, and who thus could make atonement for human sin. In practical piety, however, there has been a tendency to emphasize the human Christ, who suffered, was tempted, and overcame in the stream of human time and who is therefore both a perfect example and the compassionate savior of the soul in need. In this, too, Adventism is akin more to American Arminianism than to the Wesleyan doctrine. There lies in this tendency an invitation to legalism — not in formal doctrine, for there salvation by grace alone is clearly defined, but in Christian experience. It is recognized that in the practical life, the temptation in this direction is strengthened by the emphasis on Sabbath-keeping, law, and judgment.

An example of the unbondedness to system of early Adventist thought is provided in its doctrine of law and covenants. These follow Reformed theology fairly closely; and, given the Adventist concern with law and judgment,[21] it is not hard to see why. However, the idea of covenant is not as central to the Adventist Arminian base as it is to the Reformed system, and it is accordingly given a lesser status. The perpetuity of the moral law is maintained with vigorous endorsement of all three of the classical "uses" of the law. The law is also upheld as the divine standard of eternal judgment. But this emphasis on law does not necessarily imply legalism. There was a reduction in the role accorded law in the Christian life in dispensationalist evangelical preaching and writing in the middle of the nineteenth century. A line was drawn dividing the Old Testament dispensation of law and the New Testament dispensation of Pentecost. Those born of the Spirit were contrasted with those in bondage to the law. The prominence given to the law as a standard of judgment and righteousness in Adventist apologetic writing coincides chronologically with this emphasis and appears to be, in part, a reaction against it.

Adventist thought is characterized by a general inclusivity, as over against the binary or polarizing tendency in Reformation theologies. Law and grace are portrayed as belonging together in the scheme of salvation, rather than standing opposed to one another; and so also are "by grace alone" and "holy living," justification and sanctification, and so on. Adventists can comfortably voice the tones of both Galatians and James. There is a breadth that goes beyond a *declaring* righteous to a *making* righteous; but, as always, there is a price to pay. The clarity of the Lutheran concept of salvation, as being God's work from beginning to end, gives way to a Wesleyan synthesis of divine sovereignty and human responsibility. But again, this broader scheme, which derives in part from New Testament ideals of perfection, is not to be equated with legalism.

In addition to this broad-based Arminianism, there are those doctrines which, from a general perspective, might be designated as distinctly Adventist. These form a mutually supportive cluster, and it is the complex of ideas/beliefs that emerge from this cluster that mark Adventism off from the wider evangelical movement and inform its *raison d'etre*. These doctrines are: conditional immortality, seventh-day Sabbatarianism, a premillennial historicist eschatology which emphasizes the imminence of the Second Coming, acceptance of the gift of prophecy in the ministry of Ellen White, and teachings about the priestly work of Christ in the heavenly sanctuary. These doctrines coalesce into a distincitive eschatological theme, which lies at the heart of Adventism.

Scholars have come to regard the concept of an immortal soul as an imposition of Platonic dualism upon the more monistic Hebrew concept of personhood. The doctrine of conditional immortality is listed here because it was characteristically distinctive in an earlier age and because it has served to support other strands in Adventist thought which affirm the significance of life in the body.

Adventist understandings of the Sabbath as a day of holiness and worship owe much to Puritan Sabbatarianism. The temporal identity of the Sabbath as the seventh day and as the literal memorial of Creation was learned from the Seventh-Day Baptists. What was thus learned was submitted to the test of Scripture and refined and enlarged upon. The keeping of the Sabbath entered the Adventist movement as a practical expression of obedience to God and a personal experience of fellowship with God in holy time. It is both a celebration of creation and a proleptic experience of the age to come. The Sabbath has an additional significance for Adventists, in that the "remnant" of Rev. 12:17 is portrayed as keeping the commandments of God. For Adventists, therefore, the seventh-day Sabbath is one of the marks of the remnant, a badge signifying fidelity to God.

Early Adventists reaffirmed the historicist system of prophetic interpretation worked out by Miller and his associates. The reinterpretation of what took place in 1844 allowed them to reject date setting and to stress the imminence of the Advent in a somewhat extended eschatological scheme of events. They retained the Millerite interpretation of Babylon as apostate Christianity, and this strengthened the Adventist sense of identity as a people seeking to adhere with utmost fidelity to the true teachings of Scripture.

Ellen Harmon White (1827–1915) occupied a privileged position among the founders of the Adventist church, inasmuch as she was accepted as a special messenger of the Lord.[22] She lived to a venerable age, wrote much, and exerted a powerful influence in the developing church, although she eschewed direct leadership offices. She and her parental family had been active members in the Methodist church before they became convinced Millerites. Her subsequent experience and life work were thoroughly grounded in an underlying Arminian evangelicalism,[23] and she did much through her writing and personal influence to stabilize the movement in that tradition.

Adventist doctrine does not derive from the Ellen White writings,[24] although she did much to confirm Adventists in the doctrinal way worked out by the pioneers; but much that is distinctively Adventist derives directly from her writings and influence. Included are: the Adventist life of Bible study and piety; the Christian values that have engendered a distinctive lifestyle; ideas regarding the relationship between physical health and spirituality, which have resulted in a healthful way of living and eventually in a worldwide network of medical institutions; and ideas regarding Christian education, which led to the establishment of thousands of schools. These institutions, both medical and educational, have served to transmit and foster the complex of belief, value, and lifestyle that informs what it means to be an Adventist — and these institutions in turn have exerted a reciprocal influence on the church. In addition to all of this, Ellen White constantly encouraged the church to break out of its narrow circuit and establish institutions and outreach programs of many kinds.

As is evident from the above, Adventism is as much a way of life as a system of belief — a way of life that is informed by an Arminian piety in which the gospel has relevance for every dimension of life. The seriousness with which life in the body is regarded — the health-maintenance and educational enterprises relate to this realm of thought — is supported by the doctrine of conditional immortality. On this view, there can be no dualism between salvation of the soul and life in the body. Relevant also to this way of life is a sense of continuity between life on this earth and the next. Faithful discipleship is not regarded as earning a place in that realm, but as developing a fitness for it.

The most distinctive item in the Adventist doctrinal storehouse is its teaching about the work of Christ in the heavenly sanctuary. As already noted, this teaching arose as an explanation of what had happened in 1844. The "cleansing" of the sanctuary is understood to refer to the blotting out of the sins recorded against the people of God in the books of heaven. This requires a work of investigation or judging, in order to determine which sins should be blotted out. And this function of Christ is directly coupled with the message of the first angel of Rev. 14:7 "The hour of his judgment is come."

For Adventists, the priestly work of Christ thus is conceived of as involving two distinct ministries commencing at different times. Upon his ascension, Christ took upon himself the office of priest, to mediate the benefits of his atoning sacrifice, to forgive sins, to provide direct access to God, and to guide the church. In 1844, it is believed, a second phase began, one that added to these functions, and there commenced an examination of the records of all those who have been servants of God. By the close of this investigation, or "judgment," the company of the justified

sion has been exacerbated by other factors which have given the impression that Adventists are legalists.

If Adventism is judged on the basis of these doctrines and its missionary zeal, then surely it is evangelical in the deepest sense of the word.

The major theological differences between evangelicalism and Adventism lie in the distinctiveness that is grounded in the cluster of doctrines outlined earlier in this essay. The question about the relationship between Adventism and evangelicalism on this score cannot be given a unilateral answer. Much depends upon the attitude of both parties, the degree of latitude and distinctiveness with which each is comfortable, and the constraints which make for a united front. The message here surely is one of hope that differences will always be weighed in the light of much that is held in common and of a mutual commitment to the gospel.

NOTES

1. Edwin S. Gaustad, ed., *The Rise of Adventism: Religion and Society in Mid-Nineteenth Century America* (New York: Harper & Row, 1974); Gary Land, ed., *Adventism in America: A History* (Grand Rapids, Mich.: Eerdmans, 1986); Ronald L. Numbers and Jonathan M. Butler, eds., *The Disappointed: Millerism and Millenarianism in the Nineteenth Century* (Bloomington: Indiana Univ. Press, 1987); Ernest R. Sandeen, *The Roots of Fundamentalism: British and American Millenarianism, 1800–1930* (Chicago: Univ. of Chicago Press, 1970); and David L. Rowe, *Thunder and Trumpets: Millerites and Dissenting Religion in Upstate New York, 1800–1850* (Chico, Calif.: Scholars Press, 1985).

2. Sylvester Bliss, *Memoirs of William Miller: Generally Known as a Lecturer on the Prophecies, and the Second Coming of Christ* (Boston: Joshua V. Himes, 1853), 76–77, quoted in part in Rowe, *Thunder and Trumpets*, 13.

3. William Miller, *Apology and Defense* (Boston: J.V. Himes, 1845), 5.

4. Nathan O. Hatch, "Millennialism and Popular Religion in the Early Republic," in *The Evangelical Tradition in America*, ed. Leonard I. Sweet (Macon, Ga.: Mercer Univ. Press, 1984), 119.

5. Quoted in Francis D. Nichol, *The Midnight Cry* (Washington, D.C.: Review and Herald Publishing Association, 1944), 129.

6. A loosely-embodied federation of churched which had splintered from the baptists in New York and New Hampshire in the early nineteenth century over the issue of clerical authority, forming the Christian Connexion in 1836. They tended to be anti-formalist, anti-Calvinistic, anticreedal, antitrinitarian, and revivalist. Several Christianites became prominent Millerite leaders, and several became Seventh-day Adventists.

7. Everett N. Dick, "William Miller and the Advent Crisis, 1831–1844." Unpublished typescript volume, 1932, 268. Quoted in Land, *Adventism in America*, 34.

8. *Baptist Advocate*, 14 Sept. 1843, and 4 July 1843. Quoted in Rowe, *Thunder and Trumpets*, 119.

9. Rowe, *Thunder and Trumpets*, 115–16.

10. Ellen White described this conviction and its consequences thus: "We were firm in the belief that the preaching of definite time was of God. It was this that led men to search the Bible diligently, discovering truths they had not before perceived."

Ellen G. White, *Life Sketches of Ellen G. White* (Mountain View, Calif. Pacific Press Publishing Association, 1915), 62.

11. Ellen G. White, *Early Writings of Mrs. White* (Washington, D.C: Review and Herald Publishing Association, 1938), 13-20, and LeRoy E. Froom, *The Prophetic Faith of Our Fathers*, v. 4 (Washington, D.C.: Review and Herald Publishing Association, 1954), 981.

12. E.g., letter of Whiting to Miller, 24 Oct. 1844: "Our poor brethren were deluded into a belief of 'signs & lying wordes' gift of tongues and modern prophecies." Quoted in Rowe, *Thunder and Trumpets*, 137.

13. From the "Declaration of Principles" adopted by the Adventists of Boston in 1843. Quoted in Froom, *Prophetic Faith*, 984.

14. For further details, see app. G in C. Mervyn Maxwell, "Joseph Bates and Seventh-day Adventist Sabbath Theology," in *The Sabbath in Scripture and History,* ed. Kenneth A. Strand (Washington, D.C.: Review and Herald Publishing Association, 1982), 352-63.

15. For further details, see Froom, *Prophetic Faith*, 805-808.

16. *Second Advent Review and Sabbath Herald*, 9 Oct. 1861. Quoted in Richard Schwarz, *Light Bearers to the Remnant* (Mountain View, Calif.: Pacific Press Publishing Association, 1979), 96. At the time of the organization of the General Conference of Seventh-day Adventists in 1863, there were 3,500 members. There are today about 750,000 members in North America and 6 million worldwide. Inasmuch as the "believers' church, believers' baptism" tradition is adhered to, the number of adherents would be considerably higher than this. There is an Adventist presence in 183 of the 215 nations recognized by the United States.

17. There are several studies that may be referred to for a survey of Adventist doctrine. Three books grew out of conversations between evangelicals and Adventists: *Seventh-day Adventists Answer Questions on Doctrine* (Washington, D.C.: Review and Herald Publishing Association, 1957); Walter R. Martin, *The Truth About Seventh-day Adventism* (Grand Rapids, Mich.: Zondervan, 1960); and *Doctrinal Discussions* (Washington, D.C.: Review and Herald Publishing Association, n.d. [ca. 1962]). The first is a quasiofficial statement of Adventist beliefs. *So Much in Common* (Geneva, Switzerland: World Council of Churches, 1973 [documents of interest in the conversations between the World Council of Churches and the Seventh-day Adventist Church]), grew out of conversations with the WCC, 1965-71. An overview of many of the distinctive themes in Adventist thought can be gained from the papers read at a Bible Conference in 1952: *Our Firm Foundation*, 2 vols. (Washington, D.C.: Review and Herald Publishing Association, 1953). LeRoy E. Froom, *Movement of Destiny* (Washington, D.C.: Review and Herald Publishing Association, 1971), is an apologetic history of the development of doctrine in Adventism. Richard Rice's *The Reign of God: An Introduction to Christian Theology from a Seventh-day Adventist Perspective* (Berrien Springs, Mich.: Andrews Univ. Press, 1985), is the most systematic overview of Adventist thought to date.

18. Ellen G. White, *The Great Controversy Between Christ and Satan* (Mountain View, Calif.: Pacific Press Publishing Association, 1888), vi.

19. For instance, George McCready Price, whose flood geology, according to Bernard Ramm, formed "the backbone of much fundamentalist thought about geology, creation, and the flood." Bernard Raam, *The Christian View of Science and Scripture* (Grand Rapids, Mich.: Eerdmans, 1954), 180.

20. Ellen G. White, *Education* (Mountain View, Calif.: Pacific Press Publishing Association, 1952), 17-18.

21. See, e.g., Edward Heppenstall, "The Covenants and the Law," in *Our Firm Foundation*, 1:435-92.

22. For details of the life and work of Ellen G. White, see Arthur L. White, *Ellen G. White*. 6 vols. (Washington, D.C.: Review and Herald Publishing Association, 1981-86).

23. Almost all of Ellen White's writings betray this Arminian orientation; it is overtly evident in *The Desire of Ages* (Mountain View, Calif.: Pacific Press Publishing Association, 1898) and *Steps to Christ* (New York: Revell, 1892). The latter, as the title suggests, is thoroughly Arminian and borders on the literature of the Holiness movement.

24. For a fuller exposition of the relationship of the E.G. White writings and Scripture, see Froom, *Movement of Destiny*, 91-96 and 101-106, and *Seventh-day Adventists Answer Questions on Doctrine*, 89-104.

25. This teaching has evoked much attention, both within and outside the church. No attempt can be made here to give an exposition of the doctrine or review the arguments raised against it or in its defense. It is mentioned here because it is basic to the Adventist identity. Froom, *Movement of Destiny*, 877-79, describes the genesis of the teaching. For further details, see Edward Heppenstall, *Our High Priest* (Washington, D.C.: Review and Herald Publishing Association, 1972) and *Seventh-day Adventists Answer Questions on Doctrine*, 341-445.

26. For instance, Berkhof writes, "The concept of judgment is used above in one specific sense, namely as the judgment of the works done by believers in their earthly life; see Rom. 14:10-12; 1 Cor. 3:10-15; 2 Cor. 5:10; Gal, 6:8f. . . . In Protestant theology, this viewpoint is almost completely pushed aside by the accent on grace." Hendrikus Berkhof, *Christian Faith* (Grand Rapids, Mich.: Eerdmans, 1979), 489. There appear to be positive adumbrations regarding the judgment of believers and final justification in Wesley's theology. See Harold Lindström, *Wesley and Sanctification* (Wilmore, Ky: Francis Asbury Publishing, n.d. [ca. 1980]), 205-218.

CHAPTER 6

The Theological Identity of the North American Holiness Movement: Its Understanding of the Nature and Role of the Bible
Paul Merritt Bassett

Introduction

In 1979, Harold Lindsell called upon the North American holiness movement to enlist in his "battle for the Bible": "Given the cloudiness of today's situation, it would be well for any and all of those churches and institutions in this movement to say forthrightly whether the doctrine of Scripture teaches there are or there are not errors in the Bible."[1] Lindsell assumed that the holiness movement generally identifies itself with current American evangelicalism and saw his call as an insistence that the former be consistent in its identity. For him, though not for all evangelicals, belief in biblical inerrancy is the acid test of authentic evangelicalism.[2]

In fact, most holiness people do identify with American evangelicalism.[3] And it must be granted that the movement's theological and religious sympathies align with evangelicalism, even if not with the narrow form of it advocated by Lindsell.[4] But for all of its presumed, even self-confessed identity with evangelicalism, the North American holiness movement, strictly speaking, inherits and propagates a history and a spirituality that finally make impossible, if they do not defy, any essential synonymity, except in a very broad grassroots way of expressing relationships, and except, of course, as both are legitimate expressions of the "one, holy, catholic, and apostolic Church." The holiness movement has an identity and an inner logic all its own.

This fact suggests that the movement can be defined institutionally and theologically as distinct from other Christian traditions, including evangelicalism. This essay will attempt to construct that definition in one very critical and fundamental particular, the nature and role of Scripture, though some attention must perforce be given to the movement's *articulus stanttis vel cadentis*, the doctrine and experience of entire sanctification.

72

Defining the Holiness Movement

THE INSTITUTIONAL DEFINITION
OF THE HOLINESS MOVEMENT

Most of the North American holiness movement may be found in the denominations, churches, and other religious groups which affiliate with the Christian Holiness Association (CHA), the Interdenominational Holiness Convention (IHC), or the Canadian Holiness Federation (CHF).[5] But beyond these bodies, the movement also enjoys the explicit allegiance of large numbers of United Methodists and of smaller numbers in other groups, such as the Evangelical Friends, whose denominations as such are not "holiness" denominations.[6] Also accounting themselves part of the movement are several restorationist communions, such as the Church of God, Anderson, whose convictions prohibit belonging to any organizations such as CHA, but whose theology and understanding of religious experience encourage a sense of kinship.[7] Then, too, it must be pointed out that only racial prejudice and legitimate and illegitimate forms of preference have barred the black Methodist denominations and their offspring from overt identification with the movement. Traditionally, these bodies have differed not one whit from it in doctrine or in the mores of piety.[8]

From this point on, however, the institutional definition of the holiness movement becomes theologically and liturgically confused. To cite but two examples of the problem: even within the CHA, one finds paedobaptist and antipaedobaptist groups, and one finds as well two-sacrament, three-ordinance, and neither-sacrament-nor-ordinance groups.[9] In fact, the movement stands the usual ecumenical paradigm on its head by holding firmly together on one point only, the doctrine and experience of entire sanctification.[10] The various bodies within the movement do indeed hold tenets or engage in practices which they individually cherish and even among themselves believe inviolable, but all confess that such tenets or practices are finally adiaphora, for at the heart of their reason for being lies their call to proclaim and experience entire sanctification.

THE THEOLOGICAL DEFINITION
OF THE HOLINESS MOVEMENT

Theologically, then, the essential or fundamental definition of the North American holiness movement is quite simple. The movement consists of those who hold and proclaim what they believe to be a Wesleyan doctrine of entire sanctification. They unanimously describe the experience of entire sanctification as a divine cleansing from the tendency to sin willfully, a gifting with unconditional love to God and neighbor, and an empowerment for doing the will of God. The experience is said to be available in this life to those who are already justified by grace. They agree that it is provided for in the atoning work of Christ and brought about by the Holy Spirit. It is, they say, a gift of grace, given instantaneously and received by faith, of which the expression is unreserved consecration or surrender to the will of God. The Holy Spirit assures the seeker when the work is complete. The experience is granted instantaneously and is in itself complete, but growth in grace is inherent in it and is expected.[11]

Holiness people refer to this doctrine and experience by a number of names, often intermingling terms connoting its processional aspects with terms connoting its instantaneous aspects, and they often refer to it by metonymy and synecdoche as well. The most commonly used terms are: entire sanctification or, simply, sanctification; holiness, the second blessing or, simply, the blessing; the baptism with (of) the Holy Spirit; and Christian perfection.[12]

Adherents of the movement insist that the elements of this doctrine and experience accord strictly with Scripture, but most understand their articulation of them to derive directly from the thought of John Wesley. They tend to believe, in fact, that in this matter, if not in all of their fundamental doctrines, they are the true heirs of Wesley.[13]

The authenticity and profundity of their commitment to a Wesleyan perspective is seen best in their doctrine of entire sanctification and in what Lindsell, but not they, would call their "doctrine of Scripture." They express their Weslyan commitment as well in their understandings of grace, justification, and human nature. In their understandings of other major doctrines, its clarity and consistency sometimes have been affected by the movement's ideological struggles, internal and external. Most important to note is the fact that the Wesleyan stance of the movement always, from the earliest days of the movement, has been in tension with an equally authentic and deep commitment to the ideology and methods of nineteenth-century North American revivalism. Theirs is a John Wesley gone to camp meeting.

The Second Great Awakening, of which the rise of American Methodism was an integral part, taught people to expect sudden and radical conversions as the norm. Revivalists and pastors urged conscience-stricken hearers on to seize the moment, characteristically warning that delay in crying out for mercy could only harden the heart and lead to a more severe condemnation.[14]

Then, to this emphasis on immediacy, such evangelists as Charles G. Finney conjoined an emphasis on volition. They fervently insisted that one could and should decide whether or not to accept the proffered grace of God. In a definite break with a critical article of faith in their Calvinist upbringing, Finney and others began to talk of free will, and to talk of it as a natural human endowment. So, where the notion of gracious election to salvation long had held the field, calls for decision replaced urgings to plead for divine mercy; and where penitents formerly had testified to having received hope of salvation, they now claimed to be saved "beyond the shadow of doubt." It became a religious commonplace that the highly personal, individual enterprise of deliberately seeking justification, of seeking it in repentant remorse for past sinning, of importuning God for it, and of expecting it to come instantaneously and with certainty was what made one truly Christian, infant baptism and confirmation notwithstanding. Assurance of election came to be tied to definiteness of decision.[15]

Methodism all along had been Arminian, insisting that God calls all to redemption and grants grace to all to respond as they will. But they had made clear their agreement with the classical Protestant dogma that all is indeed of grace. Even in their talk of making a decision, thoughtful Methodists in the first half of the nineteenth century carefully grounded their proclamations in the theological notion of prevenient grace.[16] By the eve of the Civil War, however, the vocabularies of New School revivalism and Methodism sounded so similar and their evangelistic aims were so nearly alike that the theological nuances were overlooked by all but the theologically astute.[17] Grassroots Methodists, who originally had learned from Wesley to think of free will under the rubric of free grace now began to think of free will in terms supplied by New School revivalist voluntarism and to reflect on it under the rubric of natures.[18]

This influence also led Methodists to emphasize the experiential aspects of justification and sanctification, where as Wesley, and earlier Methodism, had emphasized their relational aspects. So, to cite an example of the difference, where Wesley and earlier Methodism had talked of the instantaneity of the experiences of justification and entire sanctification as a consequence of the fact that both experiences are gifts of grace, not of works, now it was understood that the instantaneity of the experiences was a consequence of the way in which the human will makes decisions.[19]

Cognitively, or formally, grassroots nineteenth-century holiness people were deeply influenced by the theology of antebellum and British Methodism, especially in their understandings of justification and sanctification.[20] But affectively, or experientially, Finney's voluntarism and revivalism's understanding of how one becomes and remains a Christian held the field among holiness people, as it did among most Methodists and large numbers of other Protestants.[21] Still (this can scarcely be overemphasized), the almost reflexive revivalism of the holiness movement seldom has had the last word in the development of faith and practice in that tradition. Sometimes quite self-consciously, sometimes quite subliminally, the movement's commitment to Wesleyanism has been put into play in ways that have kept the movement from becoming simply a congeries of revivalist sects. The movement has time and again come back to serious theological discussion and even debate about the nature and ethical implications of its doctrines of justification and entire sanctification, flying in the face of its own almost habitual revivalist perspective and its deep appreciation of the importance of religious feeling or religious experience.[22]

At the heart of this critical temper lies the holiness movement's understanding of the nature and role of Scripture. It is precisely this understanding that has kept the movement at large from going over into either fundamentalism or modernism, and that makes it most difficult to identify the movement with contemporary American evangelicalism.[23] (It makes it impossible to respond positively to Lindsell's call.) Yet it is also this understanding of the nature and role of Scripture that nurtures a positive appreciation of many of the theological and ethical concerns of evangelicalism and a sense of spiritual camaradarie with it.

Of course, it must be said that the movement has, in fact, held several understandings of the nature and role of Scripture. Often it has held several at the same time, and sometimes it has held no view consistently. But there is one discernible, constant understanding of the nature and role of the Bible that has fueled the movement all along, outlasting and sometimes actually defeating all others. It may be that here, in its "doctrine of Scripture," as Lindsell would call it, that the movement has been even truer to Wesley than it has been in the matter of Christian perfection. It is surely here that very different genealogies of the holiness movement and of evangelicalism, as currently defined, become most apparent and most crucial.

The Holiness Movement and the Nature and Role of the Bible

To understand these things, one must go back to the Thirty-Nine Articles of Religion of the Church of England. Unlike almost all other basic confessions of the sixteenth century, this document does not begin with an expression of faith in the authority of Scripture nor with an article on the nature of God and original sin. Rather, one comes to the first of two articles on Scripture only after reading articles on faith in the Trinity, on the nature of Christ, on the descent into Hell, on Christ's resurrection, and on the Holy Spirit.

Of course, the order of the articles obviously is not absolutely determinative, and the articles are not a creed in the liturgical sense, but the order seems to assert that one cannot truly understand the nature and role of the Bible until one has affirmed a living relationship with God.[24] Then, what one confesses is, in the first place, not the authority of Scripture but its sufficiency for salvation. The title of article 6 is "Of the Sufficiency of the Holy Scriptures for Salvation." By contrast, in most of the continental confessions, especially those of the Reformed tradition, the article on Scripture stands first, or, even prior to that, a preamble asserts the priority of the authority of the Bible. Such confessions seem usually to affirm that one must accept the authority of the Bible in order to come to a living relationship with God.[25]

Perhaps more telling than the order of the Thirty-Nine Articles is the fact that the Anglican commitment to the priority of sufficiency over authority served to reshape the understanding of the latter in Anglican thought. The authority of the Bible was seen to arise in the first place from its sufficiency, not from the fact that it is divine revelation. Its revelatory character is more important to its purpose than to its nature. It is the means through which the Holy Spirit would reveal salvation.[26] And that makes it the vehicle, not the object, of the *testimonium Spiritus sancti internum*. The Spirit does give witness to the truth of the Bible, but of far more critical importance is the fact that the Spirit uses the Bible to give witness to the faithfulness of God.[27] It is that *testimonium* which gives authority to the Bible.[28]

The Anglican move was quite shrewd and expressed both negative and positive sources and concerns. Negatively, article 6 was to stand over against the idea that the church and tradition are of the *esse* of salvation; it was to contradict claims to new or supplementary revelation as well. Positively, article 6, by explicitly affirming the sufficiency of the canon as a whole, provided room for exegetical variety and curtailed the then-common problem of granting superior authority to canons within the canon.

The positive purposes noted arose from the conviction that the Bible is the church's book and that therefore one must approach and undertake its study in the first instance from within the worshipping community, in the context of the community's Spirit-directed unity-in-diversity and diversity-in-unity.[29] Sixteenth-century Anglicans believed that private Bible study must arise from and be amenable to the church at worship.[30]

Anglican thought held, then, that the authority of Scripture is an experienced authority, as over against a *de iure* authority. Anglicans were convinced that, by way of its use in the worship of the church, the sufficiency of the Bible in matters relating to salvation had become known. No other would-be authority, said they, bears the message of salvation with the force and sense of truth that the Bible does. They believed it to be soteriologically sufficient, and, because sufficient, soteriologically authoritative.

Whatever might be said of its authority as a theological book or as the source or basis for revealed, transcendent metaphysical systems, they said, should be found under the heading "Sufficiency for Salvation."[31]

By the end of the sixteenth century, as a majority of Anglican leaders had come to read the Thirty-Nine Articles from a more nearly Reformed angle, and as they had come to read the word "sufficiency" as if it were the word "authority," they still did not endow the category of biblical authority with the systematic and theological absoluteness increasingly assigned it by continental thinkers. And they subordinated such other authority as the Bible was believed to have—historical, biological, geographical, etc.—to that authority which makes it sufficient for salvation.[32]

By Wesley's century, however, authority almost universally had replaced sufficiency as the controlling category for understanding the nature and role of the Bible—in spite of the original intent of article 6 of the Thirty-Nine Articles. Contention over the issues that finally produced the Relief Act of 1780, the struggles of a conventionally orthodox ecclesiastical hierarchy with what they called *enthusiasm*, and widespread, aggressive, and almost evangelistic unbelief pushed the question of biblical authority forward, past the declaration of sufficiency for salvation.

Wesley responded to this context by returning to the original perspective of the framers of the Thirty-Nine Articles and hewing closely to the letter and original intent of article 6. He maintained more or less consistently a soteriological outlook on the authority of the Bible: that is to say, he seems to have believed that the Bible is authoritative because it is sufficient for salvation.[33]

The theological authority of the Bible follows from its sufficiency for salvation, as Wesley saw it.[34] In fact, Wesley insisted, not every part of the Scripture is theologically or spiritually useful.[35] Further, while its sufficiency for salvation makes it authoritative, Wesley asserted, sufficiency and authority are quite different facets of the Bible's character. Its sufficiency is an objective datum requiring no affirmation in experience, but its authority depends absolutely on the *testimonium Spiritus sancti internum*.[36]

This is the point of view underlying Wesley's famous preface to the first edition of the standard sermons:

> I want to know one thing—the way to heaven; how to land safe on that happy shore. God himself had condescended to teach the way; for this very end He came from heaven. He hath written it down in a book. O give me that book! At any price, give me the book of God! I have it: Here is knowledge enough for me. Let me be *homo unius libri*. Here then I am, far from the busy ways of men. I sit down alone: Only God is here. In his presence I open, I read his book; for this end, to find the way to heaven.[37]

Wesley would be a "person of one book," not simply because that book is basic authority but because he finds in that one book "knowledge enough for me," i.e., sufficiency for salvation. And it is precisely as the book sufficient for salvation that it is the book of God. Through it, the living God communicates with the reader. "I sit down alone: Only God is here. In his presence I open, I read his book."

This is an allusion to what Wesley often said of the necessity for the presence of the Holy Spirit in the reading of the Bible if that reading is to be sufficient for salvation.[38] In fact, the Spirit is the sole agent of the Bible's soteriological sufficiency. Scripture's own attractiveness to reason or to experience is insufficient to lead us to salvation. For Scripture to lead us to salvation, its reading must be accompanied by the *testimonium Spiritus sancti internum*. This is given on the divine initiative, and that initiative is not fundamentally concerned with making it authoritative as it pertains to our salvation.[39]

So, when Wesley said that he wanted to be a "person of one book," he was trying to avoid what William Law had helped him to see as "philosophical religion," a religion dependent upon rationality or any authority other than that which is sufficient for salvation. Authority belongs to Scripture as the means attested by the Spirit, and the Spirit's attestation is that Scripture is sufficient to salvation.[40]

More specifically, it is the love of God for us to which the Spirit witnesses, and Scripture is authoritative because it alone calls us (the Spirit speaking through it) to that love, guides us into it, and instructs us in how we should love. As we yield ourselves to the Spirit through the book and to the book as the instrument of the Spirit, we discover the book's sufficiency for salvation, and the Spirit attests its authority.[41]

This way of looking at the matter ties biblical authority to experience, and herein lies a fundamental difference between Wesleyans and much of the rest of Christianity. In his own quest for authentic faith, Wesley had come to the conclusion that, while the Bible said that such faith should be accompanied by a sense of forgiveness, this affirmation would never be experienced in this life. Then came Peter Boehler, who introduced Wesley to three who testified "of their own personal experience, that a true and living faith in Christ is inseparable from a sense of pardon for all past and freedom from all present sins."[42] Now, experience confirmed Scripture, and Scripture must be believed.

But Wesley would not have the authority of Scripture depend upon evangelical experience. Such experience only enforces that authority. So, again, Scripture's fundamental role is to stand as sufficient for salvation, describing as nothing else does the nature of evangelical experience and pressing it personally upon the reader through the *testimonium*, pressing it to the point that one must decide whether to say "yes" or "no" to salvation.[43]

Wesley recognized the problems in talking about evangelical experience and usually limited himself to biblical language to do so.[44] This he did, not in fear but in the conviction that Scripture itself, including its very language, is sufficient for salvation. In fact, he believed that it is sufficiency itself that entails the *testimonium*, so we may rest confident that when we have spoken and lived "scripturally," the Spirit will cause our words and deeds to carry spiritual authority.[45]

All of this background lies behind the Articles of Religion that Wesley prepared for the American Methodists in 1784. And it is especially important to an understanding of articles 5 and 6, Wesley's counterparts to the Anglican articles 6 and 7. Of special significance for the purpose of this paper is the fact that, when Wesley comments on article 5, he ignores the eighteenth-century view of it and goes back to its original intentions.[46]

One of those original intentions, as we have seen, was asserting the sufficiency of Scripture for salvation, over against the claims of certain private revelations to such sufficiency. The most influential expressions of private revelation that Wesley confronted were found in what was called "enthusiasm." He responded to the enthusiasts by reminding them that in matters left undetermined in the letter of Scripture, the "general rule" given there still stood: "It is His will that we should be inwardly and outwardly holy: that we should be good and do good."[47]

As Wesley saw it, the deists, rationalists, and empiricists also claimed forms of private revelation, for they insisted that they had found in reason, experiment, and mathematics a religion far more certain and far superior to that revealed in the Bible; but, of course, this was not a religion open to all. Wesley responded that whatever the rational or scientific inadequacies of the Bible may be, it does speak of the love of God for us and it does afford us genuine spiritual direction, therein doing something that reason and science cannot do. And, what is more, says Wesley, the Bible offers that divine love and direction to all.[48]

However, while Wesley sharply criticized what he saw as the pretensions of the deists, rationalists, and empiricists, he was far more accomodating to the rising scientific disciplines than were most of his theologically orthodox compatriots. His only requirements of the new scientific and philosophical development were that they benefit humankind and that they not be posited as being sufficient for salvation.[49] In basing his understanding of the nature and role of Scripture on its sufficiency for salvation instead of on its authority, Wesley defused one of the most explosive issues of the Enlightenment and avoided the trap which usually ensnared the orthodox: given the nature of the debate, those who opened by asserting the authority of Scripture then were forced by their own terms to claim too much for that authority.[50]

Generally speaking, eighteenth-century orthodoxy had gone on the defensive and argued the authority of the Bible even in nonreligious matters. Both Lutheran and Reformed orthodoxy finally had made the Bible the "first principle" of theology and thereby incorporated theology into revelation and faith. This gave theology enormous authority, but at the expense of any sense of the Bible as quickened or quickening word. The Bible's sufficiency was adjudged in terms of its authority—not simply its soteriological authority, but its general authority in all areas of faith and knowledge.[51] Pietism, Lutheran and Reformed, refused to make the Bible a theology book but instead developed the doctrine of its authority. By the mid-eighteenth century, pietists were claiming the applicability of the authority of the Bible to a wide range of topics and attempting to provide all-inclusive theological systems. So they came to espouse the very "doctrine of Scripture" that they originally had eschewed.[52]

An illustration of Wesley's approach, set against the backdrop of the convictions of both conventional orthodoxy and pietism, will allow us to see its boldness as well as its freedom. Much of the wrangling over the authority of the Bible focused on the book's historical reliability. Especially at issue were the genealogies, for here the eighteenth century saw the Scripture as being most purely historical—at least in its claims. Here, if anywhere, the Bible's detractors believed that they could prove unreliability, and here the Bible's defenders fought most valiantly to rationalize away problems. But here Wesley allows greatest latitude for factual error.

In his note on Matt. 1:1, Wesley stated that, if there are mistakes in the genealogies, it would not even have been the responsibility of the inspiring Spirit to correct them. The Spirit's purpose in the genealogies, says he, is to show that "Jesus was of the family from which the promised seed was to come." That general purpose is all that has to be demonstrated. Sufficiency for salvation, not genealogical accuracy, is the point. What the Spirit impresses upon the reader, says Wesley, is not the historical precision of the passage but the spiritual point. In fact, the Spirit has no obligation to see to historical accuracy. From the standpoint of spirituality, says Wesley, the apparent errors might go farther to help win the Jews (to whom the book is primarily addressed) than accuracy might, for since the errors in Matthew come from errors in the Jewish tables which he used, the *testimonium Spiritus sancti internum* could impel the Jew to distrust his own sources, which are strictly historical, and see that Scripture is not meant to be a mere history book, but instead is the instrument for revealing the saving purpose of God beckoning the Jews to salvation.[53]

Of course, Wesley did declare the Bible to be "infallibly true." It is

God-given, he said, and free from "material error." The Spirit dictated the words.[54] In fact, Wesley wrote a tract on the inspiration of the Bible and gave it a title that would please the most scholastically orthodox believer in his England: "A Clear and Concise Demonstration of the Divine Inspiration of the Holy Scriptures."[55]

Yet, Wesley's was a critical temperament. Far more than enough specific instances of the exercise of that temperament, along with explicit statements of principle, could be cited to make it difficult, if not impossible, to count John Wesley among the forebears of fundamentalism or evangelicalism as these are currently defined.[56]

Wesley stands at his farthest remove from the roots of Modern fundamentalism or evangelicalism, but not at all distant from their putative mentor, Calvin, in his understanding of the *testimonium Spiritus sancti internum*. Wesley does not consider the first characteristic of the *testimonium* to be attestation that the Bible is the Word of God, but rather attestation that a given passage or biblical idea truly applies to *me* and that I am able to receive the truth of it in faith. The *testimonium* occurs whenever there is engagement with the Word (reading, hearing, reflecting), and it works from specific biblical references or ideas, not abstractly.[57] That is to say, for the Bible to exercise its sufficiency and its authority, the reader or hearer must approach it in "serious and earnest prayer" and in a spirit of self-examination. Under those conditions only — which are made possible through grace alone, not works — can the Spirit "continually inspire" and "supernaturally assist" the reader or hearer.[58] In fact, Wesley doubted that the letter of Scripture has positive value apart from the operations of the Spirit. And he doubted that the unregenerate mind has natural access to the Scripture.[59]

Behind this understanding of the *testimonium Spiritus sancti internum* lie two very significant factors, one a matter of practice, the other more formally theological. First, for Wesley, Scripture and worship, especially public worship, are inextricably linked. Scripture gains its true meaning in worship, public or private.[60] Second, strictly speaking, Christ is the revelation. Scripture is the revelation of the Revelation, as it were. Scripture is the Spirit's invention for revealing the Revelation, Christ, to us. So, it is from Christ, the true Revelation, that Scripture takes its authority.[61] There could be Christ without Scripture; there could be no authoritative Scripture without Christ.

In many ways, many in mid-nineteenth-century Methodism and the holiness movement seem to have ignored or even rejected Wesley's understanding of the nature and role of the Bible and, in consequence, his theological method as well.[62] Both moves often placed the holiness movement within a hair's breadth of Reformed theology on the two matters under discussion. Yet the data clearly show that at least the seeds of Wesley's thought remained, blossoming here and there once in a while. And when they did blossom, it became clear both that they were planted in native soil and that non-Wesleyan understandings of Scripture and non-Wesleyan methodologies do not graft easily onto an otherwise Wesleyan system. Further, by the early twentieth century, the holiness movement took deliberate and positive but not always clearly-aimed steps back in the direction of the Wesleyan understanding of Scripture developed by such technical theologians as Watson, Pope, and Miley.

The grassroots side of this inconsistency has led some holiness people, as well as some outside of the movement who have sought to understand it, to conclude that the movement is an expression of evangelicalism as currently defined, if it is not an expression of fundamentalism. But the fact is that the formal theology of the movement forms a major barricade to such an identity.

To demonstrate this assertion, we shall look at the "doctrine of Scripture," as Lindsell calls it, of Phoebe Palmer and H. Orton Wiley, respectively a most influential shaper of the grassroots understandings of the movement and its most influential formal theologian. To do both them and the topic justice, we must work with both "doctrine of Scripture" and theological method concurrently.

John Wesley had looked for his theological sources to those things that had stoked the spiritual life of the church, feeble though they might be: Scripture (as *primus inter pares*), the liturgy (which combined *traditio* and experience), tradition, and reason.[63] His concern, put pastorally, was reviving the existing church, and for that very reason, he labored long and carefully to keep his Methodists from separating from it. On the other hand, while many of the leaders of the holiness movement sought to avoid schism and spoke of "christianizing Christianity" or, less strikingly, of reviving the church, and while those theologians who gave the movement its formal systems had no thought at all of raising up new denominations, the movement as a whole, influenced by revivalism, tended to see the institutional church as increasingly problematical, spiritually, and they believed that only those sources external to, or those perceived to be independent of, the institution could revive authentic Christianity. By late in the nineteenth century, they had come to assume that such revival meant separation. Practically, this meant that those sources which had served Wesley and two or three succeeding generations as sources for theology were deliberately by-passed, for they had come to be seen as obstacles to warm-hearted, confident faith.

While liturgy had been, for Wesley, a fundamental source of theology, it now became one of the most frequent targets of the critics. The words "cold, dead, and formal," were run together as a unitary description of almost anything more ordered than the very simplest revivalist form of service. And yet there did remain among Methodists an insistence on organizational regimentation which could not help but show itself in worship as well. Tension existed among ordered worship; the liturgically amorphous services by means of which many upwardly-mobile Methodists now perceived and expressed their spirituality; and the simple, fervent patterns borrowed by many of the holiness people from revivalism. Reflecting all of this tension, Phoebe Palmer, yearning to proclaim scriptural holiness, struggled with the distinction between what she called "proxy worship" and "proxy singing" on the one hand, and "spiritual worship" and "spiritual singing" on the other. Finally, in 1859, she recorded her position in her approval of a tract entitled "How Shall We Guard Against Formality in Singing?"[64]

Late antebellum Methodism believed it to be a battle worth the effort, one that was believed to have everything to do with piety—achieving it and maintaining it. In fact, in the next year, 1860, some dissident Methodists, as firmly committed as Palmer to "spiritual worship" and "spiritual singing," as well as to the doctrine and experience of entire sanctification, organized themselves as the Free Methodist Church, the first denomination to place an explicit article on entire sanctification in its creed and one of the first in the Methodist tradition to link piety and style of worship.[65]

So, while Wesley had expressed a conviction that singing and ordered prayer should teach theology as well as encourage piety, the holiness movement turned to hymning personal religious experience. Holiness people simply did not ordinarily look upon worship as a means of nurture nor as a source of doctrine or theology. In fact, ordered, liturgical prayer— "written prayers," as they were called—was frowned on in early holiness circles, except for the Lord's Prayer, the baptismal prayer of blessing, and the eucharistic prayer of consecration. Ordered, liturgical worship was seen as a large part of the church's problem, a hindrance to true piety.[66] By the 1870s, if not earlier, holiness people were ignorant of Wesley's service books, or they looked upon them as an odd remnant of his Anglicanism. They suspected the traditional liturgies and avoided them most of the time, though they did hold to the traditional forms, simplified, for baptism and the Lord's Supper.

Traditio, of which liturgy is essentially an example and a vehicle, played almost no part in early holiness thought and practice, and it certainly was not seen as a source of theological reflection. To be sure, Wesley was quoted quite often, as were others helpful to the cause. But such quotation was almost never a matter of inculcating the idea that those who were quoted, and we ourselves, are dynamically related in a living faith. One cited "the fathers" to back up one's own point or to contradict another's. The rich, precise meaning of tradition as *traditio* went undiscussed.

For Palmer and for the early holiness movement in general, Scripture was the one and only source of authoritative doctrine. In fact, from one perspective, Palmer's taxonomy of entire sanctification, complete with its concern for the biblical language of the altar, is a clear expression of commitment to a radical doctrine of *sola scriptura*. One does what the Bible says to do, and therefore one has a right to claim what the Bible promises.[67] This radical perspective was passed on to the holiness movement's preaching. Yet its formal and official guides held no such view.[68]

For Palmer, being a "Bible Christian" meant everything. It meant trusting the word of Scripture so fully that through it God can witness that one has a pure heart.[69]

Of course, Wesley had used the term, too: "[The Methodists] resolved to be Bible-Christians at all events; wherever they went, to preach with all their might plain, old Bible-Christianity."[70] For Wesley, being a "Bible Christian" meant studying the Bible in order properly to know and to serve Christ. One does not believe the Bible in order to be a Christian, but rather because one indeed *is* a Christian.[71] So, while being a Bible Christian would include confidence in the promises of God, such confidence would not constitute the heart of the matter, for Wesley. Phoebe Palmer and the early holiness movement tended to turn this around, to say that believing the Bible is indeed what makes one Christian. In good Wesleyan language, the Bible is still called a "medium," a means; but practically it has become much more. So Palmer writes:

> Yet, if one is admonished to rely upon the *written* word as in verity the voice of God, the answer may with surprise be returned, "What, believe without any *other* evidence than the *word* of God!" O when will the truth fully obtain among professors, that "prophecy" (i.e., Scripture) came not of old time by the will of man, but holy men of old spake as they were *moved by the Holy Ghost*.[72]

In the paragraph just preceding the one quoted, Palmer was wondering why more emphasis had not been placed upon the fact that "the Scriptures are *expressly* the voice of the Spirit." In the spirit of Scottish Common Sense thought, she assumed that earlier thinkers had asked the same question that she did.[73]

Instructive, too, is a bit of Palmer's poetry from her book, *The Way of Holiness*:

> Yes, I'll to my bosom press thee,
> *Precious word*, I'll hide thee here;

Sure, my very heart will bless thee,
For thou ever sayest, 'Good cheer'!
Speak my heart, and tell thy ponderings,
Tell how far thy rovings led,
When *this Book* brought back the wanderings,
Speaking life as from the dead.[74]

Compare this selection with the Wesleys' view, expressed in the following lines from a hymn by Charles Wesley on the Bible:

Oh, may the gracious words divine
Subject of all my converse be!
So will the Lord His follower join,
And walk and talk Himself with me;
So shall my heart His presence prove,
And burn with everlasting love.[75]

The Wesley hymns on the Bible are almost always as much hymns on the Holy Spirit. Two themes recur in them: the necessity for enlightenment by the Spirit in the reading of the Word, and the bliss of coming through the written to the Living Word.[76]

Perhaps it could fairly be said that the distinction between Wesley and the grassroots of the early holiness movement, with respect to the theological authority of the Bible, is this: Wesley brought experience to Scripture in order to understand experience properly, i.e., in the light of salvation; grassroots holiness people sought to experience Scripture itself. For Phoebe Palmer and her spiritual kin, Scripture demands expression in experience; for Wesley and his kin, experience demands assessment and definition by Scripture.[77] It could be said, oversimply but accurately, that Palmer and many of the holiness people believed that to live as a Christian is to live out Scripture.

> I had read doctrinal treatises on *faith*; everything within my reach, my heart had grasped after; but, now, to my surprise, I found that I had, all the time, been overlooking its simplicity. Faith, I saw, was simply taking God at His word; not some mystical sound that was to burst upon my spirit's ear, confounding my senses; but the plain, written word of God, applied to my heart through the same power, and by the same inspirations, by which it was written: . . . . I should love to tell you how my heart apprehends the Scripture as the lively oracles, and not a dead letter, but spirit and life. O, I would love to be a living epistle, and speak, to a congregated world, of the excellency of God's word! I would love to tell that the Scriptures are living truth, and the voice of the Spirit; and that "He that believeth hath the witness in himself."[78]

For Palmer and her theological kin in the early holiness movement, the real world of the believer is the world that Scripture creates and describes. It is the authentic empirical reality in which believers live, and it shapes and gives definition and meaning to what unbelievers and unthinking believers call "the real world." So it is that the believer is to understand empirical reality or experience in biblical terms and keep that reality and experience aligned with biblical, moral and spiritual norms. So it is that the believer's "real world" has no essential independence from the world of the Bible.[79] Wesley and his theological kin, including the formal theologians of the movement, on the other hand, held that experience, evangelical or otherwise, is to be brought into line with biblical norms; but they granted that it had an essential independence from the world of the Bible.[80] To put it at an extreme, Wesley and the formal theologians could envision a person coming to evangelical experience quite apart from hearing or knowing the Scripture.[81] That segment of the early holiness movement under the tutelage of Phoebe Palmer and those who saw things as she did saw knowledge of the Scriptures, however meager, as almost absolutely necessary to the experiencing of salvation.[82] Wesley and his close theological kin could see one entering an evangelical experience without commitment to any theological proposition as such.[83] Those in the early holiness movement who were influenced by Palmer and her associates could not evision anyone entering the evangelical experience without commitment to at least some simple theological propositions.[84] So Wesley and those who followed after him invited their hearers to "receive Christ"; probably the majority of the preachers of the holiness movement invited hearers to "be saved" or to "get saved." Wesley and his closest theological kin invited believers to "love God with all of the heart, soul, mind, and strength, and neighbor as self"; Palmer and her theological kin invited believers to "be sanctified holy."[85]

The difference is subtle but profound. Wesley's is a call to experience, to personal relationship, which then will be brought to the scrutiny of Scripture by way of some theological categories already to hand in the historic faith—categories most commonly found in the worship of the church. The holiness movement also called hearers to experience and to personal relationship, but many within that movement had, in the very call, already set the theological/spiritual boundaries, so that the believer had to accept both the experience and the boundaries, however vaguely understood. And, so tightly bound were the two that refusal to accept the theological/spiritual boundaries was generally believed to be a rejection of the experience.[86] (So it was, for instance, that many a holiness evangelist packed the mourner's bench with a hot sermon on "Holiness or Hell!") When one accepted both the experience and the boundaries, one was to assume that the experience was already in line with the Bible—if it were not, one could not have accepted either the experience or the boundaries — and that theology was superfluous.[87] There would be no need to integrate Scripture and experience. They already would have been integrated in what had been received in conversion and entire sanctification. Scripture had been experienced.[88]

But was there room for difference of opinion regarding biblical interpretation? And what were the rules for interpretation?

Wesley had indicated that biblical interpretation is a matter for faith and, in a sense, a matter of the faith of the contemporary believer in the company of the church — a church encountering the still-living faith of the biblical authors, who also spoke from within the context of the elect community. But Wesley seems to have assumed no need for commitment to specific theological *dicta* or *dogmae* as a condition for faithful interpretation.

On the other hand, Palmer and those in the early holiness movement who would have agreed with her undertook their hermeneutic with a prior theological commitment. That is to say, they interpreted the Bible with some guiding propositions already in mind. Of course, they believed their theological commitment to be a commitment of faith, but its focus was clearly dogmatic.

Ironically, Palmer and her circle worried that the theologians had overcomplicated the faith, especially with reference to entire sanctification. "The great heart of the people is now crying out for the simple, unsophisticated gospel of full salvation, untrammelled by worldly sophisms," she wrote.[89]

One may find a good example of Palmer's hermeneutic in the opening section of *The Way of Holiness*. The specific question is the optimum amount of time that should transpire between justification and entire sanctification. She responded by outlining the path of one who found the "shorter way" to Christian perfection. First, one must be disposed to see that there is a shorter way. This disposition will direct one's reading and understanding, and that directed reading and understanding will induce conviction. Now one is confronted with a choice: will one affirm and conform — by grace, of course — to what has been revealed?[90]

Very significant here is the suggestion that one dispose oneself to see a biblical passage in a given way. It is a matter of bringing a particular theological commitment to the Scripture. Of course, Palmer would say that this commitment is essentially a commitment to nothing other than the truth of Scripture.

But suppose two or more disagree on the meaning of a passage? In "To the Rev. Mr. M — —," no. 52 of *Faith and Its Effects: Or, Fragments from my Portfolio*, Mrs. Palmer put this question in terms of the possibility of a pious person's being deceived concerning the meaning of a passage.

It is possible, she declared. In fact, to the truly pious, Satan is most likely to appear as an angel of light. Coming in this way, Satan proceeds to present "*detached* portions from the blessed work, as he did to our Saviour, and tell us, '*It is written.*'" One should respond to this strategem as Jesus did: "He brings us the detached portions, and by the light of truth, symmetrically arranged, Satan is vanquished."[91]

"Symmetrically arranged" seems to be Palmer's expression of confidence that Scripture is its own best interpreter. But what of those holding a "symmetry" different from her own, those who would agree with the principle she holds but still arrive at a different interpretation? She does not, in fact, come back to this broader issue. Our only explicit clue lies in this letter, which treats a rather narrow matter (the impropriety of seeking from the Bible a date for the Second Coming). Yet it does seem that Palmer would say that, in matters of faith, a passage of Scripture has but one true interpretation, and any variance from that single authentic interpretation skews all other interpretation (i.e., the symmetry) and puts the interpreter in spiritual jeopardy.[92]

Palmer's mode of biblical interpretation and her understanding of the nature and role of the Bible found deep approval among many in the holiness movement, largely because of its intimate principal connection with holiness evangelism and holiness apologetics. Probably, at base, Palmer herself had meant them to have no broader application. But, in fact, they did, and by the early 1900s, as millenarianism, movements opposed to literary-historical criticism of the Bible, and reactions to the theories of Darwin and Spencer converged and were transformed into fundamentalism, many in the holiness movement found their identities to lie there.

For example, B.F. Haynes, a former Methodist editor who, from 1912 to 1923, served as editor of the new *Herald of Holiness*, "official organ of the Pentecostal Church of the Nazarene," drew much more heavily for theological sustenance on the *Herald and Presbyter*, D.L. Moody, and Reuben Torrey than on Wesley or other Wesleyans, even while criticizing the former group for its failure to accept "second blessing holiness."[93] Writers for the *Herald of Holiness* in the years 1912 to 1920 quote Moody twice as often as they quote either of the Wesleys or any Wesleyan.

All along, however, another theological stream flowed in the holiness movement, one coming from Wesley through the formal Methodist theologians and Methodist hymnody. This stream, too, while deeply influenced by revivalism, was not absolutely dominated by it, as the current so profoundly influenced by Palmer seemed to be. This one would find its way between rising Christian liberalism and fundamentalism as a genuine alternative to both, and, from time to time, it would find itself in lively sibling debate with Palmer's kin and progeny. Strange to tell, the latter often assumed that they had been advocating all along precisely what the former did. Persons in the Palmerian stream often did not see that their theological bases conflicted with, and often contradicted, the other, and that finally their claim to be Wesleyan was tenuous. Again, an example is B.F. Haynes, who could hypostasize the Bible in grand fundamentalist fashion and then insist on the absolute priority of Christ the Living Word in ways that made the Bible instrumental only.[94]

By the 1890s, the holiness movement reflected fully Methodism's rising awareness of the need for comprehensive, systematic theology. For all that the movement threw its energies singlemindedly into the propagation of the doctrine and experience of entire sanctification. Its leaders, especially, saw the need for a broader ideological base. As the movement spawned independent bodies, it became even more aware of the need to avoid theological parochialism, and it turned without hesitation to Methodism's technical theologians: Watson, Clarke, Pope, Ralston, Raymond, Binney, Summers, Miley, and, later and with some caution, Sheldon and Curtis.[95]

Each of these theologians, in the language of his own era and his own education, carefully retained the central features of Wesley's understanding of the nature and role of the Bible, especially the following: (a) the careful linking of written word to Living Word; (b) the insistence that soteriology be the controlling hermeneutic category; (c) the belief that the Bible is authoritative because it is sufficient to salvation, not sufficient because authoritative; and (d) the understanding that, theologically, the *testimonium Spiritus sancti internum* is, in the first instance, a witness to the Bible's sufficiency to salvation and then to its authority, not first to its authority and then to its sufficiency.[96]

Whatever the pull in the direction of what became fundamentalism, the insistence of the various holiness groups that the works of Wesley, Watson, Pope, Binney, and Miley, especially, be read by those seeking ordination served as a counterweight. But by the end of World War I, the holiness people began to call for full-scale theologies done by their own scholars. Many of them now looked with suspicion upon any theological work not arising from within the movement itself, and they tended to side with the rising fundamentalists emotionally and spiritually, if not theologically, in their concern both for retaining the absolute authority of Scripture and for doctrinal "orthodoxy." At the same time, however, many in the movement's leadership understood that the pressures to align with fundamentalism could destroy the movements's essential Wesleyanism. So, for two very different reasons, the movement's scholars were encouraged to create systematic theologies.

By the early 1920s, three theologians amenable to the holiness movement had begun work on full-scale systematic theologies. R.R Byrum's *Christian Theology* appeared in 1924, A.M. Hill's *Fundamental Christian Theology* came out in 1934, and the first of the three volumes of H. Orton Wiley's *Christian Theology* came off the press in 1940.[97] All of these works drew heavily on Pope and Miley, and Wiley, especially, shows acquaintance with two theologies written from within the German-American Wesleyan tradition, J.T. Weaver's *Christian Theology*, which appeared in 1900; and S.J. Gamertsfelder's *Systematic Theology*, which was published in 1913.[98] These last two works themselves depend much on Pope and (especially) Miley; and both, in their expositions of the doctrine of entire sanctification, show clear affinities with the holiness movement, though the author's respective denominations saw no need to identify with that movement directly.

The clearest and most complete exposition of the theology of the holiness movement was that of H. Orton Wiley. While it was not published until 1940, it quite clearly reflects the formal theology of the holiness movement prior to World War I. In fact, Wiley had been urged to write it as early as 1919 and had set to work fulfilling the demand almost immediately.[99] When his *Christian Theology* finally did see the light of day, it contained few surprises, for as college president, teacher, and itinerant evangelist (all concurrently from 1913 to 1948), and as editor of the *Herald of Holiness* (from 1928 to 1936), Wiley had made his views widely known through several decades.

Christian Theology clearly reflects the formal Wesleyan theological tradition of Watson, Pope, and Miley, and is especially indebted to Miley in both form and content. It is of critical importance to this essay because of the way in which Wiley developed what Lindsell (but surely not Wiley) would have called a "doctrine of Scripture." Wiley clearly enters the lists against American theological liberalism on the one hand and against fundamentalism on the other. His aim was to present a position that would be acceptable to the holiness movement in it struggles with the former and amid its ambivalences concerning the latter.

In treating the questions of "the Christian Revelation" and, more specifically "the Christian Book," Wiley wrote of three "worthy monarchs" which the church "has forced into a false and unworthy position before God and man." These were the church, the Bible, and reason.[100] We shall look more closely at his understanding of the abuses of the Bible and reason.

In his considerations of the abuse of the idea of Scripture as revelation, Wiley explicitly castigates seventeenth-century Protestant scholasticism. But he leaves abundant clues that he is eyeing another target as well and that this target may be the primary one:

The Reformers themselves strove earnestly to maintain the balance between the formal and the material principles of salvation, the Word and
Faith, but gradually the formal principle superceded the material, and men
began unconsciously to substitute the written Word for Christ the Living
Word. They divorced the written word from the Personal Word and thus
forced it into a false position. No longer was it the fresh utterance of Christ,
the outflow of the Spirit's presence, but merely a recorded utterance which
bound men by legal rather than spiritual bonds. Men's knowledge became formal rather than spiritual. The views of God attained were merely those of
a book, not those of a living Christ which the book was intended to reveal.
As a consequence, Christ became to them merely a historical figure, not a
Living Reality; and men sought more for a knowledge of God's will than for
God Himself. They gave more attention to creeds than to Christ. They rested
in the letter, which according to Scripture itself kills, and never rose to a concept of Him whose word are spirit and life. The Bible, thus divorced from
its mystical connection with the Personal Word, became in some sense a
usurper, a pretender to the throne.[101]

In his discussion of the skewing of the relationship between reason
and revelation, Wiley leaves no doubt that one of the chief offenders is
fundamentalism, which, in its overreaction to the Enlightenment's reliance on reason and empirical evidence and the subsequent development of
biblical criticism, itself tended to insist that faith rest on logic.

Lastly, Reason itself was forced into a false authority. Severed from its
Living Source, the Bible was debased to the position of a mere book among
books. It was thus subjected to the test of human reason, and as a consequence there arose the critical or critico-historical movement of the last century known as "destructive criticism." Over against this as a protest arose a
reactionary party, which, originating in a worthy desire to maintain belief in
the plenary inspiration of the Bible, as well as its genuineness, authenticity
and authority as the Rule of Faith, resorted to a mere legalistic defense of
the Scriptures. It depended upon logic rather than life.

Wiley goes on from this point to reassert the understanding of the in-
terrelationship among faith, doctrine, and Bible that had always been
characteristic of formal Wesleyan theology, but his is an understanding
quite different from that which had been developed by such persons as
Phoebe Palmer and which had become widespread in much of the holiness movement.

Spiritual men and women — those filled with the Holy Spirit, are not unduly
concerned with either higher or lower criticism. They do not rest merely in
the letter which must be defended by argument. They have a broader and more
substantial basis for their faith. It rests in their risen Lord, the glorified Christ.
They know that the Bible is true, not primarily through the efforts of the

apologists, but because they are acquainted with its Author. The Spirit which inspired the Word dwells within them and witnesses to its truth. In them the formal and material principles of the Reformation are conjoined. The Holy Spirit is the great conservator of orthodoxy.[102]

Wiley's "doctrine of Scripture" clearly begins with the soteriological sufficiency of the Book, a sufficiency rooted in the fact that its principal and essential role is to give witness to the redemptive work of God. It is the believers' faith in that sufficiency, a faith generated by the presence of the Spirit within, that gives the Bible its authority. The theological "movement," so to speak, is from the believers' saving relationship to God in Christ to the sufficiency and then to the authority of the Bible, rather than being a movement from a conviction of either the inspiration or the authority of the Bible to saving faith. The *testimonium Spiritus sancti internum* is, in the first place, a witness to the sufficiency of the Scriptures for salvation, and only after that a witness to their authority.

This makes absolutely critical the relationship between Christ and the Bible. Here, Wiley fully reflects both the original impulses of the Protestant Reformation and Wesley's Anglicanism. The Bible is finally and essentially an instrument of revelation, not ultimate revelation itself. In this, we are at a far remove from either Phoebe Palmer, fundamentalism, or the theological expressions of Scottish Common Sense.

> In a deeper sense, Jesus Christ, our ever-living Lord is Himself the fullest revelation of God. He is the Word of God—the outlived and outspoken thought of the Eternal. Thus, while we honor the Scriptures in giving them a central place as our primary source in theology, we are not unmindful that the letter killeth but the Spirit maketh alive. Christ, the Living Word, must ever be held in proper relation to the Holy Bible, the written Word. If the letter would be vital and dynamic, we must through the Holy Spirit, be ever attuned to that living One whose matchless words, incomparable deeds, and vicarious death constitute the great theme of that Book of books.[104]

In underlining a Wesleyan understanding of the *testimonium Spiritus sancti internum*, Wiley sharply criticized the tendency of both liberal Protestantism and those forms of conservative Protestantism ideologically rooted in either Common Sense or revivalist subjectivity to interpret the venerable principle of spiritual consciousness or spiritual illumination as some sort of natural capacity. The liberals psychologized it, as did those who picked up with revivalist subjectivity; the fundamentalists and other rationalistic conservatives identified it with reason. Wiley, knowing his readership, concentrated his fire on the fundamentalists and rationalistic conservatives:

> Revelation and the written Word came to be regarded as identical. Intellectual adherence to certain received doctrines was accepted as the standard

of orthodoxy. The concept of the Church as at base a spiritual fellowship was not duly emphasized. Legalism superceded spirituality. Further still, the *testimonium Spiritus sancti*, which had been interpreted as spiritual experience, gradually came to mean nothing more than human reason.[105]

Wiley's work was quickly adopted by most of the holiness denominations as their principal theological textbook — a position which it currently retains, though the movement's students and teachers have, for several decades now, read it in the context of extended bibliographies that include the works of "friend" and "foe," ancient and modern. And, in spite of some very deep positive emotional ties to the kinds of concerns central to fundamentalism and now to evangelicalism as it is currently defined, Wiley has his effect in reminding holiness people that they really do represent, in their Wesleyanism, an alternative way of being Christian.

Conclusion

One would not make light of Lindsell's call to the holiness movement to "say forthrightly whether the doctrine of Scripture teaches [that] there are or [that] there are not errors in the Bible." That call is of critical importance to him and to vast numbers of those calling themselves evangelicals. It is also a call of critical importance to those even vaster numbers who both call themselves evangelicals and, while rejecting Lindsell's notions of inerrancy, still believe that, next to confessing some kind of personal relationship to Jesus, the truly central issue in defining evangelicalism is "the doctrine of Scripture." But Lindsell's is not a call that the American holiness movement believes to be absolutely critical to its own self-definition. Responding to it on the terms suggested by Lindsell would seriously falsify the religious and spiritual definition of the movement and create havoc in interpreting its history and inner logic.

In its own "doctrine of Scripture," the theological history and inner logic of the holiness movement have led it to conclude, with theological certainty but emotional ambivalence, that a call like Lindsell's is theologically and spiritually irrelevant. Its history and inner logic would lead it to conclude that, if the term inerrancy be used, as it is, it refers to the Bible's service as the unique creation of the Holy Spirit, intended by that Spirit to carry conviction for sin, the news of full salvation in Christ, and sure instruction in how to relate to God and neighbor in righteousness and true holiness. In these things, the Bible is understood to be wholly inerrant. The movement has largely concluded that, since empirical or scientific exactitudes certainly are not soteriologically ultimate and are not even metaphysically ultimate, they must be accounted for in terms of something other than scientific exactitude itself. That is to say, if the Bible were inerrant in all matters scientific and historical, it would only be the best of a class of writings, to be judged by a standard quite outside itself which was invented by human beings, not by God. Most holiness people would insist that all such questions must submit to the question of the ultimate purpose of Scripture itself, which is not absolutely accurate knowledge of all things in heaven and in earth but soteriological sufficiency. Scripture, they would say, is the sole representative of an entirely different order of documents.

Here, the inner logic guiding the use of the Bible in the holiness movement has centered upon the Scripture's "sufficiency for salvation." The Bible is the Spirit's unique vehicle for loving us to Christ and to Christlikeness. Scripture is the means invented by and chosen by the Holy Spirit for presenting the will of God concerning us. And that will of God, say the holiness people, is our entire sanctification—that grace be given in order that we may love God with all our heart and soul, mind and strength, and love neighbor as self. In this work, the Bible does not err, and it yields to no surrogate.

Given this way of reading Scripture, and its corollary in theological method, holiness people have not seen their differences on other matters to be hindrances to joining together and identifying themselves as a movement. In fact, they have been much more inclined to merge than to divide.[106] Currently, this aspect of their inner logic is leading to increasing understanding that, as salvation history went beyond the cross and the tomb to Pentecost, and on to what must be viewed as a divinely impelled spreading of the Gospel across all of the lines which human beings draw to distinguish themselves from others, it now seems to be leading to a crossing of the lines that have distinguished holiness people from each other and from "nonholiness" Christians. In this matter, the movement has almost come full circle, back to Wesley's understanding that the work of spreading "scriptural holiness" is not so much a work of evangelism and creating a new body of believers as it is a work of revival within already existing Christianity.

Here, then, is the center of holiness theological logic: not orthodoxy, but sanctidoxy. Not the enlightenment of the saints but the love of the Holy One.

NOTES

1. Harold Lindsell, *The Bible in the Balance* (Grand Rapids, Mich.: Zondervan, 1979), 110. A paragraph earlier, Lindsell had called upon the Church of the Nazarene in particular to "make plain which of the two incompatible viewpoints ('inerrantist' or 'errantist') represents the church and its people."

2. Ibid. 306, notes the additional doctrinal standards of evangelicalism, as he would define it. In his *The Battle for the Bible* (Grand Rapids, Mich.: Zondervan, 1976), 17–27, Lindsell argues that no question is more important than that of the basis of religious knowledge and that, since the Bible is the source of the Christian's religious knowledge, the question of its inerrancy is epistemologically prior to all other questions of doctrine.

3. For an example of this identification, see Charles W. Carter and Everett N. Hunt, Jr., "The Divine Mandate: God's Universal Redemptive Mission," in Charles W. Carter, R. Duane Thompson, and Charles R. Wilson, *A Contemporary Wesleyan Theology: Biblical, Systematic, and Practical,* 2 vols. (Grand Rapids, Mich.: Zondervan, 1983), 2:675–80. Several of the holiness bodies belong to the National Association Evangelicals (NAE).

4. Compare Harold B. Kuhn, "Wesleyanism," in *Beacon Dictionary of Theology,* ed. Richard S. Taylor, J. Kenneth Grider and Willard H. Taylor (Kansas City, Mo.: Beacon Hill, 1983), 546–47, and Willard H. Taylor, "Evangelical," in Richard S. Taylor, Grider, and Willard H. Taylor, *Beacon Dictionary of Theology,* 196–97.

5. The North American holiness movement is not itself a formally organized body, nor even a single federation. It is an amorphous affiliative group. The largest holiness bodies are the Church of the Nazarene: the Salvation Army; the Church of God, Anderson, Indiana; the Wesleyan Church; and the Free Methodist Chruch. The combined North American membership of the five largest holiness bodies is about 1.4 million. But this figure is quite misleading, because the restorationist bodies in the movement historically have resisted official membership rolls and numbering and because the behavioral expectations for those in full affiliation with holiness bodies are sufficiently demanding that many faithfully attend and financially support holiness churches, who do not wish to join them. Thus the constituencies of these groups are at least half again the size of membership. The number of persons attending a regular Sunday morning worship service in a holiness church commonly exceeds the number of members.

6. E.g., holiness people within United Methodism continue to supply the principal support for a number of independent holiness camp meetings, and Ashbury College, Wilmore, Kentucky, traditionally has drawn the largest proportion of its support from the same source.

7. Cf. John W.V. Smith, *The Quest for Holiness and Unity: A Centennial History of the Church of God (Anderson, Indiana)* (Anderson, Ind.: Warner Press, 1980), 32–42.

8. For a useful taxonomy of the black denominations and other groups in the holiness perfectionist tradition, see Charles Edwin Jones, *Black Holiness: A Guide to the Study of the Black Participation in Wesleyan Perfectionist and Glossolalic Pentecostal Movements* (ATLA Bibliography Series, no. 18; Metuchen, N.J.: Scarecrow Press and American Theological Library Association, 1987). Although the preaching of the "second blessing" in the predominantly Black Methodist denominations—African Methodist Episcopal; African Methodist Episcopal, Zion; and Christian Methodist Episcopal—is not as common as it was up until about World War II, it can hardly be said to have gone unheard since then.

9. The Free Methodist Church, the Wesleyan Church, and the Church of the Nazarene, among others, practice infant baptism; the Church of God, Anderson, Ind., among others, opposes infant baptism. Most of the movement recognizes baptism and the Lord's Supper as sacraments, although some members prefer to call them ordinances. The Church of God, Anderson, Ind., and several other smaller groups also believe foot washing to be an ordinance. The Salvation Army does not celebrate the

sacraments, though it is unclear whether this position arose from pragmatic or theological considerations. Other areas in which the several bodies within the holiness movement espouse opposing positions include premillennialism/postmillennialism/amillennialism; episcopalian/presbyterian/congregational polities; and confessionalism/ anticonfessionalism.

10. E.g., leaders from the Church of the Nazarene and from the Churches of Christ in Christian Union (CCCU) cooperate quite amicably in the CHA, but a Nazarene preacher wearing a wedding ring would not be welcome in most CCCU pulpits. Yet CCCU people would attend revival services at a Nazarene church or camp meeting and support the same preacher both financially and spiritually, and the preacher wearing the ring would not hesitate to attend and would probably be welcome among the congregation at a CCCU revival service or a camp meeting.

11. E.g., "Article 10: Entire Sanctification," *Manual of the Church of the Nazarene*, secs. 13 and 14; and "Address to the Holiness People from the General Holiness Convention in Ft. Scott, Kansas, June 27th 1888," sec 5, in Clarence Eugene Cowen, *A History of the Church of God (Holiness)* (Overland Park, Kan.: Herald and Banner Press, 1949), 219-20.

12. Cf. James Blaine Chapman, *The Terminology of Holiness* (Kansas City, Mo.: Beacon Hill Press, 1947), and W.T. Purkiser, *Sanctification and Its Synoymns: Studies in the Biblical Theology of Holiness* (Kansas City, Mo.: Beacon Hill Press, 1961).

13. Cf. the historical statements which almost every holiness body has placed at the head of its constitution, e.g., Church of the Nazarene, *Manual* (1985), p. 15; Wesleyan Church, *Discipline* (1984), secs. 1-6. Further, almost all of the bodies, in their official histories, trace their ideological/spiritual roots to the 18th-century Wesleyan Revival in England; e.g., Lee M. Haines and Paul William Thomas, *An Outline History of the Wesleyan Church*, 2 ed. (Marion, Ind.: Wesley Press, 1981), and Timothy L. Smith, *Called Unto Holiness: The Story of the Nazarenes* (Kansas City, Mo.: Nazarene Publishing House, 1962), esp. 9, 21, 42.

14. For a winsome example of such preaching, see William F. Warren, "The Gospel Invitation," in *The Gospel Invitation: Sermons Related to the Boston Revival of 1877*, ed. H.M. Grout (Boston: Lockwood, Brooks, and Co., 1877), 238-62. On p. 4, the editor notes that Warren's sermon had been preached earlier at a "Massachusetts camp-meeting." For much earlier examples, see Ralph W. Allen and Daniel Wise, eds., *Helps to a Life of Holiness and Usefulness, or, Revival Miscellanies: Containing Eleven Revival Sermons . . . Selected from the Works of The Rev. James Caughey* (Boston: n.p., 1854), esp. the sermons "Quenching the Spirit," 101-107; "The Striving of the Spirit," 108-119; and "A Call to Decision," 136-52.

15. For Finney's understanding of free will as natural ability, cf. his "Lecture XXXI: Natural Ability," in *Lectures on Systematic Theology*, ed. J.H. Fairchild (Oberlin: E.J. Goodrich, 1878), 320-41. Fairchild's is the third and most readily available edition of the *Lectures*, the first having been printed in the U.S. in 1846, the second in England in 1851. The lecture cited is virtually unchanged in all these editions. For a statement of Finney's understanding of the relationships among decision, election, and assurance, cf. "Lecture XLIII: Election," *Lectures* 495-99. Also cf. Timothy L. Smith, *Revivalism and Social Reform: American Protestantism on the Eve of the Civil War* (New York: Abingdon Press, 1975), 88-93, for a source-based discussion of this turn of affairs.

16. E.g., Richard Watson, *Theological Institutes: Or, a View of the Evidences, Doctrines, Morals, and Institutions of Christianity*, ed. J. M'Clintock 2 vols. (New York: Carlton and Porter, 1850), 2:377-80. M'Clintock's is the third and most readily available American edition of the *Institutes*, the first having been printed in 1825 (from the third

London edition), and the second in 1834. M'Clintock added extensive notes and an index but carried the text of the second edition almost untouched.

17. For a sense of the shift, compare Watson, *Institutes*, with Nathan Bangs, *The Errors of Hopkinsianism Detected and Exposed* (New York: John C. Totten, 1815), 93, and both Watson and Bangs with Daniel D. Whedon, *The Freedom of the Will as a Basis of Human Responsibility and a Divine Government* (New York: Carlton and Porter, 1864), 396–97. For discussion of the tendency to confuse terms, cf. Randolph S. Foster, *Christian Purity: Or, the Heritage of Faith. Revised, Enlarged, and Adapted to Later Phases of the Subject* (New York: Nelson and Phillips, 1869), 44–60, in which the author deals with the issue of theological anthropology, and 105–128, in which he treats the theological difference between regeneration and sanctification. The original edition of Foster's book, published as *The Nature of Blessedness of Christian Purity* (New York: Harper, 1851), did not contain these two sections but instead presented a rather classically Methodist account, without reference to possible equivocations of terms and ideas. Also cf. Robert S. Chiles, *Theological Transition in American Methodism: 1790-1935* (New York: Abingdon Press, 1965), 52–54 and 144–65.

18. For a careful analysis of the development of Arminian anthropology in 19th-century Methodism, see Chiles, *Theological Transition*, 115–63 and 144–65.

19. For an instructive example, compare Watson, *Institutes*, 2:455, with Samuel Wakefield, *A Complete System of Christian Theology: Or, a Concise, Comprehensive, and Systematic View of the Evidences, Doctrines, Morals, and Institutions of Christianity*, 2 vols. (New York: Carlton and Porter, 1862; rpt. ed. Salem, Ohio: Schmul Publishing, 1985), 2:452–53. Wakefield says ("Preface," 1:4) that his basic intention is to abridge Watson's work and to complete the system implied in it. One of the consequences of this intention is that Wakefield treats subjects which Watson simply did not have to treat in his own day. Very important among these was the two-fold character of entire sanctification, that it is both instantaneous and progressive. What had brought such a discussion to importance, as Wakefield's treatment shows, was the emphasis on voluntarism.

20. E.g., the 11th General Conference of the Wesleyan Methodist Connection (1883) stoutly reaffirmed its commitment to preaching and teaching the doctrine of entire sanctification and revised, for the first time since it originally appeared in 1860, the course of study for persons seeking ordination. Remaining on the list were Luther Lee, *Elements of Theology; Or, An Exposition of the Divine Origin, Doctrines, Morals, and Institutions of Christianity*, 2 ed. (Syracuse, N.Y.: S. Lee, 1859); Richard Watson, *Institutes*; and John Wesley, *A Plain Acount of Christian Perfection* (edition unspecified). Candidates were also urged to own a complete set of Adam Clarke's "Commentaries." The edition to be studied is not specified but it was almost surely *The Holy Bible, Containing the Old and New Testaments: The Text Carefully Printed from the Most Correct Copies of the Present Authorized Translations, Including the Marginal Reading and Parallel Texts; with a Commentary and Critical Notes, Designed as a Help to a Better Understanding of the Sacred Writings*, 6 vols. (New York: Ezra Sargeant, 1811–25). Cf. Ira Ford McLeister, *History of the Wesleyan Methodist Church of America* (Syracuse, N.Y.: Wesleyan Methodist Publishing Association, 1934), 101–103.

21. Two American Methodist theologians who had much to say on the question of theological anthropology, who clearly show the influence of revivalism in their discussions, and who were widely read and influential among late-19th-century holiness people, including many who had no background in Methodism, were Miner Raymond and John Miley. Cf. Miner Raymond, *Systematic Theology*, 3 vols. (Cincinnati, Ohio: Hitchcock and Walden; and New York: Nelson and Phillips, 1877), 2:7–174, esp.

76–89 and 140–68; John Miley, *Systematic Theology*, 2 vols. (New York: Eaton and Mains, 1892; Hunt and Eaton, 1894), 2:271–308.

22. We cite here three examples of the phenomenon: the mid-19th-century controversy over the understanding of the nature of the witness of the Spirit in the experience of entire sanctification; the turn-of-the-century millennialist controversy; and the recent controversy over Spirit baptism. In the first controversy, such persons as Nathan Bangs insisted that one ought not to claim the gift of entire sanctification until the Spirit had definitely given witness to its reality in the seeker's life, while such persons as Phoebe Palmer said that one should claim the gift and could give witness to receiving it as soon as the conditions (largely related to entire consecration) were met. Palmer did not hesitate to claim the practical efficacy of her position in revival campaigns and camp meetings. Compare Nathan Bangs, *The Necessity, Nature, and Fruits of Sanctification* (New York: Lane and Scott, 1851) with Phoebe Palmer, *Faith and Its Effects: or, Fragments from My Portfolio* (New York: For the Author, 1854). In the second controversy, such holiness advocates as the southern Methodist evangelists W.B. Godbey and L.L. Pickett fervently advocated premillennialism, while another group of Methodist holiness advocates, such as Daniel Steele and George Washington Wilson, insisted on a postmillennialist view—as did almost all of the Wesleyan theologians of the 19th century, from Richard Watson to John Miley. Most of the leading holiness evangelists from the late 1880s to the Great Depression were premillennialists, while the leaders of the National Holiness Association (nee National Campmeeting Association for the Promotion of Holiness), the majority of whom were or had been pastors, were predominantly postmillennialists. The majority of the Movement's theological scholars in the same period were postmillennialists. Compare, e.g., W.B. Godbey, *Bible Theology* (Cincinnati, Ohio: God's Revivalist Office, 1911), 279–95, with George Washington Wilson, *The Sign of Thy Coming; Or, Premillennialism, Unscriptural and Unreasonable . . . with an introduction by Rev. W.X. Ninde* (Boston: Christian Witness Co., 1899).

The third controversy, which is currently in progress, also has its roots in the late-19th-century revivalistic characterization of entire sanctification as "the baptism with the Holy Spirit." The term had been used of the experience of entire sanctification much earlier, but it had been used as well to describe any unusually vibrant spiritual occasion. Not until the late 1880s did holiness people come to use the term almost exclusively as a synonym for entire sanctification and to interpret Acts 2, esp. 2:4, as being the moment of the entire sanctification of Jesus' disciples, and Acts 8, 10, and 19 as reports of sanctificatory events. The current debate turns on two axes: the exegesis of Acts 2 and the legitimacy and theological ramifications of departure from the position of John Wesley, who did not see in Acts 2 the entire sanctification of the disciples. Compare J. Kenneth Grider, *Entire Sanctification: The Distinctive Doctrine of Wesleyanism* (Kansas City, Mo.: Beacon Hill Press, 1980), 44–90, with Robert W. Lyon, "Baptism and Spirit-Baptism in the New Testament," *Wesleyan Theological Journal* 14 (Spring 1979):14–26, and Alex R.G. Deasley, "Entire Sanctification and the Baptism with the Holy Spirit: Perspectives on the Biblical View of the Relationship," *Wesleyan Theological Journal* 14 (Spring 1979):27–44.

23. Cf. Paul M. Bassett, "The Fundamentalist Leavening of the Holiness Movement, 1914–1940: The Church of the Nazarene, A Case Study," *Wesleyan Theological Journal* 13 (Spring 1978):65–91.

24. Beside the *Thirty-Nine Articles*, the other important exceptions to the usual continental order are the *Gallican Confession* (1559), prepared largely by Calvin himself and presented finally to Charles X; and the *Belgic Confession* (1561; rev. 1619). In both of these, biblical authority is affirmed in the third and succeeding articles. The

Scottish Confession (1560), enacted by the Scottish Parliament, treats the authority of Scripture in article 19, but the reasons for the order of articles in this confession appear to have been as much political as theological. It is also important to note here three facts about the early articles of the *Thirty-Nine Articles.* (1) Article 1 is entitled "Of Faith in the Holy Trinity," not simply "Of the Holy Trinity." (2) The original title for article 2 was not "De Verbi Dei . . ." but instead retained the accusative case demanded by article 1 and was "Verbum Dei . . . ," which is to say, it bore the implied title "Of Faith in the Word of God . . . ," a point not pressed in the English translation. (3) The explicit "pro nobis" perspective of articles 2 and 3 is implicit in articles 4 and 5.

25. Compare, e.g., the *First Helvetic Confession* (1536), the *Genevan Confession* (1536), and the *Second Helvetic Confession* (1566) with the *Thirty-Nine Articles.* In fact, the Latin title for article 6 seems to point more clearly to what Scripture does with respect to salvation than to what it implies for belief and practice: "Divinae Scripturae doctrina sufficit ad salutem." But this must be viewed in the content of the article, which is concerned with the contents of Scripture and the purpose of those contents: "Scriptura sacra continet omnia quae sunt ad salutem necessaria . . ."

26. The *Thirty-Nine Articles* are unique in the 16th century in making sufficiency, not authority, the critical concept in describing the nature and role of Scripture. The English translation of the title for article 7 of the *Belgic Confession* (1561), as authorized by the Reformed Church in America, is "The Sufficiency of the Holy Scriptures to be the Only Rule of Faith," but the word translated *sufficiency* here is *perfectio,* and the article itself is concerned with the absolute and complete character of the Bible as theological compendium and rule. The *Scottish Confession* (1560), in article 19, "Of the Authoritie of Scriptures," affirms that the Scriptures are "sufficient to instruct and make the man of God perfite." But the official Latin edition makes the meaning of *sufficient* clear by using *abunde,* indicating a basic connotation nearer *superabundance* or *plenitude* than *sufficiency* as commonly understood.

27. Cf., e.g., Richard Hooker, *Of the Laws of Ecclesiastical Polity,* III.viii. 11–18, Everyman's Library ed., nos. 201–202 (London: J.M. Dent and Sons; and New York: E.P. Dutton, 1958), 1:318–24). Also see William Laud, "A Relation of the Conference between William Laud . . . and Mr. Fisher, the Jesuit . . ." (1639), sec. 14 in *The English Theological Library,* ed. C.H. Simpkinson (London: Longmans, Green, 1901), 119–132. The conference itself was held in 1622.

28. Cf. Hooker, *Of the Laws,* II.vii.5–10, pp. 1:268–76. Laud, "A Relation," says "[We must have] the assistance of God's Spirit, Who alone works faith and belief of the Scriptures and their Divine authority" (p. 120); and "The credit of Scripture to be divine resolves finally into that faith which we have touching God Himself. . . . [That faith] hath three main grounds . . . the tradition of the Church, . . . the light of nature . . .[and] the light of text itself, in conversing wherewith, we meet with the Spirit of God inwardly inclining our hearts, and sealing the full assurance of the sufficiency of all three unto us. And then, and not before, we are certain that the Scripture is the Word of God, both by Divine and by infallible proof. But our certainty is by faith, and so voluntary." (p. 131).

29. Cf. *Thirty-Nine Articles,* article 20: the Church is "testis et conservatrix" of the Scriptures, two things which it can finally and fully be only as it worships. Also see Hooker, *Of the Laws,* V.xxi–xxii, 2:76–105.

30. Cf. Hooker, *Of the Laws,* "Preface," viii. 7, pp. 1:134–36.

31. Cf., e.g., Hooker, *Of the Laws,* I.xiv.1, pp. 1:214–16:" Albeit Scripture do profess to contain in it all things that are necessary unto salvation; yet the meaning cannot be simply of all things which are necessary, but all things that are necessary in some

certain kind or form; as all things which are necessary, and either could not at all or could not easily be known by the light of natural discourse; all things which are necessary to be known that we may be saved." The entire paragraph sums up the argument of I.xiv.1–5, pp. 1:276–82. The whole of Book 2 opposes the Puritan notion that "Scripture is the only rule of all things."

32. See, e.g., Thomas Burnet, *Sacred Theory of the Earth: Containing an Account of Its Original Creation, and of All the General Changes which It Hath Undergone, Or is to Undergo, until the Consummation of All Things* (first Eng. tr. from Latin, London, 1684), I:5–6, Later but still typical would be Thomas Sherlock, *The Tryall of the Witnesses of the Resurrection of Jesus* (London, 1729). Many "orthodox" defenses of biblical authority made in the face of rising deism/rationalism really were attempts to prove the epistemological and soteriological need for (a) revelation, rather than being attempted proofs of the authority of Scripture *in se*. Cf., e.g., William Law, *The Case of Reason, or Natural Religion, Fairly and Fully Stated In answer to a book, entitled, Christianity as Old as Creation* (London, 1732), esp. no. 1. It could be argued that it was this removal of hermeneutics and exegesis from the demands of metaphysics and axiology that eventuated in the decision of the Royal Society, in the late 1660s, to inhibit theological/philosophical speculation in its own work and to limit its discussions to the measureable aspects of any phenomenon.

33. To see this in a work similar to those noted above in note 32, see John Wesley, *Compendium of Natural Philosophy*, 2 vols., 3d American ed. (New York: N. Bangs and T. Mason, 1823), 2:447–49. Also see Wesley, "Sermon XII: The Means of Grace," III.7–10, in *Wesley's Standard Sermons . . .*, ed. Edward H. Sugden, 2 vols. (London: Epworth Press, 1921), 1:248–51. Hereafter, this edition will be referred to as Sugden, *Sermons*. For a source-based discussion of this point in Wesley, see Lycurgus M. Starkey, Jr., *The Work of the Holy Spirit: A Study in Wesleyan Theology* (Nashville, Tenn.: Abingdon Press, 1962), 89ff.

34. E.g., John Wesley, "An Earnerst Appeal to Men of Reason and Religion," 55–59 in *The Works of John Wesley*, vol. 11: *The Appeals to Men of Reason and Religion*, ed. Gerald R. Cragg, (Oxford, England: Clarendon, 1978); or Thomas Jackson, ed., *The Works of John Wesley*, 14 vols. (Grand Rapids, Mich.: Zondervan Publishing House, 1958 [reprint of London: Wesleyan Conference Office, 1872), 8:21–23. Hereafter, the Jackson edition will be cited as Jackson, *Works*. Of special interest is Wesley's use of the "Homily on Salvation" in 59. Also cf. "Sermon XII: The Means of Grace," III.7–10 in Sugden, *Sermons*, 1:248–51.

35. E.g., John Wesley, *The Sunday Service of the Methodists in the United States of America. With other Occasional Services* (1784), preface, in Jackson, *Works*, 14:304: "Little alteration is made in the following edition of [the liturgy of the Book of Common Prayer of the Church of England], except in the following instances: . . . 4. many Psalms left out, and many parts of others, as being highly improper for the mouths of a Christian congregation." Also see his recognition that some verses make little sense, or even contradict the usual sense, unless they be read in light of the whole tenor of Scripture; e.g., *Explanatory Notes upon the New Testament* (London: Epworth, 1950), Rom. 12:6.

36. This is to say that "sufficiency" is not something that the reader or hearer decides. The adequacy of the Scriptures as sole presenter of the way of salvation in no way depends upon whether or not they be accepted as such. Cf. Wesley's use of the Anglican homily "Of Salvation," iii, in "An Earnest Appeal to Men of Reason and Religion," 59, in Jackson, *Works*, 8:23; "Sermon I: Salvation by Faith," 1.2, in Sugden, *Sermons* 1:39; and "Sermon II: The Almost Christian," II.4, in Sugden, *Sermons* 1:63). To consider authority's

dependence upon the *testimonium*, cf., e.g., Wesley, *Explanatory Notes upon the New Testament*, II Tim. 3:16; and Wesley, *Explanatory Notes upon the Old Testament*, preface 17–18, in Jackson, *Works*, 14:267–68.

37. John Wesley, *Sermons*, preface 5, in Sugden, *Sermons*, 1:31–32.

38. E.g., Letter to William Law, 6 Jan. 1756, in John Telford, ed., *The Letters of the Rev. John Wesley*, 8 vols. (London: Epworth Press, 1931), 3:332–33); "Sermon X: The Witness of the Spirit," II.1–14, in Sugden, *Sermons,*, 1:211–18; "Sermon XI: The Witness of Our Own Spirit," I.6, in Sugden, *Sermons*, 1:224–26.

39. Cf., e.g., Wesley's appeals to the Anglican homily "On Reading the Scripture," in "A Letter to the Right Reverend the Lord Bishop of Gloucester," 26 Nov. 1762, II.24, in Jackson, *Works*, 9:169, and "A Farther Appeal to Men of Reason and Religion," I.v.26, in Jackson, *Works*, 8:104. Throughout both of these works, which have the operations of the Holy Spirit as their theme, our point can be inferred. The citations note where it is explicitly made.

40. Cf. note 38 above.

41. Cf. John Wesley, "Sermon XI: The Witness of Our Own Spirit," 5–7, in Sugden, *Sermons* 1:223–27; and "Sermon XII: The Means of Grace," III.7–10, Sugden, *Sermons*, 1:248–52.

42. Cf. John Wesley, *Journal*, 24 May 1738, 11–12, in Jackson, *Works*, 1:471–72.

43. Cf., e.g., John Wesley, "Sermon IX: The Spirit of Bondage and of Adoption," II.1–III.4 in Sugden, *Sermons*, 1:185–93; *Explantory Notes Upon the Old Testament*, preface 18, in Jackson, *Works*, 14:252–53.

44. E.g., John Wesley, "Sermon X: The Witness of the Spirit," I.7, in Sugden, *Sermons*, 1:207–208; "Sermon XLV: The Witness of the Spirit," II.2–3, in Sugden, *Sermons*, 2:344–45.

45. E.g., John Wesley, "Sermon XLV: The Witness of the Spirit," I.1–II.1, in Sugden, *Sermons*, 2:343–44; ibid., V.1–4, in Sugden, *Sermons*, 2:357–59.

46. Conventionally orthodox 18th-century Anglican clergy most frequently used articles 6 and 7 of the *Thirty-Nine Articles* in three ways: (1) as elements in their general anti-Roman Catholic polemic; (O.2) as weapons in countering so-called "enthusiasm" (which term they applied to any attempts to internalize the biblical message and to take it personally, including those by the Methodists and the Society of Friends); and (3) as a defense of the Bible as a history book useful in neutralizing the corrosive acids of deism and rationalism. On the original intention of article 6, cf. E. Harold Browne, *An Exposition of the Thirty-Nine Articles, Historical and Doctrinal*, 5th ed. (London: John W. Parker and Son, 1860), 122–85.

47. Cf. John Wesley, "Sermon XXXII: The Nature of Enthusiasm," 22–24, in Sugden, *Sermons*, 2:96–98. Quotation is in sec. 23 (p. 97).

48. E.g., John Wesley to Mary Bishop, 7 February 1778, in Telford, *Letters*, 6:297–99; more potently, "Sermon LXX: The Case of Reason Impartially Considered," II.8–9, in Jackson, *Works*, 6:358–59.

49. Cf. "Sermon LXX: The Case of Reason Impartially Considered," esp. I.4–11.9, in Jackson, *Works*, 6:354–60.

50. For example, compare John Wesley, *A Survey of the Wisdom of God in Creation: Or, A Compendium of Natural Philosophy*, 3d ed., enlarged; 5 vols. (London, 1777), with Thomas Burnet, *Sacred Theory of the Earth*, or Richard Kirwan, *Geological Essays* (London, 1799).

51. E.g., Abraham Calov, *Apodixis Articulorum Fidei* . . . (Lüneburg, Germany, 1684), 35, and *Systema Locorum Theologicorum* . . . (Wittenberg, Germany, 1665), 1:608. Also cf. David Hollaz, *Examen Theologicum Acroamaticum* . . . (Rostock and Leip-

zig, Germany, 1718), prologue 3.13–14. Hollaz here argues that the Scriptures are not to be counted among things created, such is their divinity.

52. Cf. Martin Schian, *Orthodoxie und Pietismus im Kampf um die Predigt* (Giessen, Germany: Alfred Töpelmann, 1912), 86–87. For an example of this perspective, see F.C. Oetinger, *Theologia ex idea vitae deducta* (Halle, Germany, 1765). Oetinger, who gave evidence of deep sympathies with the mystics, was not a consistent pietist, but he was sufficiently pietist to illustrate our point here. Also see F. Ernest Stoeffler, *German Pietism During the Eighteenth Century* (Leiden, Netherlands: E.J. Brill, 1973), 217–65.

53. Cf. John Wesley, *Explanatory Notes Upon the New Testament*, Matt. 1:1; II Pet. 1:20–21; Rev. 2:1. Also see "Sermon LXIII: The General Spread of the Gospel," 25, in Jackson, *Works*, 6:286–87.

54. E.g., John Wesley, "Sermon XII: The Means of Grace," III.8, in Sugden, *Sermons*, 1:249–50: "'All Scripture is given by inspiration of God'; consequently, all Scripture is infallibly true." Also see "A Clear and Concise Demonstration of the Divine Inspiration of the Holy Scriptures," in Jackson, *Works*, 11:484. For an example of the assertion of the freedom of the biblical text from material error, cf. Wesley, *A Survey of the Wisdom of God in Creation*, 2:447–49. For an example of Wesley's understanding that the Spirit dictated to the writers what should be said, see Wesley, *Explanatory Notes Upon the New Testament*, John 19:24.

55. Cf. Jackson, *Works*, 11:484.

56. E.g., Wesley's understanding that the Apostles sometimes quoted the Old Testament incorrectly, cf. Wesley, *A Survey of the Wisdom of God in Creation*, 2:447–49 and *Explanatory Notes Upon the New Testament*, Matt. 2:6. Also see Wesley's objection that some parts of the Old Testament are not fit for Christian use in public worship, in Wesley, *The Sunday Service of the Methodists in the United States of America. With Other Occasional Services*, preface 4, in Jackson, *Works*, 14:304.

57. Cf. John Wesley, "Sermon XII: The Means of Grace," III.7–10, in Sugden, *Sermons*, 1:248–51; "Sermon VII: The Way to the Kingdom," II.9–10, in Sugden, *Sermons* 1:159–60; *Journal*, 24 May 1738, in Jackson, *Works*, 1:98–104, esp. secs. 13–14 (1:103).

58. E..g., John Wesley, *Explanatory Notes Upon the New Testament*, II, Tim. 3:16.

59. E.g., John Wesley, *Explanatory Notes Upon the New Testament*, John 3:21; "Sermon XII: *The Means of Grace*,," II.1–13, in Sugden, *Sermons*, 1:242–43, quite clearly indicates that study of Scripture is a means of grace only to those who mean to come to Christ by them. Cf. also "Sermon XXXIX: The New Birth," II.4 in Sugden, *Sermons*, 231–34.

60. E.g., John Wesley, "Sermon XIX: Sermon on the Mount IV," III:1–6, in Sugden, *Sermons*, 390–94, esp. secs. 4–5 (pp. 392–94).

61. Cf. John Deschner, *Wesley's Christology: An Interpretation* (Dallas, Tex.: Southern Methodist Univ. Press, 1960; rptd. Grand Rapids, Mich.: Francis Asbury Press of Zondervan Publishing House, 1985), 88–92, 109–111.

62. Cf. Charles Edwin White, *The Beauty of Holiness: Phoebe Palmer as Theologian, Revivalist, Feminist, and Humanitarian* (Grand Rapids, Mich.: Francis Asbury Press of Zondervan Publishing House, 1986), 106–110; Robert E. Chiles, *Theological Transition in American Methodism: 1790–1935* (New York: Abingdon Press, 1965), 92–94.

63. Cf. Chiles, *Theological Transition*, 77–87.

64. Cf. Phoebe Palmer, *Incidental Illustrations of the Economy of Salvation. Its Doctrines and Duties* (New York: Foster and Palmer, Jr., 1855), 286–91, 298–300.

65. Cf. B.T. Roberts, *Why Another Sect: Containing a Review of Articles by Bishop*

Simpson and Others on the Free Methodist Church (Rochester, N.Y.: Earnest Christian Publishing House, 1879); F.W. Conable, *History of the Genesee Annual Conference of the Methodist Episcopal Church, 1810–1872* (New York: Nelson and Phillips, 1876), 618–36; Wilson T. Hogue, *History of the Free Methodist Church of North America*, 2 vols (Chicago: Free Methodist Publishing House, 1915), 1:34–35, 80–82, 193–207, 248–64; Walter W. Benjamin, "The Methodist Episcopal Church in the Postwar Era," in *The History of American Methodism*, ed. Emory Stevens Bucke, 3 vols. (New York: Abingdon, 1964), 2:339–60. The heart of the statement on entire sanctification adopted by the organizing conference of the Free Methodist Church at Pekin, N.Y., 23 Aug. 1860, and included—theologically unaltered (though from time to time amended in form)—in subsequent editions of the *Discipline*: "Entire sanctification takes place subsequently to justification and is the work of God wrought instantaneously upon the consecrated believing soul. After a soul is cleansed from all sin, it is then fully prepared to grow in grace."

66. Charles Edwin Jones, *A Guide to the Study of the Holiness Movement* (Metuchen, N.J.: Scarecrow Press and American Theological Library Association, 1974), 63–72, lists 37 hymnals (not counting revised editions) published within the holiness movement before 1900. Quotations of hymns in holiness literature of the period would also indicate heavy use of the offical Methodist hymnals. The hymnal ordered by the General Conference of 1848, *Hymns for the Use of the Methodist Episcopal Church,* rev. ed. (Cincinnati, Ohio: Swormstedt and Power, 1850) carries 41 hymns under the specific topical heading, "Sanctification." Of the 1,148 hymns in this hymnal (omitting the supplement), 19 begin with the word *I* or *I'll*. Of 1,162 hymns in 12 of the 37 hymnals in Jones' list, 69 (with no duplications counted) begin with the word *I* or *I'll*. This does not constitute a scientific sampling, but it does give some idea of the shift toward a much more subjective and experiential hymnody. The late-19th-and early-20th century books of order or discipline of the Wesleyan Methodists, Free Methodists, and rising independent holiness groups usually include a section on ritual, with forms for baptism and the Lord's Supper, and in these rites a prayer of consecration is usual, though "written" or "read" prayers were looked upon as hindrances to spiritual freedom and as being uniquely open to affectation.

67. Examples of this could be strung out *ad infinitum*, for being a "Bible Christian," as Palmer saw it, was precisely a matter of claiming the promises of Scripture for oneself. See her account of her own experience of entire sanctification on the basis of biblical demands, promises, and warrants, in Palmer, *The Way of Holiness, with Notes by the Way: Being a Narrative of A Religious Experience Resulting from a Determination to be a Bible Christian,* 2d ed. (New York: G. Lane and C.B. Tippett, 1845), 33–39.

68. The systematic theologies used most by the holiness movement until, in the second quarter of the 20th century, it produced its own, very carefully insisted that any kind of religious assurance, most esp. the assurance of justification and entire sanctification, depended entirely upon the Holy Spirit, not simply on the "say-so" of the Bible. E.g., Miley, *Systematic Theology*, 2:342–48. In treating "errors" in the doctrine of the witness of the Spirit, Miley works with the view of Thomas Chalmers, which happens to be quite similar to that of Phoebe Palmer. Even more striking is Raymond, *Systematic Theology*, 2:364–72, in which Raymond teaches that assurance may come in an unmediated way or it may come in a mediated way, and that among the mediated ways are prayer, the sacraments, and the preached Word. Never does he even hint that it comes by trusting the "Thus saith the Lord," as Palmer would put it. Cf. Harold E. Raser, *Phoebe Palmer: Her Life and Thought*, Studies in Women and Religion, v. 22 (Lewiston/Queenston: Edwin Mellen Press, 1987), 187–90.

69. Cf. note 37 above.

70. John Wesley voices this lament on a number of occasions: e.g., "Sermon CXXXII: On Laying the Foundation of the New Chapel, Near the City Road, London," II.1, in Jackson, *Works*, 7:423.

71. E.g., John Wesley, "Sermon XI: The Witness of Our Own Spirit," 6–8, in Sugden, *Sermons*, 1:225–28.

72. Phoebe Palmer, *Faith and Its Effects: Or, Fragments from My Portfolio* (New York: For the author, 1854), 125, 152–53; also see Palmer, *Incidental Illustrations*, 309.

73. Phoebe Palmer, *Faith and Its Effects*, 152.

74. Phoebe Palmer, *Way of Holiness*, 71.

75. The hymn is #687, *Hymns for the Use of the Methodist Episcopal Church* (1848). Cf. note 66 above.

76. In Ibid. contains 15 hymns in the section called "The Scriptures." Five of them are by Charles Wesley, making this one of the sections where he is proportionally least represented: cf. hymns 679, 680, 685, 687, 689. Probably the best example of Charles Wesley's consistent efforts to link Spirit and Scripture is seen in hymn #679. Also to be noted is the fact that Wesley always moves on from written Word to Living Word in the hymns noted, and almost always does so elsewhere.

77. Compare, e.g., John Wesley, "Sermon XXXII: The Nature of Enthusiasm," 22–25, in Sugden, *Sermons*, 2:96–98, with Phoebe Palmer to Bishop and Mrs. L. L. Hamline, 10 July 1847; to Mrs. Hamline, 22 May 1848; to Professor and Mrs. Thomas Upham, 30 Apr. 1851, all in Richard Wheatley, ed., *The Life and Letters of Mrs. Phoebe Palmer* (New York: W.C. Palmer, Jr., 1875), 514–23. Also cf. Raser, *Phoebe Palmer*, 274–77. Palmer's view of the relationship between Scripture and experience owes much, probably unwittingly, to Scottish Common Sense philosophy. It is quite reasonable to believe that Palmer would have had some general idea of the Common Sense point of view and that it would have appealed to her, given her deep biblical and experiential interests and her ecclesiastical connections. Charles Hodge was the chief among her contemporaries who self-consciously developed his theology on a Common Sense foundation. His quarterly, *Biblical Repertory: A Collection of Tracts in Biblical Literature*, which began its long career in 1825, would not have been of interest to Palmer and her circle until after 1838, of course. By that time, it had become the *Biblical Repertory and Princeton Review* and was a major voice in the Reformed theological tradition, and Hodge had become the principal contributor. It is quite likely also that Palmer knew he book, *Way of Life*, for, published by the American Sunday School Union in 1841, it was written for the thoughtful layperson and carried the general approbation of both American and British evangelical denominations.

78. Phoebe Palmer, *Incidental Illustrations*, 308–309. The point being made here is the central theme of Palmer, *Faith and Its Effects*, esp. as it bears on entire sanctification.

79. On this point, Palmer's view closely parallels the view of Scottish Common Sense philosophy (cf. note 77 above). Palmer believed that, while the intellect and judgment are gifts of God in the first place, the experience of entire sanctification renovates the intellect. Cf., e.g., *Beauty of Holiness and Sabbath Miscellany* 9 (1858): 209. This, in turn, make it possible that God may speak, esp. to believers, in the ordinary experiences and impressions of life and even more singularly in dreams and visions. Cf., e.g., *Guide to Holiness and Revival Miscellany* 69 (1876):47 and Palmer, *Incidental Illustrations*, 251–54. On the other hand, the "lessons" proposed by these experiences were to be carefully scrutinized in the light of biblical teachings. Cf., e.g., *Guide to Holiness and Re-*

vival Miscellany 72 (1877):106-107. (The journal *Beauty of Holiness and Sabbath Miscellany* was purchased by the Palmers in 1864 and merged with the *Guide to Holiness* under the title *Guide to, and Beauty of Holiness and Revival Miscellany* [1864-67]. From 1867 to 1898, the journal bore the title *Guide to Holiness and Revival Miscellany*.)

80. E.g., this is clearly an essential presupposition of John Wesley's *Thoughts upon Necessity*, esp. IV.1-5, in Jackson, *Works*, 10:456-74, esp. 469-74.

81 Cf. John Wesley, "Sermon CV: on Conscience," esp. I.4-6, in Jackson, *Works*, 7:186-94, esp. 187-88.

82. E.g., Phoebe Palmer, *Way of Holiness*, 20, 54-55. The insistence that some knowledge of the Scriptures is necessary for salvation is at least analogous to the notion of Common Sense philosophy that the believer in some sense lives the Scriptures. It is possible that the relationship between Palmer and Common Sense thought is even closer than that, but, as yet, we lack a comprehensive study of the possible connections between 19th-century Wesleyan/holiness thought and the theologies built upon Common Sense bases.

83. Wesley takes care not to describe too specifically the character of our assurance of salvation or entire sanctification, since it does involve, after all, our own inmost being and the free Spirit of God. So, he is even willing to suggest that Scripture may have no direct role in it. Cf. "Sermon XLV: The Witness of the Spirit," II.2-4, in Sugden, *Sermons*, 2:344-45; also note 86 below.

84. Almost universal among 19th-century preachers of entire sanctification was the assumption that conviction of sin and the Spirit's invitation to conversion would come through either the reading or preaching of the Bible; and for Phoebe Palmer and her associates and followers, it would seem that no-one could have assurance of either justification or entire sanctification apart from committing oneself to what the Bible said (i.e., was believed to say) about the experiences.

85. Very telling here is a comparison of sermons and hymns. E.g., compare John Wesley, "Sermon LXXVI: On Perfection," in Jackson, *Works*, 6:411-23, and James Caughey, "Sermon IX: The Sting of Death," in *Helps to a Life of Holiness and Usefulness, Or, Revival Miscellanies: Containing Eleven Revival Sermons . . . Selected from the Works of Rev. James Caughey*, ed. Ralph W. Allen and Daniel Wise, pp. 120-34 (Boston: George C. Rand, 1854). Admittedly, comparing sermons entails risks, but both of these sermons on Heb. 6:1 seem to be truly representative of each preacher, and Caughey's is clearly in line with the preaching of holiness revivalism. It is also instructive to note that Wesley encouraged those seeking to "flee from the wrath to come, to be saved from their sins" to join a society, while the holiness people created no organizations for seekers. In fact, as they began to create their own denominations and other bodies, they deliberately limited membership to the already converted. Their belief that justification and sanctification are both instantaneously wrought militated against creating organizations for seekers, though the Methodists among them often retained the term "society" to refer to their groups. Revivalistic as they were, the holiness people believed that, once one really heard the Gospel, one must not dawdle. One must obey the Spirit's "Now! Confess now! Yield now!" Cf. Phoebe Palmer, *Incidental Illustrations* 304-306.

86. E.g., John Wesley, "The Nature, Design, and General Rules of the United Societies . . .," in Jackson, *Works*, 8:269-71; "Rules of the Band-Societies," in Jackson, *Works*, 8:272-73; and "Directions Given to the Band-Societies," in Jackson, *Works*, 8:273-74. It is important to remember that the only requirement for admission to the "societies" was "a desire 'to flee from the wrath to come, to be saved from [one's] sins'," with the expectation that "wherever this is really fixed in the soul, it will be shown by its fruits." For the holiness people, see, e.g., James Caughey, "Whispers to

Offended Hearers," in *Revival Sermons and Addresses* (London: Richard D. Dickinson, 1891), 327–32.

87. E.g., Phoebe Palmer, *Incidental Illustrations*, 307–312.

88. Phoebe Palmer, *Way of Holiness*, 17–39.

89. Phoebe Palmer, "Introduction," in J. Boynton, *Sanctification Practical: A Book for the Times* (New York: Foster and Palmer, 1867), 5–6. Palmer continues, "An elaborate display of doctrines or defence of technicalities, however masterly in style, or beautiful in composition, on the subject, will not satisfy the demand; but plain, earnestly practical, well-defined, and experimental teachings are just what is needed."

90. Phoebe Palmer, *Way of Holiness*, 17–22.

91. Phoebe Palmer, "To the Rev. Mr. M— —," no. 52, *Faith and Its Effects*, 319–24.

92. Ibid., 322.

93. B.F. Haynes, editorials in *Herald of Holiness* for 1916. Haynes wrote at least one editorial for almost every issue of this then-weekly paper. Forty of the 52 for 1916, chosen at random, 30 from the front page and 10 from p. 2, contain a total of 23 references to either Moody or Torrey, and 12 to Wesley or the Wesleyan theological authors Watson, Clarke, Pope, or Miley.

94. Compare B.F. Haynes, "Verbal Inspiration" (editorial), *Herald of Holiness.*, 15 Oct. 1913, p. 1, with Haynes' "Christ the Center and Source" (editorial), *Herald of Holiness*, 8 Apr. 1914. p. 4. The former: "Yes, blessed be God, this inspiration of the Bible is verbal in the most acute, intense, literal, all inclusive sense. Nothing short of this would be like or worthy of God, and nothing short of this would meet man's need." The latter: "All Scripture is His, is of Him, is for Him, is through Him, is by Him, reveals Him, exalts Him, is inseparably joined to Him in honor and integrity and validity, and no man dares invalidate or seek to invalidate this sacred Word without doing despite to the honor and majesty of the Christ. The inspired Word centers in, revolves around, points to and reveals Christ as its center and its source. All true preaching of the Word is to honor Christ. There is a path from any and every passage of this Bible to the very Christ Himself."

95. E.g., from 1911 to 1916, the "Course of Study for Licensed Ministers" (i.e., for persons seeking ordination, licensed not by a local congregation but by a district) of the Church of the Nazarene required reading and examination in Miley, *Systematic Theology*. From 1916 to 1932, it ordered either Miley or Thomas Ralston, *Elements of Divinity; Or, A Concise and Comprehensive View of Bible Theology; Comprising the Doctrines, Evidences, Morals and Institutions of Christianity; With Appropriate Questions Appended to Each Chapter*, ed. T.O. Summers, (Nashville, Tenn.: A.H. Redford, 1871). (This was the third edition of Ralston's work, which had been published originally in 1847. From about 1911 to 1940, Olin Alfred Curtis, *The Christian Faith, Personally Given in a System of Doctrine* (New York: Eaton and Mains; and Cincinnati: Jennings and Graham, 1905) was a standard text in undergraduate theological studies in the several Nazarene colleges. William Burt Pope, *Compendium of Christian Theology; Being Analytical Outlines of a Course of Theological Study, Biblical, Dogmatic, Historical*, 3 vols.; 2nd ed., rev. and enlgd. (London, Wesleyan Conference Office; New York: Phillips and Hunt; and Cincinnnati: Walden and Stowe, 1880), was required collateral reading in introductory courses in systematic theology on each of the 23 Nazarene college reading lists that I have seen for the period 1909 to 1923. From 1883 to 1915, the Wesleyan Methodist Connection (now, after several mergers and schisms, the Wesleyan Church) instructed those preparing for ordination to study and stand examination on Richard Watson's *Institutes* along with their own Luther Lee's *Elements of Theology: Or, An Exposition of the Divine Origin, Doctrines, Morals and*

Institutions of Christianity (New York: Miller, Orton, and Mulligan; and Syracuse, N.Y.: S. Lee, 1856). The 11th and latest edition of Lee's work was the first printed in 1892, 25 years after Lee himself had returned to the Methodist Episcopal Church and three years after his death. From about 1890, Wesleyan college students were reading Amos Binney, *Binney's Theological Compend, Improved; Containing a Synopsis of the Evidences, Doctrines, Morals, and Institutions of Christianity, Designed for Bible Classes, Theological Students and Young Preachers*, ed. Daniel Steele (New York: Eaton and Mains, 1874); or ed. T.O. Summers (Nashville, Tenn.: Southern Methodist Publishing House, 1885). Pope, *compendium*, also seems to have been a standard requirement.

96. It must be noted, however, that from 1914 (perhaps from 1911) to 1944, the Nazarenes had added to their list of required reading Sidney Collett, *All About the Bible: Its Origin — Its Language — Its Translation — Its Canon — Its Symbols — Its Inspiration — Its Alleged Errors and Contradictions — Its Plan — Its Science — Its Rivals* (New York: Fleming Revell, n.d.). For discussion of Collett's understanding, which was prefundamentalist and essentially late-19th-century evalgelical Anglican, cf. Bassett, "Fundamentalist Leavening," 71–72.

97. Cf. R.R. Byrum, *Christian Theology* (Anderson, Ind.: Gospel Trumpet Co., 1924). Byrum affiliated with the Church of God, Anderson. Also see A.M. Hills, *Fundamental Christian Theology*, 2 vols. (Pasadena, Calif,: C.J. Kinne, 1934. Hills was a Nazarene. And see H. Orton Wiley, *Christian Theology*, 3 vols. (Kansas City, Mo. Nazarene Publishing House, 1940, 1941, 1943). Wiley was a Nazarene.

98. Cf. Jonathan T. Weaver, *Christian Theology: A Concise and Practical View of the Cardinal Doctrines and Institutions of Christianity* (Dayton, Ohio: United Brethren Publishing House, 1900). Weaver was a bishop in the United Brethren Chruch. Also see S.J. Gamertsfelder, *Systematic Theology* (Cleveland, Ohio: C. Hauser, 1913). Gamertsfelder belonged to the Evangelical Association of North America (in 1922–46, the Evangelical Church).

99. Wiley, *Christian Theology*, remains required reading in the courses of study for those seeking ordination in the Church of the Nazarene, the Wesleyan Chruch, the Free Methodist Chruch, and a number of smaller holiness groups. As early as 1919, at least, various administrative entities within the Church of the Nazarene were requesting that Wiley write a systematic theology. Cf. ibid., 1:5.

100. Ibid., 1:140–42.

101. Ibid.

102. Ibid.

103. Cf. Bassett, "Fundamentalist Leavening," 65–67, 80–85.

104. H. Orton Wiley and Paul Culbertson, *Introduction to Christian Theology* (Kansas City, Mo.: Beacon Hill Press, n.d.), 27. Also see Wiley, *Christian Theology*, 1:33–34.

105. Wiley, *Christian Theology*, 1:36–37.

106. E.g., the Church of the Nazarene is the result of the merging of at least two dozen smaller denominations, the latest merger (still not completely consummated) involving an indigenous denomination of several score congregations in Nigeria. The Wesleyan Church is the result of another thirteen or so mergers, the latest being that of the Wesleyan Methodist Church and the Pilgrim Holiness Church in 1968. Of late, sentiment is growing, though fitfully, and various kinds of conversations and projects are being undertaken which bring merger of the Wesleyans and Nazarenes closer. Doctrine is definitely not an issue, although the Wesleyan article of faith on Scripture is more congenial to fundamentalist interpretation than is that of the Nazarenes.

CHAPTER 7

Are Restorationists Evangelicals?
Richard T. Hughes

If one inquires into the relationship between restorationism and evangelicalism, the answer seems inevitably to be both ambiguous and problematical. In the first place, as Leonard Sweet observed, practically "everyone at times has either been drawn into the loosely twined evangelical camp or claimed the label, thereby stripping the concept of Evangelicalism of much analytic purchase."[1] Much the same can be said for the theme of restoration, since practically all Protestants, and certainly all evangelicals, appeal to the Bible and the earliest Christian traditions in one way or another. In fact, a variety of scholars in recent years have noted the importance of the restoration sentiment in such widely diverse traditions as Mormons, baptists, and Episcopalians.[2] One is tempted to despair of addressing the question at hand with any precision at all.

Yet competent scholars assure us that there is a relation between evangelicalism and restorationism. Timothy Weber, for example, argued that "historical primitivism" characterized first evangelicals and then premillennialists, who, as Weber put it, "held on to the first century with a passion." Grant Wacker judged that "historical primitivism served as the logical and emotional foundation for dispensational premillennialism [in pentecostalism], not the reverse." And Mark Noll thought that fundamentalists exhibited "an intense primitivism in their defense of the Book, of the Blood, and of the Blessed Hope" and even "in their struggle to recapture a lost Christian America."[3]

At one level, this issue seems to resolve itself into a tautology. Both evangelicals and restorationists view Scripture as normative; therefore, evangelicals are restorationists and vice versa. But this is far too easy a resolution to a very difficult problem and ignores some important distinctions which can help bring considerable precision to our task.

We might begin sharpening the issue by making the commonplace observation that both Protestant evangelicals and Protestant restorationists ultimately descend from the sixteenth-century Reformation. That simple fact suggests that the sixteenth century may offer clues important for unraveling our dilemma. Most Protestants of the sixteenth century held firmly to the principle of *sola scriptura*. But two fundamentally different ways of embracing that principle emerged. For some, these two perspectives were mutually exclusive. For others, they merged and blended indiscriminately.

At one extreme stood the theology of Martin Luther, whose allegiance to Scripture was beyond dispute. Yet Luther's ultimate allegiance was not to Scripture for its own sake, much less to primitive ordinances and practices as normative in any sense. Luther's ultimate allegiance was to a merciful God, to the power of grace that breaks in from outside one's self and that one grasps only through faith. Scripture was important, to be sure, but only insofar as it proclaimed this *euangelion*, this evangelical gospel, which heralded deliverance from sin, death, and despair. Luther therefore placed the gospel in judgment on Scripture and demoted the book of James, which he viewed as "an epistle of straw, for it has nothing of the nature of the gospel about it."[4]

At the other extreme stood the Reformed tradition of Zurich, led first by Huldreich Zwingli and then by Heinrich Bullinger. Christian humanism, with its profound reverance for antiquity, informed this tradition to an enormous extent, and the humanist battlecry, *ad fontes* (to the sources), inspired Zwingli's ministry in Zurich from its inception. If Luther's ultimate question had been "How can I find a merciful God?", Zwingli's question was "What was the ancient practice?" From this perspective, God became the supreme lawgiver and the Bible an ancient, albeit divine, legal code that had to be followed in exacting detail, in keeping with Zwingli's covenant theology. Accordingly, Zwingli condemned both singing and organs in the churches, since Scripture commanded neither; reduced the mass to a simple memorial supper; and provided for destruction of images, abolition of relics and vestments, and elimination of pilgrimages, along with a host of medieval laws and prohibitions, including clerical celibacy.[5] To be sure, Zwingli also spoke of faith and grace, but it is clear that Zwingli's conception of the *euangelion* had been tempered and chastened by the *restitutio* ideal.

To grasp just how different Luther was from Zwingli on this point, one need only recall Luther's response to the radical reforms undertaken in Wittenberg while he was hiding in the Wartburg Castle. Luther was furious when he learned that Andreas Karlstadt had abolished practices he considered unauthorized by Scripture. Karlstadt's restorationist approach, Luther complained, "destroys faith, profanes the blood of Christ, blasphemes the gospel, and sets all that Christ has won for us at naught."[6]

While *sola scriptura*, therefore, was a common Reformation theme, there were radically differing applications of that motif. Based on those differences, we can distinguish between reformation (*reformatio*) and restitution (*restitutio*) as ideal types of belief and behavior among sixteenth-century Protestants.[7] *At its irreducible core*, reformatio *signifies a perspective that takes seriously human frailities and imperfections and that trusts in the power of God for redemption, healing, and empowerment.* The notion of justification by faith and grace was the most prominent sixteenth-century expression of this theological core. But other themes also have reflected, to various degrees, this basic orientation. Themes such as Holy Spirit empowerment and premillennial eschatology, while open to human control and manipulation, nonetheless, at their theological core, reflect an openness to the power of God in the lives of believers. *Therefore*, reformatio *points fundamentally to any biblically-informed Christian orientation wherein the believer relies on the power of God rather than on one's self.* By any measure, this perspective surely lies at the heart of the traditional evangelical witness.

The *restitutio* sentiment is altogether different. It may appear to be simply a neutral tool, devoid of theological valences, by which a variety of primitive practices and/or beliefs may be restored. In fact, however, the *restitutio* sentiment always has as its starting point human initiative and activity. Its fundamental presupposition is that there is something which Christian faith and/or practice has lost and which human beings must restore. It is certainly true that the *restitutio* sentiment may have as its object the divine initiative, and in that case the *restitutio* sentiment may *move toward* a *reformatio* posture, although it never becomes identical with the *reformatio* posture. In such cases, the believer views the divine initiative as a dimension of early Christian life which one must actively seek to recover. Holiness advocates, for example, have spoken of restoring spiritual empowerment, and pentecostals and Mormons have spoken of restoring miraculous gifts. In such cases, the *reformatio* perspective, while clearly discernible, nonetheless is weakened by its dependence on the human initiative inherent in the *restitutio* sentiment. On the other hand, *restitutio* may have as its object the restoration of ancient Christian traditions that are essentially unrelated to the divine initiative (*reformatio*). In such cases, the *restitutio* sentiment simply may be incidental to the evangelical witness or, in certain instances, even may constitute the antithesis of that witness.[8] Further, restoration movements often intensify the human initiative which is the starting point for the *restitutio* sentiment, finally moving in profoundly self-reliant directions. In such cases, the *restitutio* sentiment can stand altogether at odds with the *reformatio* orientation.

If we seek, therefore, to generalize about the *restitutio* sentiment, we might simply observe that, *at its innermost core,* restitutio *depends on human potential and the ability to discern and implement the ancient Christian traditions, and often results in postures of profound self-reliance.* If, therefore, one understands the heart of the evangelical witness to consist in reliance on the power and grace of God, then it is clear that the *restitutio* sentiment, while sometimes standing on the fringe of the evangelical witness, is in no sense at the theological core of that heritage.

If one desired to examine the relationship between *restitutio* and *reformatio* in concrete, historical terms, one could examine a variety of Protestant traditions in which these themes have intermingled in numerous ways. While *restitutio*, for example, dominated the anabaptist witness, some historians have argued that aspects of the *reformatio* perspective were present as well.[9] And while *reformatio* dominated all other themes in Calivn's outlook, it did not altogether eliminate *restitutio* strands.[10] Traditions that built on the Reformed heritage in later years also mixed these ideals in interesting configurations. Thus, Puritans learned from Calvin, and Luther of the sovereignty of God and of faith and grace, while ultimately they learned from both Martin Bucer and Heinrich Bullinger the importance of restoring the ancient practices of the Christian church. Puritan allegiance to these two perspectives was part and parcel of the Puritans' covenant theology, by which they sought to preserve both the sovereignty of divine grace and the integrity of human nature. At the same time, the Puritan emphasis on repristinating biblical models for both church and state, standing alongside the Puritans' allegiance to the absolute sovereignty of God, involved them in profound theological ambiguities.[11] Many baptists perpetuated this ambiguity, although some — such as Particular Baptists and Primitive Baptists — resolved the ambiguity in favor of *reformatio*, while others — especially the Landmark Baptists — resolved the issues in favor of *restitutio*.[12] Even Methodists, as Albert Outler has pointed out, while standing squarely in the evangelical heritage, still embraced elements of restorationist orientation.[13]

My purpose here is not to question the legitimacy of the *restitutio* orientation. Historically, this perspective has undergirded a profound allegiance to Scripture and has produced a host of Christian heroes noted for their moral purity, their ethical commitments, and the doctrinal integrity of their congregations. All of this must be acknowleged. The question here, therefore, is not whether *restitutio* possesses legitimacy, which is a complex and legitimate question in its own right. The question here pertains instead to the relationship between *restitutio* and *reformatio* — between the concern to restore first times, on the one hand, and the gospel of God's initiative, which stands at the heart of the evangelical witness, on the other. The question here is simply this: Are restorationists evangelicals by virtue of their restorationist orientation?

There are many traditions in Christian history in which one might perceive the *restitutio/reformatio* relationship in various configurations, as we have observed. If one wished, however, to discern the *restitutio* perspective in almost pure form, almost completely unmixed with the *reformatio* orientation, one could do no better than to observe closely the American-born Churches of Christ — a people who called themselves simply "Christians" — between roughly 1870 and 1950. In this tradition, the *restitutio* sentiment, rooted in human initiative, was greatly intensified by both experiential and philosophical factors and became, in these years, a profoundly self-reliant outlook.

But why the dates 1870–1950? By 1870, the process of division in the Christian movement launched by Alexander Campbell and Barton W. Stone was well under way, and by 1906 the United States Bureau of the Census formally had recognized that this division had produced the Disciples of Christ, centered mainly in the Midwest, and the Churches of Christ, centered chiefly in the border states of the South running from Tennessee to Texas. While social factors — the Civil War, sectionalism, and economics — certainly exacerbated the division, the root and core of the division was theological.[14] Simply put, Disciples took one side of Alexander Campbell's agenda — his insistence on ecumenism — and made that the central plank of their theological platform. Churches of Christ, on the other hand, made the idea of restoration their defining characteristic, their very *raison d'etre*. Further, since the division often was bitter and rancorous, and since Disciples, in city after city, retained possession of church buildings and, at least in urban areas, took the majority of members, Churches of Christ were forced virtually to begin again from a rural base in tents and store front churches. Churches of Christ in the early twentieth century, therefore, grew extremely defensive. More often than not, that defensiveness centered on their first priority, the call to restore the primitive church. During those years between 1870 and 1950, therefore, Churches of Christ embodied the restorationist heritage in an amazingly pure form and most often proclaimed a message that was essentially antagonistic to the *reformatio* orientation.

One must hasten to add that the theological landscape has shifted among Churches of Christ since 1950. In the first place, theological defensiveness, while still present, has diminished greatly. Second, while still staunchly restorationist, more and more preachers in this tradition have discovered, not in Luther or Calvin but in the New Testament, the theme of justification by grace through faith. In fact, in the 1960s, 1970s, and 1980s, a slow but certain renewal movement has occurred among segments of the Churches of Christ, focusing attention increasingly on the *reformatio* orientation. Still, Churches of Christ by and large continue to define themselves in terms of the *restitutio* ideal.

The remainder of this paper will focus on the *restitutio* sentiment among Churches of Christ from 1870 to 1950. But why? What objectives might this exploration accomplish? First, such an inquiry will help us determine whether Churches of Christ historically have belonged within the evangelical spectrum, as several scholars either explicitly or implicitly have suggested. Perhaps the first scholar to designate this tradition as evangelical was Robert Baird, in his *Religion in America* (1844), though he did so, as he put it, "with much hesitation." Baird acknowledged that these Christians in many way appeared orthodox.

> Yet I understand that there is much about their preaching that seems to indicate that all that they consider necessary to salvation is a cold, speculative, philosophical faith, together with immersion as the only proper mode of baptism; so that there is little, after all, of that "repentance towards God," and "faith towards our Lord Jesus Christ," which are the indispensable terms of the gospel.

A few scholars, writing in more recent years, have been far less reluctant than Baird to classify this tradition as evangelical. Both Timothy Smith and George Marsden, for example, have suggested that Churches of Christ in some way fit into the "evangelical kaleidoscope." David Edwin Harrell confirmed that judgment with a lengthy discussion of Churches of Christ in a volume he edited, *Varieties of Southern Evangelicalism*. And Wayne Flynt, writing in that same volume, indicated that Disciples of Christ, along with Presbyterians, Baptists, and Methodists, comprise "the four evangelical churches" in the American South.[15] But are these judgments correct? Do Churches of Christ really fit within the evangelical spectrum? Second, focusing on Churches of Christ will illumine the persistent tendency of the *restitutio* perspective to move toward self-reliant postures. And third, assessing Churches of Christ in the context of the *reformatio* and *restitutio* traditions will help sharpen our understanding of the meaning of evangelicalism and evangelical heritage.

While Churches of Christ[16] had their earliest roots in the Second Great Awakening, under the tutelage of Barton W. Stone, it was their second-generation leader, Alexander Campbell, who contributed most to the enduring patterns of their thought. In the present context, four aspects of Campbell's thought are especially important: his understandings of the millennium, the Bible, the gospel, and the Holy Spirit.

The millennial theme takes us quickly to the heart of the Campbell movement. Campbell believed that human traditions and inventions, codified in creeds, had badly divided the Christian church. He sought, therefore, to unite Christians simply by returning to the common store of faith and practice found in the New Testament and the first Christian age. Significantly, Campbell firmly believed that Christian union, won through a restoration of primitive faith and practice, would launch the millennial dawn.[17] Important here is the profound sense of self-reliance so central to Campbell's thought. Campbell had no doubt that the human mind could perceive the primitive patterns of the faith, that the human will could implement those patterns, and that sheer human exertion could transform this world into the universal kingdom of God. Although the guns of the Civil War virtually blew Campbell's postmillennial eschatology away, his highly optimistic assessment of human potential endured among Churches of Christ for many, many years.

Scottish Common Sense Realism, euphemistically known in the nineteenth century as "Baconianism," profoundly shaped Campbell's understanding of Scripture.[18] Deeply impressed by the ability of natural facts to bring consensus in the realm of natural science, Campbell surmised that an emphasis on biblical "facts" would likewise bring union among Christians. For this reason, Campbell emphasized his view that the Bible was "a book of facts, not of opinions, theories, [or] abstract generalities."[19] If one sought biblical truth on any topic, Campbell thought, one should simply collect and classify all the pertinent "facts" according to the inductive method taught by Francis Bacon. In his debate with the skeptic Robert Owen, Campbell remarked that "the principles of investigation on which the inductive philosophy of Lord Bacon is founded . . . are those which should govern us on this occasion. . . . 'We first ascertain the facts, then group them together, and after the classification and comparison of them, draw the conclusion.'" Or again, Campbell declared in 1850 that the "inductive style of inquiring and reasoning, is to be as rigidly carried out in reading and teaching the Bible facts and documents, as in the analysis and synthesis of physical nature." As Jesse Kellems observed years ago, for Campbell, "every verse and every fact in the Biblical record is to be treated as so much scientific phenomena."[20]

With this scientific view of Scripture, it was easy for Campbell finally to view the New Testament as a sort of legal constitution, a perspective Campbell thought essential to the task of restoration. "*To restore the ancient order of things* this [New Testament] must be recognized as the only constitution of this kingdom." Later he proclaimed that "the constitution and law of the primitive church shall be the constitution and law of the restored church." Campbell's father, Thomas, made a similar point in his *Declaration and Address.* "The New Testament," he wrote, "is as perfect a constitution for the worship, discipline, and government of the New Testament Church . . . as the Old Testament was for the worship, discipline, and government of the Old Testament Church."[21]

In addition, Campbell urged that Christians should speak of Bible facts with Bible words. In 1825 he argued that, since "all correct ideas of

God . . . are supernatural ideas," therefore "no other terms can so suitably express them as the terms adopted by the Holy Spirit." For this reason, he declared, "*We choose to speak of Bible things by Bible words*, because we are always suspicious that if the word is not in the Bible the idea which it represents is not there; and always confident that the things taught by God are better taught in the words . . . which the Holy Spirit has chosen."[22]

Not only was the Bible a collection of facts; for Campbell, the gospel itself was fundamentally factual and propositional, and he frequently spoke of the "gospel facts."[23] The "gospel facts," he said, included all the sayings and doings of Jesus but consisted especially in his death, burial, resurrection, and ascension.[24]

Clearly, Campbell understood that the gospel declared what God had done for humankind, not what humankind had done for itself. But since Campbell apparently assumed that most Protestants understood this already, he directed his zeal not so much toward proclaiming the divine initiative as toward stating the gospel in factual and propositional terms, in the interest of Christian union. As it turned out, this way of doing theology emphasized more the ability of humankind both to understand and to give intellectual assent to "the facts" than it emphasized the divine initiative that comprised the heart of the gospel. Many among later generations of Churches of Christ would tend almost to forget the divine initiative which Campbell simply assumed and would focus more and more on giving intellectual assent to the "gospel facts."

This was profoundly ironic for two reasons. First, Campbell acknowledged the passion narrative as central and proclaimed that one fact alone comprised the core of the gospel: the fact that Jesus is the Messiah. Second, Campbell often insisted that mere intellectual assent to "gospel facts" is not saving faith. The faith that saves, he urged, "is not the belief of any doctrine, testimony, or truth, abstractly, but belief in Christ; trust or confidence in him as a person, not a thing." Again, he argues that "the man that merely assents to them [facts], and does not confide in them, and give himself up to them, is, with me, an infidel, rather than a disciple of Christ." Yet, despite all this, Campbell emphasized time and again that faith can only begin with facts sustained and supported by testimony and evidence. Thus, "Faith is the simple belief of testimony, or of the truth, and never can be more or less than that." Again, "evidence alone produces faith," and faith can be increased only "by affording additional evidence, or by brightening the evidences already produced." In Campbell's view, therefore, a Christian was one who "believes this *one fact*, and has submitted to *one institution* [immersion], and whose deportment accords with the morality and virtue of the great Prophet."

This rational understanding of the gospel clearly reinforced the self-reliant dimensions of the Campbell movement and became normative among Churches of Christ for at least 125 years. Further, while Campbell emphasized the relational dimension of the gospel to which the facts pointed, the relational dimension sometimes escaped later members of Churches of Christ. In fact, in later years, members of Churches of Christ would emphasize that the gospel consisted simply of "facts to be believed, commands to be obeyed, and promises to be enjoyed."[25]

Like his understanding of the gospel, Campbell's view of the Holy Spirit was far more complex than many of his later followers recognized. Campbell rejected the notion, prevalent on the American frontier in his day, that the Spirit might work in miraculous ways, totally apart from the written or preached word, in conversion. Instead, he insisted that the Spirit always worked *with* the word which appeals to our rational faculties. Word and Spirit "are always united in the great work [of conversion]," Campbell argued. "No one is converted by the Word alone, nor by the Spirit alone." But Campbell often was misunderstood. Many heard him to say, despite his disclaimers, that the Spirit was shackled to the Word. Indeed, he argued in 1824 that "since those gifts [of the Spirit] have ceased, the Holy Spirit now operates upon the minds of men only by the word." Or again, "Whatever the word does, the Spirit does; and whatever the Spirit does in the work of converting men, the word does." He even claimed in 1835 that "if the Spirit of God has spoken all its arguments" in Scripture, then "all the power of the Holy Spirit which can operate on the human mind is spent." Further, Campbell suggested that the Spirit is heard only when we exercise the Baconian principle of induction. "When the induction is perfect and complete and fully comprehended on any one point, we can never have any more divine light upon that subject. This is our method of learning and of teaching what the Holy Spirit has taught on any given subject."[26] With this emphasis, it is no wonder that Campbell was misunderstood. While he meant to emphasize that the Spirit always works in conjunction *with* the word, many of his later followers contended that the Spirit works only *in* the pages of Holy Writ.

These four themes — millennialism, the nature of Scripture, the nature of the gospel, and the role of the Holy Spirit — not only were important to Campbell but also have been fundamental to all Christians claiming the evangelical label. For this reason, these themes are important tests of the extent to which Churches of Christ are in fact evangelical. We shall inquire later concerning the role of these themes, both in Churches of Christ and in evangelicalism at large. For now, it is enough simply to say that, when Campbell had finished his work, he had constructed a restorationist agenda deeply rooted in the sixteenth-century heritage of Christian primitivism, the Enlightenment heritage of Baconianism, and the postmillennial tradition of confident self-reliance.

For all of this, there were those who perceived Campbell as at least a potential ally of the evangelical witness. After all, did he not preach the Bible and the Bible alone? And did he not hold a high view of biblical authority? No wonder that organizers of the Evangelical Alliance, meeting in London in 1846, urged Campbell to attend. And Campbell was tempted to go, commenting that "no convention that has met since the Protestant Reformation has had so strong a hold upon my affections and esteem."[27] Nonetheless, he declined the invitation. And within a few months, Campbell thought it important to distance himself further from the alliance. In the first place, he complained, the alliance was simply a gathering of sectarians searching for common ground. "I had rather be digging through the ruins of the fallen temple of primitive Christianity and be clearing off the rubbish from the ancient foundations," he told his readers. Then he launched a critique of the theological statement adopted by the alliance. When the alliance stated that "justification of the sinner [is] by Faith alone," Campbell objected. In good Baconian fashion, he ransacked the Bible for the causes of justification and found six: grace, blood, name, knowledge, faith, and works. He emphasized works, however, citing James to the effect that "a man is justified by works, and not by faith only." When the alliance affirmed "the work of the Holy Spirit in the conversion and sanctification of the sinner," Campbell agreed but offered one disclaimer: "Where the word is not announced the Spirit sanctifieth not." With all these objections, however, Campbell congratulated the alliance on its first proposition: "The divine inspiration, authority, and sufficiency of the Holy Scriptures."[28]

In this response to the Evangelical Alliance, one finds the basic terms that were to characterize attitudes of Churches of Christ toward evangelicals and evangelical theology for many years to come. A chief difference between Campbell and the later Christians, however, was the latter's growing exclusivism. While Campbell could praise the evangelicals and dialogue with them, later Christians occasionally denigrated them but mainly ignored them. Evangelicals, they contended, were sectarians, persisting in sectarian error. On the other hand, Churches of Christ had restored the primitive Christian institution to which evangelicals refused to return. One catches a glimpse of this perspective as early as 1844, when Thomas Taylor wrote to Alexander Campbell, to inform him that Robert Baird, in his *Religion in America*, had classified Campbell and his followers as evangelical. "At last it is admitted you are *evangelical*," Taylor sarcastically wrote. "May I congratulate you on this vast accession of honor? Yes, our churches are admitted amongst the *evangelical denominations*." Members of Churches of Christ in later years exhibited similar disdain for the evangelical tradition.

John F. Rowe, for example, wrote in 1844 that seventeenth-century baptists "had a clearer perception of apostolic teaching . . . and approximated more nearly the New Testament order of things, than the modern school of Baptists, who have spoiled . . . by contact with 'Evangelical Churches.'"[29] In the early twentieth century, Churches of Christ routinely allied themselves with fundamentalism in opposition to modernism but rebuked the fundamentalists for their failure, as they put it, to be primitive and biblical Christians. N.B. Hardeman was one of the most influential preachers among Churches of Christ in that period. In one of his famous "Tabernacle Sermons," preached before thousands in Nashville's Ryman Auditorium between 1922 and 1938, Hardeman charged that "a man is in a powerfully bad light trying to defend the Bible against the evolutionists and infidels while at the same time . . . he does not conform thereto. If I won't wear Bible names, if I won't subscribe to the Bible as my only creed, if I won't take it, and it alone, I am at a disadvantage in trying to defend it against the enemy."[30] Most of the time, however, Christians in the conservative Campbell lineage simply ignored the evangelicals and, especially from 1870 to 1950, existed in virtual isolation from the evangelical traditions. This fact alone helps answer our question, Do Churches of Christ belong in the evangelical spectrum? Members of Churches of Christ during these years would have answered with a resounding "no."

Is it possible, however, that Churches of Christ could in some sense be considered evangelical in spite of their own intent and affirmation to the contrary? There are several ways to approach that question. First, one might ask if Christians in this tradition felt any common ground with the Protestant Reformation. How did they appraise the Reformation? Did they look to Luther, Calvin, or Zwingli as important for their work in any sense at all?

Here again, Campbell set the standard for assessment. Campbell made two fundamental judgments about the Reformation and the reformers. First, he viewed the reformers simply as restorers like himself, whose efforts unfortunately had aborted, and he cast them all in the same restorationist light. He imagined that "the Protestant reformers, one and all, made very little account of the experience, learning, and success of the church for 1400 years."[31] He therefore saw his own work of restoration as continuing the work of the reformers and often spoke of the movement he led as "the nineteenth-century Reformation." Second, Campbell, viewed the reformers as biblicists and praised Luther especially for liberating the Bible into the common tongue. "The Bible was brought out of prison, and Luther bid it march," he wrote. "He made it speak in German and thus obtained for it a respectful hearing." But the Bible, like the reformers' attempts to restore, quickly fell on hard times. "It was soon loaded with immense burdens of traditions . . . [and] became unable to travel with its usual speed, and then stopped the Reformation."[32]

Campbell's perspective in this regard became normative among Churches of Christ. This becomes apparent when one samples assessments of the Reformation rendered by some of the church historians who emerged among Churches of Christ.[33] One of the earliest of these historians was John F. Rowe, who in 1884 wrote *A History of Reformatory Movements, Resulting in a Restoration of the Apostolic Church.* Rowe's title says it all. Rowe, and most of the chroniclers who followed him until the very recent years, were not seriously interested in charting the course of Christian history. Instead, most sought simply to conform the Christian story to a preconceived pattern of fall and restoration. The fall they identified with the rise of the Roman Catholic Church. On the question of restoration, they developed two predominant interpretations. For some, Luther had launched the restoration which Alexander Campbell and the Churches of Christ only had recently completed. Others argued that the reformers had not sought to restore at all but had simply reformed specific abuses, leaving restoration altogether to Alexander Campbell and his colleagues. In neither instance did most of these chroniclers reflect the slightest understanding of the theological work undertaken by either Luther or Calvin.

In his book, John F. Rowe argued the latter position at considerable length. Thus, "Luther, Zwingle [*sic*], Calvin, . . . Knox, [and] Wesley never made any attempt to return to apostolic practice, nor did . . . these Reformers even suggest the idea of reproducing the Church of Christ as established by the apostles. They simply aimed to *re-form* existing ecclesiastical institutions." Luther at least had translated Scripture into the common tongue. But "then came the Augsburg Confession [and] . . . the Bible became once more a sealed book, then a cessation of Bible investigation, and finally the imposition of human dogmas and ecclesiastical contraction, in which condition of stagnation the Lutheran Reformation has stood ever since." Then Rowe spoke of his own tradition. In his view, Churches of Christ stood in "a movement as radical and far-reaching as that which was inaugurated by Christ and his apostles. . . . We propose more than a *reformation of reformations.* We go back of all reformations, and plant ourselves upon apostolic ground." Indeed, Alexander Campbell "sought the complete *restoration* of apostolic principles and practices, and . . . actually raise[d] up a body of people identical with primitive Christians, both in faith and practice."[34]

In 1929, J.W Shepherd wrote another history of Christianity, *The*

Church, The Falling Away, and The Restoration. Shepherd clearly saw that Luther's reform revolved around the theme of justification by faith and grace. But for Shepherd, that notion was of little consequence. Indeed, Luther's failure to restore the forms and structures of the apostolic church presented, as Shepherd put it, "a sore need for Zwingli and a Carlstadt. . . . Had it not been for what they did, 'Luther's writing and preaching might have ended in preaching and writing.'" Luther's failures and Karlstadt's success revolved around the argument from biblical silence. While Karlstadt rejected what the Bible did not authorize, Shepherd said, Luther accepted what the Bible did not forbid. In this context, Shepherd especially praised Zwingli, who "contended that nothing should be practiced that was not expressly commanded by the Scriptures." Yet, Shepherd said, the Second Helvetic Confession (1566) and the errors of Calvinism finally swallowed Zwingli's attempt to restore. Shepherd finally concluded that the "Reformation was a vast stride from Rome, but it fell far short of a return to Jerusalem."[35]

In 1961, F.W. Mattox wrote yet another church history, called *The Eternal Kingdom: A History of the Church of Christ.* For Mattox, Luther was a restorationist making rapid progress in his return to Jerusalem until he permitted codification of his perspective in the Augsburg Confession in 1530. After that, Mattox wrote, "he was forced to spend the rest of his life defending what he had written. If he had not been forced to write his convictions in creedal form, he would have continued to pursue his course toward a restoration of the New Testament church." Mattox clearly admired Zwingli, who, Mattox wrote, "relied on the Bible as a book of rules. His view of the Scripture would allow in church services only what the Bible approved," a position Mattox contrasted with that of Luther, who "would remove only what the Bible condemned."[36]

These assessments of the reformers and their theology were not confined to church history texts. They informed the proclamations of several generations of preachers in Churches of Christ. Typical was N.B. Hardeman, who preached a series of sermons on the Reformation to a vast audience of some six thousand people in Nashville's Ryman Auditorium in 1928. Hardeman praised Luther for giving "to the world an open Bible." But that was the limits of his praise. "Instead of turning back to original principles," Hardeman complained, Luther "sought simply a reformation of the things that then existed." As a result, the Bible was "a stranger" to the Lutheran faith. "Not one shoot, phase, wing, or branch [of the Lutheran tradition] was ever thought of, dreamed of, or hinted at, by holy men that penned this Book. . . . When you want to study Lutheranism," he told the crowd, "you have no more use for the Bible than you have for an almanac." He concluded with a similar judgment regarding every Christian tradition other than his own. "The Bible," he triumphantly proclaimed, "knows nothing about Catholics, Lutherans, Presbyterians, Episcopalians, Baptists or Methodists."[37]

The conclusion is obvious. Most members of Churches of Christ during those years never understood the *reformatio* tradition of the sixteenth century, and those, such as J. W. Shepherd, who did understand, thought that tradition of small theological significance. If *reformatio*, therefore, comprised in some sense the theological core of the evangelical heritage, the evidence so far suggests that Churches of Christ, from the Civil War until very recent years, simply did not belong.

But there is yet another way to assess this issue. Earlier in this chapter, when searching for a broad theological definition of evangelicalism, I suggested that *reformatio*, at its irreducible core, points to "any biblically-informed Christian orientation wherein the believer relies on the power of God rather than on one's self." This orientation not only embraces justification by faith, but also can embrace two other themes that have been important components of most recent understandings of evangelicalism: the indwelling Holy Spirit and the premillennial Second Coming of Christ. From the outset it should be stated that it is possible for these two themes to stand diametrically in opposition to the *reformatio* orientation, particularly when they become the object of psychological and social manipulation. Still and all, at the most basic level, both themes reflect a sense of radical dependence on the power of God that breaks in on the believer from the outside. The question now is simply this: Where did the mainstream of Churches of Christ stand on these three issues during the period under consideration? We already have examined Alexander Campbell's understandings of these themes. Did later Churches of Christ agree, or did they develop perspectives more compatible with the evangelical tradition?

Since one's view of Scripture helps determine one's theological orientation, we first must ask how these Christians viewed the Bible. Did they perpetuate Alexander Campbell's Baconian perspective, wherein the Bible was a collection of divine facts and a rational guide to righteousness and salvation? The answer most emphatically was "yes." If anything, later Christians intensified this perspective. Especially important in this regard was Moses Lard, who worked out a careful and systematic defense of the restoration position in the mid-nineteenth century. Lard began with the Baconian premise that knowledge of biblical truth is fully possible: "We are not only conscious, in many instances, that we know a thing; but conscious that we know it correctly, truly, as it was intended to be known," he wrote. "To know that we know, is the proof that we know; . . . It is the truth thus known that makes us free." From this premise, Lard explained the vision and task of Churches of Christ:

> The reformation for which we are pleading consists, 1st. *In accepting the exact meaning of Holy Writ as our religious theory* . . . [and] 2d. *In the minute conformity of our practice to the revealed will of Chirst* . . ., accepting as doctrine, precisely and only what is either actually asserted or necessarily implied in the Bible; to speak the same things by speaking what the Bible speaks, and to speak them in the language of the Bible; and to practice the same things by doing simply the will of Christ. Thus it is proposed continually to construct the body of Christ after the divine model.[38]

By 1884, John F. Rowe judged that Alexander Campbell not only had restored the primitive church; he also had "restored to the people the only correct and approved rules of [biblical] interpretation." Further, Campbell had "simplified the whole matter by showing that facts are to be *believed*, commands to be *obeyed*, and the promises of the gospel to be *enjoyed*." By 1934, W. Clyde Odeneal echoed the old Campbellian refrain that "in 'rightly dividing the word of truth' the New Testament may . . . be viewed as the constitution of the church." In a lengthy article on that topic, Odeneal likened the New Testament to the United States Constitution and finally concluded that "the church can do nothing without an express command, an approved example or a necessary inference found in the New Testament. To do so is to cease to be the church and to become a sect or denomination."[39]

From these premises, which demanded human initiative, intense human exertion, and exacting conformity to the law of God, it would be surprising if Churches of Christ in that era had tolerated justification by faith alone, empowerment by the indwelling Holy Spirit, and premillennial eschatology. In fact, they did not.

Regarding justification by faith alone, John Rowe, pretty much summed up the Christians' position when he concluded simply "that there is no such doctrine in the Word of God." What Wesleyan Methodists called justification by faith alone, Rowe complained, was actually nothing more than "justification by *sensuous feeling* — an ecstasy, an illusion, a dream, a vain imagination, the delights of animal magnetism — which they tell us is wrought directly by the mystic impulse of the Holy Spirit, without illumination and conviction by the testimones of God's word."[40]

N.B. Hardeman not only rejected the notion of justification by faith alone; he also ridiculed its theological counterpart, the idea of human depravity. In his first series of "Tabernacle Sermons," he preached in Nashville in spring 1922, Hardeman told his audience: "Rob the world of the idea of depravity, and there would never have been any kind of reason for the preacher's laying his dirty ecclesiastical hands upon a spotless babe." Further, Hardeman told the crowd, Luther was "the first man on this earth who taught . . . justification by faith alone." Desperate to find this doctrine in Scripture, Hardeman contended, Luther "ransacked the pages of Holy Writ from first to last, and found no such consolation." He then simply "added the word 'alone' to the Book of God." While some find this doctrine full of comfort, Hardeman warned, "to people who respect the Bible, . . . no comfort from Luther's addition can come."[41]

In his second series of "Tabernacle Sermons" in 1923, Hardeman reiterated what had become by now the standard definition of the gospel among Churches of Christ: facts to be believed, commands to be obeyed, and promises to be enjoyed. But Hardeman also explained how the gospel addresses itself to the human temperament. Gospel facts, he said, "come as a challenge to my intellect." Gospel commands "come as a direct challenge to my will power." And gospel promises "appeal to my sentiments and emotions."[42] In this analysis Hardeman simply underscored the extent to which traditional theology among Churches of Christ emphasized human understanding, human ability, and, finally, self-reliance.

Hardeman's "Tabernacle Sermons" were strategically important. Not only did Hardeman present these sermons to thousands in the Nashville area, but also the sermons were published in five separate volumes which received wide distribution among members of Churches of Christ. In fact, at least two generations of preachers in this tradition cut their theological teeth on Hardeman's materials. Hardeman contributed significantly, therefore, to Church of Christ orthodoxy in the 1930s, 1940s, and 1950s. At the same time, he reflected an orthodoxy that was well in place by the 1920s.

Just how firmly in place it was can be measured by an episode involving K.C. Moser, an Oklahoma preacher among Churches of Christ from the 1920s to the 1970s. In the late 1920s and early 1930s, Moser's study of the New Testament convinced him that justification comes by faith and not by works. In 1932, he published his views in a book, *The Way of Salvation*, which received little notice in the Churches of Christ fellowship. Then, in 1934, Moser contributed an article to the *Firm Foundation*, an immensely influential periodical among Churches of Christ, published in Austin, Texas. Going directly against the traditional Baconian perspective, Moser declared that "the gospel concerns a person, not mere facts." Further, he wrote, obeying the gospel did not mean simply obeying commands. To obey the gospel was "to believe the gospel," and "to believe the gospel is to believe in, trust in, Christ crucified, buried and raised for our justification." Moser concluded his article with a warning: "Brethren, for the sake of souls, let us never get too big to restudy our position."[43]

The response to Moser, swift and almost unanimously negative, revealed that leaders among Churches of Christ had difficulty even comprehending what Moser had in mind. Their failure to comprehend testified to the enduring power of the Baconian epistemology in this tradition. G.H.P. Schowalter, editor of the *Firm Foundation*, understoood Moser to say that while the gospel can be believed, it cannot be obeyed. In Schowalter's traditional editorial page, he urged Moser to "speedily abandon such fantastic speculation and urge the lost not only to believe, but to obey."[44]

This exchange created a storm of controversy which was to haunt Moser well into the 1960s.[45] Though he refused to engage in the ongoing controversy, he did respond to Showalter in 1934, pointing out that the editor totally had misunderstood his point. To this, Showalter simply affirmed that "I . . . did not misunderstand or misrepresent him but . . . simply . . . drove home a solar plexus blow." Then Showalter revealed what perhaps concerned him most: "Ben M. Bogard, the [Landmark] Baptist debater of Texarkana, understood . . . [Moser] the same way [I did] and with a broad smile of satisfaction asked me, 'What are you folks going to do with Moser?' . . . I told him that we would treat the doctrine the same whether taught by Moser, a professed Christian, or Bogard a professed Baptist."[46]

Numerous other responses to Moser appeared in the *Firm Foundation*, and all reflected the Baconian perspective. John W. Hedge typified most, when he argued that "the plan of salvation" calls for "faith, repentance, confession . . . , and baptism, in their order. . . . [and with] equal emphasis on each item contained in that plan." And Logan Buchanan assured Moser that "the position my brethren occupy [the gospel tradition] has been studied and restudied from every angle, and there has never been anyone able to upset it since the days of the apostles, nor will there ever be, because it is founded on the word of the Lord Jesus Christ."[47]

As it turned out, Moser's proved to be a pivotal voice in Churches of Christ. Though barred from participation in numerous church events for some forty years,[48] Moser continued to preach and teach and eventually found a few strategic allies among both preachers and Bible professors in Church of Christ–related colleges.[49] Through their work and his, the theological face of Churches of Christ began to change. The publication in 1957 of Moser's influential and evangelical book, *The Gist of Romans*,[50] spurred additional change in the 1960s and the 1970s.

By 1979, Thomas H. Olbricht, professor of Bible at Abilene Christian University, had moved even beyond Moser's position and called for something quite foreign to Churches of Christ up to that time: attention to biblical theology. Olbricht lamented the historical Churches of Christ preoccupation with the specific details of church life and the resulting aversion to theology, and he suggested that this emphasis had obscured the central message of Scripture: "The predispositions against the overarching message of the Scripture, fostered by many of our forefathers including Campbell, has improverished the effort to restore New Testament faith," he observed. He therefore called for a restoration perspective which would focus on "that core message for which biblical theology searches," a message found in "the mighty acts of God and his final and crucial act in the death, burial, and resurrection of Jesus Christ." Clearly, some among the Churches of Christ were moving toward a more evangelical perspective.[51]

Concerning the Holy Spirit, an extreme version of Campbell's perspective prevailed among most members of Churches of Christ until the very recent past. N.B. Hardeman provided a classic statement of the orthodox position in 1923. God's role in human redemption, he said, was "to originate the plan, draft the scheme . . . and furnish . . . blueprints, together with certain specifications as to how the matter should be finally executed upon the earth." Jesus was "the great master mechanic" to whom "were delivered the plan and the specifications." Finally, the Spirit's task was simply to guide "the apostles into all truth," so that humankind might know "what God had planned and Christ had executed."[52] In other words, when the Spirit had informed the biblical text, its work was essentially through.

Finally, how have Churches of Christ regarded premillennialism? As we have noted, Alexander Campbell held a strong postmillennialism position. Most in Churches of Christ shared his view during the first half of the nineteenth century. In the years just preceding 1843, some Christians embraced a premillennial viewpoint, which Campbell labored to refute. Campbell rooted his objection squarely in the *restitutio* perspective: "With me, the Christian's hope is just the same now, in 1843, that it was in Anno Domini 43."[53] In any event, premillennialism among Churches of Christ collapsed with the failure of William Miller's predictions.

Premillennial perspectives emerged again, however, during World War I. R.H. Boll, a coeditor of the highly influential Nashville publication, the *Gospel Advocate*, began a series of articles on prophecy near the end of 1914. An enormous controversy ensued. The *Gospel Advocate* owners suspended Boll from his editorial post, and in January 1916, Boll became editor of a journal dedicated to the premillennial position: *Word and Work*.[54] There, Boll and his staff revealed their skepticism of human sufficiency and their affirmation of the sovereign power of God. "The world," they complained, "has a big man and a little God. But the Bible sets forth a very little man and a great and wonderful God, in whom the only hope of man lies."[55] Clearly, *Word and Work* was moving toward a *reformatio* perspective.

The mainstream of Churches of Christ vehemently attacked *Word and Work* and its premillennial position and continued its attack for many years. The issue was still sufficiently contested in 1938 that N.B. Hardeman, preaching his fourth series of "Tabernacle Sermons," attacked premillennialism head on and typified the orthodox position. What most concerned Hardeman was the standard view of dispensational premillennialists that Jesus came to establish a kingdom but failed in that effort and instead established the church. Such a view completely undermined the standard view of Churches of Christ that the church *was* the kingdom, that the kingdom fell from its pristine purity after the apostolic age, and that Churches of Christ now had restored that kingdom in its fullness to the earth, or at least were in the process of moving toward a full and complete restoration. Dispensational premillennialism, Hardeman complained, made "the church of Christ absolutely an accident."[56] It therefore completely undermined both the legitimacy of the Church of Christ restoration movement and the premise of self-reliance upon which this tradition finally rested. That was the nub of the matter.

What, then, can we conclude about Churches of Christ? Measured by most contemporary understandings of evangelicalism, Churches of Christ throughout their history have appeared evangelical indeed. After all, they resolutely held to the authority of an inerrant Bible and resisted modernism with astounding zeal. More than this, they advocated the complete restoration of apostolic Christianity, a goal shared by many in evangelical traditions and one that seems intensely evangelical at first blush.

But is it? If we measure evangelicalism by the *reformatio* tradition and allow that tradition to signify "any biblically-informed Christian orientation wherein the believer relies on the power of God rather than on one's self," then what might we conclude, both about the *restitutio* sentiment and about the Churches of Christ between 1870 and 1950? In the first place, the *restitutio* sentiment fails the test, since it is born in the womb of human initiative and often tends toward postures of self-reliance. And most often, Churches of Christ in the period under consideration failed the test, because (1) they implicitly denied that they were evangelical, (2 they misunderstood and often attacked the Reformation roots of the evangelical tradition, (3) they often transformed the relational dimension of the gospel into a rational "system of facts," and (4) they steadfastly resisted the major evangelical doctrines that pointed to the grace and power of God breaking into the lives of women and men from outside themselves.

This is not to say, however, that Churches of Christ historically have been unaware of a gracious and providential God. Though the burden of most of their preaching from 1870 to 1960 has focused on the human response to God's commands, still, most in this tradition have maintained that God demonstrates his grace in a variety of ways. They have believed, for example, that God acts providentially, especially in response to prayer, and that God manifested his grace by devising a plan of salvation, by inspiring the Scriptures through the Holy Spirit, and by providing Christians today with a constitution for the church. While little of this bears much resemblance to the classic notion of justification by grace through faith, members of Churches of Christ have not been altogether without some sense of a gracious God.

Further, it should be stated clearly that there has been a minority in Churches of Christ, since the birth of this movement in the early nineteenth century, that has embraced fully the themes of justification by grace through faith and empowerment by the indwelling Holy Spirit. These have included both church leaders and members. But this persistent minority report should not obscure the fact that the burden of the tradition among Churches of Christ until very recent years has been distinctly nonevangelical and even antievangelical.

Finally, the analysis of the years 1870 to 1960 should not imply that Churches of Christ in more recent years stand entirely outside the evangelical orbit. In fact, since 1960 Churches of Christ increasingly have stood within that theological spectrum. Many members of Churches of Christ increasingly view the Bible not so much as a book of facts, but more as a chronicle of God's mighty deeds on behalf of humankind; many pulpits in this heritage increasingly proclaim the traditional evangelical message of justification by grace through faith, affirming baptism as a faith response to God's grace; and more and more members of Churches of Christ have taken seriously in recent years the Holy Spirit as a living reality in the lives of Christian women and men.[57]

But let us be clear. Those in this heritage who stand within the evangelical orbit stand there not because of their biblicism, not because of their Common Sense rationalism or intense antimodernism—themes that all correlate in one way or another with the *restitutio* sentiment. Nor do they belong there because of their allegiance to the *restitutio* sentiment itself. They belong there only to the extent of their allegiance to the various manifestations of the *reformatio* heritage and especially to the cornerstone of that heritage: the theme of justification by grace through faith.

This argument also contains implications for understanding and defining evangelicalism at large. Thus, for example, pentecostals belong in the evangelical orbit not because of their allegiance to the *restitutio* tradition, but rather because of their reliance on spiritual empowerment breaking into their lives through the grace of God. Again, premillennialists belong in the evangelical heritage as well, though not because, as Weber points out, they "held to the first century with a passion." They belong instead because of their openness to the sovereignty of God in human affairs. Even fundamentalists, whose first allegiance most often is to an inerrant Bible rather than to a sovereign and gracious God, still may be viewed as evangelicals to the extent that the *reformatio* perspective plays some role in their thought. But fundamentalists most assuredly are not evangelicals because of their allegiance to biblical inerrancy, their opposition to modernism, or their Baconian epistemology.

In the final analysis, I suspect that I and Donald Dayton, who in this volume proposes a "pentecostal" rather than a "presbyterian" model for measuring evangelicalism, are saying much the same thing. I differ with Dayton only because I sense that a "pentecostal" model is too narrow and implicitly imposes on evangelicalism certain themes peculiar to the pentecostal tradition. In my view, it is far preferable to return to the sixteenth-century Reformation for a model which can embrace a number of perspectives congenial to the *reformatio* tradition. In any event, to distinguish clearly between *reformatio* and *restitutio*, as I have sought to do here, should bring considerably more precision to our efforts to understand who belongs in the evangelical spectrum, who does not, and, perhaps more important, why.

NOTES

1. Leonard Sweet, ed., *The Evangelical Tradition in America* (Macon, Ga.: Mercer Univ. Press, 1984), 85.

2. See essays by Jan Shipps on Mormons, Robert T. Handy on baptists, and David Holmes on Episcopal evangelicals in *The American Quest for the Primitive Church*, ed., Richard Hughes (Urbana: Univ. of Illinois Press, 1988), 181–95, 143–52, 153–70.

3. Timothy P. Weber, *Living in the Shadow of the Second Coming* (New York: Oxford Univ. Press, 1979), 38–39; Grant Wacker, "Playing for Keeps: The Primitivist Impulse in Early Pentecostalism," 196–219 and Mark Noll, "Primitivism in Fundamentalism and American Biblical Scholarship: A Response," 120–28, in Hughes, *American Quest*.

4. Martin Luther, "Preface to the New Testament" (1522) in *Luther's Works*, vol. 35: *Word and Sacrament*, ed. E. Theodore Bachmann, *1* (Philadelphia: Muhlenberg Press, 1960), 362.

5. See Bernard J. Verkamp, "The Zwinglians and Adiaphorism," *Church History* 42 (Dec. 1973):486–504. On Zwingli's rejection of music in Christian worship, see Charles Garside, Jr., *Zwingli and the Arts* (New Haven: Yale Univ. Press, 1966), esp. 43–47.

6. Martin Luther, "Against the Heavenly Prophets" (Dec. 1524 and Jan. 1525) in *Luther's Works* vol. 40: *Church and Ministry*, ed. Conrad Bergendoff, 2 (Philadelphia: Fortress Press, 1958), 90–91, 150.

7. Gordon Rupp and George Yule make a similar distinction. See Rupp, "Patterns of Salvation in the First Age of the Reformation," *Archiv für Reformationsgeschichte* 57 (1966):60; and Yule, "Continental Patterns and the Reformaton in England and Scotland," *Scottish Journal of Theology* 18 (1969):305

8. For a discussion of some of the ways the restoration sentiment has been formulated, see Samuel S. Hill, Jr., "A Typology of American Restitutionism: From Frontier Revivalism and Mormonism to the Jesus Movement," *Journal of the American Academy of Religion* 44 (Mar. 1976):65–76; and Richard Hughes, "Primitivism and Perfectionism: From Anabaptists to Pentecostals," in *Reaching Beyond: Chapters in the History of Perfectionism*, ed. Stanley Burgess (Peabody, Mass.: Hendrickson Publishers, 1986), 213–55.

9. Walter Klaassen, e.g., has argued that "anabaptist writings are full of statements insisting that they, like other evangelical Christians, hold to and teach salvation by grace through faith," though Klaassen also notes that anabaptists sometimes resorted to a spirit of legalism. Klaassen, *Anabaptism: Neither Catholic nor Protestant* (Waterloo, Ontario, Canada: Conrad Press, 1973), 29, 34. On the other hand, Hans Hillerbrand claimed that, according to the anabaptist vision, human beings "by living in obedient discipleship pull the lever which extracts . . . grace." Hillerbrand, "Anabaptism and the Reformation: Another Look," *Church History* 29 (1960):415.

10. See, e.g., John C. Olin, ed., *John Calvin and Jacopo Sadoleto: A Reformation Debate* (New York: Harper and Row, 1966), 88.

11. Bullinger's impact on England and Puritanism came esp. through his *Decades of Sermons* and through the proto-Puritan John Hooper. Bucer pointed the English reform in a primitivist direction chiefly through his *De Regno Christi*, presented to King Edward VI in 1550. For Puritan covenant theology, see Willaim K. B. Stoever, *"A Faire and Easie Way to Heaven": Covenant Theology and Antinomianism in Early Massachussetts* (Middletown, Conn.: Wesleyan Univ. Press, 1978). For Puritan primitivism, see T. Dwight Bozeman, *To Live Ancient Lives: The Primitivist Dimension in Puritanism* (Chapel Hill: Univ. of North Carolina Press, for the Institute of Early American History and Culture, 1988).

12. On baptist primitivism, see Robert T. Handy, "Biblical Primitivism in the American Baptist Tradition," in Hughes, *American Quest*, 143–52. On Primitive Baptists, see Byron Cecil Lambert, *The Rise of the Anti-Mission Baptists: Sources and Leaders, 1800–1840* (New York: Arno, 1980). On Landmark Baptists, see James E. Tull, *A History of Southern Baptist Landmarkism in the Light of Historical Baptist Ecclesiology* (New York: Arno, 1980), and Richard Hughes and Leonard Allen, *Illusions of Innocence: Protestant Primitivism in America, 1630–1875* (Chicago: Univ. of Chicago Press, 1988), 79–101.

13. Albert Outler, "Biblical Primitivism in Early American Methodism," in Hughes, *American Quest*, 131–42.

14. The best statement of the role of social factors in bringing division is David Edwin Harrell, Jr., *The Social Sources of Division in the Disciples of Christ, 1865–1900* (Atlanta, Ga.: Publishing Systems, Inc., 1973). In the 20th century, the Disciples of Christ underwent a second major division, largely a by-product of the fundamentalist/modernist controversy. The resulting denominations were (a) the more liberal Christian Church (Disciples of Christ) and (b) the more conservative Christian Churches/ Churches of Christ, sometimes labeled Independent Christian Churches. On this division, see James Brownlee North, "The Fundamentalist Controversy Among the Disciples of Christ, 1890–1930," Ph.D. diss., Univ. of Illinois, 1973. See also James DeForest Murch, *Christians Only: A History of the Restoration Movement* (Cincinnati, Ohio: Standard Publishing, 1962), 223–77, 293–307; and Leroy Garrett, *The Stone-Campbell Movement: An Anecdotal History of Three Churches* (Joplin, Mo.: College Press, 1981), 615–729. Regarding the Disciples of Christ, see W.E. Garrison and A.T. DeGroot, *The Disciples of Christ: A History* (St. Louis, Mo.: Bethany Press, 1958), and Lester G.

McAlister and William E. Tucker, *Journey in Faith: A History of the Christian Church (Disciples of Christ)* (St. Louis, Mo.: Bethany Press, 1975).

15. Robert Baird, *Religion in the United States of America* (1844; rptd., New York: Arno, 1969), 573; Timothy L. Smith, "The Evangelical Kaleidoscope and the Call to Christian Unity," *Christian Scholar's Review* 15. no. 2 (1986):126, 128, 133, 134; George Marsden, ed., *Evangelicalism and Modern America* (Grand Rapids, Mich.: Eerdmans, 1984), viii–ix; David Edwin Harrell, Jr., "The South: Seedbed of Sectarianism," in *Varieties of Southern Evangelicalsim*, ed. David Edwin Harrell, Jr. (Macon, Ga.: Mercer Univ. Press, 1981), 45–57; and Wayne Flynt, "One in the Spirit, Many in the Flesh: Southern Evangelicals" in Harrell, *Varieties*, 23ff. Flynt speaks specifically of Disciples of Christ, though one assumes, given the prevalence of Churches of Christ in the Mid-South, that he uses that term to designate all the heirs of the Stone-Campbell movement.

16. On Churches of Christ, see Earl Irvin West, *The Search for the Ancient Order*, v. 1 (Nashville, Tenn.: Gospel Advocate, 1964); v. 2 and 3 (Indianapolis, Ind.: Religious Book Service, 1950 and 1979); and v. 4 (Germantown, Tenn.: Religious Book Service, 1987). For a social history of Disciples of Christ and Churches of Christ to 1900, see David Edwin Harrell, Jr., *Quest for a Christian America: The Disciples of Christ and American Society to 1866* (Nashville, Tenn.: Disciples of Christ Historical Society, 1966), and Harrell, *Social Sources of Division*.

17. On Campbell's view of the millennium, see Robert Frederick West, *Alexander Campbell and Natural Religion* (New Haven, Conn.: Yale Univ. Press, 1948), 163–217; Carl Wayne Hensley, "The Rhetorical Vision of the Disciples of Christ: A Rhetoric of American Millennialism," Ph.D. diss., Univ. of Minnesota, 1972; and Hughes and Allen, *Illusions of Innocence*, 170–87.

18. On Baconianism, see T. Dwight Bozeman, *Protestants in an Age of Science: The Baconian Ideal and Antebellum American Religious Thought* (Chapel Hill: Univ. of North Caroline Press, 1977). On the impact of Baconianism on Campbell and the movement he led, see Hughes and Allen, *Illusions of Innocence*, 153–69; Samuel Morris Eames, *The Philosophy of Alexander Campbell* (Bethany, W.V. 2.: Bethany College, 1966), esp. 19–32; and Michael Wilson Casey, "The Development of Necessary Inference in the Hermeneutics of the Disciples of Christ/Churches of Christ," Ph.D. diss., Univ. of Pittsburgh, 1986, 54–64.

19. Alexander Campbell, "Tracts for the People—No. 3," *Millennial Harbinger*, ser. 3, no. 3 (Jan. 1846):13; "Millennium—No. 1," *Millennial Harbinger* 1 (1 Feb. 1830):56–58; and *The Christian System*, 3d ed. (Pittsburgh, Forrester and Campbell, 1840), 18.

20. Alexander Campbell, *The Evidences of Christianity* (Cincinnati, Ohio: Jethro Jackson, 1852), 262; "Schools and Colleges—No. 2," *Millennial Harbinger*, ser. 3, no. 7 (Mar. 1850):172; and Jesse Kellems, *Alexander Campbell and the Disciples* (New York: Richard R. Smith, 1930), 170.

21. Alexander Campbell, "A Restoration of the Ancient Order of Things—No. 3," *Christan Baptist* 2 (4 Apr. 1825):174; "A Restoration of the Ancient Order of Things—No. 4," *Christian Baptist* 2 (6 June 1825):221; and Thomas Campbell, "Declaration and Address," in *Historical Documents Advocating Christian Union*, ed. Charles A. Young (Chicago: Christian Century Co., 1904), 109.

22. Alexander Campbell, "A Restoration of the Ancient Order of Things—No 4," *Christian Baptist* 2 (6 June 1825):222; *Christian System*, 125; and "Millennium—No. 2," *Millennial Harbinger* 1 (5 Apr. 1830):147.

23. Cf., e.g. Alexander Campbell, "Prefatory Remarks," *Millennial Harbinger* 1

(4 Jan. 1830):7–8; "Millennium—No. 1," *Millennial Harbinger* 1 (Feb. 1, 1830):58; "Millennium—No. 2," *Millennial Harbinger* 1 (5 Apr. 1830):145; *Christian System*, 91; and *The Christian Preacher's Companion, or, The Gospel Facts Sustained* (Centerville, Ky.: n.p., 1891).

24. Alexander Campbell, *Christian System*, 111.

25. Alexander Campbell, "The Foundation of Hope and Christian Union," *Christian Baptist* 1 (5 Apr. 1824):177; *Christian System*, 57ff; "A Review of a Review," *Millennial Harbinger*, new ser., no. 3 (Nov. 1839):505; "Extracts From My Sentimental Journal—No. 1," *Christian Baptist* 1 (5 Apr. 1824):173. Cf. *Christian System*, 122. For a discussion of Campbell's view of the relation of faith to reason, see Thomas H. Olbricht, "Alexander Campbell's View of the Holy Spirit," *Restoration Quarterly* 6 (1st Qtr. 1962):4–7. For the "facts . . . commands . . . promises" formula, see, e.g., John F. Rowe, *History of Reformatory Movements, Resulting in a Restoration of the Apostolic Church*, 5th ed. (Cincinnati, Ohio: John F. Rowe, 1892), 182–83.

26. Alexander Campbell, *A Debate Between Rev. A. Campbell and Rev. N.L. Rice on Christian Baptism* (Lexington, Ky.: A.T. Skillman and Son, 1844), 747; "Address to the Readers of the Christian Baptist—No. 4," *Christian Baptist* 1 (1 Mar. 1824):148; *Christian System*, 64; *Christianity Restored* (Bethany, Va.: 1835), 350; and *Christian Baptism, With Its Antecedents and Consequences* (St. Louis, Mo.: 1882; rptd Nashville, Tenn.: Gospel Advocate, 1951), 184–85. Cf. Thomas H. Olbricht, "Alexander Campbell's View of the Holy Spirit," *Restoration Quarterly* 6 (1st Qtr. 1962):1–11; Patrick Leon Brooks, "Lockean Epistemology and the Indwelling Spirit in the Restoration Movement" (M.A. thesis, Abilene Christian Univ., 1977), 44–55, 71–77, and 87–103; and Brooks, "Alexander Campbell, The New Holy Spirit, and the New Birth," *Restoration Quarterly* 31 (3rd Qtr. 1989):149–64.

27. Alexander Campbell, "Christian Union—No. 8. Evangelical Alliance—No. 3," *Millennial Harbinger*, ser. 3, no. 4 (Mar. 1847):166.

28. Alexander Campbell, "Evangelical Alliance—No. 2," *Millennial Harbinger* ser. 3, no. 3 (Aug. 1846):445–47; "Christian Union—No. 8. Evangelical Alliance—No. 3," *Millennial Harbinger*, ser. 3, no. 4 (Mar. 1847):168–69; "Christian Union—No. 19. Evangelical Alliance—No. 4," *Millennial Harbinger*, ser. 3, no. 4 (Apr. 1847):217; and "Christian Union—No. 7. Evangelical Alliance—No. 2," *Millennial Harbinger*, ser. 3, no. 4 (Feb. 1847):79.

29. Thomas Taylor, "Our Brethren in Danger of Turning Evangelical," *Millennial Harbinger*, ser. 3, no. 1 (June 1844):268; John F. Rowe, *History of Reformatory Movements Resulting in a Restoration of the Apostolic Church*, 5th ed. (Cincinnati, Ohio: G. W. Rice, 1884), 101.

30. N.B. Hardeman, *Hardeman's Tabernacle Sermons*, v. 2 (Nashville, Tenn.: McQuiddy Printing, 1923), 250. In all, Hardeman preached 5 series of Tabernacle sermons. The first 4 series, preached in 1922, 1923, 1928, and 1938, were all delivered in Nashville's Ryman Auditorium. The fifth and final series was preached in 1942 in the War Memorial Building and the Central Church of Christ, Nashville. Five Separate volumes resulted: 1 (Nashville: McQuiddy, 1924); 2 (Nashville: McQuiddy 1923); 3 (Nashville: McQuiddy, 1928); 4 (Nashville: Gospel Advocate, 1938); and 5 (Nashville: Gospel Advocate 1943).

31. Alexander Campbell, "Methodistic Calumny," *Millennial Harbinger* 4 (July 1833):301.

32. Alexander Campbell, "Prefatory Remarks," *Millennial Harbinger* 1 (4 Jan. 1830):4. For an excellent assessment of Campbell's understanding of the 16th-century Reformation, and esp. of Luther, see Richard L. Harrison, "Alexander Campbell on

Luther and the Reformation," *Lexington Theological Quarterly* 19 (Oct. 1984):123–52.

33. Preachers and members of Churches of Christ have written an assortment of church histories over the past century. A partial list of these would include John F. Rowe, *History of Reformatory Movements*; George Adam Klingman, *Church History for Busy People* (Cincinnati, Ohio: F.L. Rowe, 1909); J.W. Shepherd, *The Church, The Falling Away, and the Restoration* (Cincinnati, Ohio: F.L. Rowe, 1929); Eli Monroe Borden, *Church History, Showing the Origin of the Church of Christ, and Its History from the Days of the Apostles to Our Time* (Austin, Tex.: Firm Foundation, 1939); John Dee Cox, *A Concise Account of Church History* (Murfreesboro, Tenn.: DeHoff Publications, 1951); F.W. Mattox, *The Eternal Kingdom: A History of the Church of Christ* (Delight, Ark.: Gospel Light, 1961); Monroe Hawley, *Redigging the Wells: Seeking Undenominational Christianity* (Abilene, Tex.: Quality Printing, 1976); Homer Hailey, *From Creation to the Day of Eternity: God's Great Plan for Man's Redemption* (Las Vegas: Nevada Publications, 1982); and Leonard Allen and Richard Hughes, *Discovering our Roots: The Ancestry of Churches of Christ* (Abilene, Tex.: Abilene Christian Univ. Press, 1988).

34. Rowe, *History of Reformatory Movements*, v–vi, 30, 35, 119. This volume, which in its 1889 edition bore the main title *The Apostolic Church Restored*, was immensely popular and by 1913 had gone through nine editions.

35. Shepherd, *The Church*, 93–94, 114–15, 121, 123, 125.

36. Mattox, *Eternal Kingdom*, 252–53, 256.

37. Hardeman, *Tabernacle Sermons*, 3:91–92, 97.

38. Moses Lard, "The Reformation For Which We are Pleading—What Is It?" *Lard's Quarterly* 1 (Sept. 1863):14, 22. Lard claimed to be absolutely presuppositionless with regard to the Bible: "We do not mean that a mere resemblance shall exist between the elements or particulars of our theory and the contents of His word; but that these contents shall themselves constitute these elements or particulars." Ibid., 13. On Lard, see Casey, The Development of Necessary Inference," 302–12.

39. Rowe, *History of Reformatory Movements*, 182–83; and W. Clyde Odeneal, "The Constitution of the Church," *Firm Foundation* 51 (24 July 1934):1 and 8.

40. Rowe, *History of Reformatory Movements,* 123.

41. Hardeman, *Tabernacle Sermons*, 3:90–94.

42. Ibid., 2:94–95.

43. K.C. Moser, *The Way of Salvation* (Nashville, Tenn.: Gospel Advocate, 1932; rptd. Delight, Ark.: Gospel Light, 1933); and "Can the Gospel Be Obeyed?" *Firm Foundation* 51 (6 Feb. 1934):2.

44. G.H.P. Showalter, "Obedience and Salvation," *Firm Foundation* 51 (13 Feb. 1934):4.

45. Interview with Mrs. K.C. Moser, Abilene, Tex., 22 Nov. 1987.

46. K.C. Moser, "Reply to Brother Showalter," *Firm Foundation* 51 (3 Apr. 1934): 8; and G.H.P. Showalter, "The 'Faith Alone' Idea," *Firm Foundation* 51 (3 Apr. 1894):4.

47. John W. Hedge, "Simplicity of the Gospel of Christ," *Firm Foundation* 51 (8 May 1934):5; and Logan Buchanan, "Review of K.C. Moser's Article," *Firm Foundation* 51 (3 Apr. 1934):8.

48. Interview with Mrs. K.C. Moser.

49. Esp. important in this regard were G.C. Brewer, for many years an influential preacher among Churches of Christ; R.C. Bell, professor of Bible at Abilene Christian College; F.W. Mattox, author of *The Eternal Kingdom*, already mentioned, and president of Lubbock Christian College; and J.D. Thomas, professor of Bible at Abilene

Christian College and author of *The Biblical Doctrine of Grace* (Abilene, Tex.: Biblical Research Press, 1977). Thomas, who directed the Abilene Chirstian College Bible Lectureship from 1952 to 1969, invited G.C. Brewer to speak on "Grace and Salvation" at the 1952 lectureship and views that sermon as a pivotal turning point for Churches of Christ (conversation with J.D. Thomas, 17 Feb. 1988.) For Brewer's sermon, see G.C. Brewer, "Grace and Salvation," *Abilene Christian College Bible Lectures,* 1952 (Austin, Tex.: Firm Foundation Publishing House, 1952), 101–27.

50. K.C. Moser, *The Gist of Romans* (Oklahoma City: K.C. Moser, 1957).

51. Thomas H. Olbricht, "Biblical Theology and the Restoration Movement," *Mission Journal* 13 (Apr. 1980):9.

52. Hardeman, *Tabernacle Sermons,* 2:147–48; see also 2:151–52. For Hardeman, the principle task of the Spirit was to assure a complete, authoritative, and infallible Bible. He therfore supposed the Spirit might have said to the apostles, "My relation to you as apostles shall not be simply to remind you of the past; but I will guide you unto all truth, and hence see that no mistake is made.'" Then Hardeman affirmed, "I have perfect confidence in the all-sufficiency, in the absolute perfection of that guiding, so that there is not a single, solitary thing God would have you and me do today but that the Spirit guided those apostles unto the proclamation of that truth." Ibid. 2:150–51.

53. Alexander Campbell, "The Coming of the Lord—No. 23," *Millennial Harbinger,* new ser. no.7(May 1843):219f. See also Campbell, "The Coming of the Lord—No. 21," Millennial Harbinger, new ser., no. 7 (Feb. 1843):73f. On the outbreak of premillennialism among Churches of Christ about 1843, see Hughes and Allen, *Illusions of Innocence,* 130–31.

54. See e.g., R.H. Boll, "Studies in Prophecy," *Word and Work* 10 (Aug. 1916):362; and Boll, "The Olivet Sermon," *Word and Work* 10 (Nov. 1916):487–91.

55. "The Lord's Day Lesson," *Word and Work* 10 (Jan. 1916):40.

56. Hardeman, *Tabernacle Sermons,* 4:157. Hardeman also objected that premillennialists among Churches of Christ compromised with the "denominational world. . . . There's the harm. It's the sacrifice, brethren, of the old landmarks." Ibid., 162–63.

57. Most in Churches of Christ continue to resist premillennial eschatology, chiefly because they judge this perspective to be unbiblical. For recent discussions within Churches of Christ on the question of the Holy Spirit, see Brooks, "Lockean Epistemology and the Indwelling Spirit," 139–91.

CHAPTER 8

Black Religion and the Question of Evangelical Identity

Milton G. Sernett

The distinctive inner logic of African-American religion is the telling of the story of travail and triumph — of the coursing of the river of freedom, to use Vincent Harding's dominant metaphor.[1] More a matter of being than of being right, black theology, however defined, appeals to the experience of a people of long memory rather than to dogma or textbook theology. The communal song, not catechetics, has been the principle hermeneutic of the African-American religious experience. Never at ease in the American Zion, yet part of the struggle to define and perfect the American experiment, black Americans have expressed their theology in dialectical fashion, constantly reflecting upon the present moment in light of the past. In this reflective mode, interpretations of black destiny and divine providence in the face of the vagaries of human existence and the realities of oppression signify more than debates concerning liturgical practice or scriptural inerrancy.

In 1941, the novelist Richard Wright observed, "We black folk, our history and our present being, are a mirror of all the manifold experiences in America. What we want, what we represent, what we endure, is what America *is*."[2] The mirror of African-American history reflects the contradictions between American ideals and American practices. The same may be said of black theology. C. Eric Lincoln writes: "Black theology is in some sense what is missing from white theology. To the degree that it fulfills its own best intentions, it is the restoration of a deficit incurred through the habitual malfunctioning of a racist calculus."[3] Whether one has in mind the "black theology" articulated in the classroom, the pulpit, or the folk culture, the primary thrust has been toward full liberation, both spiritually and politically. However, the song of liberation has been sung by varied voices with different emphases at separate historical moments.

In attempting to define its uniqueness over against the dominant European-American religious establishment, African-American religion has been at the crossroads of similarity and dissonance. On the one hand, the black church can be thought of as a self-contained tradition, albeit one constantly modified by changing social conditions—constantly "becoming," yet, as Lincoln writes, "with no convenient place in the existing parameters of American pluralism."[4] On the other hand, recognition of differences, of varieties of African-American religious identity and expression, "problematizes" the notion of a single entity conceived of as *the* Black Church."

Black Methodism and black pentecostalism afford examples of the tension between similarity and dissonance. A black pentecostal congregation may in certain contexts signify its uniqueness according to racial or cultural criteria and in other contexts stress its theological and liturgical similarities with a neighboring white pentecostal assembly of believers. Bishop Richard Allen, pioneering African Methodist, retained the white Methodist discipline and forms of polity even after separating from the structure of white Methodism in 1816. Yet he demonstrated a different sense of mission and purpose as he sought to minister without interference from the white elders among his people at Mother Bethel in Philadelphia.[5]

All theological ideologies struggle faithfully to reflect the aspirations of the communities that give them birth. The religious heritage of black Americans is a creative synthesis born of New World experiences in which African and European-American traditions worked in a symbiotic tension. The very presence of the black church as a sociological phenomenon is testimony to the historical failure of white Christians to break free of the captivity of theology to ethnology.

In attempting to sketch the points of contact between black religious traditions and evangelicalism, we must keep in mind the dialectical tensions between theology and ethnicity, between religion and group identity.[6] Some blacks, as C. Eric Lincoln observes in *Race, Religion and the Continuing American Dilemma*, identify themselves primarily as "Protestant" or "Catholic" or "Jewish," while others argue that "black religion" is a *fourth force in American religious pluralism.*[7] Nevertheless, I would argue that the theology of freedom, in which interpretations of the providence of God are of paramount concern, is a common thread one can trace throughout African-American religious history.

Having to endure both chattel slavery in the South and discrimination in areas north of slavery, black Christians necessarily became stalkers of meaning. They sought out power in the Spirit and read history for signs of the providence of God. Absalom Jones, Allen's early coadjutor and later this country's first ordained black Episcopal priest, in 1808 preached a thanksgiving sermon celebrating the abolition of the slave trade, in which he stated, "The deliverance of the children of Israel from their bondage, is not the only instance, in which it has pleased God to appear in behalf of oppressed and distressed nations."[8] Spirituals also testify to linking the providence of God with the historical struggle for black liberation. Lawrence Levine has concluded that the "single most persistent image" in the spirituals is that of the "chosen people." The slaves sang, "We are de people of de Lord."[9]

This desire for salvation and assurance, both collectively and individually, became the paramount theological concern as African-American Christians spoke "another word" about themselves in relation to their experiences at the hands of white Christians. All religious options had to be assessed according to the extent to which they offered witness to God's providence on behalf of those yet under the yoke of oppression. Varieties of evangelicalism, no less than varieties of nonevangelicalism, proved attractive to African Americans to the degree that they offered assurance that God was a time-god working in history for the deliverance of all those held in the house of bondage, figuratively and literally.

Evangelical nomenclature, with a significant exception to be noted later, is not common currency among African-American Protestants. William Bentley writes, "To blacks, at least the mainstream ones within the major black denominations, the word [*evangelical*] has little historical relevance. Instead, 'Bible believing' is the more widely used descriptive term."[10] Most black Bible-believers do not "*think* of themselves as 'evangelicals'," George Marsden observes.[11] Contemporary black theologians do not seem much interested in the question this forum addresses. White evangelicals are the ones who seem troubled by competing varieties of evangelicalism and the accompanying identity confusion. Our rather formal endeavor is, we must admit, born of disarray primarily among white Protestants who have been elbowing each other for the right to march in the evangelical parade.

Nonetheless, as a historian I am intrigued as much by the absence of significant black participation in the scholarly controversy as I am in the debate itself. This curiosity is heightened by assertions such as the following. William Pannell writes: "The origins of the black Christian experience in America were evangelical in nature."[12] Obviously, *something* happened along the way from the beginning of the black spiritual odessey to the present moment.

Given the brief compass of this essay, the full story cannot be told, even if it were within my ability to do so. But since the charge given to me is to explore the connections between "evangelicalism" and the "black church," I propose to limit this essay to an examination of the compatibility of three meanings of evangelicalism with African-American religious history and its dominant theme, as earlier expressed — the theology of freedom. Donald Dayton's typology of evangelicalism will be used as an initial filtering device.[13]

As a Lutheran affiliated with the Evangelical Lutheran Church, my personal familiarity with the term *evangelical* derives from the Reformation theme of justification by grace and not by works. There are now third- and fourth-generation black Lutherans in the United States. Yet, as Lutherans readily acknowledge, African Americans have not flocked in great numbers to the banner of the liturgical and doctrinal heirs of the German Reformation. Until at least the late nineteenth century, American Lutherans made few efforts to extend their understanding of being evangelical to African Americans.[14]

Prior to the popularity of black holiness and pentecostal churches, largely a phenomenon of twentieth-century urbanization, most African American Christians identified themselves as baptist and, to a lesser extent, Methodist. Using data from the special *Census of Religious Bodies of* 1926, Carter G. Woodson concluded that the "rural Negro church" still dominated the black religious ethos. "It is the simple Protestant faith," he wrote, "largely of Methodists and Baptists, who, with the exception of the difference of opinion on immersion, are very much alike everywhere among Negroes."[15] Neither the liturgical traditions, Anglicanism, Roman Catholicism, and Lutheranism, nor the doctrinal descendants of Calvin in the continentally-derived Reformed churches, had much success in winning the allegiance of blacks, slave or free, in antebellum America. Instead, African Americans had been drawn to the preaching of those evangelicals whom Dayton describes as practicing "convertive piety" in its Anglo-American manifestations during the religious awakenings in the South, beginning with the baptist revivals of the mid-1700s.

Donald Matthews, Albert Raboteau, and others have written persuasively concerning how African-American slaves appropriated the language and rituals of white evangelicalism for themselves.[16] European forms were made to serve African functions. With the gradual weakening of the African cosmology and the loss of community necessary to sustain traditional religions, the slaves, the most dispossessed of the dispossessed, rejoiced at the good news of a new life offered freely to all people. The evangelical rejection of earthly status and authority, coupled with an emphasis upon an intense personal conversion experience, proved attractive to thousands of black slaves. They, like the poor whites who organized the early baptist churches and Methodist class meetings, responded to the theme, as voiced by the Methodist itinerant Francis Asbury, "Disallowed indeed of men but chosen of God and precious."[17]

Donald Mathews correctly argues that antebellum black and white evangelicalism in the South cannot be understood apart from each other. Evangelicalism is here to be understood as a social-historical process whereby "the old distinction of family and class was rejected for the new distinction of piety and morality."[18] "From interaction with and participation in this process," Mathews maintains, "blacks created the measure by which southern Evangelicalism itself could be judged, and through their appropriation of Evangelical Christianity expressed a religious-social ethos that could best convey its significance in the Evangelical promise to 'preach liberty to the captives.'"[19]

Though initially bound together by an emphasis upon the need for an inward conversion experience and the desire to create new communities based upon equality in the spirit rather than the conventional social canons, black and white evangelicals probably understood the evangelical message in different ways. This should not surprise us, for the slaves applied the "good news" to their own situation of being under the yoke of bondage, in ways which whites could not, no matter how dispossessed they felt. Mathews makes the interesting observation that black Christians were not as burdened with the sense of original sin as were whites. "While whites might rightfully be said to have 'broken down' under preaching," he suggests, "blacks were lifted up, enabled to celebrate themselves as persons because of their direct and awful contact with divinity which healed their battered self-esteem with the promise of deliverance, the earnest of which was the vision itself."[20]

Despite initial convergence around the banner of convertive piety, over against establishment religion, black and white evangelicals soon went their separate ways. Blacks had their own millennial dream of freedom. "The ineluctable tendency of the black evangelical ethos," Albert Raboteau concludes, "was in the direction of asserting 'manhood' rights, which were understood as a vital form of self-governance."[21] Independent black baptist congregations emerged and retained a surprising degree of autonomy, at least until the 1820s and the insurrection of Denmark Vesey. During the era of independent black preaching, approximately 1760–90, according to Peter Wood's periodization, African Americans in the South established the foundations of a distinctly black evangelical tradition and began building communities of faith.[22] "The opportunity for black religious separatism," Raboteau tells us, "was due to the egalitarian character of evangelical Protestantism; its necessity was due, in part, to the racism of white Evangelicals."[23]

The black theology of freedom ran counter to the narrowing definition of what white southerners deemed "evangelical" as they rose in social standing within the plantation economy. Once the majority of white evangelicals had a vested interest in the maintenance of slavery, even as a necessary evil in a fallen world, the gap between black and white evangelicalism widened. Though the black evangelical creed could lead to quietism and a disposition to refrain from openly challenging the political props of slavery, it could also inspire resistance, as Nat Turner's prophetic visions did. More commonly, black Christians used the egalitarian impulse of evangelicalism to affirm their psychological "somebodiness" in the midst of a hostile environment, and to assess the failures of whites to practice the egalitarian ethic.

Frederick Douglass, angered by the hypocrisy of slaveholding Christians, asserted that revivals of religion and revivals of the slave trade went hand in hand. Yet Douglass, like many of the slaves, made a distinction between "the pure, peaceable, and impartial Christianity of Christ" and "the corrupt, slaveholding, women-whipping, cradle-plundering, partial and hypocritical Christianity" which gave support to the South's peculiar institution.[24]

One reason, then, for the historical predilection of black Christians for evangelical convertive piety has to do with where the majority of blacks were located in the eighteenth and early nineteenth centuries and with whom they came in contact. The evangelical takeover of the South by the baptists and Methodists provided the occasion, but the ability of African Americans to tease out the message of freedom in the evangelical gospel proved to be the decisive factor. Black Christians then turned their oppressor's religious discourse against the "peculiar institution," to situate themselves within the moral universe.

Antebellum black Christians discovered that nineteenth-century white evangelicals were divided among themselves. The slaveholding and the anti-slavery advocates went into ideological battle armed with an appeal to evangelical traditions. The non-Garrisonian abolitionists drew heavily upon the implications of convertive piety in their attack upon slavery. They took up abolition's axe to demonstrate the authenticity of their own conversions and soon found themselves, as Donald Scott has shown, possessed of a "sacred vocation."[25] Beriah Green, abolition's moral theologian and president of Oneida Institue, believed that, by exposing the loathesome facts of slavery, he could convince the supporters of slavery of their need for repentance and change.[26] Slavery became a symbol of all that was sinful and prevented the fulfilment of the kingdom of God. "Immediatism," Donald Scott reminds us, "was less a program of what to do about slavery than, in evangelical terms, a 'disposition,' a state of being in which the heart and will were set irrevocably against slavery."[27]

While some abolitionists gave slavery only metaphorical significance, others employed the rhetoric and the spiritual energy of the Second Great Awakening to organize themselves for an attack upon both church and state. The national evangelical communions eventually split along sectional lines, widening the gulf between evangelical abolitionists and evangelical slaveholders.[27] This division, however, afforded blacks, especially in the North, evidence that being evangelical did not necessarily mean that one had chosen popularity over purity in the cause of freedom. Indeed, black abolitionists, such as David Walker and Henry Highland Garnet, themselves employed antislavery evangelical rhetoric.[29]

Contemporary observers of what has been called the "new evangelicalism," especially as manifested by television preachers of the gospel of success, no doubt have little awareness of the reformist spirit in the evangelical heritage. White evangelicals associated with the "born-again" movement had little interest in social activism until after World War II. Thus the social conscience of evangelicalism had to be "rediscovered."[30] The problem with all such searches for a usable past is that they use history selectively. I find few, if any, continuities between the renewed interest of some evangelicals in politics and social reform and the pre–Civil War evangelicalism of even such a tentative abolitionist as Charles G. Finney, not to mention such radical ecclesiastical "come-outers" and political abolitionists as Beriah Green.[31] Those who would argue for a direct line of descent from the evangelical reformers of the pre–Civil War era to the contemporary renewal of interest in social activism somehow must explain what happened after emancipation. Donald Dayton puts it succinctly and well: "What had begun as a Christian egalitarianism was transformed into a type of Christian elitism. Revivalistic currents that once had been bent to the liberation of the slave now allied themselves with wealth and power against the Civil Rights movement."[32]

The loss and deflection of the pre–Civil War social conscience in support of black freedom in the North was paralleled in the postemancipation South by an almost complete separation of black and white Christians along racial lines. In 1876, the editor of the Raleigh *Biblical Recorder* gave expression to the general white Protestant sentiment. Permanent church partnerships between blacks and whites were as inconceivable as influencing "fire and gunpowder to occupy the same canister in peace."[33] Black Christians in the post-Reconstruction South developed their own institutions, separate and apart from the white power structure. Black churches became the single most important vehicle for the exercise of an independent social and cultural life. This was true not only of rural isolates but also of urban blacks, whose churches served as town halls and community centers as well as houses of worship.[34]

Meanwhile, southern white Protestants skewed evangelicalism in defense of racial superiority. Few white evangelicals dissented from the notion, as H. Shelton Smith has written, "that the system of black-white separatism represented the normal development of a divinely implanted instinct."[35] The individualist, verticalist character of southern white Protestantism, Samuel S. Hill, Jr., has argued, prevented white evangelicals from making connections between theology and social ethics. "According to the pervasive revivalistic ideology," Hill wrote in 1966, "justification (conceived as forensic) is usually thought of as an act which is self-contained, having no organismic relation to anything else."[36] White revivalists such as Samuel P. Jones expected blacks to stay in their place and reduced religion to a decision of the sinner to "quit his meanness."[37]

Black churches, though theologically conservative, did not become significantly involved in the twentieth-century controversy of fundamentalists versus modernists. Consequently, the emergence of neo-evangelicals out of the fundamentalist fold since World War II has been predominantly a white phenomenon. During the revivals of the classical evangelical period, blacks were drawn into the evangelical circles because the evangelical message could be used as a basis for building community. Black Christians rarely engaged in doctrinal debates over, for example, predestination or unitarianism. Correct praxis, not correct doctrine, was of importance to those hungry for liberation. But white fundamentalists let their eschatology govern their social theory; they lacked the will to apply theology to ethics and quarreled endlessly among themselves over the hallmarks of evangelical identity.[38]

The white fundamentalist preoccupation with the question of inerrancy made the Bible a cultural icon. In contrast, black Christians, while appealing to biblical authority, rarely have developed rigid doctrines of inerrancy. As Henry Mitchell writes in *Black Preaching*, black preaching employs an "intuitively flexible approach" to the Bible. "A Black preacher is more likely to say, 'Didn't He say it!' than to be officious about what 'the word of God declares!'[39] James S. Tinney has suggested that, even though black and white pentecostals may share common ground in an emphasis on tongue-speaking, black pentecostals do not attempt to define themselves with an appeal to the fundamentalist view of Scripture, nor have they felt as inhibited by classical trinitarianism. He argues that the fundamentalist view of Scripture "falls on deaf ears in the black community," and consequently Oneness doctrines (Jesus Name, Apostolic) have had greater popularity among black than white pentecostals.[40]

Though black and white pentecostals may have differed in their approach to the Bible, they occupied, at least in the early years of the modern pentecostal revival, common ground. The Azusa Street mission led by William J. Seymour was interracial in nature, and many of the early white pentecostal clergy were ordained by black pentecostals.[41] If we view pentecostalism as a subcategory of "classical" or revival evangelicalism and look at it as a social movement, much as southern evangelicalism was before 1800, then its appeal to the black and white disinherited becomes intelligible. The early years of pentecostalism were, it might be argued, similar to those during the evangelical revivals in the South, when blacks and whites shared the fellowship of interracial communities of the twice-born. But once again, the incubus of racism matured, and eventually black and white pentecostals went their separate ways.

Thus far, following Dayton's typology, we have examined the possible connections between African-American religion and three historic expressions of evangelicalism: the Reformation, Anglo-American revivalism, and its subset, fundamentalism. Contemporary evangelicalism, while having roots in all three historic types, often is seen as a broad cultural phenomenon which encompasses diverse groups that share common tendencies.[42] If we adopt James Davison Hunter's view that an orientation toward salvation, revival, holiness, and biblical literalism are hallmarks of contemporary evangelicalism, then it might be assumed that black religion, which frequently has been thought of as a "religion of the disinherited," would fit the profile. And Hunter's attitudinal survey, drawn from data collected by the Princeton Religious Research Center in 1978–79, indicated that whites outnumbered blacks in the contemporary evangelical subculture approximately ten to one (88.2 to 11.8 percent). This ratio approximated the ratio of whites to blacks in the general population (90.4 to 8.9 percent).[43]

Hunter's profile indicates that, although the vast majority of black Bible-believers in the traditionally black denominations can be considered evangelical in a very broad sense, they are not participants in the contemporary evangelical subculture. Nor had they been included in the "Victorious Life" or "Manly Christianity" of the Billy Sunday era. The post–World War II renaissance of evangelicalism, sometimes referred to as the "New Evangelicalism," has been predominantly a white religious phenomenon. Though William Bentley would like to categorize black holiness and pentecostal groups as "entirely evangelical," he admits that "among blacks who are of this persuasion the term as such is not in widespread use."[44] The National Association of Evangelicals does not include any of the predominantly black denominations.

A number of black evangelicals have identified with the evangelical community, understood in a transdenominational sense. One thinks of individuals such as Ben Kinchlow of the "700 Club"; Tom Skinner, of Tom Skinner and Associates; William Bentley, the first black graduate of Fuller Seminary; and Howard O. Jones, the first (as of 1958 the only) black associate in the Billy Graham Evangelistic Association.[45] In the late 1960s, black leaders in the predominantly white mainline denominations organized black caucuses to push black causes, as did, for example, Black Methodists for Church Renewal. The National Black Evangelical Association (NBEA) was founded in 1963 in Los Angeles, as an umbrella organization for black evangelicals dissatisfied with the predominantly white National Association of Evangelicals. William H. Bentley, pastor of Calvary Bible Church in Chicago, served as president. In 1975, the NBEA convention in New York City emphasized evangelical pan-Africanism; assisting black youth, especially college students; and increased involvement in social-action projects such as Operation LIVE, a street-level counseling ministry. The NBEA reportedly had a mailing list of five thousand and a constituency of between thirty thousand and forty thousand in 1980.[46]

Dedicated to bringing liberal blacks to a more evangelical position, especially regarding the authority of Scripture, the NBEA was not without internal controversy. Tensions reportedly surfaced in 1976, when theology workshops were initiated to discuss the wisdom of pursuing a distinctively black theology. At the San Francisco convention in 1977, leaders debated whether evangelicals should emphasize biblically-based "expositional" theology or culturally-based black "experiential" theology. Anthony C. Evans, pastor of Oak Cliff Bible Fellowship in Dallas, argued for an "expositional" theology in which emphasis was to be placed on the authority of biblical declarations, rather than, as Henry Mitchell advocated on black cultural traditions. "If the Bible message and blackness bump heads," Evans declared, "blackness must go."[47] Proponents of the need for a distinctive black theology such as William H. Bentley, former president of the NBEA, contended that there was "no totally objective revelation of truth" and cited the writings of advocates of "experiential" theology, such as James H. Cone.[48]

Described as a "theology-culture rift" by *Christianity Today*, by 1980 the discord had resulted in the resignation of three members of the board of directors, including Ruben S. Conner, outgoing president and pastor of Community Bible Church in Dallas. The resignations were tabled, and efforts subsequently were made to resolve the differing theological perspectives. Conner and outgoing first vice-president Anthony Evans wanted to strengthen the doctrinal basis of the NBEA by including an explicit statement confirming inerrancy. Bentley supported what he called "Black Evangelical Christian Nationalism" and resisted the adoption of what he called an "a priori approach."[49]

It is not surprising that leaders within the NBEA have had difficulty in locating the critical norm for the theological stance of their organization. James Cone, of all the current black theologians, has given greatest attention to the problem of articulating a distinctive "black theology." But as Theo Witvliet perceptively points out in *The Way of Black Messiah: The Hermeneutical Challenge of Black Theology as a Theology of Liberation*, Cone himself still struggles to clarify the hermeneutical-methodological relationship between the biblical witness and black theology. Witvliet writes:

In order to be able to reflect critically on the praxis of proclamation in the black church, the black theologian needs a deep knowledge of the situation, history and culture of the black community. To achieve this he or she is pointed towards, among other things, the results of historical investigation, and there is no way in which these may be treated arbitrarily and one-sidedly. But on the other hand the renewing power of the Spirit in the praxis of the black church and community calls for ongoing reflection on the sources in which the messianic praxis of the Jew Jesus of Nazareth is documented. Everything here depends on the way in which the relationship between the two elements — black experience and biblical witness — is given a hermeneutical basis and is worked out methodologically — unconfused and undivided.[50]

At a more general level, the debate within the NBEA constituted a paradigm of the competing forces which historically have been at play in the relationship of African Americans to American evangelicalism. The theology-culture rift was reflective of the larger question of how blacks and whites should work out their interrelationships in a common Christian enterprise. If the past is a fair indicator of the future course of this dialectic, then black Christians will continue to measure evangelicalism, of whatever definition and identity, by a very simple but demanding yardstick. Albert Raboteau wrote that, for antebellum black evangelicals, "doing good and avoiding evil were proofs of racial equality as well as signs of justification and sanctification."[51] The same may be said of the black perspective on the evangelicalism of the present and future. Evangelical theology and evangelical ethics must meet on the common ground of equality and justice if the evangelical identity is to bridge racially discrete Christian communions.

NOTES

1. Vincent Harding, *There is a River: The Black Struggle for Freedom in America* (New York: Vintage, 1983).

2. Quoted in Mary Frances Berry and John W. Blassingame, *Long Memory: The Black Experience in America* (New York: Oxford Univ. Press, 1982), ix.

3. C. Eric Lincoln, *The Black Church Since Frazier* (New York: Schocken, 1974), 145.

4. C. Eric Lincoln, *Race, Religion, and the Continuing American Dilemma* (New York: Hill and Wang, 1984), 135.

5. See Richard Allen's 1833 autobiography, in Milton C. Sernett, *Afro-American Religious History: A Documentary Witness* (Durham, N.C.: Duke Univ. Press, 1985), 135–49. Also, Carol V.R. George, *Segregated Sabbaths: Richard Allen and the Emergence of Independent Black Church, 1760–1840* (New York: Oxford Univ. Press, 1973).

6. See Milton C. Sernett, "Believers and Behavers: Religion and Group Identity," in *Introduction to the Study of Religion*, ed. T. William Hall (New York: Harper and Row, 1978), 217–30.

7. Lincoln, *Race, Religion,* 133.

8. Absalom Jones, *A Thanksgiving Sermon, Preached on January 1, 1808, in St. Thomas', or the African Episcopal Church, Philadelphia: On Account of the Abolition of the Slave Trade* (Philadelphia: Fry and Kammerer, 1808), 10.

9. Lawrence W. Levine, "Slave Songs and Slave Consciousness: An Exploration in Neglected Sources," in *Anonymous Americans: Explorations in Nineteenth-Century Social History,* ed. Tamara K. Hareven (Englewood Cliffs, N.J.: Prentice—Hall, 1971), 106.

10. William H. Bentley, "Bible Believers in the Black Community," in *The Evangelicals,* ed. David F. Wells and John D. Woodbridge (Nashville, Tenn.: Abingdon, 1975), 110.

11. George Marsden, ed., *Evangelicalism and Modern America* (Grand Rapids, Mich.: Eerdmans, 1984), xv.

12. William Pannell, "The Religious Heritage of Blacks," in Wells and Woodbridge, *The Evangelicals,* 99.

13. Donald W. Dayton, "The Limits of Evangelicalism: The Pentecostal Tradition," ch. 4, this book.

14. Milton C. Sernett, "A Question of Earnestness: American Lutheran Missions and Theological Education in Alabama's 'Black Belt'," in *Essays and Reports: The Lutheran Historical Conference, 1980* (St. Louis, Mo.: Concordia Historical Institute, 1982), 80–117.

15. Carter G. Woodson, *The Rural Negro* (Washington, D.C.: Association for the Study of Negro Life and History, 1930), 152.

16. Albert J. Raboteau, *Slave Religion: The "Invisible Institution" in the Antebellum South* (New York: Oxford Univ. Press, 1978). Donald Matthews, *Religion in the Old South* (Chicago: Univ. of Chicago Press, 1977). Charles Joyner, *Down by the Riverside: A South Carolina Slave Community* (Urbana: Univ. of Illinois Press, 1984).

17. Cited in Matthews, *Religion in the Old South,* 35.

18. Ibid.

19. Ibid., xv.

20. Ibid., 215.

21. Albert J. Raboteau, "The Black Experience in American Evangelicalism: The Meaning of Slavery," in *The Evangelical Tradition in America,* ed. Leonard I. Sweet (Macon, Ga.: Mercer Univ. Press, 1984), 186.

22. See Peter H. Wood, "'Jesus Christ Has Got Thee at Last': Afro-American Conversion as a Forgotten Chapter in Eighteenth-Century Southern Intellectual History," *Bulletin of the Center for the Study of Southern Culture and Religion* 3 (Nov. 1979):6.

23. Raboteau, "Black Experience," 183.

24. Frederick Douglass, "Narrative of the Life of Frederick Douglass, An American Slave," in *Frederick Douglass: The Narrative and Selected Writings,* ed. Michael Meyer (New York: Random House, 1984), 121–22.

25. Donald Scott, "Abolition as a Sacred Vocation," in *Antislavery Reconsidered,* ed. Lewis Perry and Michael Fellman (Baton Rouge: Louisiana State Univ. Press, 1979), 51–74. See also, James D. Essig, *Evangelicals Against Slavery, 1770–1808* (Philadelphia: Temple Univ. Press, 1982).

26. Milton C. Sernett, *Abolition's Axe: Beriah Green, Oneida Institute, and the Black Freedom Struggle* (Syracuse, N.Y.: Syracuse Univ. Press, 1986), 23.

27. Scott, "Abolition as a Sacred Vocation," 72.

28. See John R. McKivigan, *The War Against Proslavery Religion: Abolition and the Northern Churches, 1830–1865* (Ithaca, N.Y.: Cornell Univ. Press, 1984), and C.C.

Goen, *Broken Churches, Broken Nation: Denominational Schisms and the Coming of the American Civil War* (Macon, Ga.: Mercer Univ. Press, 1985).

29. See *Walker's Appeal, With a Brief Sketch of His Life*. Also, *Garnet's Address to the Slaves of America* (New York: J.H. Tobit, 1848).

30. See, e.g., Donald Dayton, *Discovering An Evangelical Heritage* (New York: Harper and Row, 1976).

31. On Finney, see James D. Essig, "The Lord's Free Man: Charles G. Finney and His Abolitionism," *Civil War History* 24 (Jan. 1978):25-45. For a case study of radical evangelical abolitionism dividing northern evangelicals, see Sernett, *Abolition's Axe*, ch. 6.

32. Dayton, *Evangelical Heritage*, 134.

33. Kenneth K. Bailey, "The Post-Civil War Racial Separations in Southern Protestantism: Another Look," *Church History* 46 (Dec. 1977):463.

34. Howard N. Rabinowitz, *Race Relations in the Urban South, 1865-1890* (New York: Oxford Univ. Press, 1978), 223-25.

35. H. Shelton Smith, *In His Image, But . . . Racism in Southern Religion, 1789-1910* (Durham: Duke Univ. Press, 1972), chs. 5 & 6.

36. Samuel Hill, Jr., *Southern Churches in Crisis* (New York: Holt, Rinehart and Winston, 1967).

37. Samuel P. Jones, "Personal Consecration: 'Quit Your Meanness'," in *The American Evangelicals, 1800-1900*, ed. William G. McLoughlin (New York: Harper and Row, 1968), 186.

38. Harold J. Ockenga, "From Fundamentalism, Through New Evangelicalism to Evangelicalism," in *Evangelical Roots*, ed. Kenneth S. Kantzer (Nashville, Tenn.: Thomas Nelson, 1978), 43.

39. Henry H. Mitchell, *Black Preaching* (New York: Harper and Row, 1979), 113.

40. James S. Tinney, "Exclusivist Tendencies in Pentecostal Self-Definition: A Critique from Black Theology," *Journal of Religious Thought* 36 (Spring-Summer 1979):32.

41. James S. Tinney, "William J. Seymour: Father of Modern-Day Pentecostalism," in *Black Apostles*, ed. Randall K. Burkett and Richard Newman (Boston: G.K. Hall, 1978), 213-25.

42. Marsden, *Evangelicalism*, x.

43. James Davison Hunter, *American Evangelicalism: Conservative Religion and the Quandry of Modernity* (New Brunswick, N.J.: Rutgers Univ. Press, 1983), 49-50.

44. William H. Bentley, "Bible Believers," in Wells and Woodbridge, *The Evangelicals*, 113.

45. Howard O. Jones, *White Questions to a Black Christian* (Grand Rapids, Mich.: Zondervan, 1975). See also Richard Quebedeaux, *The Worldly Evangelicals* (New York: Harper and Row, 1978), 156-59.

46. James S. Tinney, "Black Evangelicals: Expanding the Fold," *Christianity Today* 19 (25 Apr. 1975):758. John Maust, "The NBEA: Striving to Be Both Black and Biblical," *Christianity Today* 24 (27 June 1980):785.

47. Cited by Roger Koskela, "The NBEA: When the Bible Bumps Blackness," *Christianity Today* 21 (6 May 1977):902.

48. James Locklear, "Theology-Culture Rift Surfaces Among Evangelical Blacks," *Christianity Today* 24 (23 May 1980):64.

49. Theo Witvliet, *The Way of the Black Messiah*, trans. John Bowden (Oak Park, Ill.: Meyer Stone Books, 1987), 218.

50. Raboteau, "Black Experience," 191.

CHAPTER 9

Baptists and Evangelicals

Eric H. Ohlmann

Delineating and defining evangelicalism have become increasingly difficult. Especially during the last few decades, this phenomenon has grown
more pluralistic, diverse, and complex. Whereas there used to be general
agreement on what constituted evangelical theology, today that is a matter
of considerable debate. Whereas the fellowship used to have a fairly homo-
geneous infrastructure, now it is quite diverse. Whereas differences between evangelicals and nonevangelicals were thought to be fairly clear-cut,
now they are nebulous and controversial. It has become so difficult to
agree on the identifying marks of evangelicalism and to ferret out what
constituent groups have in common that many persons disagree on who
belongs and who does not, and some are despairing of the term itself.

In a work of this length, one cannot hope to address all of the relevant
issues. Here, the focus will be on the relationship between baptists and
other evangelicals, in the hope that comparing and contrasting the two
will clarify the identity of both entities as well as the relationship between
them. More specifically, the writer will concentrate mainly on some underlying dynamics of both movements, which gave rise to and shaped the emphases characteristic of each one.

Many descriptions of evangelicalism and most accounts of baptists
have tended to reiterate the most noticeable characteristics of these bodies
and too infrequently have attempted to unearth their underlying principles and dynamics. Further, such accounts generally have provided snap-
shots of only the present state of affairs in each fellowship, rather than
movies of their entire historical lifespans. They have extracted theological
characteristics from their historical roots and shaping influences and have
tended to neglect the growing diversity within each fellowship. Consequently,
some foundational and vital factors have been overlooked.

This study will attempt to ascertain and compare those underlying
principles and dynamics of both fellowships, to unearth some of their
roots, to note at least some of their developments through the years, to
consider some of their nontheological dimensions along with theological
ones, and to keep in mind their diversities and complexities.

Sources of Baptist Life and Thought

Theologically, baptists have drawn heavily upon seventeenth-century Puritanism. Most early baptists, including their leaders, had been Puritans before becoming baptists.[1] Nor did they abandon their Puritan ideals and aspirations upon identifying with the baptists. According to their most widely-used confessions of faith,[2] commonalities with the Puritans, even after centuries of separate existence, still far exceeded differences between the two bodies. Rather than abandon their Puritan roots, baptists usually intensified those characteristics, resulting in their being designated the left wing of the Puritan movement.

The deepest motivations and inner dynamics of the baptists also were strongly provoked and profoundly shaped by the social realities of their early adherents. Characteristic baptist emphases in theology and polity naturally and logically flow from their Puritan roots, conditioned by those social influences. Therefore, to understand baptists, one also needs to examine the social matrix from which they emerged and the sociological influences that initially shaped them. Most important among these was their status as dissenters and sectarians.

Underlying Principles and Dynamics of Baptists

The religious dynamics which became most meaningful for the baptists under those circumstances included: a strong aspiration toward spiritual and ethical ideals, a strong conviction[3] of personal responsibility for the Christian life, an emphasis on religious experience, deep concern for religious freedom, and an emphasis on biblical authority.

I. ASPIRATION TOWARD SPIRITUAL AND ETHICAL IDEALS

If one presses the inner logic of baptists back to its basis, one discovers a strong conviction of the need to strive toward Christian spiritual and ethical ideals. As is common in the believers' church tradition, early baptists appropriated the discipline and mission of the New Testament church, believing that the biblical instructions to the primitive church applied equally to Christians in all ages.[4] And, like most sectarians, they tended to personalize and absolutize their ethics, straining after them with focus and intensity.

While maintaining that only God can justify and regenerate, baptists went beyond the mainline reformers in their emphasis on Christ the example, in addition to Christ the gift, and on the consequent need for human effort in sanctification. Calvin had gone beyond Luther in this regard, the Puritans beyond Calvin, and the baptists went even beyond many Puritans.[5] For them, salvation involved not only the forgiveness of sin, but also walking in newness of life. As descendants of the radical Puritans, they further tied assurance of true faith to visible manifestations of active obedience to moral laws and to laws of God with respect to the Church.[6] It was generally agreed to be the case that "a major motive for membership of an individual [in a] congregation was to keep each other pure and to clear the profession of the Gospel from scandal.'"[7] Hence, baptists became deeply committed to vigilant conformity to biblical ethics in outwardly manifested conduct.

Seventeenth-century baptist confessions of faith are among the most reliable records of these aspirations.[8] While they do not explicitly label striving for Christian maturity as the foundation of all baptist life and thought, they do reveal the authors' passions and convictions on the subject. Article 52 of "The Faith and Practice of Thirty Congregations" (1651), for instance, declared "that the *chief or only* ends of a people baptised according to the counsel of God . . . are, or ought to be, *for to walk subtably [sic]; or to give up themselves unto a holy conformity to all the Laws or Ordinances of Jesus Christ"*[9] (italics added). Besides noting that Christ is our law giver, who has given rules to live by (article 18), and that faith produces conformity to the will, graces, and virtues of Christ (article 23), the Somerset Confession (1656) uncharacteristically inserted twenty-one specific commandments of Christ, by which Christians are to glorify God and comfort their souls (article 25).[10] This same aspiration comes through in the most influential Second London Confession (1677). Although essentially a paraphrase of the Westminster Confession, in a preface its baptist authors declared their confession to be a statement of doctrine "which with our hearts we most firmly believe, and *sincerely indeavour to conform our lives to*" and expressed the hope that "the *only care and contention* of all upon whom the name of our blessed Redeemer is called, might for the future be, *to perfect holiness in the fear of the Lord . . . , vigorously to promote in others the practice of true Religion and undefiled in the sight of God and our Father*"[11] (italics added). In different ways, this deep concern for quality Christian living, individually and corporately, pervades most early baptist confessions.[12]

Since their disadvantaged status was abolished by the first amendment to the Constitution of the United States, this sectarian trait has waned some among baptists in America, but it has not been lost. One can take a dissenter out of sectarianism, but not sectarianism out of a dissenter. Even though the legal restrictions were lifted, the social stigma of being sectarians has persisted, to a greater or lesser degree, to this day, and the sectarian mentality is still very apparent in baptist thought.

2. CONVICTION OF PERSONAL RESPONSIBILITY
FOR THE CHRISTIAN LIFE

Closely related to—indeed a corollary of—the first underlying principle of baptists has been a strong conviction of personal responsibility for the Christian life. Along with other Protestants, and more than most of them, baptists have shifted the responsibility for salvation from the institutional church and its functionaries to the individual believer. They have tenaciously claimed the right of personal access to God, apart from any human intermediary, and have stressed the obligation of exercising that responsibility. Becoming a believer and living the Christian life have been viewed less as the product of some institutional rites or knowledge of a catechism than the result of personal, subjective appropriation of grace and diligent obedience to God.

Several precedents and inducements contributed to this development among early baptists. Equally important were some concurrent and powerful incentives in the English environment. Baptists were born in a period of major demoncratizing forces. As Christopher Hill put it:

> Copernicus's theory had "democratized the universe" by shattering the hierarchical structure of the heavens; Harvey "democratized" the human body by dethroning the heart. In the social sphere, Bacon's method went "far to level men's wits. . . . " The new experimental philosophy . . . made all men equal, as Hobbes was soon to proclaim. . . . Every man could be his own expert. In just the same way the radicals used the Protestant doctrine of the priesthood of all believers to justify preaching by laymen, and not merely by university-trained specialists.[13]

All these leveling influences upon the baptists, plus their need as despised sectarians to demonstrate some self-worth, resulted in a radical antiinstitutional and personal stance, reflected in their emphases on soul liberty, individual interpretation of Scripture, the priesthood of all believers, and the autonomy of the local church, as over against the more churchly alternatives. Ecclesiastically, the outcome was greatly diminshed authority and power for the clergy and the institutional church, and greatly increased choice and responsibility for individual believers. Sacraments came to be viewed as ordinances, with less focus on what God does for the recipients and more on the significance of their response. Soteriologically, too, the result was a shift toward personal responsibility for salvation.

Rather than diminishing, adherence to this conviction of personal responsibility has intensified among baptists over the years. That trend is not surprising, in light of rationalism's insistence on religion as a personal matter between the individual and God, the chronic shift in theology from the sovereignty of God to freedom of the will, the pietist and revivalist emphasis on the importance of individual decisions of faith, and the enormous impetus provided by American democracy, capitalism, and many other similar influences. Given the baptist propensity toward personal responsibility, however, baptists responded more readily to these stimuli than most other groups. As an astute analyst of baptists notes: "Here is a form of the Christian community which rests upon an experience of the Gospel which is personal, rather easily intelligible, vividly symbolized, calling for personal dedication, and open to the promptings of the Spirit."[14]

3. EMPHASIS ON RELIGIOUS EXPERIENCE

As sectarians, baptists had reasons for emphasizing religious experience. Having questioned and rejected hierarchial authorities, they needed a self-authenticating form of religion; and generally having less than the average education, they benefited from a religion demonstrated by something non-scholastic, such as experience. Having minimized the importance of objective means of grace dispensed by institutions, it was natural to shift to subjective and experiential religion, appropriated personally. Having rejected infant baptism as the rite of initiation into the church and having adopted the principle of regenerate church membership, baptists also needed some verification of regeneration. An experiential approach provided that measurement. As Walter Rauschenbusch assessed the outcome, "Experience is our sole requisite for receiving baptism; it is fundamental in our church life."[15]

As persons whose primary concern was to live out the spiritual and ethical injunctions given to the primitive church, early baptists imbibed the biblical paradigms of Christian living and diligently sought to relive them in their own experience. As heirs of Puritanism, they were also solicitous of experiential verification of their salvation in outward Christian conduct.

Although experiential religion generally has been characteristic of sects,[16] formation of the early baptists during the seventeenth century surrounded them with additional and powerful incentives for this perspective. The Reformation already had advanced the idea by "the principle of *sola fides*, which removes the center of authority from ecclesiastical institutions and relocates it in the elect soul."[17] The immediate context in England, however, further bolstered this approach. The practical mathematics and sciences were mushrooming. And by synthesizing experimentation and the inductive method, Francis Bacon and some of his contemporaries popularized the notion that one "arrives at useful knowledge by experience, not by scholastic disputation."[18]

"The quest for personal religious *experience* . . . is closely akin to the

experimental spirit in science,"[19] according to Christopher Hill. It is also a
form of pushing up from below, against the authority of books and learning, and of asserting that one's own experience is the best part of learning.
Consequently, the new experimental method contributed to an analogous
demand for firsthand religious experience,[20] especially by dissenters such
as the baptists. It provided a demonstration of religious commitment by
a "test of the senses and the heart as against intellectual exercises divorced
from practice."[21]

Immersion in such ideas during their most impressionable years had
a profound impact upon the baptists. The Second London Confession
reveals that baptists, like the experimental predestinarians, were greatly
concerned that "none might deceive themselves, by resting in, and trusting
to, a form of Godliness, without the power of it, and inward experience
of the efficacy of those truths that are professed by them."[22] This concern
so dominated their view of the Christian life that one insightful analysis
of them has alleged: "Experimental religion was then for the early Baptists
a fundamental tenet; it was more than that, it was their *raison d'etre.*"[23]

This is one characteristic of early baptists that definitely has been
enhanced among their successors over the years. Baptists may not have
been consistently experiential, but they always have had an affinity for
that position, so that "wherever and whenever special homage was paid
to experimental religion, there and then Baptists prospered."[24] And from
each of those successive awakenings and spurts of growth, they gained further impetus for emphasizing the experiences of conscious repentance,
new birth, and assurance of salvation. Thus Walter Ruschenbusch observed:

> The Christian faith as Baptists hold it sets *spiritual experience* boldly to the
> front as the one great thing in religion. . . . Take our churches right through
> and nothing so draws and wins them in preaching as the note of personal ex-
> perience of God; nothing so touches and melts them in the social meeting
> as the heart-note of experience.[25]

4. SOLICITUDE FOR RELIGIOUS FREEDOM

A necessary corollary to dissent and personal religion is religious liberty.
As unlawful dissenters from established churches in England, the majority of American colonies, and most other countries, baptists constantly
stood in danger of arrest, fines, imprisonment, confiscation of property,
torture, or banishment. Consequently, their circumstances naturally aroused
a powerful passion for religious liberty, the freedom to follow their own
consciences in matters of religion.

Personal religion, especially when accompanied by a desire for high
ethical achievement, also requires religious liberty. How can one relate to
God personally and assume some responsibility for the quality of that rela-

tionship, if one is not free to follow conscience? One is denied the very means of salvation if deprived of the opportunity for voluntary, intentional responses to God's grace.

Hence, baptists placed a high premium on religious liberty, adhering to it tenaciously and advocating it strenuously. "They popped out of the womb kicking and screaming for liberty."[26] Nothing else energized them more, was the subject of more writing,[27] or was undertaken at greater cost to life and property. Baptist and nonbaptist writers have acknowledged baptists as the most vocal, active, and persistent champions of the cause in colonial America.[28] And to this day, they cooperate more with each other in this regard than in any other venture.

5. EMPHASIS ON THE SUPREME AUTHORITY OF SCRIPTURE

Like most Protestants, baptists adopted the Reformation principle of *sola scriptura* and discovered that advancing Scripture as the sole source of their faith and practice was a strategic method of challenging certain beliefs and practices that they believed were based more on tradition than on the Bible. In addition, several concurrent developments in England produced an environment in which "truth could no longer be imposed from above, by authority: it had to be rebuilt from below, on individual conviction."[29]

The distinctive emphases of baptists further buttressed their dependence upon the Bible. Having separated themselves from the conventional authorities of church and tradition, for instance, they were more dependent upon the remaining authority of Scripture than less sectarian types. Because of their sense of personal responsibility for the Christian life and their view that all generations need to reappropriate the mission of the apostolic church,[30] they had a greater need to consult the manual for Christian living, namely the Bible, especially since it was believed to contain everything necessary to know about salvation, to believe in, and to observe. Because of their emphasis on religious liberty, they claimed the right to interpret Scripture for themselves and needed to assume the accompanying responsibility. And as aspirants for Christian ideals, they tended to treat Scripture as absolute law.

Accordingly, baptist confessions of faith regularly refer to the Bible as the supreme or sole source of faith and practice.[31] And in reaction to developments such as historical criticism, they have increasingly shifted to the expression, *"sole* source of faith and practice."

Comparing Baptists and Evangelicals

How do evangelicals compare with baptists on these underlying principles and dynamics? Similarities and differences on these foundational items are very significant, because they represent core values and commitments which originally gave rise to and subsequently have shaped the other facets of each group.

Before addressing that comparison, however, we need to indicate how the term *evangelical* is being used here. In this comparison, the label is employed in an Anglo-American sense, primarily to designate a trans-denominational coalition of Christians who share the basic ethos and central commitments of those movements within Protestantism (such as Puritanism, German Pietism, Wesleyanism, New Lightism of the Great Awakening, and New Sideism of the Second Great Awakening) which commonly have been designated evangelical for etymological reasons.[32] This historical approach is considered important in that it brings to the subject a perspective broader than the present-day expression of the evangelical phenomenon — which is, so to speak, only the last frame in a long movie.

Within this fellowship there are theological diversities, varieties in denominational and other organizational affiliations, distinctions in racial and ethnic origins, and other differences — nearly to the point of obscuring any common characteristics — so that there is considerable disagreement about the particulars of its commonalities. Yet there is also a common spirit, and there are some broader values and mutual attractions — about which there is wider agreement — which draw evangelicals together into an identifiable entity, warranting the designation of a fellowship. Among these are the same ones found among the baptists.

I. ASPIRATION TOWARD SPIRITUAL AND ETHICAL IDEALS

Evangelicals generally share the believers' church ideal of spiritual and ethical maturity and committed striving toward that end. Many of them have not been formed by the same influences as baptists, but most of them have had an affinity for the believers' church position on several issues, with the result that the outcome in this particular characteristic is similar.

Supplementing shaping influences coming from the believers' church tradition have been those of the evangelical heritage itself. They include the Puritan emphasis on obedience as part of the covenant of grace and their diligent efforts to prove their election;[33] the anabaptist and pietist stress on separation from the world; the Wesleyan accentuation of sanctification (even to perfection), which since has been supplemented by the holiness and pentecostal emphases; and the analogous or resultant influences of the American awakenings.

The revivalist emphasis on conversion also has been important. In American revivalism, conversion has been seen as more than an objective and often inperceptible act of regeneration on the part of God. Instead, it has been viewed as "a complete transformation, an overhaul from the inside out, which results in our reversing directions, transferring loyalties, and changing commitments."[34] It initiates a process of conscious and observable sanctification, which is expected to continue and progress.

Given all these incentives for exemplary Christian living, it would be surprising if evangelicals did not share this concern. Indeed, evangelicals as a whole may exemplify it more than baptists as a whole do. The causes and particulars of this characteristic vary between baptists and some evangelicals, but the general thrust is largely shared.

2. EMPHASIS ON PERSONAL RELIGION

Historically, evangelicals especially have imbibed the Reformation shift to personal religion and have increasingly embellished it. How individuals personally respond to God's offer of grace always has been considered most decisive. Means of grace have been viewed as important, but from the evangelical perspective, they avail nothing unless individuals personally appropriate the grace which is proclaimed.

Many of the forces that induced baptists to move in this direction have been experienced by other evangelicals as well. Most significant has been the evangelical emphasis on a personal conversion experience. Whereas baptists for many years had been influenced strongly by their sectarian status, evangelicals have been drawn to personal religion primarily by their views on conversion. They have shared the good news in anticipation of eliciting a personal response, which has been premised on the assumption that persons are free to respond and have a responsibility to do so. In fact, the emergence and growth of evangelicalism closely paralleled shifts of emphasis in theology, from the divine to the human role in salvation. That is not to say that all evangelicals view justifying faith more as a decision than as a gift. Calvinist evangelicals, for instance, have associated personal responsibility more with Christian discipline and sanctification than with making a decision of faith. But we must note a correlation between evangelicalism and an emphasis on personal response to the gospel. Evangelicalism has had a propensity to expand the limits of human freedom in salvation, and with that freedom has come a growing sense of personal responsibility.

3. EMPHASIS ON RELIGIOUS EXPERIENCE

An experience of conversion has come to be almost synonymous with evangelicalism. While experience is not the source of evangelical theology, as Kenneth S. Kantzer has noted, "without experience by which it is personally appropriated, good theology is not only unattainable but is utterly worthless."[35] From the evangelical perspective, "a person becomes an evangelical Christian by having a subjective conversion experience, which is described by such terms as: 'born again,' 'saved,' 'regenerated,' or 'initial sanctification,'"[36] and the Christian life is essentially a lifelong process of active, experiential sanctification. The other side of this coin is a tendency "to diminish the significance of the sacraments, a sacerdotal clergy, authoritative hierarchical structures, and doctrinal complexities."[37]

Puritanism already had moved decisively in this direction. The "experimental predestinarian tradition,"[38] for instance, generated intense exertions to gain assurance of saving faith through visible godliness. In their use of Scripture, according to Norman Pettit, Puritans also "never consciously separated experiential from biblical religion, but always assumed they were one and the same."[39] Probably few, accordingly, ever have depicted the symptoms of repentance in as vividly experiential terms as William Perkins did when he portrayed them as "a change and alteration of the body as it were burning anew — and it causes the entrails to rise, the liver to rowle in the body and it sets a great heat in the bones and consumes the flesh more than any sickness can."[40] Most Puritan morphologies of conversion, like that of Perkins, are full of conscious experiences.

What had developed as standard practices in anabaptism, Puritanism, German pietism, and Wesleyanism received a massive and brilliant defence in Jonathan Edwards' *Religious Affections*.[41] Combined with the added stimulus of the First and Second Great Awakenings, this experiential thrust in Christianity became a permanent and prominent feature of American evangelicalism.[42]

Not all evangelicals are equally experiential. Nevertheless, the impetus given by the Puritans to visible Christian conduct as a means of verifying supernatural regeneration also has continued to grow over the years and seems to be a powerful motivation for most evangelicals.

4. SOLICITUDE FOR RELIGIOUS LIBERTY

Concern for and advocacy of religious liberty have not been as prominent among other evangelicals as they have been among baptists. But some of the motivations for the baptists' fervor also were experienced by other evangelicals. If the Christian life is a matter of personal religion, as they believed it is, then the freedom to exercise that responsibility is imperative. Nor do persons strongly strive for ethical achievement unless given the freedom to follow their consciences in determining what those goals are, and a free rein to pursue them.

Therefore, while evangelicals have not always advocated religious liberty or even approved of it (e.g., the New England Puritans), they usually have had an affinity for it. The German pietists resisted state and ecclesiastical restrictions on their personal faith, to a point often verging on advocacy of separation of church and state. Wesleyans had the same struggle, ultimately resulting in separation. And the revivalism of the Great Awakening generated widespread evangelical support for civil and religious liberty, even warranting cooperation with the rationalists in an effort to achieve it.[43] In other words, although not cleaving as tenaciously to this principle as the baptists, evangelicals have shared the spirit.

5. EMPHASIS ON BIBLICAL AUTHORITY

With the reformers' reassessment of the authority lodged in tradition and ecclesiastical hierarchies came a heavier reliance on Scripture. And with the shift from the church as primary agent for the Christian life to more personal responsibility came a shift from institutional means of salvation (the sacraments) to a means available to all, namely, the Bible. Having some responsibility for one's Christian life called for more freedom to examine the basic handbook and to be familiar with its stipulations.

Evangelicals, both past and present, usually have agreed with this emphasis. Besides having their roots in the Reformation, their stress on personal religion (which requires informed Christians) has reinforced it. Of course, numerous other factors, such as the Enlightenment's dependence upon reason, also have contributed to the evangelical insistence that Scripture must be our supreme (or only) authority for faith and practice. But so consistent is the agreement on this feature of evangelicalism that no further evidence is needed.

Conclusions

Similarities between baptists and other evangelicals on these underlying principles and dynamics are critical, because they represent some commonalities on a very germinal level. These convictions determined the spirit of each movement and were the source of their other doctrines and practices, or at least strongly influenced or shaped them. Different views and behaviors may emerge from this same basis, but the prevailing spirit of the two traditions is similar, making for significant affinities between them, such as tendencies toward believers' churches, believers' baptism, diminishing divine action in the sacraments, concern for the many ramifications of religious liberty, emphasis on evangelism and missions, social concern, and ecumenicity.

There are differences between baptists and other evangelicals regarding some characteristic baptist emphases. These two movements were shaped by different influences and at times took somewhat different directions. Further, there are varying degrees of commitment to some of these beliefs and practices among evangelicals. At the same time, the similarities between them exceed the differences, and most evangelicals consider these emphases important. One of the major reasons for that agreement is an extensive and vital commonality on underlying principles and dynamics, which in turn have done much to shape the rest of the two movements along similar lines.

NOTES

1. Winthrop S. Hudson, "Baptists Were Not Anabaptists," *The Chronicle* 16 (Oct. 1953):173.

2. The Second London Confession, the Orthodox Creed, the Philadelphia Confesion, and the New Hampshire Confession.

3. The term *convictions* is used here in the sense of beliefs which are a part of one's essential nature, without which that nature would be different. Cf. James William McClendon, Jr., *Systematic Theology: Ethics* (Nashville, Tenn.: Abingdon, 1986), 22–23.

4. Ibid., 31–35.

5. For an expanded account of this case, see Eric H. Ohlmann, "The Essence of Baptists: A Reexamination," *Perspectives in Religious Studies* 13 (Winter 1986):83–104.

6. Stephen Brachlow, "Puritan Theology and General Baptist Origins," *Baptist Quarterly* 31 (Oct. 1985):179–89.

7. B.R. White, *The English Baptists of the Seventeenth Century* (London: The Baptist Historical Society, 1983), 69.

8. Confessions of faith are not the only records. Among others are: polemical writings, sermons, devotional materials, and spiritual biographies. But confessions of faith are the most important because they are the most broadly representative sources.

9. William L. Lumpkin, *Baptist Confessions of Faith* (Chicago: Judson Press, 1959), 183.

10. Ibid., 208–11.

11. Ibid., 246–47.

12. Ibid., 165 and 285, provide some examples of concern for the life of entire congregations.

13. Christopher Hill, *Intellectual Origins of the English Revolution* (Oxford, England: Clarendon Press, 1965), 112.

14. Daniel D. Williams, "The Mystery of the Baptists," *Foundations* 1 (Jan. 1958):9.

15. Walter Rauschenbusch, "Why I am A Baptist," *The Baptist Leader*, revised reprint of series from *Rochester Baptist Monthly*, edited and introducd by H.H. Barnette (Jan. 1958):8.

16. Ernst Troeltsch, *The Social Teachings of the Churches*, 2 vols., trans. Olive Wyon (New York: Harper & Bros., 1960), 1:692.

17. Sacvan Bercovitch, *The Puritan Origins of the American Self* (New Haven, Conn.: Yale Univ. Press, 1975), 10.

18. Hill, *Intellectual Origins*, 183.

19. Christopher Hill, *The Century of Revolution,* 1603-1714 (Edinburgh, Scotland: Thomas Nelson and Sons, 1961), 180.

20. Hill, *Intellectual Origins*, 112-13.

21. Ibid., 294.

22. Ibid., 247.

23. Edwin S. Gaustad, "Baptists and Experimental Religion," *The Chronicle* 15 (July 1952):111. Gaustad uses the term *experimental* in much the same way as more recent usage employs *experiential.*

24. Gaustad, "Baptists and Experimental Religion"; cf. McClendon, *Systematic Theology*, 38; Edwin S. Gaustad, "Where are the Lions?", *Christian History* 4 (1985):28.

25. Rauschenbusch, "Why I Am a Baptist," 8.

26. James Leo Garrett, E. Glenn Hinson, and James E. Tull, *Are Southern Baptists "Evangelicals"?* (Macon, Ga.: Mercer Univ. Press, 1983).

27. See, e.g., H. Leon McBeth, *English Baptist Literature on Religious Liberty to* 1689 (New York: Arno, 1980).

28. William G. McLoughlin, *New England Dissent,* 1630-1833 (Cambridge, Mass.: Harvard Univ. Press, 1971), xvi; Leo Pfeffer, *Church, State, and Freedom* (Boston: Beacon, 1953), 99.

29. Hill, *Intellectual Origins*, 294.

30. White, *English Baptists*, 11.

31. Lumpkin, *Confessions;* G. Keith Parker, *Baptists in Europe: History and Confessions of Faith* (Nashville, Tenn.: Broadman Press, 1982).

32. Cf. George Marsden, ed., *Evangelicalism and Modern America* (Grand Rapids, Mich.: Eerdmans, 1984), ix-xvi.

33. R.T. Kendall, *Calvin and English Calvinism to* 1649 (Oxford: Oxford Univ. Prss, 1979), 51-138.

34. Jon Johnston, *Will Evangelicalism Survive Its Own Popularity?* (Grand Rapids, Mich.: Zondervan, 1980), 21.

35. Kenneth S. Kantzer, "Unity and Diversity in Evangelical Faith," in *The Evangelicals*, ed. David F. Wells and John D. Woodbridge (Nashville, Tenn.: Abingdon, 1975), 52.

36. Johnston, *Will Evangelicalism Survive*, 21. See also Marsden, *Evangelicalism*, x.

37. Sydney E. Ahlstrom, "From Puritanism to Evangelicalism: A Critical Perspective," in Wells and Woodbridge, *The Evangelicals*, 270.

38. Kendall, *Calvin and English Calvinism*, 79-138.

39. Norman Pettit, *The Heart Prepared: Grace and Conversion in Purian Spiritual Life* (New Haven, Conn.: Yale Univ. Pres, 1966), 9.

40. Cited in John T. McNeill, *Modern Christian Movements* (Philadelphia: Westminster, 1954), 31.

41. Jonathan Edwards, *Religious Affections*, ed. John E. Smith (New Haven, Conn.: Yale Univ. Press, 1959).

42. Cf. Alan Heimert, *Religion and the American Minds: From the Great Awakening to the Revolution* (Cambridge, Mass: Harvard Univ. Press, 1966), 40-42.

43. Sidney E. Mead, *The Lively Experiment: The Shaping of Christianity in America* (New York: Harper and Row, 1963), 27-35.

CHAPTER 10

Pietism: Theology in Service of Living Toward God

C. John Weborg

Introduction

Pietism and evangelicalism are critiques — pietism of orthodoxy, whether Lutheran and/or Reformed; and evangelicalism of both fundamentalism and liberalism. Pietism has sought the life and liveliness of faith, evangelicalism more the truth of faith. Pietism has sought after a public and relational coherence between Scripture and the life of the believer. Its apologetic therefore is more sociological in character, while evangelicalism's apologetic seeks to show a doctrinal coherence between Scripture and theological statements. Because both the objects of reform and the sources of the two movements, particularly that of the "new evangelicalism" in America, are varied, it may be indicated that evangelicalism has more to do with pietism than pietism with evangelicalism. I will use one form of pietism (classical Lutheran) to foster this engagement, seeking to show pietism's commitment to practical, not polemical and philosophical, theology.

Practical Theology

Piety has to do with godliness. The focus of its concern is a way of life that is pleasing to God, the embodiment of which is loving the Lord God with all one's heart, soul, and mind, and one's neighbor as one's self. Few have stated this definition of theology with more clarity than William Ames (1576-1633), in *The Marrow of Theology*, one of the most persuasive and pervasively read of Puritan books: "Theology is the doctrine or teaching of living toward God,"[1] and "nor is there anything in theology which does not refer to the final end or to the means related to that end — all of which refer directly to practice."[2]

On the German and Lutheran side, Philip Jakob Spener (1635-1705) had asserted that theology was a practical discipline.[3] There is no thought here, either on the Puritan or pietist side, that "practical" refers to what is workable as opposed to what is ideal. In American usage, this concern for practicality often gets reduced to a question: "Will it work?" The implication is that the "workability" of the proposal or project is the latter's sole justification. Pietists tend to say that the Christian faith is "done" just as much as it is believed. It is practiced just as much as it is proclaimed, and, as this essay will seek to show, the practice of the faith is a form of proclamation. The issue here is not "Will it work?" as much as it is the will to work and the task of working the will. The Christian faith is to be practiced by all who name the name of Christ.

There is a context for this emphasis on the practical. In the realm of theology, Reformed and Lutheran pietism formed a reaction to a highly systematized theology, influenced as to form by the philosophy of Aristotle and cast into permanent shape in the form of books of confession, e.g., for the Lutherans, the Augsburg Confession. It was often the custom to write these confessions in a way so as, on the one hand, to state clearly what is believed and, on the other hand, to state whom and what is repudiated — a form and method used currently by the framers of the Chicago Statement on Biblical Inerrancy. In the development of Reformation theology, these named repudiations were referred to as the *damnamus* clauses. When theology is done in this fashion, it cannot help but be highly polemical. Along with that comes the need for theologians constantly to develop their skills in polemics, i.e., the exposure of error.

On the Dutch scene, for example, the conflict between, on the one hand, the orthodox party of Calvinism and, on the other, those of Arminian persuasion or the growing number of followers of Cocceius, reached tragic, if not comic, proportions. The followers of Jacobus Arminius (1560–1609) questioned the prevailing notion of predestination, while the followers of Johannes Cocceius (1603–1669), began developing a system of biblical interpretation that much later would be referred to as a salvation-history perspective. This latter view did not treat the Bible as a storehouse of proof-texts for dogmatic assertions, but rather thought of the Bible as an unfolding history of God's work for human salvation. So bad did the polemics get that admirals who commanded ships for the Dutch East India Company threatened to dock chaplains one month's pay for dogmatic argumentation aboard ships. One admiral even threatened a chaplain with confinement for his polemical demeanor![4]

The Lutheran side fared no better. Can you imagine a year's diet of Jacob Andreae's sermons, devoted as they were to an attack on papalism, Zwinglianism, Schwenkfeldianism, and anabaptism, each series lasting three months in the year 1658? Allan C. Deeter's 1963 dissertation cites examples from educational systems whereby students were assigned to keep notebooks on preachers, later to be turned in to various inspectors for analysis.[5] Often the sermons contained lengthy quotations in Latin and Greek, placing them beyond the comprehension of most laypeople. The upshot was a climate of suspicion, sophistication, and alienation. Polemics, even concerning the gospel, are not necessarily a proclamation of the gospel. The pietists knew that and sought to change the situation. There was a need for *theologia practica*, i.e., the teaching of faith, hope, and love as primary theology, to replace *theologia Spinosa*, i.e., prickly, thorny teaching which only irritates the soul.[6] Had faith, hope, and love been stressed as the fruits of a Christian life, indeed as indices of it, there would have been far less to single out for lament, both in the lives of Christians and in the life of the church. The following sections will pick up the matter of ecclesiology, develop the notion of community as symbol, and show the theological shift pietism made in stressing the fruits and not the origin of faith.

Laments

Spener also turned his observations to the common life of Germans. Beyond lamenting spiritual lethargy spawned by territorial churches, drunkenness, indifference by clergy to spiritual concerns, and the prevalence of lawsuits, he took note of a pervasive lack of love and neighborliness.[7] It was everyone for herself or himself, a mode of life contrary to the Jerusalem community of Christians described in the Book of Acts. In Acts one finds a community of goods practiced among the believers. What Spener lamented was that the people of his day knew little about care for the poor and their place in the community. All that people knew how to do was to throw a few coins to the poor and let them be. Then, when this somewhat "restorationist" view of the primitive church was preached, it was dismissed as strange teaching.[8] For Spener, this very reaction was what summoned him to call for more use of the entire Bible in the church and for the discussion of it in conventicles. To the extent that Scripture was used primarily for support of dogmatics, to that extent biblical support for the practice of theology was severely curtailed. Consequently, the German people lacked a comprehensive view of Scripture and of how all of life was comprehended in Scripture. Pietism sought to remedy that.

Ecclesiology

It is often thought that pietism concerns itself most with the spiritual re-
birth and renewal of individuals. Charges of subjectivism and individualism are rampant. While it is true that pietists tended to stress the regener-
ative power of the gospel more than the external and forensic benefits of
justification, their goal was not just new persons. The goal was a renewed
church, as the full title of Spener's work shows: *Pia Desideria, or Heartfelt Desire for a God-Pleasing Reform of the True Evangelical Church,
Together with Several Simple Christian Proposals Looking Toward this
End* (1675). Ecclesiology has not received its due in pietism studies. Had
it done so, perhaps the charges of excessive inwardness and rampant subjectivity would have been mitigated to some extent. I argue that pietism
seeks a sociological apologetic for the gospel, where coherence is looked
for between Scripture and life. A fruitful Christian life is evidence of the
power and therefore of the truthfulness of the gospel. Hence the call for
holiness of life, both of persons and of congregations, is not to promote
a negative separatism but to show forth faith, hope, and love as signs of
the gospel's triumph over unbelief, hopelessness, hate, and indifference.
It takes congregations, not just individuals, to achieve this triumph. The
reason is that the fruit of the Holy Spirit cannot be in evidence where people are not in relation. Spener's perspective and proposals for church renewal bear this out and acquire a forceful technology.

In Part 1 of the *Pia Desideria*, Spener discusses the offenses caused
by the unholy state of the church. For one thing, the Jews, whom he des-
perately wants to see converted, are not moved to seek the faith taught
by Christians, due to the unholy life evident in the church. He notes that
Jews could not possibly know that Christians believe that Jesus is God,
because Christians do not obey his commandments. A second group of
people kept from the true faith by the dissolute character of congregational life includes the papists and other persons who do not share the
faith of what Spener thought to be true Christianity. Spener notes in part
2 that if the Jews are to be converted, the church will have to manifest
a holier state. Much the same sentiment pertains toward the conversion
of other persons.[9] To that end, Spener speaks of his longing that a renewed church, one in which there is more "wheat than tares," might be
an "occasion" for the conversion of others. The German word he uses for
"occasion" is *Verlassung*,[10] a word that carries intimations of instrumentality but not causality.

It is in this context that Spener returns to a fascination with the primitive church. While not a "restorationist," Spener does see a model, if not

a norm, for the work he sets out to do. His extensive citations from early church history clearly support his thesis that such times of congregational purity, love, and mutual support did exist and did exert powerful influences over persons and social conditions. His citations from Scripture show his conviction that, since God is able to do what God commands of us, namely, to be sanctified, and since God has promised the conversion of the Jews and the downfall of Rome, it is not enought to wait idly for these promises to be fulfilled. It is incumbent upon Christians, and in particular the church, to be the occasion for the fulfillment or working out of these promises. The Holy Spirit is the one who effects this work of obedient faith, making possible a "life together," to use Bonhoeffer's words, powerful enough to commend the gospel to any who have eyes to see and ears to hear.[11]

Community as Symbol

The biblical character and roots of this mode of thinking have not always been noticed, nor has the power of it been acknowledged. A recent study of the Book of Deuteronomy by S. Dean McBride, Jr., is suggestive. He notes that Josephus uses the term *politeia*, not *nomos*, to describe the "judicial substance" of the book. When Torah is represented this way, it takes the form of, and functions as, a constitution for the community. This is a covenantal law, "the divinely authorized social order that Israel must implement."[12] In a related study, J. Gerald Janzen argues that the "covenant relation becomes in effect the vocation of the human society to image God," and that "the laws are a socially ordering extension of God's redemption in the Exodus."[13] The references to a social order needing to be implemented and a social ordering as an extension of God's redemption also can be used to name Spener's concern for a renewed church, models for which he found in Acts and in primitive church history. In fact, as a key text Spener used Deut. 15:4–5, which reads: "But there will be no poor among you (for the Lord will bless you in the land which the Lord gives you for an inheritance to possess), if only you will obey the voice of the Lord your God, being careful to do all this commandment which I give you this day" (RSV). Spener then went on to laud the institution of tithing as a way of making distribution to all of the poor. This one example indicates how much Spencer would be amenable to the life-giving and life-preserving character of a polity that gives a place to all and that extends the benefits of creation to each who has need.[14] When this happens, it can be said of that community, as was said of the church in Acts 4:32ff, that the social and spiritual unity of the people, the nonpossessive attitude of the believers, was such that there was no needy person among them. The text then notes that the apostles gave testimony to Jesus with great power, and great grace was upon them all. The very embodiment of this grace is a form of its communication. When thus embodied, the Christian gospel of grace cannot help but attract attention — another biblical note sounded by Saint Paul and implicitly recognized by Spener.

Nowhere in the writings of Saint Paul does this theme come to the fore more than in Romans 9–11, the well-known passage that relates the church to Israel. How shall the Israelites be brought to a confession of Jesus Christ as Lord? In Rom. 11:11, he says that, through the trespass of the Jews, salvation has come to the Gentiles in order to make the Jews jealous. In Rom. 11:14, Saint Paul explains his apostleship to the Gentiles as a way, through Gentile believers, of making the Jews jealous of the gospel. Hans Küng speaks of a ministry of "jealousy-making":

> The Church, in its whole existence, must be a token of the salvation it has received. In its whole existence it must bear witness to the messianic fulfillment. In its whole existence it must vie with Israel in addressing itself to a world that has turned its back on God, and in demonstrating to it, with authority and love, the word that has been fulfilled, the righteousness that has been revealed, the mercy that has been accepted, the reign of God which has already begun. Its whole life, lived in a convincing way, would be a call to all men to believe the good news, to experience a change of heart and to unite themselves with its Messiah.[16]

Ernst Käsemann has picked up the immensity of this theme in his work, *Romans*. The theme of the Jews made jealous by other nations is a Deuteronomic theme (32:21) made current by Saint Paul in Rom. 10:19, the background for Romans 11. Käsemann has traced the apocalyptic features of this issue, particularly how the conversion of the Jews signals the approaching end. Hence Saint Paul's ministry to the Gentiles and his zealous concern for a church righteous in its ways is directed toward a "jealousy-making" ministry, since God will bring the Gentiles to repentance in order that the Jews might be made jealous of what has been given to them. "It is," writes Käsemann, "the apocalyptic dream of a man who had tried to do in a decade what two thousand years had not managed to do."[16] Käsemann's point would not have been lost on Spener, who placed the conversion of the Jews and the downfall of Rome in the category of the apocalyptic activity of God.[17]

Another way of understanding the concern of pietists for a holy church can be provided by current work in sociology and anthropology. The work of F.W. Dillistone[18] regarding the nature and function of symbols has called attention to Victor Turner's understanding of the dynamic and processual nature of symbols. In such systems, there is a concern for "symbols operating as dynamic systems of signifiers," particularly related to periods of, and persons in, transitions.[19]

University of Arizona anthropologist Peter Stromberg did a study of a congregation deeply rooted in pietism, the Immanuel Church (*Immanuelskyrkan*) of the Swedish Mission Covenant in Stockholm, Sweden. His book bears the provocative title, *Symbols of Community,* and finds the material delineated in Dillistone and Turner useful in understanding the character of a pietistic congregation. Stromberg notes that in the heritage of Pietism an inner and personal relationship with God is foundational. Each self is unique and relates to God personally. Orthodoxy's failure was that it did not "build a bridge between the uniqueness of the self and the symbol of faith. The relationship is thus impersonal."[20]

The community derives its sense from the prior relation to God. Those participating in this fundamental relation share it in common with others who know the same experience.[21] Relatedness, apart from its intrinsic value, becomes symbolic because it is a form, embodiment, and signifier of a new life. In this sense, the life of Jesus can be termed symbolic, in that what he said and did invites and enlivens faith, hope, and love.[22] In fact, to study the life of Jesus is to study a life in relation to all sorts and conditions of persons. Considered from that standpoint, Jesus was a "set of relations." As such these relations were indicators, symbols of what might happen to persons who open themselves to Jesus, as presented in the Gospels and in the gospel. Jesus not only "symbolizes" what God has become and has done for persons in Jesus, but also what persons can become before God, themselves, and others in Jesus. Stromberg writes, "The significance of religious symbols to which believers are committed is that the believers enter into relationships with those symbols . . . believers immerse themselves in the symbol so that the person-symbol relationship is much more than an aspect of thought; it is an experience."[23] Again, "a relationship of commitment occurs when the symbol and the self are, at least momentarily, merged. Such a relationship therefore always entails the possibility of self because it enables the self to be seen in terms of the symbol it has collapsed into."[24]

Thus, for Stromberg, the set of relations which a congregation "is," is the symbolic presentation of the gospel. These transformed people are an embodiment of the work of God in Christ through the power of the Holy Spirit. Turner's notion of "symbols operating as dynamic systems of signifiers" fits Stromberg's observations of the life of Immanuelskyrkan. It also sets this life off from the confessional tradition, which also speaks of the creeds and confessions as "symbols." A symbol embodied as a system or statement of faith entails a relationship different from the one demanded by a symbol embodied as a relation of care and concern. The former is less personal and more intellectual in character, while the latter not only is more personal, it is self-involving. A congregation is a kind of symbol different from a confession of faith.

The ideas of a "divinely authorized social order" (McBride), the social order as an extension of God's redemptive work (Janzen), a "jealousy-making ministry" (Küng), and the congregation as a symbolic activity and embodiment of the grace it signifies (Stromberg)—all serve to highlight in particular Spener's call for a reborn church and in general pietism's interest in the regenerate church. The power of such a congregation is incalculable and is intrinsic to the communication of the gospel. Pietism has a high view of the church as symbol. Spener could have rested happily with Küng's notion of a "jealousy-making ministry," for that is what he found in the life of the Jerusalem church. For good or ill, relations, relating, and relationship acquire at least a quasisacramental character in pietistic communities.

Fruitfulness

No-one who reads the *Pia Desideria* will fail to notice the frequent use of the term "fruit."[25] In one passage, Spener says that the perfection demanded of the church does not mean the elimination of hyprocrites. What is required is the absence of "manifest offenses," and anyone who is guilty of such should not be let off without reproach, because, if attention is not paid to this matter, the weeds will cover the grain. What should dominate is the fruit of the faith of the people.[26] Fruit includes all that pertains to godliness, but especially the initiative of love. The practice of true Christianity has to flow from a deep, inward source in order to be a positive force. Otherwise, it is negative, in that it only avoids what is openly offensive and lives an outwardly moral life.[27] Martin Schmidt has taken note of this emphasis on the fruit of faith by showing that, whereas during the Reformation the major issue was the origin of faith, for pietism the issue was the outcome of faith.[28] The same Holy Spirit who provided the gift of faith to undeserving and impotent sinners, the pietists argued, is able to bring about the transformation of life. Hence there was every reason to stress the regeneration of persons, repentance of sin, and heartfelt service to God and neighbor.

The stress on fruitful faith is in keeping with the narrative unfolding here. Fruit is visible on trees in the orchard and available to any who want to pick it. The fruit of faith is made visible and available in the lives of persons and congregations. Spiritual fruit is needed in a jealousy-producing ministry. This metaphor leads to at least three additional concerns: Lutheran pietism's interpretation of the eschatological assertions in article 17 of the Augsburg Confession, the effect of this eschatology on the idea of the church, and the doing of the word of God as a way to understand the Word of God.

Augsburg Confesion, Article 17

It has already been noted that Spener placed his concern for a renewed church in an apocalyptic setting, namely, in the plan of God to convert the Jews, bring about the downfall of Rome, and reach out to the alienated. None of these events would happen until the church got its house in order and became a sign of life. Hence, Spener found article 17 of the Augsburg Confession a problem to deal with, because it appeared to the conventional interpreters of the confession to forbid belief in an earthly millennium, on grounds that it is a worldly kingdom of just that sort that the Jews were seeking. Lutherans also said that such a kingdom would flirt with anabaptist notions of building the kingdom by works — or worse, by protest methods, raising the ghost of Thomas Münzer!

Spener[29] and Bengel[30] (1687–1752) replied that the article forbade only a *false* belief in an earthly kingdom of Christ, a millennium that humans would build. But for pietists there was another way to argue the case. If the doctrine of justification by grace through faith is used as a model, then the very monergism that brings about justification can bring about the kingdom. God will do it and, in the case of Spener, in a post-millennial form. Concrete fruit of the gospel, present and active in the lives of persons and churches, was intrinsic to God's prophetic program. Since God had promised better times for the church, any activity in that regard was not a human effort trying to usurp what was rightfully God's work. It was the obedience of faith, and it was faith active in love, first as love of God and his Word and then as love of neighbor. The millennium would be a period of maximum fruitfulness.

Ecclesiology Revisited

If the church were to have this significant role in eschatology, it stands to reason that ecclesiology would come in for scrutiny. In the Augsburg Confession, article 7 confesses that the church is the "assembly of all true believers among whom the gospel is preached in its purity and the holy sacraments are administered according to the Gospel." Article 8 acknowledges that even hypocrites and open sinners may be present. The implication is that, at the end of the gospel era, the true church will be known. Until then, the church is a mixed company of saints and sinners, wheat and tares. In contrast to this, the pietists sought to "de-eschatologize" the church a bit, by stressing the fruit of faith in the lives of the believers. This historicizes the church, making the "true" church more visible now as a sign of promise, in order that it might evoke jealousy and be a symbol "operating as a dynamic system of signifiers," to cite Turner again and retrieve the Stromberg thesis. To the orthodox party, this intention contained two threats. First, it can lead to separatism, so that the conventicles, the small groups used to renew the church, easily could turn into dissident churches. Second, instead of constituting the church objectively in the Word and sacraments, the door is opened to giving the decisive place as the constituting factor and the criterion for the church to the human experience of God.

The Bible

Finally, the Bible comes into play here. It has already been noted that Spener called for a more comprehensive use of the entire Bible and asked that it be discussed by people in the conventicles. Several features are noteworthy in this use of Scripture. James Stein has pointed out that both Francke and Spener considered the apostles, not the text, to be inspired, which in this instance gave the character of illumination to the work of the Holy Spirit. This attribution resulted in the notion that it was when the Scripture was in the use that its power came to be known, rather than putting the emphasis on the formal character of Scripture.[31]

In Francke's (1663–1721) "Scriptural Rules of Life," this same point comes to expression. The Scripture is given to make one wise unto salvation. To that end one needs to be mindful of what one is to believe, do, and hope — that is, to be mindful of what is taught, commanded, and promised. It is in doing the will of God that one knows whether or not the teaching is from God. Then follows a biological metaphor: "Remember that you may know no truth in Scripture for which you will not have to give an account (I Tim. 6:14) of whether you have transformed it into life as one transforms food and drink into flesh and blood."[32]

Spener's "The Necessary and Useful Reading of the Holy Scriptures" argues a similar line of advice. Anyone who wishes to read fruitfully must be in a state of repentance and have a heartfelt desire to know the divine will; yet knowledge of God does not consist in a mere knowing but requires praxis and action. In order to grow in the knowledge of Scripture and understand its teaching, one seeks to do what it says. If such practice is missing, even what one has will be taken away.[33]

These two references bring to light a significant point. In addition to the "Scripture Rules of Life," Francke wrote *A Guide to the Reading and Study of the Holy Scripture*. In both documents he teaches that if one is to understand the Scriptures, one needs to enter the mind and the affections of the apostles and prophets. This is the case for several reasons. First, God worked those affections in their hearts, making them intrinsic to the apostles' or prophets' communication. Second, there is an indissoluble link between affections and language, words being the "index" of a person's affections. Third, since one seeks to know the affections of the apostles in order to know the meaning of their language, so one seeks to know the kernel of Scripture in order to know its husk. This is why the unregenerate do not understand Scripture: they do not share the same affections with the writers of Scripture. What one understands to be the truth, one undertakes to do.[34]

Interestingly, Gadamer discusses this feature of pietism in relation to hermeneutics. He argues that, in addition to understanding and interpretation, the pietists added application.[35] Here the effort is not to turn something into objective knowledge or to perceive knowledge as domination of a text, an expression Gadamer owes to Max Scheler. One does not take the text into possession as if one (the interpreter) owned it. By application, I do not take Gadamer to mean skill in applying texts to cases, which allows the texts to retain a certain detachment. Gadamer writes, using the interpretation of law as an example, "To interpret the law's will or the promises of God is clearly not a form of domination, but of service. They are interpretations — which includes application — in the service of what is considered valid."[36] The understanding is arrived at, in part at least, by the doing, the application. Taken in this sense, then, when one understands Scripture, one understands more than texts, one understands the apostolic submission to the work and words of Christ. This is what it means to enter the affections of the apostles, for in doing so, one joins them in their commitments and in their relation to God in Christ, thus participating in the experiential character of the Christian life with the apostles.

Experiential Character

Much has been made of the personal, inward, subjective side of pietism. Conventional interpretation often leaves the impression that a "saved individual" is the end of the pietistic call for regeneration. Both Karl Olsson[37] and F. Ernest Stoeffler[38] have argued cogently for preference for the notion of "experiential" piety over terms like inwardness, subjective, and personal, Stoeffler even arguing that it was pietistic influences in eighteenth-century America which transformed the Puritan tradition into a kind of life-centered evangelism. This assertion is in keeping with Ernst Benz's discussion of pietism's critique of the way the Lutheran doctrine of justification by grace through faith fared among the German people of the seventeenth century. Benz spoke of an "indolence" that had come over the people, due in large measure to just such an external and forensic doctrine of justification.[39] It came across easily to persons that this was a transaction external to them and with little self-involvement, and hence they had little or no expectation of personal transformation. Jay Rochelle, writing about contemporary Lutheranism, speaks of "complacency" as the Lutheran sin.[40]

My view is that the stress on regeneration and transformation in pietism of whatever stripe sought to restore a religious dimension to justification, a depth, a recovery of the primal elements of all religious experience. I refer to the fear of God, not as terror but as a fear born out of deep gratitude for grace one did not earn and favor one did not expect. To presume on such grace, to take it so for granted, to become complacent in it, is to cut the umbilical cord of the Christian life, which is, at its heart, a relationship of grateful trust in the promise of God and the pledge of the Godhead to us. Moreover, it is to mock the holiness of God and to ignore the difference between transcendent holiness and human sinfulness. Nor, on the other side, could one collapse the friendship of God into an intimacy that led to identity with God. This was an experiential piety in which two poles—human and God—never merged. If such ever happened, it would destroy the relationship and thus the basis for experience.[41] But it is to be left to the genius and grace of God to lure persons to approach, using whatever media are available as vehicles of the divine condescension.

Relationship as Media

Peter Stromberg, to whom extensive reference was made earlier in this paper, spoke of "relationship" as a foundational category for pietism. This notion then was broadened into the concept of "processual symbolic activity" with regard to the power of a congregation's influence. But the same thinking was applied to persons.

Among classical pietists, Johann Albrecht Bengel comes closest, as far as I can tell, to developing a phenomenology of religion. His discussions of the holiness and glory of God are among the richest in Christian edification literature.[42] For Bengel, the glory of God is the chief ground of conversion, and it can be manifested in a variety of ways, from reading Scripture to experiencing a tragedy. The glory of God reveals God's holiness and triggers a process Bengel calls *Nachdenken*,[43] the capacity for, and process of, thinking back over one's life, having now been confronted by the holiness and glory of God. He writes that the experience of the glory and holiness of God brings about awareness of an immeasurable difference between God and humans, yet it also engenders an incomparable pleasantness. The experience is somewhat akin to a person's feeling of relief that he or she has been found out in her/his sin while still dreading the very same fact. The flight from sin is over, but facing it has just begun. Both freedom and fear are present in the experience. Rudolf Otto spoke of the "holy" as having the simultaneous capacity for fascinating people and frightening them.[44] Abraham Joshua Heschel's memorable words claim that "the sense of the ineffable does not hush the quest of thought, but, on the contrary, disturbs the placid and unseals our suppressed impressionability."[45] Needless to say, the two chief examples in the Bible of *Nachdenken*[46] are associated with David and the prodigal son. The phenomenon of "coming to oneself"[47] was for pietists a key issue in anthropology, because they geared their "processual symbolic activity" to this God-given capacity.

What I have identified as a "phenomenology of religion," rooted in a system of symbolic signifiers, can be identified in two illuminating examples of how pietists "theologized" about the decisive role of human relations. When Spener discussed the priesthood of believers in his *Explanation of Luther's Small Catechism*, he did so in two places: under the commandment prohibiting murder and under Christology.[48] The former is most intriguing. Spener first negatively assesses how persons are killed: by deeds, words, and looks. One of the more effective ways of killing people is by killing hope, for killing hope deprives persons of their future. Positively, he notes that Christian priests give life, largely with the same tools through which life can be taken away, but wielded with a different spirit. To give hope by deed, word, or look is to create life where little or no life exists. Relations are media, occasions of *Nachdenken*. When accompanied by the word of God, they are what "disturbs the placid and unseals our suppressed impressionability," to use Heschel's words. Francke said that his child-care workers at the Halle Orphanage would be either hirelings or shepherds, an obvious reference to John 10. A hireling was not necessarily either abusive or negligent, and could be professional to the core without entering into any bond with the children. Hirelings quit when the going gets rough. Shepherds are just the opposite. There is bonding, a proper kind of distance and intimacy, and discipline. Shepherds do not flee from the sheep. The way of the shepherd occasions the onset of *Nachdenken* and can usher such children into the mystery of love that "disturbs the placid and unseals . . . impressionability." So glory, that which fascinates and yet evokes fear, begins its work in and among dispossessed children, drawing them to the center of a love that will not let them go.[49]

Transition

This essay has attempted to identify motifs that emerged in one expression of pietism. By taking note of these motifs, one is in a position to see immediately that a movement which sets out to reform life, not doctrine, will view its character differently than one will whose purpose is to reform doctrine and call the church back to a true faith. It may be the case that evangelicalism has more to do with classical pietism than pietism with evangelicalism. Scholars point to the period of classical pietism as a major source of contemporary evangelicalism. But this must refer to pietism's call for new life, spiritual fruitfulness, and a sense of difference both from the lethargic life of the territorial churches and from the worldliness of the members.[50] While the "new evangelicalism"[51] emerged as a critique — on the one hand, of the fundamentalistic churches, with their intellectual and cultural strictures, and their separateness from the world to the point of indifference, and, on the other hand, of the liberal churches — it had as a major thrust the reform of doctrine. To the extent that the reform of doctrine dominated, the "new evangelicalism" found the contributions of Scottish Common Sense Realism and the Princeton Theology highly formative.[52]

Evangelicalism of the 1980s, perhaps retrieving some themes from a previous postmillennial phase, goes beyond concern for theological orthodoxy and expresses increasing concern for a holistic understanding of the gospel's application of life. Ronald Sider has pressed claims for economic justice, Wesley Michaelson for environmental concerns, the Evangelical Women's Caucus for feminist concerns, Robert Webber for liturgical renewal, and Thomas Sine for future planning for hunger relief, agricultural reform, etc. One wonders if, in those churches that identify themselves as evangelical, there is an eschatology of "future better times," so crucial to Spener's vision and commitments, to give support and structure to the people who seek a future better time for their generation. Perhaps the hints of renewed interest in postmillennial theology, as exemplified in the work of John Jefferson Davis of Gordon-Conwell Theological Seminary, bode well for a renewed interest in this line of thought. Otherwise the eschatology of twentieth-century evangelicalism, and fundamentalism in particular, has been pessimistic about history, seeing only a downward spiral in the future. In such conceptions it is too easy to concede the world to a dismal end and to exempt oneself from service to the world, seeing that it has been judged already.

Yet evangelicalism still seeks an identity. Robert Webber has identified fourteen groups of evangelicals.[53] My view is that the term *evangelical* is more connotative than denotative, more descriptive than definitional. Even if these groups hold in common a high view of Scripture, a highly structured atonement theology, a belief in a specific form of eschatological vision, etc., the views are not uniform. The Finney tradition and the Princeton tradition, with their conflicts over free will, perfection, new measures, etc., make strange bedfellows. Are both evangelical? John Gerstner could speak of Finney as the nineteenth century's greatest evangelist and evangelicalism's greatest foe![54] What is connoted in the term *evangelical*, at a minimum, is a confession that persons are redeemed solely by God's grace in Jesus Christ, the fully divine and human person, for no reason other than God's sovereign will to do so; that the hope of the world lies in God's redemptive deed at the end of history; that the Scripture contains all that is needed for life and salvation; and that persons need to be reborn by the power of the gospel. These elements are at best a circumference of a circle. For numerous evangelicals, this core is insufficient for a center. Areas of contrast between pietism and evangelicalism can be noted in matters related to Scripture, conversion, and revivals.

Scriptural Issues

Certainly the debate over inerrancy is a key issue of identity. For some it is a watershed issue, the dividing line between one who is an evangelical and one who is not. Some would blur the line of demarcation a bit and speak of non-inerrantists as inconsistent evangelicals. Still others would not find inerrancy to be a criterion at all. But for those who do, it seems that the end product of such a conception is to make it the key issue, if not the center, of evangelical concerns. The net effect is to make epistemology a part of the evangel, to merge the formal and the material principles of the Reformation, namely, the roles of authority and redemption.

Pietists did not do that. They spoke more of the inspiration of persons than of texts, certainly a divergence from much current evangelical thinking. Moreover, there was a wariness with ideas such as the doctrine of inerrancy.[55] But perhaps an even more significant difference is suggested by the reflections of Francke cited earlier in this paper. The supposition that only the regenerate truly understand the Scripture means that the material principle supercedes the formal character of the Bible.[56] This implies further that if the word *epistemology* is used, pietists will use it to mean that the power and truthfulness of the Word of God are known as the Word of God is obeyed and as it comes to pass in God's providential work in history. The implication then is more that God is true to his word, than that the Word of God is true, which of course they would not deny. Allowing for some artificiality in that sentence, we still may say that pietists shy away from isolating the Word of God from God, resist allowing it to be a self-contained entity.

One of the reasons for this point of view no doubt was how pietists experienced orthodoxy, whether of a Reformed or a Lutheran stripe. Orthodoxy was formally correct, precise to the highest degree with regard to theological formulation. The puzzle was why formal correctness did not yield faithful and fruitful Christians. Pietists apparently concluded that even an air-tight theological system was no guarantor of true Christianity. A true faith without true Christians as an enigma of immense proportions. The one apparently did not imply the other.

On the basis of the foregoing, the pietists likely would not have been congenial to the "domino theory," which says that if the formal character of Scripture is compromised (and especially if inerrancy is made the touchstone of true evangelical faith), then the whole faith is in danger. The experience of orthodoxy would make them cautious of an equation that made an indubitable epistemological foundation the only security of true faith. When such an epistemology is present and the fruits are not, something is amiss.

For pietists, it is insufficient to speak of truth claims apart from another function of truth. Theology, based on Scripture, does make truth-claims, but more than a hyphenated noun is here. Remove the hyphen, and one has both a noun and a verb: "Truth claims," i.e., lays hold on a life and calls it into service. The subjective side of this process is the life and witness of one claimed by the truth.

The conventicles were started to an occasion for this claim by the Word of God to do its work. Here the priesthood of all believers had an opportunity for application, as people discussed, investigated, and applied the Word of God. The relation to the Word of God was more immediate than in hearing a sermon. By questions and stories, all of life could be brought into relation to the Word of God and comprehended in it. Inevitably, what comes in for judgment and grace, law and gospel, condemnation and consolation is one's life. Both the authority and the power of God were present and active as truth began to claim lives, sometimes engendering resistance, sometimes repentance and transformation. This was the garden where the seed of the Word of God was planted, cultivated, and pruned. The fruit was harvested. Hence the Word of God is treated not in isolation but in an environment which itself conditions others to hear, repent, and be reborn. The favorite metaphor of these people was "nursery," the horticultural kind, that is, where conditions are part of the communication of the gospel. The Christian faith cannot be reduced to symbols, but must, at the same time, be symbolized in people claimed by the truth. The quality of symbolization is what Spener meant by fruitfulness, where the gospel is commended in the lives of those whose lips profess Jesus' name.

Another aspect of this doctrinal issue needs explication. To the extent that much mainline evangelicalism has its roots in the doctrine of inerrancy forged by the Princeton Theology and buttressed by Scottish Common Sense Realism, contemporary evangelicalism will nuance its understanding of the Scripture question differently than much of classical pietism. The root system is different. Francke, for example, will find Saint Bernard a worthy companion in the study of Scripture, because he identifies with Saint Bernard's goal.[57] By introducing the word "habit," Francke has identified the notion of a renewed person, created by the Holy Spirit, capable of knowing and enjoying the affections of the apostles who wrote Scripture. In order to sense the import of this root-system, one needs to read the magisterial work of Jean Leclercq, O.S.B., *The Love of Learning and the Desire for God.* There the contrast between scholastic and monastic theology is traced out. But, in particular, Leclercqu's profuse citations from Saint Bernard show why Francke would find a soul-friend in him. The epistemological character of sanctity is explicated, and the priority of fear of God as preparation for knowing God. The distinction between wisdom and knowledge, and the crucial role played by experience, are traced out in their various ramifications.[59]

Furthermore, the "Johann Arndt" of the Scandinavian lands, Eric Pontoppidan—whose *Mirror of Faith* was the staple of much Scandinavian Lutheran piety and was the instrument of the conversion of pietistic leaders, e.g., Carl Olof Rosenius — employed many of the sources Francke found congenial.[60] A listing in that work of the people formative in Pontoppidan's life reads like a *Who's Who* of the history of spirituality. Some of them are the shapers of the Wesleyan evangelical tradition and its various offshoots in America. It is this group, for example, that Donald Dayton, in his ongoing discussion with George Marsden, says bids fair for being paradigmatic for the identity of evangelicalism.[61] For that group, the epistemological issue is not implied in the term evangelical, as it is in the tradition formed by the Princeton Theology. Rather, major attention is centered on the "sanctification gap," as Richard Lovelace has termed it.[62]

Conversion

Pietism offers caution to the American revival tradition with which it is often identified. For one thing, classical pietism, while acknowledging a strong belief in conversion, did not necessarily make conversion a discernible moment of decision. Francke comes closed to doing so, while Spener and Bengel definitely did not. But even Francke was leery of imposing his experience on others, as his own words indicate: "We do not ask, 'Are you converted? When were you converted?' But we ask, 'What does Christ mean to you? What have you experienced personally with God? Is Christ necessary to you and your daily life?' And it is, to be certain, very likely that one does not know at all the period of time."[63] This reference may be attributed to several sources. The Lutheran doctrine of baptism as a means of grace surely is significant. Ole Hallesby, whose devotional books published by Augsburg Press have been enormously popular, wrote a book on *Infant Baptism and Adult Conversion,* setting out in modern dress how the two correlate, a book quite amenable to a pietist mode of conceptualizing. Another clue is that the reliance on organic and biological language tends more toward process than to decisive moments. A third source may be what I termed a phenomenology of religion, in which case the entire process of *Nachdenken* makes it enormously difficult to specify a "when," a "before," or an "after" of conversion. The issue is that the religious dimension of justification and the experiential aspect of faith are relational categories. A pertinent question among the immigrant Swedes who founded the Evangelical Covenant Church was, "Are you living yet in Jesus?" Compare that with the question "When were you saved?" or "Are you saved?", and the difference in tone and assumption becomes apparent. More interest was expressed in living faith and its fruit than in the nature and time of its beginning.

Revivals

Pietism would engage the revival movement critically to the extent that revivals are understood as caused. Finney's suggestion of a philosophical connection between causes and the onset of revivals would give some pietists pause.[64] Such a view implies a synergistic notion of building the kingdom of God and thus snatching God's eschatological initiative from him. Pietists would be more at home with the awakening language attached to the works of Jonathan Edwards and John Wesley. While it is true that many initiatives were made by pietists, e.g., missions, social service, etc., it is clear that such activities were seen not as causing revival but only as the obedience of faith, a faith active in love. My earlier reference to pietistic millennial theology supports this position. We do God's work. We obey God's word. But God's "better times" still belong to God's inner counsel. They are not ours to bring in. Thus, for Finney, the relation between means and ends is more direct; for the pietists, the relation tends to be more indirect.

In a cemetery in Jyväskylä, Finland, there is a stone monument with the following inscription: "In a blacksmith shop that stood on this spot, Paavo Ruotsalainen[65] met in 1799, for the first time, Jaako Hogman, the Jyväskylä blacksmith whose words, 'One thing you lack and with it everything, the inward knowledge of Christ,' made him the awakener of our people." Pietists rejoice in the transforming power of that inward knowledge and find it to be the heart of the gospel, that which makes possible a theology in service of living toward God.[66]

NOTES

1. William Ames, *The Marrow of Theology,* trans. and with introduction by John Dykstra Eusden, foreword by Douglas Horton (Durham, N.C.: Labyrinth Press, 1968), 77.1.

2. Ibid., 78.11.

3. Phillip Jacob Spener, *Pia Desideria,* trans., ed., and introduction by Theodore G. Tappert, Seminar Editions (Philadelphia: Fortress Press, 1964), 112. Spener's middle name will be spelled differently depending on English or German usage.

4. Martin Prozesky, "The Emergence of Dutch Pietism," *Journal of Ecclesiastical History* 28 (Jan. 1977):29–37. F. Ernest Stoeffler, *The Rise of Evangelical Pietism,* Studies in the History of Religions 9 (Leiden: E.J. Brill, 1971), 109–179. George Brown, Jr., "Pietism and the Reformed Tradition," *Reformed Review* 23 (1970):143–52.

5. Allan C. Deeter, "An Historical and Theological Introduction to Phillip Jacob Spener's *Pia Desideria*" (Ph.D. diss. Princeton Univ., 1963), 10–12, 22ff.; Harold O.J. Brown, *Heresies* (Garden City, N.J.: Doubleday, 1984), chs. 17 and 18; Jaroslav Pel-

ikan, *From Luther to Kierkegaard* (St. Louis, Mo.: Concordia Publishing, 1950), 49–84.

6. Spener, *Pia Desideria*, 53 and 115–16.

7. Ibid., pt. 1.

8. Ibid., 61.

9. Ibid., 68–75.

10. See the German text of Spener, *Pia Desideria*, ed. Kurt Aland, Kleine Texte für Vorlesungen and Übungen (Berlin: Walter De Gruyter, 1955), 47.

11. Spener, *Pia Desideria*, 76–85.

12. S. Dean McBride, Jr., "Polity of the Covenant People: The Book of Deuteronomy," *Interpretation* 41 (July 1987):229–33.

13. J. Gerald Janzen, "The Yoke That Gives Rest," *Interpretation* 41 (July 1987): 256–61.

14. Spener, *Pia Desideria*, 60–62.

15. Hans Küng, *The Church*, trans. Ray and Rosaleen Ockenden (New York: Sheed and Ward, 1967), 149.

16. Ernst Käsemann, *Commentary on Romans*, trans. and ed. Geoffrey W. Bromiley (Grand Rapids, Mich.: Eerdmans, 1980), 307, but see 304–311 for Käsemann's illuminating discussion.

17. Spener, *Pia Desideria*, 76–77.

18. F.W. Dillistone, *The Power of Symbols in Religion and Culture* (New York: Crossroad, 1986), 110–14 and ch. 1.

19. Victor Turner and Edith Turner, *Image and Pilgrimage in Christian Culture* (Oxford, England: Basil Blackwell, 1978), app. A, 243ff.

20. Peter G. Stromberg, *Symbols of Community: Immanuelskyrkan* (Tucson: Univ. of Arizona Press, 1986), 17.

21. Ibid., 18.

22. Ibid., 51.

23. Ibid. 50.

24. Ibid., 52.

25. Spener, *Pia Desideria*, see 46, 49, 63, 65, 78, 102, and 116 for examples of references to fruit.

26. Ibid., 81.

27. Ibid., 27.

28. Martin Schmidt, "Phillip Jakob Spener und die Bibel," in *Pietismus und Bibel*, ed. Kurt Aland, Arbeiten zur Geschichte des Pietismus (Witten, Germany: Luther-Verlag, 1970), 14, 15, and 27.

29. Emmanuel Hirsch, *Geschichte der neueren evangelische Theologie*, 5 vols. (Gutersloh, Germany: C. Bertelsmann Verlag, 1951), 2:125–27.

30. Johann Albrecht Bengel, *Bekräftiges Zeugniss der Wahrheit in vielen und mancherley nöthigen Stücken insonderheit gegen Hn. Kohlreiff und Hn. Drümel* (Stuttgart: Johannes Nicholaus Stoll, 1748), vol. 30–31, nos. 72–73; *Eklärte Offenbarung Johannis oder vielmehr Jesus Christi*, 3d. ed. (Stuttgart: Johann Christoph Erhard, 1758), 945; *Tischreden*, ed. by Ch. Ehmann (Reutlingen, Germany: Carl Rupp Verlag, 1869), vol. 128, no. 370.

31. K. James Stein, *Phillip Jakob Spener: Pietist Patriarch* (Chicago: Covenant Press, 1986), 152. Stein notes that Erich Beyreuther traces Spener's shift from verbal inspiration to personal inspiration to the lectures Spener heard from Sebastian Schmidt at Strassburg Univ. See Beyreuther's *Geschichte des Pietismus* (Stuttgart: J.F. Steinkopf Verlag, 1973), 71. Cf. also Martin Schmidt, "Phillip Jakob Spener und die Bibel,"

32, and the illuminating discussion of the Scripture issue in Dale Brown, *Understanding Pietism* (Grand Rapids, Mich.: Eerdmans, 1978), ch. 3.

32. In Gary Sattler, *God's Glory, Neighbor's Good* (Chicago: Covenant Press, 1982), 199–237, esp. 222–23.

33. Spener, "The Necessary and Useful Reading of the Holy Scriptures," in *Pietists: Selected Writings*, ed. and with introduction by Peter C. Erb and preface by F. Ernest Stoeffler, Classics of Western Spirituality (New York: Paulist Press, 1983), 71–75.

34. August Herman Francke, *A Guide to the Reading and Study of the Holy Scripture*, trans. and augmented with notes by William Jacques (Philadelphia: David Hogan, 1823), app., pp. 125–31

35. Hans Georg Gadamer, *Truth and Method*, trans. and ed. Garrett Barden and John Cuming (New York: Seabury, Continuum Books, 1975), 29 and 274–75.

36. Ibid., 278.

37. Karl A. Olsson, "Pietism and Its Relevance to the Modern World," *The Bulletin, Moravian Theological Seminary* (Fall 1965):33.

38. F. Ernest Stoeffler, *Rise of Evangelical Pietism*, 13–16; and "Epilogue," in *Continental Pietism and Early American Christianity*, ed. F. Ernest Stoeffler (Grand Rapids, Mich.: Eerdmans, 1976), 268.

39. Ernst Benz, *Die Protestantische Thebias* (Wiesbaden, Germany: Franz Steiner Verlag, 1963), 16–19, 129–31.

40. Jay Rochelle, "Lutheran Piety: History and Prospect," *Lutheran Forum* 16 (Lent 1983):11.

41. I have developed these themes in C. John Weborg, "Pietism: 'The Fire of God Which Flames in the Heart of Germany,'" in *Protestant Spiritual Traditions*, ed. Frank C. Senn (New York: Paulist Press, 1986), 183, 193, and 195–97.

42. Johann Albrecht Bengel, *Erklärte Offenbarung*, 310–12, 544, and *Sechzig Erbauliche Reden über die Offenbarung Johannis oder vielmehr Jesu Christi samt einer Nachlese gleichen Inhalts*, 2d ed. (Stuttgart: Johann Christian Erhard, 1758), 238–39.

43. Bengel, *Sechzig Erbauliche Reden*, 750–52, 845.

44. Rudolph Otto, *The Idea of the Holy*, tans. John W. Harvey (New York: Oxford Univ. Press, Galaxy Books, 1958), 12–40 and 136–42.

45. Abraham Joshua Heschel, *Man is Not Alone: A Philosophy of Religion* (New York: Farrar, Straus and Giroux, 1951; First Noonday Printing, 1976), 15.

46. Bengel, *Sechzig Erbauliche Reden*, 64, 85, 129.

47. Johann Albrecht Bengel, *Gnomon*, trans. C.F. Werner, with foreword by Egon W. Gerdes and Johann Albrecht Bengel, 2 vols. (Stuttgart: J.F. Steinkopf Verlag, 1970), 1:365.

48. Phillip Jakob Spener, *Einfältige Erklärung der Christlichen Lehr Nach der Ordnung dess Kleinen Catechismi des Theuren Mann Gottes Lutheri*, (Frankfurt: Johann Dietrich Friedgen, 1677), 135, questions 232 and 233; cf. questions 599 and 600 for Christological references.

49. August Hermann Francke, *Pietas Hallensis or a Publick Demonstration of the Footsteps of a Divine Being Yet in the World in a Historical Narration of the Orphan House and Other Charitable Institutions at Glaucha Near Halle in Sacony*, n.t. (London: J. Downings, 1705), 192–95, nos. 3 and 4.

50. On the conflictual character of this relation, see George Marsden, *The Evangelical Mind and the New School Presbyterian Experience* (New Haven, Conn.: Yale Univ. Press, 1970), 3, 31–33, and *Fundamentalism and American Culture* (New York: Oxford Univ. Press, 1980), 4–8, 44–45.

51. Harold John Ockenga, "From Fundamentalism, through New Evangelicalism,

to Evangelicalism," in *Evangelical Roots: A Tribute to Wilbur Smith*, ed. Kenneth Kantzer (Nashville, Tenn.: Thomas Nelson, 1978), 35–46.

52. See William G. McLoughlin, ed., *The American Evangelicals, 1800–1900* (New York: Harper and Row, Harper Torchbooks, 1968), "Introduction," 1–4, and, as an instance of the determinative influence of Reformed theology in shaping Fuller Seminary, see George Marsden, *Reforming Fundamentalism: Fuller Seminary and the New Evangelicalism* (Grand Rapids, Mich.: Eerdmans, 1987), 119–20, showing that some at Fuller had the self-understanding of carrying on the old "Princeton" tradition.

53. Robert Webber, *Common Roots* (Grand Rapids, Mich.: Zondervan, 1978), 32.

54. John Gerstner, "Theological Boundaries of Evangelical Faith," in *The Evangelicals*, ed. David F. Wells and John D. Woodbridge (Nashville, Tenn.: Abingdon, 1975), 27.

55. Fredrick Holmgren, "The Pietistic Tradition and Historical Criticism," *Covenant Quarterly* 28 (1970):49–59, esp. 53. Professor Holmgren calls attention to Erich Beyreuther, *Die geschichtliche Auftrag des Pietismus in der Gegenwart* (Stuttgart: Calwer Verlag, 1963), 19, 22.

Bengel did have an inerrancy doctrine which was crucial to (1) his organic view of the biblical narrative, so that all parts held together and led to final consummation; and (2) supporting his arithmetical calculations for the crucial date of 1836. At the same time, he held to a view of graded inspiration which taught that the prophets, esp. the John of the Book of Revelation, received exact information while the apostles functioned a bit like secretaries who knew the mind of their employer and could express the meaning the employer intended. For the nuances of this subject and how it fits in Bengel's system, see Gottfried Malzer, *Johann Albrecht Bengel: Leben und Werk* (Stuttgart: Calwer Verlag, 1970), 362–68, and Ernst Ludwig, *Schriftverständnis und Schriftauslegung bei Johann Albrecht Bengel* (Stuttgart: Chr. Scheufele Verlag, 1952), 28–32.

56. See the work of Donald Frisk, "Theology and Experience in Early Pietism," *Covenant Quarterly* 28 (1970):15–30.

57. Francke, *Guide to Reading and Study,* 129, 131.

58. Ibid., 134. For reference to similar influences in the Reformed tradition, see James Tanis, "The Heidelberg Catechism in the Hands of the Calvinistic Pietists," *Reformed Review* 24 (Spring 1971):154–61.

59. Jean Leclercq, O.S.B., *The Love of Learning and the Desire for God*, trans. Catherine Misrahi (New York: Fordham Univ. Press, 1961, 1974), 266–69.

60. Eric Pontoppidan, *Härlinga tros-Spegel* (Wästerås, Sweden: John Laurentius Horrn, 1977), 3d. ed. Dr. Sigurd Westberg, archivist of the Evangelical Covenant Church, translated the pertinent texts for me. See also Trygve R. Skarsten, "Erik Pontoppidan and His Asiatic Menoza," *Church History* 50 (March 1981):33–43. Pontoppidan's influence on the Norwegian pietist Hans Nielsen Hauge is described in Andreas Aarflot, *Hans Nielsen Hauge: His Life and Message*, trans. Joseph M. Shaw (Minneapolis, Minn: Augsburg Publishing House, 1979).

61. See the discussion between Marsden and Dayton in George Marsden, "Demythologizing Evangelicalism: A Review of Donald Dayton's *Discovering an Evangelical Heritage*" (with a reply by Donald Dayton) *Christian Scholar's Review* 7 (1977):203–11; and between Marsden and Ernest Sandeen on the problem of the origins of fundamentalism in Sandeen's review of Marsden's *Fundamentalism and American Culture: The Shaping of Twentieth Century Evangelicalism* in *Christian Scholar's Review* 10 (1981): 255. More recently, Dayton has published "Yet Another Layer of the Onion, or Opening the Ecumenical Door to Let the Rifraff In," *Ecumenical Review* 40 (Jan. 1988):87–110, and "An Analysis of the Self-Understanding of American Evangelicalism with a Cri-

tique of Its Correlated Historiography" (unpublished paper prepared for the Wesleyan/ Holiness Study Project, First Fellows Seminar, 28-30 Jan. 1988. Similar historiographical concerns have been raised by Joel Carpenter, e.g., "The Fundamentalist Leaven and the Rise of an Evangelical United Front," in *The Evangelical Tradition in America*, ed. Leonard I. Sweet (Macon, Ga.: Mercer Univ. Press, 1984), 257-88.

62. See Richard Lovelace, "The Sanctification Gap," *Theology Today* 29 (Jan. 1973):363-69. My colleague Richard Carlson called this reference to my attention.

63. Quoted in Brown, *Understanding Pietism*, 118, from Erich Beyreuther, *August Hermann Francke* (Marburg, Germany: Francke-Buchhandlung, 1956), 51.

64. Charles Finney, *Revival Lectures* (New York: Fleming H. Revell, n.d.), 29, cf., 5, 27.

65. Paavo Ruotsalainen, *The Inward Knowledge of Christ*, trans. with introduction by Walter J. Kukkonen, Publication of Luther Agricola Society, B10 (Helsinki, Finland: 1977), 6-7.

66. I would be remiss if I did not acknowledge dependence on the research done for my doctoral dissertation, "The Eschatological Ethics of Johann Albrecht Bengel: Personal and Ecclesial Piety and the Literature of Edification in the Letters to the Seven Churches in Revelation 2 and 3," (Ph.D. diss., Northwestern Univ., June 1983).

CHAPTER II

Evangelicalism: A Mennonite Critique

C. Norman Kraus

Broadly speaking, anabaptist-Mennonites always have been within the evangelical Christian tradition, i.e., they were not spiritualists, rationalists, antitrinitarian, etc., as some have claimed. However, they represent a distinct hermeneutical community which, as Walter Klaassen has pointed out, is "neither Catholic nor Protestant."[1] Jesus, as he is interpreted by the apostolic witness, is the hermeneutical norm, and the church gathered around the biblical record seeks to understand and obey this authority. But to understand what this means, one must describe more carefully the Mennonite experience within American evangelicalism.

In the late 1970s, the Goshen College Center for Discipleship sponsored a series of lectures on the general theme of evangelicalism and anabaptism. In my contributions to that symposium, I defined evangelicalism as a postfundamentalist coalition of conservative Protestant Christians who wished to return to the more centrist position of an earlier generation of conservative denominational theologians such as A.H. Strong, James Orr, Charles Hodge, B.B. Warfield, Herman Bavinck, and E.Y. Mullins.[2]

Anabaptism was described as a diverse movement in the sixteenth century which represented a variety of related theological and ethical positions. The Swiss Brethren and later the Dutch leader, Menno Simons, represent the most literally biblical position, while leaders such as Hans Denck in South Germany were influenced more by the mystical tradition and made distinctions between the "inner" and the "outer" word.[3] The former tended to see the Bible as a literal authority for the contemporary church, while the latter trusted the Spirit's word coming to them through the Bible for guidance. There were, however, common characteristics and concerns, as well as historical relationships, that enable us to see anabaptism as a movement and to speak of an "anabaptist perspective."

American Mennonitism is the historical outcome of a migration to America by Dutch- and German-speaking anabaptists. The movement had already turned sectarian in the seventeenth century, under the pressure of heavy persecution, and this sectarian character was heightened by the group's cultural adjustment to the new dominant English culture in

America. Thus Mennonitism is already the product of interaction with evangelical Protestant and revivalistic influences.

Now, some ten years after the symposium, we need to clarify and expand our analysis and critique. I frankly see no reason extensively to revise the earlier assessment, but it needs to be updated in light of the vigorous discussion that has been in progress, both on the Mennonite experience in America and on fundamentalism's self-understanding vis-à-vis evangelicalism.[4]

Defining Evangelicalism

According to its own self-definition, fundamentalism definitely has re-emerged as a distinct movement alongside and within evangelicalism. At the other end of the spectrum, the question of whether we should speak of a "postevangelical" development has been raised by Robert Price, and in 1980, Richard Quebedeaux already had raised the question of whether "today's evangelicals" will be "tomorrow's liberals." Somewhere in the middle of this continuum, the debate goes on whether the term *evangelical* should be given a broad, social-historical definition or be more precisely and theologically defined according to the Augustinian norms of the Reformed tradition.[5]

I think that we must allow for variations and a certain ambiguity in the use of the term *evangelicalism*. The situation is not unlike that in early-twentieth-century English evangelicalism. Men such as James Orr and P.T. Forsyth, for example, clearly held an evangelical interpretation of Christ and salvation by faith based upon scriptural authority, but they did not subscribe to the dualistic supernaturalism of an earlier orthodoxy. Indeed, the idea that there exists a fine but logically clear line distinguishing "evangelical liberal" (postevangelical) from "liberal evangelical" (radical evangelical) may need to be dropped, unless we simply equate evangelicalism with the rational dualistic supernaturalism which B.B. Warfield claimed is the life breath of orthodox Christianity.[6] In my judgment, such an option is no more feasible today than it was when B.B. Warfield, James Orr, E.Y. Mullins, James Strong, et al. argued the issues within conservative Protestantism nearly a century ago.

With such considerations in mind, I propose the definitional classification within which to assess the relation of Mennonites to evangelicalism. (See Figure 1).

From its emergence in the 1940s, the evangelical movement has been an uneasy coalition. If one takes the membership of the National Association of Evangelicals (NAE) as a definitional guide, the coalition was made up of different and conflictual groups. However, the group which I have labeled "neofundamentalist," represented by the early Fuller Seminary, soon dominated the movement.[7] The NAE was not an interdenominational council but a postfundamentalist, nondenominational association of individuals, parachurch organizations, individual congregations, and denominations. The new element was the divergence and tension within the core group of neofundamentalists itself.

Conservative Protestants
(Evangelicals)
    | \
Conservative   Fundamentalist
(Denominationalism)   (Nondenominationalism)

                    Neofundamentalists

                    Neo-Evangelicals

                    Radical Evangelicals

Figure 1

_____

As early as 1980, Harold Lindsell was ready to drop the term *evangelical*, because of self-contradictions within the ranks. Differences had arisen concerning the definition of inerrancy, and the neofundamentalists had formed the International Council on Biblical Inerrancy to preserve and propagate a strict definition of inerrancy. Now, ten years later, that group has recognized that the questions of hermeneutics and the application of these inerrant Scriptures also are major issues. Kenneth Kantzer's description of the ICBI Summit III (1986) indicates that extreme diversity was the order of the day.[8]

Previous discussions in the Evangelical Theology Section of the American Academy of Religion similarly indicate a significant divergence among scholars in both the interpretation of inerrancy and in the use of the Bible. The point of agreement within evangelicalism seems to be a common commitment to the authority of the Bible, but what is the nature of that authority? And what is the form of revelation in the Scriptures? Opinions range from those of J.I. Packer, who clearly holds to traditional inerrancy theory and a "canonical" principle of interpretation, to those of Donald Bloesch, who makes Christ the normative touchstone for interpretation and freely uses higher critical methods.[9]

The neo-evangelicals and radical evangelicals as a whole have been influenced more by contemporary social concerns, anthropological understandings of culture and language, existentialist corrections of rationalist philosophy, and anabaptist concern for the centrality of Jesus and discipleship. Nevertheless, they continue to find their self-identity in the nonliberal circle by deliberate choice. They affirm the personal reality of God's self-revelation in Jesus Christ as it is recorded in Scripture. Thus Scripture continues to have normative authority for them across cultural relativities.

Contemporary Mennonite Dialogue

During this same decade, Mennonites have intensified their dialogue within and outside the denominational boundaries. Inter-Mennonite cooperation in seminary education, missions, and publication, along with continued discussion and fellowship at the Mennonite World Conference level, have given rise to a new sense of shared worldwide identity. Serious theological and biblical publications during the last ten years show a growing awareness of the anabaptist heritage and an increasing freedom from older fundamentalistic inhibitions. Dialogue with other denominational groups, especially from the Reformed tradition; increased fellowship with the Russian baptists; and participation with evangelicals in conferences, missionary ventures, publishing projects, and social witness — all have given Mennonites a new self-awareness and self-confidence.

Mennonites now are able to affirm their plurality across the cultures of America, Europe, Africa, and Asia. Indeed, the dynamic plurality within Mennonitism parallels that of the evangelical movement as a whole, and the relationship of the two movements might be diagrammed on a parallel continuum as follows: (See Figure 2).

In light of the above considerations, I now want to concentrate more directly on the American Mennonite response to and understanding of fundamentalism and evangelicalism. I shall take the position of one within the tradition, who affirms an anabaptist perspective on the Mennonite denomination and its relation to Protestant evangelicalism.[11]

Radical Evangelicals ——▶ Neo-Evangelicals ———▶ Neo-Fundamentalists

| | |

Anabaptist Mennonites   Mainstream Mennonites   Anabaptist Fellowship of
                                                Concerned Mennonites[10]

Figure 2

A Shared Dream?

While Mennonites cannot simply be equated with anabaptists, they are lineal descendants and have tried to maintain something of the original vision. Since we are all products of our history as well as our contemporary environment, even those areas of similarity and seeming agreement between groups sometimes prove to be significantly distinct in mood, perspective, and even intention. Thus we might well begin our comparison and critique with a comparison of the original "dreams" of anabaptism and of evangelicalism.[12]

Do sixteenth-century anabaptism and twentieth-century neo-evangelicalism share an original perspective and vision? For example, were the apocalyptic hopes of Melchior Hoffmann and of W.E. B(lackstone), the nineteenth-century Plymouth Brethren author of *Jesus Is Coming*, the same? Can we compare the evangelistic exploits of men such as Michael Sattler, Hans Hut, and Balthazar Hubmaier with the mass rallies of modern evangelists? Was Menno Simons' basic concern the same as that of fundamentalists in the 1920s, as John Horsch, a Mennonite scholar, suggests? I am convinced that, despite surface similarities, there are major differences in the two visions.

The first difference is signaled in the subtle shades of meanings in the synonyms *renaissance* and *revival*. In his irenic introduction of the neo-evangelical movement, Donald Bloesch called the new movement a "renaissance." In a unitive mood, he included fundamentalism, neo-orthodoxy, and neo-evangelicalism in his definition.[13] But in doing this, he described the ideal rather than the historical reality.

One cannot help questioning whether *renaissance* is the right word here. Historically, evangelicalism represents the instinct of American revivalism to bring spiritual renewal within and by means of nineteenth-century American Protestant orthodoxy. Accordingly, its aim is *recovery*, not *discovery*; return, not revision. And even as a *post*fundamentalist movement, evangelicalism is largely the revival of an earlier theological position that was lost in the heat and din of battle with secularism and liberalism.

The major theological debates within the evangelical movement thus far have concerned the logically necessary minimum required in statements of the evangelical position. Clark Pinnock's vision of a genuinely "postliberal" statement of evangelical theology[14] apparently has not been part of the revivalist vision of neo-evangelicalism. Up to this point, attempts at revisionism have been rather consistently labeled "liberal" or "radical left." This is not "renaissance" either in mood or intention.

By way of contrast, the Reformation, of which anabaptism was a dynamic part, arose in the context of the humanist renaissance of learning and the breakup of the old culture. It developed out of a new experience of grace and a new discovery of biblical truth. It was a radical challenge to traditional orthodoxy and an attempt to formulate new patterns of church and theology.

Anabaptism was the direct result of the discovery of the original Bible, which had been made available through Renaissance scholarship. Its call to make the New Testament the sole authority for the revision of church life and theology was an appeal for a new hermeneutic that would give the witness of Scripture its true authority and relevance. It was not an appeal to the inerrancy of sacred writings in order to support a revival of orthodox theology. Anabaptism was clearly an attempt at discovery and revision, not merely at recovery and revival. It was precisely this openness that made it seem so *radical* and so threatening to establishment Protestantism, and that in many cases led to the charge of "spiritualism." While American Mennonitism has had its share of traditionalism, the rediscovery of its roots has introduced a fresh "anabaptist" spirit into its life.

A second, related difference in orientation between anabaptism and evangelicalism is denoted by the words *prophetic* and *evangelistic*. American evangelicalism has put great stress on evangelism, but very little emphasis on prophetic witness. In this regard it continues the pietistic emphases on the individual experience of new birth and the assurance of salvation. Its evangelistic appeal has been to make one's "calling and election sure" (2 Pet. 1:10). Discipleship continues to be interpreted almost entirely as a spiritual relationship with Jesus, and emphasis is given to personal morality. Relatively little attention has been given to social witness against injustice.

The Evangelicals for Social Action have been a prophetic minority within the movement, but they do not characterize the dominant thrust of evangelical social witness. The so-called "Moral Majority" is much more representative. In this respect, Billy Graham as evangelist epitomizes the movement. While one may be appreciative of his testimony against social injustice, e.g., racial injustice and militarism, the tardiness of his witness hardly entitles him to be called a prophet. Indeed, he himself has claimed a calling as evangelist rather than as prophet.

Anabaptism, on the other hand, was a prophetic movement in the full-blown biblical sense of that word. Anabaptists were heralds of a new social order. Their evangelism — and they were the Reformation's first evangelists — was a call into the new order of Christ. Baptism, based on conversion and on commitment to the *lordship* of Christ, was the sign of entering this new creation order. Anabaptists called *individuals* to a new convenant relation to God and their fellowmen, through participation in Christ. They called the *church* to recognize anew the authority of Jesus Christ for a life of disciplined obedience. And they called the *secular order* to a new recognition both of the supreme claims of Christ and of the freedom of individual Christians and the church to live according to those claims.

Yet a third shade of difference between evangelicals and anabaptists may be seen in the apologetic and polemic approach of American evangelicals in communicating the Christian message. At the heart of anabaptism, in contrast, is a new hermeneutical approach to Scripture and a confessional approach to witness.

Evangelicalism, especially in its neofundamentalist form, continues to maintain a rationalistic approach to the Bible and to theology.[15] God is identified with the supreme being of philosophical theism. Revelation is conceived as the rational transfer of ideas by words. Biblical authority is defined as a *logical* sanction — perfection, absolute agreement, and the inerrancy of its words are required. Belief thus inevitably becomes a kind of intellectual assent to doctrines about God and Jesus, and converts must be won by verbal argument and logical persuasion. The present argument among evangelical scholars over whether the proper term for the Scriptures' veracity is "truthfulness," inerrancy," or "infallibility" has little significance, so long as the message of the Bible is treated as a piece of religious philosophy and trust is defined as literally correct statements.

Our point here, however, is to note that when one takes this perspective, the proclamation of the gospel inevitably takes on an apologetic character. It is no coincidence that the chair of a great conservative professor, B.B. Warfield, combined "Biblical and Polemical Theology" into one title. Or that the subjects of apologetics and Christian evidences retain their priority in the curriculums of most Bible schools even in transcultural settings. Or that over the years the evangelists of the movement have managed to combine their proclamation of the gospel with a host of "anti" campaigns against the rationalistic and ideological enemies of the faith. Or that 1 Pet. 3:15b continues to be a favorite proof-text to justify this priority. When the gospel is understood in rationalistic and ideological terms, formally speaking its proclamation becomes not only an announcement (*evangel*), but a rational argument (*apologia*).

By contrast, anabaptism arose out of the philological and historical discoveries of the Renaissance scholars and was prompted by the reforming zeal of the times. It was part of the protest against scholastic logic and ecclesiastical dogma. Its primary thrust, therefore, was to present a new and more authentic biblical interpretation. Its concern was *hermeneutical*, i.e., for the meaning and application of Scripture. Its genius was a new nonscholastic hermeneutic related directly to the lifestyle of the believers in the church.[16]

The polemical side of anabaptism was concerned with defense of this new hermeneutic and the new church style which it demanded. While individuals like Menno Simons at times engaged in verbal polemics, the final appeal usually was to the life of true believers, rather than to a theological apologetic. The new hermeneutic would be authenticated in the life of obedience to Christ.

Finally, the two movements, anabaptism and evangelicalism, do not share identical visions of the church and its role in the kingdom of God. Protestant theologians of the sixteenth and seventeenth centuries characterized the church as the sacramental sign of the spiritual kingdom in heaven. The pietistic movement added individual spiritual discipline to these signs, and its great biblical scholar Bengel added a future millennial kingdom to the present spiritual phase. The anabaptists, however, had a distinctly different emphasis. They thought of the church as the sphere of obedience to kingdom authority. The church, in its social life and relationship to the world, is to be an anticipatory expression of the kingdom of its Lord.

The Plymouth Brethren further emphasized the spiritualization of the church and its divorce from the kingdom, in their dispensationalist system. This nineteenth-century movement, which was so much like the anabaptists in its zeal for a pure church, nevertheless resulted in a separatist ecclesiology quite different from that of anabaptism. The Plymouth Brethren taught that the true church is a "heavenly" reality which has been substituted for a sociopolitical kingdom which will be introduced as a future dispensation. With such a spiritualized view, the visible church was reduced to intermittent meetings of those who confessed orthodox faith — later called the "fundamentals." The faithful were encouraged to separate from denominational Babylon and to avoid all political activity.

Present-day evangelicalism remains heavily influenced by the pietist tradition, as it was modified by dispensationalist teaching. It is this spiritualistic concept of the church as a faith reality within the heart of the individual that continues to furnish the theological rationale for the *non*-denominational, parachurch network of the evangelical movement.[17]

Within evangelicalism, the goal of the church is the spiritual renewal of the nation. This is to be accomplished through evangelism and moral reform of individuals, rather than through a clear call for kingdom alternatives. Thus the incorporation of a moral and political campaign such as Jerry Falwell's "Moral Majority" or Pat Robertson's call of God to run for president of the United States is to be understood as *Christian* politics. What seems implicit here is the identification of the *visible* church as a *national* institution, and the nation rather than the kingdom of God as the embodiment of the salvific realm on earth.

Given this conceptual presupposition, along with the glorification of individual enterprise, a vast network of parachurch and nondenominational religious institutions, such as Bible schools, evangelistic crusades, missionary organizations, television and radio "ministries," independent churches, youth organizations, and publishing companies, has developed as the benchmark of American evangelicalism.

While all this may seem like the simple outcome of a "free church" concept such as the anabaptists advocated, it actually has a twist all its own that gives it a demeanor quite different from that of original anabaptism. This is most evident in its acclaim of "God and country," its approval of the nation's ideological and military goals, and its rejection of the biblical peace witness which is so central to the anabaptist-Mennonite tradition.

From the anabaptists' perspective, the problem was not a spiritually dead church that needed revival, but a *false* church that needed replacement. And the false character of the church was directly related to its nationalization, i.e., its identification with the "kingdoms of this world." Thus the task was to reconstitute the new church order as a social-spiritual option for human society. Such an option must be voluntary and transnational. The anabaptist strategy for this reconstitution was to create a voluntary community of faithful obedience to Christ, in the confidence that Christ himself would fulfill the promise of "a new heaven and new earth in which dwells righteousness." Thus, on the one hand, anabaptism was not sectarian, withdrawing from responsibility for and witness to the world; on the other, it did not attempt to renew and reform the existing political order. Thus its goal and rationale were considerably different from the more pietistic vision of contemporary American evangelicalism.

Anabaptism understood the relation between the church and the kingdom of God to be close and integrated. The church in its visible, social expression was to be an authentic reflection of God's will "on earth as it is in heaven." It was, of course, an anticipatory expression and sign, and not the final one. But it was the realm in which the "peace, justice, and joy of the Holy Spirit" were experienced in this world (Rom. 14:17). Thus the church was essential in the anabaptist understanding of salvation. And the question of the *true visible church* was crucial.

In the course of its history, abetted by severe persecution, the anabaptist movement took on a sectarian character. Thus the current unitive movement within the anabaptist-Mennonite tradition begins from a *de facto* sectarianism, but not sectarianism by design. Roughly speaking, then, this unitive thrust runs parallel to the evangelical movement but has an important difference. Anabaptism's view of salvation as a new creation in Christ, and the church as a social expression of that new creation order, call for more than spiritual unity among varied ecclesiastical groups. It calls for nothing less than the formation of the authentic community (*koinonia*) of Christ in the midst of human society.

The Mennonite Experience in America

One cannot speak of a single Mennonite church of North America today, but must speak in the plural of Mennonite denominations which share a common history and orientation. Of the three largest groups, the Mennonite Church, the General Conference Mennonite Church, and the Mennonite Brethren Church, the theology and programmatic approach of the last seem most compatible with evangelicalism. However, segments within each denomination differ considerably in their convictions and approaches. The positions range from strictly fundamentalist (anticommunist and anti-liberal) to radical evangelical. Liberalism as technically defined is rare and remains more an implicit bias among lay representatives whose major concern is social justice.

American Mennonites, as we have noted, were influenced very early by the German-speaking pietistic revivalist movement in Pennsylvania and Virginia. In fact, they already had been under such influence in Europe.[18] This brush with revivalism in the 1880s and 1890s had a twofold effect. On the one hand, it caused division and the formation of several new small denominational groups, which tended to solidify the mainline Mennonites in their traditional ways. On the other hand, it introduced certain revivalistic vocabulary and emphases into the mainstream Mennonite churches. For example, an increased emphasis on salvation as a single personal crisis experience challenged the traditional anabaptist emphasis on a new birth which was identified with the start of a life of discipleship.

In spite of a certain confluence of American Mennonitism with evangelical Arminianism and holiness piety, Mennonites maintained a distinct self-image and hermeneutical perspective. Earlier in the century, that perspective might have been characterized with a phrase, "the all things," which was popular in Mennonite circles in the 1920s and 1930s. These "things" included scriptural doctrines, practices, and ceremonial ordinances which were "neglected" by other Christian groups, but which characterized the Mennonite community. Central among "the all things" were the twin doctrines of *nonconformity* and *nonresistance*.

Nonconformity is the negative face of a commitment to discipleship (*Nochfolge Christi*) and places emphasis upon obedience to Christ, not just verbal assent and a crisis conversion experience. Nonconformity is an attitude and a reflex that has been conditioned by centuries of opposition and persecution. The "world," defined by pride, self serving, and violence, includes the social-religious institutions which adapt to and even use these sinful human proclivities to control society. And in the experience of the Mennonites, these social institutions included the evangelical churches! They did not, of course, include all individuals who belonged to these churches, but the institutions themselves rather consistently had taken part in the opposition Mennonites had experienced.

In nineteenth- and twentieth-century American Mennonitism, nonconformity included more than the traditional cultural practices and adopted holiness restrictions. Prohibition of slavery, the rejection of the civil oath, opposition to secret orders, restriction of business alliances and investments with non-Christian companies, and general avoidance of economic institutions like the stock market and insurance companies were central. Evangelical revivalists considered such issues secondary to the new birth and did not consistently oppose such practices.

Nonresistance, or biblical pacifism, specifically meant nonparticipation in war and violence, but the overtones had a much wider significance. Historically, war in the western "Christian" nations has been fought under the banner of "God and country." There also has been a symbiotic relation between wars of conquest and missionary conquest.[19] Thus, at least implicitly, war and violence have been baptized as legitimate means not only to defend the "Christian nation" but to further the cause of Christ as well. The Mennonite rejection of all participation in war included the total rejection of this interpretation of Christ's mission. James Juhnke (1989) has pointed out how this concern became even more crucial during and after World War I, when war became total.[20]

The failure of fundamentalists and evangelicals to deal seriously with this *peace* message of Christ, and their naive identification of national values with the Christian gospel, not to mention their support for the nation's military causes, have constituted continuing obstacles to Mennonite participation in these movements. Even among the more fundamentalistic Mennonite leaders in the 1930s, this concern was a major stumbling block. In the first issue of his new periodical, *The Sword and Trumpet*, published in January 1929, George R. Brunk noted, "Even the so-called 'Fundamentalists' forsook the Gospel principles of peace and went into the business of human butchery. Nonresistance and nonconformity are two great fundamentals that are excluded by the fundamentalists."[21]

In the post–World War II period, Guy F. Hershberger, who clearly spoke for the majority of Mennonites at that time, continued and strengthened the witness to nonresistance while at the same time seeking ways to become involved redemptively in the problems of society. And long before C.F.H. Henry wrote *The Uneasy Conscience of Modern Fundamenatlism* (1947), his concern with social issues, especially peace issues, made him suspect among the fundamentalists.[22]

While Mennonites generally have agreed with the basic doctrinal tenents of evangelicalism, they always have been suspicious of a too-exclusive emphasis on orthodox doctrine. They themselves did not have a fully-developed, explicit theology to hold the movement together. Indeed, as S.F. Pannabecker pointed out in *Faith in Ferment* (1968), the Mennonite tradition never has been "doctrine-oriented."

John C. Wenger, a well-known Mennonite historian and theologian, accounted for this nontheological tendency with a reference to anabaptist sensitivities. He wrote that "the Anabaptists were somewhat uneasy that the theological enterprise somehow was likely to partake of the wisdom of this world — a danger which appeared very real to them. . . . And the persistent way in which the state churchmen urged the princes forward in the program of wiping out Anabaptism by persecution . . . added to the anxiety of the Anabaptists about theology as such."[23] Thus anabaptists tended to be suspicious of all Christendom's theological movements, whether theologically conservative and evangelistic or more liberal and social service-oriented. Their own best instincts led them to espouse a simple biblicism with emphasis on genuine conversion, and a discipleship that wedded gospel witness and gospel service.

We must add that Mennonite doctrine has been inclined more toward evangelical Arminianism than toward Calvinistic theology. Indeed, already in the sixteenth century, the anabaptists' emphasis on the necessity for obedient response to the call of the gospel caused them to be classified as synergist. Thus in the nineteenth and twentieth centuries, Mennonites have felt far more comfortable with the Wesleyan and Free Will Baptist traditions than with the more sharply-defined Calvinism of centrist fundamentalism and contemporary evangelicalism. This, of course, also has been a major point of tension within the evangelical movement itself, and the dominance of the Calvinist faction, especially in its dispensationalist guise, has discouraged many Mennonites from too close identification.[24]

Finally, the Mennonite understanding of social service in the name of Christ as a fundamental part of the gospel itself historically has created tension in the relation of Mennonites to fundamentalists. From the beginning, fraternal sharing of goods and even communalism have been integral to the anabaptist understanding of the church. Further, anabaptists have insisted that sharing the "cup of cold water" with those outside the church in relief and development projects is an essential part of sharing the gospel.[25]

While this sharing was part of the original vision of pietists such as A.H. Francke (1663–1727), it was lost in the fundamentalist emphasis on salvation as a purely spiritual and supernatural experience. One of the significant developments in contemporary evangelicalism has been a recovery of the social-service dimension of the gospel. This recovery of a social-service vision has rendered Mennonite cooperation more tenable.

In summary, the traditional Mennonite understanding of what is primary and what is secondary in the gospel differs from the American evangelical consensus. To characterize the position of the centrist group of Mennonites, perhaps the best we can do is follow J. Denny Weaver's suggestion of their three "priorities." He lists as first *the normativeness of Jesus for truth*. This places the emphasis on *praxis* and discipleship, rather than on *doxis* and rational thought, in determining "truth." Those who would follow Jesus must adopt his way of being in the world, namely, "take up his cross."

Second, Weaver lists *community*, or the new social reality in Christ, versus individualism. This places emphasis on reconciliation and relationship to our fellows as integral to salvation. To be "in Christ" means to be in the social body (the *koinonia*) of Christ. And last, Weaver lists *peace,* or *shalom*. The Mennonite "peace position" insists that "peace on earth" is a fundamental part of the good news of Christ, and that this peace cannot come through more violence. This stance breaks with the apocalyptic idea that peace can only be established by the violent overthrow and destruction of those who oppose our political and religious values. While there are differences on the fine points of this position, these priorities do represent a contemporary anabaptist-Mennonite consensus.[26] And such a consensus remains peripheral in American evangelicalism.

Concluding Critique

Against this background of historical comparisons, let me close by offering a critique of evangelicalism from an anabaptist-Mennonite perspective.

In the first place, as we have noted, the evangelical movement defies a precise theological definition. Indeed, theological divisions have become more evident during the last ten years. Thus we have no option but to identify the movement in terms of its social-historical context and its religio-cultural characteristics. In any case, anabaptists always have been opposed to the idea that a truly Christian movement can be understood simply in terms of its intellectual belief patterns.

From this perspective, how might one assess American evangelicalism? Certainly we should begin by acknowledging the new surge of confidence and interest it has stimulated in the churches. For example, the world evangelism conferences at Berlin, Lausanne, Amsterdam, and Manila certainly have had a significant impact. Further, the National Association of Evangelicals undoubtedly has been a positive unitive influence.

At the same time, we must also note that the movement seems to have had minimal effect on public morals and the intellectual zeitgeist. As Carl F.H. Henry pointed out in his address at the fortieth anniversary of Fuller Theological Seminary, evangelicalism has not effectively slowed the growth of secular humanism and relativism. Indeed, Henry rather pessimistically concluded that, in less than a generation, evangelicalism has been swamped by the moral relativism of the very culture it sought to change.[27] The nation and its churches seem to be more ideologically conservative, but how does this translate into authentic New Testament Christianity?

From an anabaptist-Mennonite perspective, the evangelical movement exhibits several major weaknesses which, in spite of the integrity of most of its leaders, have undercut its effectiveness as a genuine renewal movement.[28] Let me mention four.

The first is its accommodation to nationalistic American culture and its tacit espousal of nationalism and capitalism as *Christian* values. The movement has unabashedly waved the flag of "God and country." It generally has been critical of international movements such as the United Nations and the European Common Market, and fearful of any movement that might threaten American hegemony. On the other hand, its preachers have uncritically supported Israel's *nationalistic* supremacy as prerequisite to Christ's victory. Evangelicalism consistently has supported an ever-stronger American military establishment and in general has allied itself, at least tacitly with the political right.

The movement has lacked a clear moral critique of American political and social policy based on a distinctively New Testament Christian ethic. In short, it has tended to reinforce capitalistic nationalism in the name of Christian moral values, harking back to a nineteenth-century "Golden Age" when the evangelical social establishment dominated religion in the United States. Today its leaders seem willing, at least tacitly, again to become the dominant element in a civil establishment and to "set the political agenda for the twenty-first century."[29] This stance has given the movement an ethnocentric, defensive demeanor at a time when international understanding, justice, compassion, and reconciliation are the urgent needs of the moment.

Second, for all its emphasis on evangelism and church growth, the mission ideology and approach of its representative mission boards have remained basically imperialistic. Indeed, this position on missions is simply an extension of the basic nationalism and ethnocentricity. The fact that evangelicalism's call for personal conversion does not really challenge basic cultural values in the American setting has hidden this essentially imperialistic character of its missions in the rest of the world. In overseas settings, its theological definitions, cultural goals, and operational patterns all clearly carry the label "Made in America." Its missionary organizations continue to operate from a position of power and control of the mission.

Contextualization is still a suspect concept, as the battle which focuses on the ideas of Charles Kraft and the Fuller School of World Missions indicates. Eugene Nida's "three-language model of communication," which points out that Western Christian culture and biblical culture cannot be equated when we translate the gospel in crosscultural settings, still has made little headway in evangelical missionary practice.

This nationalistic presentation of the Christian witness has created an unnecessary offense and continues to link Christianity to Western political hegemony in the minds of people in Asia and the Third World. In countries such as Japan, where Christianity is still viewed as a "foreign" religion, it unnecessarily ties the fortunes of missionary activity to fluctuations in political relations.

The movement's third weakness is its capitulation to the spirit of individualism, which results in an inadequate theology of the church. It is not merely accidental that the contrasting movements within Protestantism have come to be labeled "evangelical" and "ecumenical" (or conciliar). Theologically speaking, these two are not necessarily opposed to each other. One can certainly be both evangelical and ecumenical. But the terminology indicates a significant difference of understanding concerning the nature of the church and its relation to the salvation of the individual. The contrast is between the nondenominational ideal of the church as a spiritual association of individually "born again" believers, and a more traditional "churchly" or denominational ideal of individuals finding salvation in and through the ministry of the church.

Evangelicalism's insistence on an individualistic stereotype of salvation, and on the value of aggressive competition in evangelism, has spawned a host of parachurch institutions that have no lines of responsibility to a sponsoring ecclesiastical body. This has greatly compounded the problem of irresponsible independency which was already so evident in American Christianity, and it has weakened the congregational base of the church. Lines for responsible conciliar consensus in decision making are almost completely absent, leaving the movement vulnerable to the fragmentation and contradiction that have eroded its influence.

Further, the theology of dispensational premillennialism continues to influence evangelicalism's understanding of the relation of the church and the kingdom of God, in spite of some neo-evangelicals' earlier break with it. Thus, evangelicals still tend to view the church as an emergency *substitute for*, rather than as a *continuation of*, Christ's own mission under his lordship in the world. This affects their strategic priorities and undergirds the movement's nondenominational stance, as mentioned above.

Priority remains on a verbal proclamation which calls disparate individuals to a private salvation. Evangelicalism does not understand the church as the Spirit's alternative community, bearing witness to Christ's lordship over the "principalities and powers" (Eph. 3:9–10). Instead of being the anticipatory community of salvation, expressing the rule of God among us, the church remains an adjunct institution more or less peripheral to the message of the gospel.

Saddled with its inadequate theology of the church, evangelicalism's options for social witness are between sectarian withdrawal and political activism. Having chosen the latter, evangelicalism's social witness has taken on a more strident political tone, as the movement demands prayer in the public schools, laws against abortion, etc., and vigorously defends capitalistic democracy. Its goal is to change national policy, rather than to create an authentic "kingdom" community in the church. This posture has further divided and weakened the prophetic effectiveness of the movement.

The anabaptist-Mennonite tradition always has been convinced that the church is central in God's plan and insists on the separation of church and worldly governments. For this reason, it has struggled to avoid political involvement in the sense of active politicking, but at the same time it has sought to give a relevant ethical witness on social and political issues. Such a stance requires, first, that the church itself, as a social institution, exemplify the new order of the kingdom of God within its own life. Second, this stance means noncompliance with unjust laws and social practices. It might also involve protest and advocacy of ethical political policy, but short of demanding legal enactment and enforcement of "Christian" moral codes or religious practices. The church as the body of Christ must live *in the world* and witness *to* the world, but it does so from a position of political weakness. Indeed, in this sense its weakness is its strength.

Finally, on a more theological note, evangelicalism continues to have a problem defining its working concept of authority. This has affected both its apologetical value and its hermeneutical method. On the one hand, following its scholastic and fundamentalist precedents, evangelicalism has been extremely reluctant to admit that its epistemological stance is confessional. And it continues to insist that the ultimate formal authority for theological statements is the words of God as they appear in written documents, and not the Word spoken in Christ. As a consequence, its apologetical value has been seriously limited. In the past it has been lured into making rationalistic and quasiempirical claims on the basis of biblical interpretations that some of the more "radical" evangelicals now are beginning to call into question.

Hermeneutically, the movement has been involved in a "scribal" approach to both the interpretation and the application of Scripture, which hampers its flexibility in making cultural adaptations. The inadequacy of this approach becomes most evident in its missionary attempts to produce a duplicate theology and similar churches across cultures.

The problem, much like that of the Jewish scribes in the pre-Christian era, lies in the fact that inerrancy theory makes something other than God absolute. Just as the scribes made Torah absolute and thus in effect limited God to his own law, so the inerrancy advocates have made the Scriptures absolute. In order to invest them with absolute authority, they define them as the words of God, who cannot speak a falsehood. But so long as the meaning of verbal symbols (words) is culturally conditioned, we must speak simply of God limiting himself to our finite situation.

In order to develop a postliberal evangelical position, we must escape the tyranny of the rationalistic assumptions that are characteristic of both liberal and fundamentalist methodology alike, and we must locate the authority for theology in God himself, as he is revealed in Christ. Until the movement deals more radically with this problem and those mentioned above, we cannot expect to see a genuine "evangelical *renaissance*."

NOTES

1. Walter Klaassen, *Anabaptism: Neither Catholic nor Protestant* (Waterloo, Ontario, Canada: Conrad Press, 1981).
2. See "The Evangelical Family Tree" as I diagrammed it in C. Norman Kraus, *Evangelicalism and Anabaptism* (Scottdale, Penn.: Herald Press, 1979), 44.
3. Werner O. Packull has given an excellent description of this part of the movement in his *Mysticism and the Early South German-Austrian Anabaptist Movement, 1525–1531* (Scottdale, Penn.: Herald Press, 1979).
4. Richard K. MacMaster, *Land, Piety, Peoplehood* (Scottdale, Penn.: Herald Press, 1985), is the first of a projected series on the Mennonite experience. Other volumes are in preparation. See also Beulah Stauffer Hostetler, *American Mennonites and Protestant Movements* (Scottdale, Penn.: Herald Press, 1987). For fundamentalism, see George W. Dollar, *A History of Fundamentalism in America* (Greenville, S.C.: Bob Jones Univ., 1973), and Jerry Falwell, ed., *The Fundamentalist Phenomenon* (Garden City, N.J.: Doubleday, 1981).

5. Robert Price, "Inerrant the Wind: The Troubled House of North American Evangelicals," *Evangelical Quarterly* 55, no. 3 (July 1983):129–44; Richard Quebedeaux, *The Worldly Evangelicals* (New York: Harper and Row, 1978), 163ff.; Robert E. Webber, *Common Roots: A Call to Evangelical Maturity* (Grand Rapids, Mich.: Zondervan, 1978). For a theological assessment, see John Gerstner, "The Theological Boundaries of Evangelical Faith" (21–37), and Kenneth Kantzer, "Unity and Diversity in Evangelical Faith" (36–67), in *The Evangelicals*, ed. David Wells and John Woodbridge (Nashville, Tenn.: Abingdon, 1975).

6. Where, for example, is one to classify Donald Bloesch and Bernard Ramm, who have moved in a Barthian direction?

7. George Marsden tells the story of the struggles between the fundamentalists and neofundamentalists in his *Reforming Fundamentalism* (Grand Rapids, Mich.: Eerdmans, 1987).

8. See Kantzer's foreword to the report of the summit, *Applying the Scriptures* (Grand Rapids, Mich.: Zondervan, 1987).

9. Robert K. Johnston, ed., *The Use of the Bible in Theology: Evangelical Options* (Atlanta, Ga.: John Knox, 1985).

10. The rightwing conservative elements in contemporary Mennonitism usually make issues of fundamentalist doctrines such as inerrancy and dispensationalist premillennialism. They often take a more defensive, patriotic stand on political issues, using the "two kingdom" doctrine as theological justification. And they generally support the most conservative nondenominational missionary societies, TV evangelists, etc.

11. A number of evangelical authors have attempted to include the anabaptist-Mennonites within evangelicalism, but generally this is done with broad strokes and by inference. For example, Ed Dobson and Ed Hindson assert that "fundamentalism is the spiritual and intellectual descendant of the nonconformist Free Church movement" (p. 57) and pay tribute to the anabaptists of Hubmaier's variety and to the Mennonites. They thus imply that fundamentalism stands in the baptist-anabaptist tradition, without really facing the troubling issues that separate those of the anabaptist tradition from American neofundamentalism. See Falwell, *Fundamentalist Phenomenon,* 27–57.

Robert Webber's inclusion of "anabaptist evangelicalism" as one of the subcultural evangelical groups similarly avoids the tension and even the contradictions that exist between this position and others on his list. See Webber, *Common Roots*, 38. Kenneth Kantzer's incidental comment that the distinguishing feature of anabaptists is the "gathered" versus the "folk" church really does not touch the issues at all. We may continue to hope that Ron Sider's comment that "evangelicals and Mennonites need each other to correct distortions" represents the attitudes of both partners in the dialogue. But the differences are deeper than Sider indicated in his article "Evangelicalism and the Mennonite Tradition" (in *Evangelicalism and Anabaptism*, 149–68). While Franky Schaeffer represents an extreme rightest position, his lengthy and biting attack on Ron Sider for his peace position indicates the nature and the depth of the conflict. See Franky Schaeffer, *Bad News For Modern Man* (Westchester, Ill.: Crossway Books, 1984).

12. John H. Yoder points out the limits of historical comparisons in his article, "The Hermeneutics of Anabaptism," in *Essays on Biblical Interpretation*, ed. Willard Swartley (Elkhart, Ind.: Institute of Mennonite Studies, 1984).

13. Donald Bloesch, *The Evangelical Renaissance* (Grand Rapids, Mich.: William B. Eerdmans, 1973), 51–52.

14. David Wells and Clark Pinnock, eds., *Toward A Theology for the Future* (Carol Stream, Ill.: Creation House, 1975), 96.

15. In this regard the movement is genetically faithful to Protestant orthodoxy, its 17th-century forebear. Of course, not all evangelical preachers and teachers are urging a rationalistic approach to the gospel. Men like Thomas Finger, Charles Kraft, Donald Bloesch, and John Yoder certainly are not, but Carl F.H. Henry's insistence on "inscripturated revelation" and the propositional character of truth seems to imply a rationalist assumption. To see the explicit logic of the position, one has only to read the works of men like the late Francis Schaeffer (whose writings continue to be a staple evangelical commodity), Harold Lindsell, J.I. Packer, and Kenneth Kantzer.

16. This practical hermeneutical concern for discipleship was the same for literalist Conrad Grebel or spiritualist Hans Denck.

17. Nondenominationalism was, in the first place, a rejection of the claims of denominational bodies as ecclesiastical organizations to be representatives of the true church. But it also was a rejection of the idea that the church has a social base. It is a heavenly reality and a "spiritual fellowship." Since the true church is a spiritual concept, only truly spiritual persons can represent it. Further, since the true church can be theologically defined only by the "fundamentals," a denomination, as a social structure organized on the basis of distinctive religious convictions, has no ecclesiastical significance.

18. See Richard K. McMaster, *Land, Piety, and Peoplehood: The Establishment of Mennonite Communities in America, 1688–1790* (Scottdale, Penn.: Herald Press, 1985), 175–82; and Robert Friedmann, *Mennonite Piety Through the Centuries* (Goshen, Ind.: Mennonite Historical Library, 1949).

19. Robert Handy documents this in his *Christian America: Protestant Hopes and Historical Realities* (New York: Oxford Univ. Press, 1971), 117ff.

20. Juhnke is preparing the third volume in *The Mennonite Experience in America* series, on the period 1890–1930, to be published by Herald Press, Scottdale, Penn. See esp. chs. 7 and 8. See also S.F. Pannabecker, *Faith in Ferment* (Newton, Kan.: Faith and Life Press, 1968), 227–39; and Rodney J. Sawatsky, *The Influence of Fundamentalism on Mennonite Nonresistance, 1908–1944* (M.A. thesis, Univ. of Minnesota, 1973).

21. The original *Sword and Trumpet*, edited and published by George R. Brunk of Newport News, Virginia, appeared in Jan. 1929; quotation on p. 22. Brunk follows this quote by recounting a recent incident involving his home congregation. "At Newport News, Virginia, in the great Billy Sunday meetings recently, seats were reserved one night for Mennonites, but they were left empty; a fitting rebuke to the preacher's proud, egotistical man-pleasing spirit; the irreverent, clownish, belligerent manner, and interweaving of saving truth with destructive error." As an example of such error, he quotes from an earlier prayer of Sunday, "Jesus! you're sure taking a lot of back talk from Kaiser. . . . Count Billy Sunday in up to his neck when war comes. . . . Jesus will be our Commander-in-chief, and he has Hindenburg beat to a frazzle." Then Brunk adds, "Is it not a great sin to encourage such blind guides by honoring and enriching them?" ("Notes and Items," *Sword and Trumpet* 1, no. 1).

22. Hershberger has been a prolific writer. See Theron Schlabach's biographical article, "To Focus a Vision," in *Kingdom, Cross and Community*, ed. J.R. Burkholder and Calvin Redekop (Scottdale, Penn.: Herald Press, 1976), 15–50. A full bibiliography of Hershberger's works is also included in this volume. They throw much light on the relation of Mennonites to the fundamentalist movement.

23. Pannabecker, *Faith in Ferment*, 221f; and John Christian Wenger, *The Mennonite Church in America* (Scottdale, Penn.: Herald Press, 1966), 255.

24. According to John Gerstner, American evangelicalism is represented at its pristine best in Jonathan Edwards, Charles Hodge, and B.B. Warfield ("Theological

Boundaries, 27). Using this criterion, he notes that Charles Finney, "the greatest of nineteenth-century evangelists, became the greatest of nineteenth-century foes of evangelicalism." According to this definition, most anabaptists of the 16th century should not be included, and neither should most contemporary Mennonites. The more conservative faction of the Mennonite Brethren, a group strongly influenced by baptist revivalism while still in Russia, is perhaps an exception.

25. One should note the importance to the Mennonite self-identity of organizations such as the Mennonite Central Committee, Mennonite Mutual Aid, Mennonite Disaster Service, and Mennonite Voluntary Services. One could plausibly argue that it is these service organizations within the church that define the distinctly Mennonite character and provide much of the glue holding the various Mennonite groups together.

26. J. Denny Weaver, *Becoming Anabaptist: The Origin and Significance of Sixteenth Century Anabaptism* (Scottdale, Penn.: Herald Press, 1987), 120ff.

27. Carl F.H. Henry, "Evangelical Trends in Theology and Ethics," 3 Nov. 1987. Compare Nathan Hatch's similar evaluation, "Evangelicalism as a Democratic Movement," in *Evangelicalism and Modern America*, ed. George Marsden (Grand Rapids, Mich.: Eerdmans, 1984), 81–82.

28. Of course, the scandals of popular figures such as the Bakkers, and the inherent contradictions of an Ollie North piously claiming a new birth but at the same time justifying the most blatant political immorality and even illegality, have hurt the movement's image, but the problem lies deeper.

29. There is protest and challenge of this position within the movement, but by the evangelical scholars' own reckoning, it represents the "radical" minority. More recently key figures such as Billy Graham, who in 1970 spoke explicitly of America as the embodiment of Judeo-Christian values, seem to have taken a less nationalistic line. And people like Jerry Falwell and Pat Robertson, in the thick of political battle, seem to have retracted their earlier positions. Both have publicly disavowed any intention of making America "Christian." The phrase, "to set the agenda for the twenty-first century," is part of the Robertson campaign rhetoric.

CHAPTER 12

Evangelicals and the Self-Consciously Reformed

Mark A. Noll

Cassandra Niemczyk

Dutch Calvinist immigrants to America's heartland in the nineteenth century had a word for the burgeoning evangelicalism of their new land: "Methodistic."[1] In fact, however, the evangelicals to whom the Reformed Dutch referred usually were not Methodists at all, but "democratized Calvinists." John Nevin, the German Reformed theologian from Mercersburg, Pennsylvania, had a sharper eye for the nuances of popular American religion. His catchall designation, "Puritans," was intended to designate the descendants of seventeenth- and eighteenth-century Congregationalism and eighteenth-century Presbyterianism. But it was meant to be every bit as critical as the Netherlander's expression.[2] In the twentieth century, the distancing term would become "fundamentalist." Transplanted Europeans of Reformed commitment, or Americans who aspired to the doctrinal purity of sixteenth-century Geneva or Scotland, used these words to set themselves apart from what one Christian Reformed commentator has recently described, with self-conscious overstatement, as "intellectually slovenly, heart-on-the-sleeve American revivalism."[3]

When leaders of America's self-consciously Reformed communities have spoken of "evangelicalism," they usually have been referring to a limited sector of popular Protestantism of the nineteenth and twentieth centuries. For these Reformed Protestants, "evangelicals" usually are other heirs of the Protestant Reformation—Congregationalists, Presbyterians, Baptists—who have lived for a longer time in North America. In the twentieth century, the self-consciously Reformed also have reflected at some length on their relationship with the fundamentalists and the neo-evangelical heirs of fundamentalism, that is, with individuals and groups associated with Moody Bible Institute, Dallas Seminary, Gordon College and Seminary, *Christianity Today,* Billy Graham, Wheaton College, Fuller Seminary, and similar organizations. In the full range of American evangelicals—including Methodists and other Wesleyans, the holiness groups, and the pentecostals — the Reformed have taken less direct interest.

Reformed attitudes toward even a delimited range of evangelicals, however, still are instructive for understanding the broader phenomenon of evangelicalism in America. What they illustrate most generally is the process whereby the very act of criticizing a mainstream religious movement draws the critic closer to the banks of that stream.

More particularly, Reformed assessments of evangelicalism show how conceptions of Christianity inherited from Europe clash with the practice of the faith as it has developed in America. This paper is not able to canvass the full array of self-consciously Reformed reactions to American evangelicalism.[4] Rather, by focusing on three important examples, it describes a common Reformed resistance to the American definitions of Christianity in terms of personal piety and individual ethics. Against such definitions, the nineteenth-century Orthodox Presbyterian church has stressed the maintenance of traditional doctrine, and one strand of the contemporary Christian Reformed church has advocated an ecclesiastical-cultural perspective in Christian life in the world.[5] From these perspectives, the self-consciously Reformed have criticized, yet also gradually accommodated themselves to, the prevailing tendencies of at least some American evangelicals.

"Puritanism" and the Mercersburg Theology of Nevin and Schaff

Joseph Berg, Philadelphia pastor and outspoken leader in the German Reformed denomination from which he eventually withdrew, wrote in 1846, "Religion is a personal matter from beginning to end. . . . The church does not make the believer. Believers constitute the church." No idea could have more directly opposed the convictions of Mercersburg theologian John Williamson Nevin (1803–1886) and his colleague, the church historian Philip Schaff (1819–93). To these architects of a Romantic Reformed idealism, Christianity "in its very conception . . . is the power of a common or general life; which can never appear therefore as something isolated and single, simply, but always includes the idea of society and communion, under all its manifestations."[6]

In the mid-nineteenth century, the Mercersburg theology of Nevin and Schaff took firm hold of the German Reformed church, centered in south-central and eastern Pennsylvania. In this theology, strongly supported by nineteenth-century continental convictions about organic development, the church occupied a lofty position. It was the medium through which faith was brought to the believer, and it was the necessary society in which the recipient would live out that faith. The visible, institutional, liturgical, and sacramental body was indispensable to the whole process of conversion and sanctification. In short, "No church, no Christ."[7] The position was as close, ecclesiastically, to Roman Catholicism as American Protestantism would ever come. In the Mercersburg theology, Christianity was *communal*. It comes as no surprise that one modern historian of the movement has seen it as a reaction against Jeffersonian democracy.[8] The Mercersburg perspective assuredly cut across the grain of nineteenth-century American culture, including the grassroots revivalism of the day.

Nevin and Schaff harbored no ill will toward evangelical piety. What they could not tolerate were certain "new measures" of revivalism, associated with Oberlin College and originating with the New Haven Theology, an Americanized offshoot of Puritanism.[9] The Mercersburg men reserved particular disdain for the efforts of Charles Grandison Finney, whose "right use of the constituted means" had turned the sawdust trail into an American institution. For Nevin and Schaff, the tent meetings of Finneyite revivalism spawned a circus atmosphere in which the following questionable outcomes prevailed: "loud groaning, crying and shouting, clapping of hands, jumping, falling down, permitting women to pray in mixed assemblies, admitting unlearned ministers and frequent attacks on educated, and the assumption that all who came to the anxious seat and declared they had found peace there in the midst of the animal excitement were truly converted."[10]

As these German Reformed theologicans saw America's religious situation in the mid-nineteenth century, they felt that frontier evangelists had emphasized conversion at the expense of sanctification, fragmented the major denominations into sects, demonstrated an exaggerated hostility toward form and tradition in religion, encouraged interdenominational animosity, supported a morbid cultural asceticism, and replaced ancient Christian creeds with modern, *ad hoc* summaries of personal and capricious opinion. Nevin lamented:

> Blind outward authority, and mere private judgment are alike insufficient as a key to the Bible. What we desire is, that this should be acknowledged, and a true conciliation at least aimed at between the great tendencies, which are here placed in opposition and conflict. It is not by the simple assertion of its own life, but in *so* asserting this life as to leave no room for the other side of religion that Puritanism [i.e., evangelicalism] seems to us to be too often in fault.[11]

Evangelicalism, then, was viewed as dogmatically one-sided in its strident individualism and as very much the product of the cultural conventions of the American nineteenth century.

For their part, the Mercersburg theologians exhibited an unreflective attachment to the intellectual conventions of Hegelian Germany. Nonetheless, they still illustrate well a persistent Reformed perception of American evangelicalism—that its stress on the individual leaves little room for a biblical and traditional view of the church. At the same time that Mercersburg was taking American evangelicalism to task, however, it too was proceeding along a path of Americanization. Mercersburg's philosophical idealism eventually became a point of contact with liberalizing forces in the Congregational church. A complicated denominational story evolved, but the identification of the German Reformed with American, if not necessarily evangelical, patterns of church life culminated in 1957, when the remnant of the German Reformed church united with a "puritan" denomination, the Christian Congregational Churches, to become the United Church of Christ.[12]

Fundamentalism, Evangelicalism, and the Orthodox Presbyterian Church

The story of the Orthodox Presbyterian Church (OPC) illustrates another kind of manuevering between a self-consciously Reformed body and the larger world of American evangelicalism. In this case, a tension between the Reformed and the evangelical is as old as the denomination. For Orthodox Presbyterians, *Reformed* has meant the purity of Calvinist doctrine as codified initially by the Westminister Confession and Catechisms of the 1640s and defended in the nineteenth century by the Old School Presbyterian theologians at Princeton Theological Seminary (Archibald Alexander, Charles Hodge, and B.B. Warfield). *Evangelical*, on the other hand, is a more ambiguous term. It may have positive connotations with reference to popular representations of conservative Protestantism. But it may also speak negatively of "Arminian," "charismatic," or other tendencies thought to detract from the purity of Reformed faith. The history of the Orthodox Presbyterian Church reveals a significant shift on questions posed by the intersection of evangelical and Reformed. For its first quarter-century or so, the "true Reformed" position won out in the denomination, while advocates of a more "evangelical" stance were forced to depart. In the last quarter-century the roles have been reversed. Now denominational leaders edge toward fuller fellowship with evangelicals, and a smaller dissenting faction holds out for an uncompromising defense of Reformed faith. In both phases, however, the key issue has been the acceptable limits of evangelical influence in the life of a truly Reformed church.

On 11 June 1936, J. Gresham Machen and his small coterie of fellow conservatives seceded from the Presbyterian Church in the U.S.A. to form what eventually was to become the Orthodox Presbyterian Church. In the decade before 1936, Machen, a New Testament scholar from Princeton and Westminster seminaries, had led a losing battle against the parent denomination's growing tolerance of theological liberalism. If *true* Presbyterianism, as the finest expression of historic orthodox Christianity, were to survive in this country, Machen and a few of his colleagues felt, then a whole new ecclesiastical system would be needed to replace the diseased denomination. The fledgling group would become *the* Presbyterian Church of America, in effect — the old denomination stripped of its impurities.[13]

The opening statement at the First General Assembly in 1936, by Rev. H. McAllister Griffiths, made this intention crystal clear. They had gathered, said Griffiths, "to continue what we believe to be the true spiritual succession of the Presbyterian Church in the U.S.A., which we hold to have been abandoned by the present organization of that body."[14] The year before, members of the Constitutional Convenant Union, which conservatives had formed to defend adherence to the Westminister Confession, had pledged themselves "to maintain the Constitution of the Presbyterian Church in the U.S.A., . . . making every effort to bring about a reform of the existing church organization, . . . but . . . if such efforts fail . . . holding ourselves ready to perpetuate the true Presbyterian Church in the U.S.A, [PCUSA] regardless of cost."[15] Once the deed was done, Machen could say, "On Thursday, June 11, 1936, the hopes of many long years were realized. We became members, at last, of a true Presbyterian Church; we recovered, at last, the blessing of true Christian fellowship."[16] The name by which these truly Reformed Presbyterians called themselves was simply "The Presbyterian Church of America."

The sense that this new, as-yet tiny group was *the* Presbyterian Church of America — charged with preserving both the Reformed faith and a broad reach into America — remained strong throughout the months before the Second General Assembly in November 1936. At that gathering, the statistical report was encouraging. In only five months the number of ministers had leaped from 34 to 108, and there were now congregations in sixteen states.[17] The avalanche, perhaps, had begun. The tide within the Northern Presbyterian Church, perhaps, had begun to turn. Maybe now the great host in the PCUSA that shared an aversion to liberalism would overcome its toleration of pluralism and come out to fulfill the vision of *the* Presbyterian Church of America.

In late 1936, the self-identity of the new group hung at least in part upon the possibility that it might supplant the old denomination as the recognized heir of the great Presbyterian tradition, as the public expounder of the Westminster standards, and as the acknowledged representative in twentieth-century America of the faith of John Calvin, John Knox, and John Witherspoon.

Yet it was not to be. The hosts did not come out. The big Presbyterian Church remained the big Presbyterian Church. And within a year of the new group's formation, its vision of becoming in fact, as well as in name, *the* Presbyterian Church of America irretrievably collapsed. In spring 1937, *the* one true Presbyterian Church of America divided into two. Even as the Second General Assembly in 1936 reported optimistically on the growth in ministers and congregations, long and acrid debate took place on the new body's stance toward issues at the core of self-identity for fundamentalist evangelicals.[18] Chief among these issues was the premillennial eschatology associated with despensationalism, a theological system with recent but very strong roots among a broad range of northern conservative Protestants. The other sensitive issues that troubled the new denomination were also matters defined by America's conservative evangelical tradition. These included the question of drinking alcoholic beverages and the question of agencies independent of General Assembly authority.

The division of 1937 certainly helped clarify the self-identity of those who reamined in the Presbyterian Church of America. Supporters of the new splinter, the Bible Presbyterian Synod, were also antiliberal and antipluralist, but they tolerated the mores and the doctrinal emphases of American fundamentalism more willingly. Earlier, in 1929, Machen had founded Westminister Seminary to protest a reorganization of Princeton Seminary that left that institution in the hands of doctrinal inclusivists. On that occasion, he had received much commendation from Presbyterian and non-Presbyterian conservatives, who were delighted to see an institution like Westminster arise. Some of these leaders urged Machen to adopt a doctrinal basis that made room for premillennialists, but Machen, despite impressive pledges of support if only he could make this nod in the direction of the larger evangelical world, would hear nothing of it. To Machen, as he put it in a letter, premillennialism was "a very serious heresy" that greatly encouraged the doctrinal weakness and practical compromises to which American churches were so prone.[19] If the Westminster standards did not permit dispensationalism, neither would Machen and his closest associates. If the Bible did not condemn all drinking, neither would they. The price of this clarification was a drastic slowing of momentum. Almost at the very inception of *The* Presbyterian Church of America came the division that mocked its aspirations to become a large conservative church and a dynamic influence upon America.

Then insult was added to injury. The northern Presbyterian church (PCUSA) took the smaller denomination to court over its name and won a judgment forbidding the new group from calling itself "The Presbyterian Church of America." This circumstance brought out into the open the conundrum of self-identity. The new denomination was definitely Reformed, as defined by faithful adherence to the Westminster standards. It was antimodernist. It was antipluralist. It was Old School rather than New School. But how did it fit into the American scene?

The Fifth General Assembly of February 1939 wrestled with the question of self-identity, as it considered what the denomination's new name would be. Were they, as various ones suggested, the Orthodox Presbyterian Church, the Evangelical Presbyterian Church, the Presbyterian and Reformed Church of America, the North American Presbyterian church, the Presbyterian Church of Christ, the Protestant Presbyterian Church of America, the Seceding Presbyterian Church of America, the Free Presbyterian Church of America, the American Orthodox Presbyterian Church, or even the True Presbyterian Church of the World? In the end, sentiment was divided nearly equally between the Orthodox Presbyterian Church and the Evangelical Presbyterian Church, with only lesser support for names retaining the word America. By one vote, "Orthodox" prevailed over "Evangelical," and so the name has remained.[20]

The early leaders of the Orthodox Presbyterian Church (OPC) were willing to stand *with* fundamentalists *against* modernists, but only during the crisis of separation and its immediate aftermath. Thereafter, the new church tended to be more self-consciously Reformed. Its tendency was to view Arminianism and dispensationalism, no matter how prevalent among fundamentalist allies, as un-Reformed heresy.

The OPC's subsequent ecumenical activity followed the lines of those earliest General Assemblies. While some contact continued with generally evangelical and antiliberal groups, the OPC has experienced closest fellowship with small, self-consciously Reformed bodies. Like the OPC, most of these groups have some history of combative division over their faithfulness to historic Reformed confessions.

From the first, the leadership exerted by Westminster Theological Seminary in the denomination helped to define the OPC's ecumenical partners as well. Thus, through John Murray links were forged with the Free Presbyterian Church of Scotland. More important by far, however was the bond with the Christian Reformed Church (CRC), a bond symbolized by the Christian Reformed ministers — R.B. Kuiper, Ned B. Stonehouse, and Cornelius Van Til — who, after Machen's death in 1937, became the mainstays of the Westminster faculty. When the synod of the CRC sent a telegram to the first OPC General Assembly, extending an invitation for the new denomination to commision a fraternal delegate to its meetings, the assembly appointed Corenelius Van Til to that task. Later in 1936, Van Til reported back on the cordial reception he had received from the CRC.[21]

The OPC's informal ties with other exclusively Reformed bodies were cultivated through the years and eventually formed the basis for more permanent organizations, including the Reformed Ecumenical Synod, an international body founded under the leadership of the CRC in 1946, and the North American Presbyterian and Reformed Council, established in 1975.

Despite its determination to be Reformed, the OPC did not entirely cut itself off from evangelical associations. The General Assembly of 1941 elected a Committee of Nine to study the denomination's relationship to American culture in general and to other ecclesiastical bodies in particular. Cornelius Van Til and Gordon H. Clark, who later in the decade came to represent irreconcilable factions in the church, were members of this committee. It placed two recommendations before the 1942 General Assembly. That body adopted a proposal to work toward the creation of a federation of Presbyterian and Reformed churches, but failed to sanction a move toward cooperation with broadly evangelical bodies.[22]

In that same year, the OPC received an invitation to join the American Council of Christian Churches, Carl McIntire's fundamentalist analogue to the more liberal Federal Council. The General Assembly set up a committee to investigate the council. In 1945 this committee drafted a statement spelling out the principles that would channel the OPC's fellowship with other churches in the years to come. According to this statement, Lutheran, Baptist, and Methodist denominations merited the name of Christian churches; but "Presbyterianism has historically insisted on its being the most consistent manifestation of Christ's body. Therefore, it could not grant that other churches are equally pure." Again, "It must be assumed that the Orthodox Presbyterian Church is convinced that its principles and practices are more Scriptural than are the principles and practices of such churches as are not Reformed or Presbyterian." Most far-reaching of all, "In no case may the Orthodox Presbyterian Church in its cooperation with other churches sacrifice, or even compromise, its distinctiveness. Its distinctiveness is its reason for existence."[23] Under this umbrella, cooperation could exist only with Reformed and Presbyterian groups. Non-Reformed evangelical churches were not just "different," they were clearly inferior to the spiritual defenders of truly Reformed faith.

Thus it came about that, in an era during which evangelical parachurch and ecumenical activity revived, the Orthodox Presbyterian Church retreated to the sidelines. In 1949, the OPC did join the International Council of Christian Churches, but with list in hand of un-Reformed things that needed to be changed. When the council refused to make concessions, the stalwart Calvinists withdrew their membership.[24] They also stepped back from the ever-widening circle of the National Association of Evangelicals.

Although this policy of separation, grounded in a self-conscious doctrinal purity, was formally adopted by the political machinery of the OPC during the 1940s, it by no means reflected a unanimity of opinion. The dissenters stepped forward during the years of controversy that surrounded the ordination to the ministry of Gordon H. Clark. Clark was a professor of philosophy, and the problems that surfaced during his vocational transition concerned esoteric points of theology. One of Clark's commitments that made him suspect to the Van Til faction was that Clark's philosophy was not the presuppositional variety that Van Til had adapted from Dutch sources for use at Westminster. Suspicion of Clark reflected in part suspicion of the American provenance of his thought.

During the latter half of the 1940s, when the Clark controversy came to a head, nondoctrinal issues became as important as doctrinal ones. As the sides lined up on Clark's ordination, it became apparent to some observers that the division cut widely. The young philosopher and his supporters — in contrast to the Van Til coalition — affirmed a vision of the OPC that was at odds with the prevailing denominational policy on ecumenicity. Specifically, certain ministers and elders in the OPC were unhappy with the retreat from cooperation with evangelical churches. The goal of this faction pointed beyond a merely principled unity, in line with "conservative American Presbyterian tradition," to a full, pragmatic coalition that would — in alliance with a wide range of fundamentalistic and evangelical allies — trounce modernism once and for all. Clark claimed that the denomination had unfavorably changed its attitude toward evangelicals during its first decade of existence. In the beginning, he said in reproaching the opposition, "we held them to be brethren . . . and looked on their churches as sister churches."[25]

The faction led by the Westminster faculty supported the formation of ties with other Reformed denominations but shied away from evangelical churches for fear of an Arminian influence. To the Westminster group, Arminianism, was the tantamount to a denial of historic Calvinism. Supporters of Clark, on the other hand, did not construe Arminianism as "another gospel; rather, they saw it as an "inconsistent statement of the true gospel." Not Arminians themselves, they nonetheless wanted the OPC to assume a character and appearance more in keeping with American evangelicalism. From their perspective, the little denomination was becoming too sectarian, too European, and too narrow in its doctrinal disputation.[26]

Toward the end of the decade, Clark and several of his closest associates withdrew from the Orthodox Presbyterian Church and affiliated themselves with other Reformed groups which were more tolerant of mainstream evangelical religion. Arthur Kuschke, librarian at Westminster Seminary during the period of their departure, reflected on the situation in a letter to a friend in 1951: "Their actual goal was the control of the OPC in order to direct it along a general evangelical line, rather than a specifically Reformed line. Accordingly, all of this point of view who finally left did so not because of the failure to establish Dr. Clark's views as orthodox but because they could see their attempt to control the OPC had failed."[27] Whether or not this analysis is correct, the departure of the Clark coalition from the denomination fixed the identity of what was left behind. The OPC was then a Reformed and not an evangelical church.

Over time, however, the hard line against non-Reformed believers has mellowed, so much so that more recently, the "true Reformed" factions have fallen from power in the denomination. In 1961, an interchurch relations committee acknowledged that differences among denominations may arise from extratheological sources and are not necessarily bad for the promulgation of the Christian faith. These "differences that exist often manifest the diversity which the church of Christ ought to exemplify and make for the enrichment of the church's total witness." Jack J. Peterson, a chairman of this committee, has confessed, "We believe in the unity of the body of Christ and strive to work toward the realization of that unity in the fullest way possible. . . . But the command of Christ to dwell together in unity has motivated us to face the difficult and the impossible."[29]

And what is "the difficult and the impossible"? Orthodox Presbyterian John P. Galbraith gives us a clue:

> There is one church. All of God's elect trusting in Christ as their one and only Savior are members of that church. As such they should show it in fellowship and mutual care. Therefore, the fact that one is "Reformed," and others are, say, "Arminian," does not mean that they are not members with us of the one body which is Christ, and, thus, of one another. As members of that body with us we have responsibilities to them. They are two-fold: to express our common membership in Christ and our family love for them in every way we can, and to instruct and learn from one another to the end that we may supply to each other what each is lacking in love, faith, knowledge, and obedience.[30]

Lest we assume that the OPC pendulum has swung too far, it is necessary to point out that Galbraith's ecumenical conception refers more to inter*personal* relations than to inter*church* affairs. But it does represent a clear movement on the part of the OPC toward non-Reformed American evangelicals. In the 1980s, the more strictly Reformed factions have experienced a loss of power. Their representatives now complain that "instead of the [separated Reformed] seminaries really inculcating Reformed think-

ing into the masses, the masses have 'evangelicalized' the Reformed seminaries. . . . Men flow from the seminaries without a real understanding of
how they are (or *should be*) distinctive from evangelicalism."³¹ And once
again the denomination is being challenged to say whether it is "Premillennial or Reformed?"³²

The difference between the late 1930s and the late 1980s, however, is
significant. Where once "true Reformed" positions dominated the OPC's
General Assembly, they are now heard in fugitive periodicals. The voices
more open to cooperation with American evangelicals now come from the
denomination's officials.

The larger significance of the OPC's history of discussion about evangelicals certainly must be that it is very difficult to remain a strictly Reformed *American* denomination. To the extent that a group does not seal
itself off from the country's larger religious life — as the OPC never has
done — and to the extent that a group seeks to promote its position in the
wider culture — as the OPC and especially Westminster Seminary have
tried to do, to that extent it is very difficult to remain pristine. The very
effort to maintain a Reformed position in America seems to lead inevitably to some accommodation of Reformed doctrine to the more practical
pieties of the American experience.

Neo-Evangelicalism and the Christian Reformed Church

The effort by the Christian Reformed Church (CRC) to preserve its Dutch
Calvinism in the context of America's broader evangelicalism is not, as
with the OPC, primarily a question of doctrine, but is more a matter of
culture and ecclesiology. Especially in the story of relations between American neo-evangelicals and the progressive wing of the CRC, we see once
again why Reformed Christians have been suspicious of evangelicalism,
but also how they have come to feel at ease with the objects of their
suspicion.

Unlike the Orthodox Presbyterian Church, which is geographically
and ethnically dispersed, the predominantly Dutch Christian Reformed
denomination is concentrated in pockets across the Upper Midwest, where
its immigrant founding fathers and mothers first settled in the middle of
the nineteenth century. Two secessions from the established Reformed
Church in the Netherlands and two subsequent waves of emigration from
the old country contributed theological diversity as well as numbers to the
new American denomination.

The CRC, which separated in 1857 from the longstanding Reformed Church in America, reflected three distinct varieties of Dutch Calvinism: defensive *confessionalists* who rested their case on traditional denominational creeds, *antithetical Calvinists* whose attitude of extreme separation allowed no neutral ground to exist between the church and the world, and the Kuyperian *positive Calvinists* whose penchant for "common grace" undergirded the party's movement toward denominational education, missionary and social outreach, and a measure of cooperation with the world in its redemptive transformation. Despite theoretical differences, all three groups at first were united in their disinclination to join the American evangelical mainstream.[33]

When the fundamentalist-modernist debates arose in mainline Protestant denominations during the 1920s and 1930s, "antithetical Calvinists" such as Cornelius Van Til and Ned B. Stonehouse identified themselves so strongly with the seceding Orthodox Presbyterian Church that they joined it. In the period between these eruptions and World War II, doctrine and separation were bywords in the CRC. Yet when neo-evangelicalism, with its purpose of exerting a more positive impact on American life, arose out of the fundamentalist movement in the late war years, there was a parallel development among the CRC. At that time the "positive Calvinists," with their greater openness to more general American trends, came to prominence in the denomination. This group positioned itself self-consciously over against the neo-evangelicals. But after years of analysis and criticism, these progressive Calvinists began to call themselves "evangelicals." The CRC Reformed did not repudiate the communal, traditional, credal, sacramental, and organic traditions of their heritage.[34] But, especially as reflected in the pages of one "positive Calvinist" periodical, the *Reformed Journal*, they began to define a self-image that was consciously Reformed *and* evangelical.

The neo-evangelical heirs of fundamentalism attained visibility when they mobilized into large-scale religious organizations whose membership transcended church and denominational loyalties. Youth for Christ, the Billy Graham Evangelistic Association, and *Christianity Today* became well known. Of particular institutional significance to the new coalition were the National Association of Evangelicals (NAE) and the young evangelist Billy Graham. Those conservatives who joined the NAE and who supported the public ministry of Graham were, in the main, the "neo-evangelicals" against whom the "positive Calvinist" wing of the Christian Reformed Church measured itself.

In the early years of the neo-evangelical movement, the CRC stepped onto the bandwagon with astonishing alacrity. By means of synodical decision, the denomination joined the NAE in 1943. But the church was not able to reconcile itself to its own impulsive action. The CRC's eight-year relationship with the NAE was punctuated by "uneasiness, uncertainty, distrust, and sharp division of sentiment."[35] Thus, a distracting ambivalence belied the denomination's lofty 1944 expression of ecumenical principles, which stated, "The CRC is closely related to other Christian churches as being with them a manifestation of the church, which is the one body of Christ."[36] In 1951 the synod voted to terminate its membership in the NAE. The CRC would not yet be evangelical. Instead, it would preserve its identity and bring to America "the power of a full and undiluted Reformed witness."[37]

Even to the most ecumenically minded of the "positive Calvinists," the evangelicals of the NAE seemed a different breed, Christians who express their faith *"in different terms* than we do."[38] In an echo of Mercersburg, the CRC progressives felt that evangelicals came up short on the meaning and centrality of the institutionalized church. As they saw it, evangelicals seemed to equate the church and the parachurch, "a voluntary association of like-minded people loosely united for practical action."[39] To the Reformed, such an arrangement was unthinkable, at odds with the purposes for which God had sanctioned and ordained his body as an institution of society.

In neo-evangelicalism, the traditional role of the church freely spilled over into the parachurch agencies. The Reformed have made, at best, an uneasy accommodation to this situation. The logic, according to James Daane, was simple. Preaching, sacraments, and discipline "are not only the tasks of the church, . . . they are not the proper tasks of any other organization; and any organization that does any one of these three things should do all three." Nor was the parachurch to be the focus for ecumenicity. Daane continued, "Whenever evangelicals find their unity in parachurch, para-ecumenical organization, they are searching for unity alongside, that is, outside of, the church, and therefore outside the biblical conception of unity."[40] The heirs of fundamentalism were not only misdirected, but also deluded, because, as another "positive Calvinist" claimed, "it is in the church, not an *ism*, where the evangel, evangelists, and evangelicals find their true home. Evangelicalism is a fantasy — acted out perhaps, but still a fantasy. The church is still real."[41] And that rock-solid, visible church needed to function according to clear-cut, traditional principles, in contrast to "the ecclesiastical principle with which individualistic, congregationalistic, 'evangelical' churches operate."[42]

The doctrine of the church loomed as a major fork in the road for the Reformed and "individualistic, congregationalistic" evangelicals. The resulting divergence reflected a larger problem, which the CRC pinpointed as the "untheological and creedless spirit of American evangelicalism."[43]

The evangelicals did maintain what Nathan Hatch has called an "ideological tradition," but this orientation, in contrast to that of the Dutch Calvinists, was pragmatic and subjective and was not self-consciously rooted in historic Christianity.[44] The ahistorical, nontraditional heritage of American evangelicalism fit hand-in-glove with more casual and innovative forms of worship. One CRC journalist contrasted a traditional hymn with a modern chorus, both of which treat the same theme of Christ as friend. The "Jesus, priceless treasure, source of purest pleasure" of the tradition becomes, in the chorus, a true-blue "friend of mine" who "walks with me and . . . talks with me" in "Fellowship Divine."[45] If Christ Himself was so easily brought down to the level of common humanity, there was no room at all for a Christian elite in the evangelical tradition, which, as Hatch put it, followed the "impulse . . . to throw open theological questions to any serious student of Scripture, trusting the common sense intuition of people at large to be more reliable than the musings of an educated few."[46] Among evangelicals, authority simply was spread too thin.

If evangelical doctrine and tradition were problematical, the practical side of Christianity presented what seemed to be nearly insurmountable barriers to fellowship between the two groups. In the eyes of the Dutch, evangelicals had imbibed too many of the dominant cultural values. The latter were materialistic, positivistic, and uncritically patriotic. They glorified in the American way of life, in a manner tantamount to idolatory of the self. "How can we get evangelicalism off the stage and back to the highways and hedges?" queried one Reformed critic. "We might start," he ironically recommended, by reading John Wesley and his fears of increasing wealth among the people called Methodists. Unless something is said and done the present evangelical upsurge might conceivably be the last hurrah."[47]

The despicable spirit of modernity that had infiltrated American Christianity in the second half of the twentieth century could be summed up in a word, *individualism*. It was the same criticism that the Christian Reformed had leveled against "Methodism" in a previous generation. Individualism explained many facets of evangelicalism which the Reformed disdained, including its Arminian flavor, the private interpretation of Scripture, its atomistic view of the church, and the artificial apparent separation from the world.[48] But the product of individualism that piqued the ire of the positive Calvinists more than anything else was the notion that social reform came only through the conversion of individuals.

In the late 1940s, Carl F.H. Henry faulted his own fundamentalist camp for lacking a social ethic. Henry, who became an influential leader in the neo-evangelical movement, balanced his ethic on a common-sense aphorism: "Evangelical Christianity recognizes that a good society turns upon the presence of good men."[49] Only God can make people good, the argument ran, and his means to that end are individual conversion and personal sanctification. Therefore, conversion and sanctification are the straight highways to a good society. In the first two decades of his public ministry, Billy Graham — neo-evangelical spokesperson par excellence — believed and preached this viewpoint exactly.[50]

A "positive Calvinist," Lewis B. Smedes, commended Henry for his long-overdue social concern. But Smedes did not believe that "good men, rather than good laws, are the key to social ethics." Henry's way was "conservative, reactionary, individualistic"; it was "a call to keep the church out of social questions." What was needed, Smedes insisted, was a truly *social* ethic: "We insist that environmental forms are terribly important to any social ethics. And we insist that government has a positive calling to see that the various segments of the organic society share properly in the social and economic privileges and responsibilities of the common wealth."[51] Henry's proposal lacked a concrete and specific plan for social involvement of the church in the affairs of America's poor and needy.

In the 1970s, the neo-evangelicals made several disorganized attempts at formulating such a plan. Christian Reformed representatives attended these caucuses, but ended up echoing Smedes' call for a more detailed blueprint to impact economic, social, and political life in America. Still, social *concern* was visibly present in these discussions. Billy Graham also began to plead for social justice. The CRC had always supported Graham on account of his stand against liberalism.[52] Now the gap between the evangelical and Reformed traditions closed another notch.

When the neo-evangelicals emerged from their closet of social isolation in the late 1960s, the Christian Reformed, feeling a little smug, were ready to shake their hands. Said Smedes, "What we heard . . . came down to this: man is not merely a soul to be saved, but a total creature-in-relationship, needing to be healed *en toto*. We admit to wondering why it could have taken evangelicals so long to admit this. . . . This is what we . . . have been saying all along."[53] The evangelicals had finally seen the light. They had always been "brethren," but more in the sense of "my enemy's enemy is my best friend."[54] Now perhaps they were family. As early as 1966, statements such as the following began to appear in the "positive Calvinist" *Reformed Journal*: "But unless *we evangelicals* do come to terms with these and similar questions about the nature of men's rights, we are not going to advance into a relevant social ethic for our time."[55] Twenty years later the identification is hardly complete. But it is now much closer than it was.[56] Three of the most persistent CRC critics of neo-evangelicalism, James Daane, Lewis Smedes, and Richard Mouw, eventually came to teach at the evangelical Fuller Seminary. And many other "positive Calvinists" from the CRC have contributed fulsomely to neo-evangelical projects in the 1970s and 1980s.

"Antithetical Calvinists" within the CRC may think that too much of the Reformed faith has been given away in the growing association of their denomination with evangelicals. Whatever conclusions one draws about that possibility, the recent history of the CRC suggests that taking time to criticize American evangelicals may be the most direct road to becoming one of them.

Historically, Reformed conceptions of Christianity have differed significantly from the multiple varieties of such conceptions found among American evangelicals. The ecclesiological, cultural, and doctrinal convictions of Europe's Reformed traditions fit awkwardly in the American environment. For that reason, Calvinistic Protestants have had much to criticize in American evangelicalism. That course of criticism, however, has not been without its unintended consequences. Because of the criticism, at least some strands of America's broader evangelicalism have bent in a Reformed direction. But also, in the very process of criticism, some of the Reformed themselves have become more like evangelicals.

NOTES

1. James D. Bratt, *Dutch Calvinism in Modern America: A History of a Conservative Subculture* (Grand Rapids, Mich.: Eerdmans, 1984), 59.
2. James Hastings Nichols, *Romanticism in American Theology* (Chicago: Univ. of Chicago Press, 1961), 2.
3. Marlin J. Van Elderen, "A Chosen Race," *Reformed Journal* 32 (March 1982):13.
4. Full coverage would also include treatment of smaller Presbyterian denominations of Scottish covenant origin, the Theonomist movement, the Canadian Reformed Church, the Toronto Institute for Christian Studies, and several other bodies.
5. For a related discussion of how more general perspectives — doctrinal, pietist, cultural, moralist — shape the use of Scripture, see Richard J. Mouw, "The Bible in Twentieth-Century Protestantism: A Preliminary Taxonomy," in *The Bible in America: Essays in Cultural History*, ed. Nathan O. Hatch and Mark A. Noll (New York: Oxford Univ. Press, 1982).
6. Both quotations, Nichols, *Romanticism*, 153.
7. Ibid., 152, 292, 298.
8. Ibid., 260.
9. On the theological side of those developments, see Bruce Kuklick, *Churchmen and Philosophers from Jonathan Edwards to John Dewey* (New Haven, Conn.: Yale Univ. Press, 1985), 94-111.
10. Quoted in Nichols, *Romanticism*, 53-54.
11. Quoted in ibid., 189.
12. See Sydney E. Ahlstrom, *A Religious History of the American People* (New Haven, Conn.: Yale Univ. Press, 1972), 615-21, 921.

13. Some of the material in the following paragraphs is adapted from Mark A. Noll, "The Pea Beneath the Mattress: Orthodox Presbyterians in America," *Reformed Journal* 36 (Oct. 1986):11–16.

14. *Minutes of the First General Assembly of the Presbyterian Church of America* (Philadelphia: The Presbyterian Church of America, 1936), 3.

15. Quoted from Ned B. Stonehouse, *J. Gresham Machen: A Biographical Memoir* (Grand Rapids, Mich.: Eerdmans, 1954), 495–96.

16. Quoted from ibid., 502.

17. Minutes of the Second General Assembly of the Presbyterian Church of America (Philadelphia: The Presbyterian Church of America, 1936), 9.

18. For this debate and an authoritative general picture of the schism among the separates, see George M. Marsden, "Perspective on the Division of 1937," in *Pressing Toward the Mark: Essays Commemorating Fifty Years of the Orthodox Presbyterian Church, 1936–1986*, ed. Charles G. Dennison and Richard C. Gamble (Philadelphia: Committee for the Historian of the Orthodox Presbyterian Church, 1986).

19. See Darryl G. Hart, "Doctor Fundamentalis: An Intellectual Biography of J. Gresham Machen, 1881–1937" (Ph.D. diss., Johns Hopkins Univ., 1988), ch. 8, "The Founding of an Orthodox Presbyterian Church," quotation at note 16.

20. *Minutes of the Fifth General Assembly* (Philadelphia: Presbyterian Church of America, 1939), 7–8.

21. *Minutes of the First General Assembly*, 15, 16: *Minutes of the Second General Assembly*, 6.

22. Charles G. Dennison, *The Orthodox Presbyterian Church, 1936–1986* (Philadelphia: Committee for the Historian of the Orthodox Presbyterian Church, 1986), 49

23. John P. Galbraith, "The Ecumenical Vision of the Orthodox Presbyterian Church," in Dennison and Gamble, *Pressing Toward the Mark*, 418–24; quotations, 423, 423–24, 420.

24. Ibid., 418.

25. Quoted in Michael A. Hakkenberg, "The Battle Over the Ordination of Gordon H. Clark, 1943–1948," in Dennison and Gamble, *Pressing Toward the Mark*, 345. This article is the best introduction to a complicated episode.

26. Ibid., 343.

27. Quoted in ibid., 347.

28. Quoted in Galbraith, "Ecumenical Vision of the OPC," 424.

29. Ibid. and Dennison, *Orthodox Presbyterian Church*, 59.

30. Galbraith, "Ecumenical Vision of the OPC," 419.

31. William White, "What's Wrong with Our Reformed Seminaries: A Summary of Conservative Reformed Comment," *Journey Magazine* 2, no. 1 (Jan.-Feb. 1987):5.

32. Donald J. Duff, "Premillennial or Reformed?" *Clarion* 35, no. 23 (14 Nov. 1986):472–73.

33. Bratt, *Dutch Calvinism in Modern America*, 43–54.

34. See James Daane, "No Individualistic Salvation," *Reformed Journal* 32 (Feb. 1982):17–19.

35. George Stob, "Eight Years of N.A.E. Membership," *Reformed Journal* 1 (Apr. 1951):7.

36. Quoted in Van Elderen, "A Chosen Race," 16.

37. George Stob, "The Synod of 1951," *Reformed Journal* 1 (July 1951):2.

38. George Stob, "Our N.A.E. Dilemma," *Reformed Journal* 1 (May 1951):4.

39. Lewis B. Smedes, "The N.A.E. and the Church of Christ," *Reformed Journal* 11 (May 1961):5–6.

40. James Daane, "Para-Church: A Final Note," *Reformed Journal* 25 (Oct. 1975): 6; and Daane, "Fragmented Evangelicals," *Reformed Journal* 26 (Nov. 1976):28.

41. Lewis B. Smedes, "Evangelicalism—A Fantasy," *Reformed Journal* 30 (Feb. 1980):3.

42. George Stob, "The Christian Reformed Church in the American World," *Reformed Journal* 1 (June 1951):3.

43. George Stob, "Our N.A.E. Dilemma," 4.

44. Nathan O. Hatch, "Evangelical Colleges and the Challenge of Christian Thinking," *Reformed Journal* 35 (Sept. 1985):13.

45. John Hammersma, "Tradition and Trend in Our Hymnody," *Reformed Journal* 12 (Dec. 1962):10.

46. Hatch, "Evangelical Colleges," 11.

47. Robert W. Lyon, "Evangelical Superstars," *Reformed Journal* 30 (July 1980):4.

48. See Henry Stob, "Fundamentalism and Political Rightism," *Reformed Journal* 15 (Jan. 1965):13.

49. See Carl F.H. Henry, *The Uneasy Conscience of Modern Fundamentalism* (Grand Rapids, Mich.: Eerdmans, 1947). Henry is quoted here from Lewis B. Smedes, "The Evangelicals and the Social Question," *Reformed Journal* 16 (Feb. 1966):10.

50. See the analysis by Reinhold Niebuhr, "Liberalism, Individualism, and Billy Graham," *Christian Century* 73 (23 May 1956):641

51. Smedes, "Evangelicals and the Social Question," 10, 13.

52. See Sidney Rooy, "The Graham Crusades—Shall We Participate?" *Reformed Journal* 8 (June 1958):6. Rooy's answer was yes.

53. Lewis B. Smedes, "Evangelicals, What Next?" *Reformed Journal* 19 (Nov. 1969):4.

54. Bratt, *Dutch Calvinism in Modern America*, 127: "That formula was established in the early '30s and reiterated constantly over the next twenty years. Fundamentalists were 'brethren in Christ.' Modernists were 'enemies of the cross'."

55. Lewis B. Smedes, "Where Do We Differ?" *Reformed Journal* 16 (May-June 1966):9. See also Smedes, "An Appeal to Billy Graham," *Reformed Journal* 22 (Sept. 1972):3.

56. Also important for bridging the gap between the CRC and American evangelicals was cooperation, along with British evangelicals, in Bible scholarship, often published by William B. Eerdmans Co. in Grand Rapids, Mich. See Mark A. Noll, *Between Faith and Criticism: Evangelicals, Scholarship, and the Bible in America* (San Francisco: Harper & Row, 1986), 100-101.

CHAPTER 13

Lutheranism

Mark Ellingsen

For numerous observers, Lutheranism represents a paradigmatic example of evangelicalism. However, if the assumption is that the Lutheran heritage and the churches still faithful to that heritage properly belong to the family of Christians often identified as the "evangelical movement," then the relationship between Lutheranism and that particular evangelical family is much more complex. To be sure, in Europe and elsewhere in the world, a number of Lutherans explicitly identify themselves as part of the evangelical movement, even forming organizations which identify with this evangelical family. But in North America, the number of Lutherans who do this is infinitesimally small. No North American Lutheran denomination, not even the champion of theologically conservative Lutheran orthodoxy, The Lutheran Church–Missouri Synod, officially identifies with the evangelical family usually associated with the National Association of Evangelicals (NAE). And one finds a similar hesitancy among some theologically conservative Lutherans on other continents.[1]

In fact, the general Lutheran tendency to distance itself from the evangelical movement has led to a kind of linguistic crisis (which connotes elements of an identity crisis) within all segments of American Lutheranism. Historically, the Lutheran church has been identified as "evangelical," in the sense of being rooted in the *evangelium* (gospel). This identification is rooted in the fact that several Lutheran churches in the United States (including the largest Lutheran denomination) have employed the adjective "evangelical" as part of their corporate titles. And in Germany, the German equivalent *evangelisch* is virtually synonymous with the term "Lutheran."

Of course, in Germany no threat to Lutheranism's "ownership" of the German equivalent of the term "evangelical" has surfaced as a result of the emergence of the evangelical movement. A new term to identify the movement, *evangelikal*, has been coined, largely by members of that movement. (Their rationale has been to distinguish conservative evangelicals from Lutheranism or, more generally, from all the Protestant *Landeskirchen*.[2]) But in English-speaking nations, where there is no distinction between the use of the term *evangelical* by the family of Christians outside the ecumenical establishment (but more aligned with the National Association of Evangelicals [NAE]) and the use of the term by Lutherans, the problem is that the two uses have been collapsed, with the Lutheran use of the term being rendered archaic in the broader culture. For the term *evangelical* has come to be the sole property of the group of theological conservatives clustered around the NAE. It has come to a point where Lutherans in America no longer can lay claim to the title "evangelical" without being regarded as somehow endorsing the NAE or the theological agenda of the Evangelical Theological Society. (Perhaps a not unrelated dynamic haunts efforts by the holiness and pentecostal traditions to lay claim to the term "evangelical.")

What is it about the nature of Lutheranism that brings about its complex relationship to evangelicalism? An examination of these characteristics may provide significant insights concerning the nature of American evangelicalism, as well as the character of the conservative evangelical coalition.

Justification by Grace through Faith: The Center of Lutheranism

As the subtitle of this section suggests, no legitimate presentation of Lutheranism can fail to begin with the doctrine and reality of justification by grace through faith apart from works of the Law. To be sure, all evangelicals and Roman Catholics endorse this Pauline, bibical doctrine in some form. But none do so with the passion and single-minded emphasis of the Lutheran heritage. According to the Lutheran Confessions (*The Book of Concord*—a collection of sixteenth-century documents which are understood by Lutherans as being in some degree or other accurate expositions of Scripture and therefore authoritative for defining the Lutheran version of Christian faith), justification by grace through faith is the main or chief aritcle of Christian doctrine.[3]

Of course, the circumstances which first occasioned this Lutheran emphasis are well known to readers and do not require exposition. Granted, the Lutheran Reformation was related somewhat to Luther's spiitual turmoil and quest for the security that seemed to elude him in the medieval church's sacrament of penance. But the real occasion for the genesis of the Lutheran movement was the struggle of Luther and his colleagues against certain aberrant practices of the late medieval Roman Catholic church pertaining to the buying and selling of indulgences for the deceased. These practices greatly troubled the young Augustinian monk, and not only because they seemed to undermine his emerging insights concerning the Pauline teaching of justification and the righteousness of God. He was also troubled by the negative impact on the Christian praxis of the faithful which the marketing of indulgences was causing.[4] (This interaction of doctrinal and practical concern in the genesis of the Lutheran movement serves as a reminder that justification by grace through faith is never to be regarded simply as a doctrine. For Lutherans, it is the norm for evaluating and criticizing the Church's praxis as well as all aspects of its teaching.) Underlying all of the Lutheran Reformers' concerns was the observation that the contemporary Roman Catholic practice of the day seemed to be compromising a commitment to the primacy of God's grace and the doctrine of justification through faith alone.[5] Given these concerns, the characteristic Lutheran doctrinal commitments follow quite logically.

Insofar as Pelagianism is regarded the great adversary, be it understood originally in its medieval scholastic and penitential forms or seen as the characteristic malady of the human condition (often manifesting itself in despair or spiritual anguish), an emphasis on justification by grace through faith — the conviction that salvation comes from a source outside us, through God's use of the external means of Word and sacrament — is the most amenable conception for proclaiming the gospel.[6] This conception's emphasis on the primacy of God's external action in bringing about salvation equips it better to combat the Pelagian heresy or the anguished conscience than are other traditions, with their characteristic themes of perfection, baptism with the Spirit (manifested in glossolalia), cooperation with grace, or the puritan work ethic. (These alternatives convey the notion of what Geoffrey Wainwright has labeled the "active receptivity" of faith, which is endorsed by all denominational traditions except Lutheranism.[7]) For, in the Lutheran conception of the doctrine of justification, Christians are not saved *by* faith. On the contrary, faith is more like the instrument, perhaps even the receptacle, of God's redeeming work of grace in Christ.[8] This is evident from the fact that, on occasions, the concept of justification is used interchangeably with Christology, as Christology also, like justification through faith, is identified as "the first and chief article.[9]

Given these Lutheran commitments to critiquing Pelagianism by means of an emphasis on God's sole agency in saving human beings (*sola gratia*), other characteristic Lutheran theological positions become necessary consequences. This result is entailed by Lutheranism's insistence that justification through faith alone is the criterion by which all matters of doctrine and faith are to be judged.[10]

Certainly, the Lutheran commitment to justification through faith alone, apart from works of the Law, i.e., the affirmation that the Christian is free from the Law, surfaces in the corresponding Lutheran insistence on the distinction between the Law and the Gospel. In all proclamation, it is argued, the Law (the Word of God which demands obedience and so condemns sin) must not be confused with the Gospel (The Word of God which gives life and forgiveness to the sinner). Correspondingly, Lutherans argue, the Two Kingdoms, the Kingdom of the Law (civil government) and the Kingdom of the Gospel (the proclamation of the Gospel), must always be distinguished from each other, in theory as well as in the praxis of formulating concrete political strategies. As distinct from the Gospel, such strategies always are ambiguous and never can be identified unambiguously with God's redemptive will.[11] (The Law-Gospel distinction may be one of Lutheranism's most practical ecumenical contributions, insofar as it offers a conceptuality by which preachers may critque how Gospel-centered their proclamation really is. Likewise, the Two-Kingdom Ethic, though often maligned due to distortions of the model in the past, provides a helpful model for Christian political involvement in a pluralistic society, since on its grounds all political wisdom belongs to the realm of the Law and is accessible to all human beings.)

The commitment to justification through faith alone, as a means of affirming God's sole agency in saving human beings, is reflected in the Lutheran doctrine of the Church. Lutherans insist that the Church is not upheld by the piety of the believers (is not defined in terms of the faithful). Rather, inasmuch as spirituality is the work of God, only given through the external means of Word and sacrament, the Church must be created by God's actions — by his Word and the sacraments.[12]

These commitments are reflected in the Lutheran doctrine of ministry as a ministry of Word and sacrament. The ministry does not belong to officeholders by virtue of some special charisma or essential quality (bestowed on the minister by ordination). Rather, the office of the ministry is God's work, created by Word and Sacrament.[13] As such, God's call to ordained ministry is mediated through the priesthood of all believers. (This strong emphasis on the universal priesthood, though, does not entail that the ordained ministry is derived from it. In fact, *The Book of Concord* asserts that an evangelical episcopacy is the most desirable sort of church polity [though not necessary for the essence of the church] and that a reformed papacy, understood as an office which has not been divinely instituted, would be appropriate for the sake of enhancing Christian unity.)[14]

The Lutheran emphasis on the primacy of God's action and the correlated insistence that he only works through external means are also manifest in Lutheran views on the Sacraments. It should be noted, parenthetically, that the Lutheran tradition is open to recognizing more than two Sacraments. Thus at several points, the Lutheran Reformers identified the Roman Catholic Sacrament of confession as a Sacrament. In his 1539 treatise, *On the Councils and the Church*, Luther lists *seven* Sacraments. These commitments are reflected in the authoritative *Book of Concord* at several points, not least of all where it is stated that "no intelligent person will quibble about the number of Sacraments."[15]

In addition to these Catholic elements in Lutheran Sacramentology, others may be noted. At a number of points, the Lutheran view of the Church exhibits the kind of sacramental ecclesiology typical of the Roman Catholic heritage. This posture is evident in the Lutheran definition of the church in terms of Word and Sacrament.[16] God creates the church and binds it together, in part through the right administration of the Sacraments. This theme was explicitly endorsed by Martin Luther at several points during his career. The similarities between his articulation and the Roman Catholic conception of the Church as Sacrament (enunciated by Vatican II) are striking.[17]

Catholic elements, emphasizing on the primacy of God's action, reflect at other points in Lutheran Sacramentology. As in the Roman Catholic tradition, infant baptism is normative for Lutheran praxis, and baptismal regeneration (even though the one baptized is still thought to be marred by sin) is affirmed. The primacy of God's act in saving his people is given testimony by this practice, inasmuch as, in baptizing infants, the Church gives testimony to the fact that God alone saves, that the Sacrament is valid even apart from faith.[18]

The same emphases are reflected in the Lutheran view of the Lord's Supper (the Eucharist) and in its insistence on the Real Presence of Christ "in, with, and under" the elements.[19] Unlike the Reformed heritage, Lutherans insist that Christ is present and is received not only by the godly, but also (albeit to one's detriment) by the wicked.[20]

Of course this insistence on the Real Presence of Christ in the Sacrament is not an endorsement of transubstantiation (the traditional Roman Catholic idea that the Communion elements in their essence only *resemble* bread and wine. But it is equally important to observe that Lutherans do not advocate the position of consubstantiation with regard to the Sacrament. The elements are not a hybrid substance of Christ's Body and bread, his Blood and wine. Rather, the elements are considered to be both Body and ordinary bread, both Blood and ordinary wine, simultaneously.

To be sure, this conception requires explication, lest the Lutheran view to be dismissed as mere nonsense. Perhaps one could find analogues to the mystery that the Lutheran view is striving to explicate in the mystery of an embrace of a devoted husband and wife. As love is really present in that embrace, while the physical action of embracing retains its own integrity, so Christ is really present in the bread and wine, though the elements retain their own integrity.

Luther himself employed Christology as an analogue for illuminating this mystery. As the person of Christ can be both divine and human without confusion of his two natures, so the sacramental element can be both ordinary bread and Christ's Body without confusion.[21] The Lutheran doctrine of the Real Presence is as closely related to Christology as it is a consequence of the Lutheran insistence that God acts on behalf of human salvation, apart from works done by believers or the quality of their faith.

These Lutheran commitments pertaining to the Eucharist have implications for the characteristic Lutheran treatments of Christology and the doctrine of the Trinity. In order to respond to the Reformed critique that the Body of Christ cannot be present in the elements of the Sacrament, inasmuch as Christ's earthly body cannot be omnipresent in the manifold celebrations of the Eucharist at any given time, since it remains in heaven, Luther appealed to the Patristic concept of the *communicatio idiomatum* (communication of properties). According to this conception, whatever can be affirmed of one of Christ's natures can be affirmed of the other in a derivative sense. Thus it can be argued that omnipresence may be ascribed not just to Christ's divine nature, but also to his human nature. As such, Christ's body can intelligibly be conceived of as present in every celebration of the eucharist in all times and places.[22] Appeal to the concept of the *communicatio idiomatum* provides an intelligible way for Lutherans to deal with the concerns raised by most evangelicals concerning the rationality of an affirmation of Christ's Real Presence in the Eucharist.

The *communicatio idiomatum* entails emphasis on the unity of Christ's person, which in turn has implications for the characteristic Lutheran treatment of the doctrine of the Trinity. For, just as the unity of Christ's person is emphasized, so it follows that the unity of the three persons of the Trinity on one Godhead is a characteristic emphasis of Lutheranism.[23]

To the extent that the trinitarian and Christological propensities of Lutheranism are consequences of its Sacramentology (its insistence on Christ's Real Presence in the Sacraments), which is itself a consequence of the Lutheran emphasis on justification by grace through faith, it follows that even these Nicene doctrinal construals are related to the Lutheran commitment to the centrality of justification by grace through faith. The impact of the doctrine of justification on all the characteristic doctrinal formulations of the Lutheran tradition is apparent once again. The impact of this commitment surfaces in at least two other loci — the Lutheran doctrine of election and its eschatology.

With regard to election, it is hardly surprising that the Lutheran emphasis on the primacy of God's action in bringing about salvation manifests itself in an affirmation of the doctrine of predestination—the idea that salvation is a consequence of God's election of the faithful in eternity. It is true that, at certain points in his career, especially when he was polemicizing against virulent forms of Pelagianism, Luther did endorse a kind of double predestination.[24] But this is not the official Lutheran position authorized by *The Book of Concord*. Rather, the official position is that of single predestination—a belief that God predestines only the elect and that damnation is the unbeliever's own fault.[25]

The Lutheran position on this point illustrates the tradition's often paradoxical mode of thinking. At its best, Confessional Lutheranism is not a tradition concerned with speculative questions.[26] As long as the centrality of justification by grace through faith is properly proclaimed and reflects in the life of the Church, doctrinal questions and matters of polity will take care of themselves.

This inattention to speculative detail, as long as justification by grace through faith is properly in place, also surfaces in Lutheran eschatology, specifically in the Confessional Lutheran attitude towards the millennium. Granted, a number of prominent Lutheran pietists, including the father of pietism, Philip Jacob Spener, engaged in millennial speculations at some point in their careers.[27] But the Confessional Lutheran position tends towards amillennialism, presumably because millennial speculation among sixteenth-century Jews was leading to a belief that before the eschaton, the saints would possess a worldly kingdom. Such a belief would seem to be rejected because it connotes a return to legalism, to the idea that material prosperity is the reward for faithfulness.[28] Once again it is apparent how, on all the classical doctrinal loci, from Trinity and Christology to sanctification, social ethics, ecclesiology, sacramentology, and even eschatology, the agenda for Lutheranism is set by its commitment to the centrality of justification by grace through faith.

Another Look at Justification by Grace through Faith: Clarifying Misconceptions — The Limits of Evangelicalism

Generally speaking, evangelicals and the rest of the Christian world think of Lutherans as not being sufficiently concerned with sanctification or not able to deal adequately with the Christian life, due to an undue Lutheran concentration on the doctrine of justification. My suspicion is that this widely-accepted criticism has emerged because evangelicals and others have understood Lutheran references to justification by grace through faith in terms of exclusively forensic categories.

Of course, in one sense all Lutheran conceptions of the doctrine of justification have a forensic character. The juridical metaphor, of being pronounced righteous by the (divine) judge rather than being "made righteous" as a condition for completing justification, underlies all Lutheran thinking about justification by grace through faith.[29] However, if by forensic justification one means that justification is only a "legal fiction," distinct from sanctification not just logically but also temporally, then one must insist that the Lutheran conception of justification is not merely limited to the forensic view.

It is true that at times Lutherans (particularly those influenced by Lutheran orthodox theology) treat justification as a forensic justification, in the sense of separating justification and sanctification, even to the point of regarding them as distinct temporal events.[30] Most members of the evangelical coalition — notably those from the holiness tradition, the holiness-influenced segments of pentecostalism, and the orthodox Presbyterian wing of the coalition — tend to endorse such a view of the doctrine of justification.[31] Thus it is hardly surprising that they would judge this forensic view to be what Lutherans mean in speaking of justification by grace through faith. Given such interpretive suppositions, it is little wonder that Lutherans, in pointing to the doctrine of justification, would be accused of neglecting sanctification. On grounds of this forensic view of justification, sanctification has nothing to do with justification. But in fact this is not the prevailing Lutheran view of justification by grace through faith.

The more characteristic Lutheran conception is to view justification in terms of conformity to Christ or union with Christ (see Eph. 4:23–27; Rom. 6:1–11). This is the idea that, in the event of justification, believers receive all that Christ has and become intimately united with him, as a bride does to her spouse. Though distinct from justification, sanctification is regarded as happening simultaneously with justification, not just as a forensic reality. This conception of justification as conformity to Christ maintains that, in the justification event, believers are given a new identity, are made Christ-like, much like what happens in the close bond of a marital relationship. Just as marriage partners who have spent a lifetime sharing with and loving each other come to take on some of the positive characteristics of their mate, and spontaneously care and serve each other, so it is with Christians who are conformed to Christ in the event of justification by grace through faith. In this sense, the content of the Christian life is given in justification and in baptism, so that Christian life is nothing more than living out one's baptism, that is, a living out of one's new Christlike identity which has been given in baptism.[32]

This conception of justification seems to respond to a characteristic evangelical concern about the Lutheran emphasis on this doctrine. Such a conception could make some contribution to the evangelical coalition, among other ways, insofar as it provides a conceptual framework for relating the Lutheran emphasis on justification, and its critique of Pelagianism in all its forms, to a concern with holiness and sanctification. In addition, as was already suggested, this conception relates justification by grace through faith and its effects to the Sacraments, more closely knotting the Sacraments to the practice of the Christian life. The image of justification as union with Christ is conveyed by seeing baptism as an event of regeneration by virtue of being joined to the body of Christ. Baptism puts a mark on those baptized, a mark which they can never totally eradicate and which forever characterizes how the Christian life is to be lived. Likewise, the same image correlates with a Real Presence view of the Eucharist. In the Lord's Supper, one receives Christ, is further united with him, in a most intimate physical union. As the food we eat nourishes us, so the Christian life is nourished by the intimate contact Christians have with Christ when they receive him in the Lord's Supper. Sanctification may not receive the self-conscious attention from Confessional Lutherans that it does from other segments of the Christian family. For Lutherans the Christian life, sanctification, takes care of itself, happens spontaneously when justification is rightly proclaimed and grasped in faith. However, it is equally evident that sanctification is by no means bypassed by the Lutheran emphasis on justification and its high Sacramentology, as long as observers and Lutherans themselves proclaim justification in terms of this union-with-Christ (conformity-to-Christ) model.

Of course this conception of justification by grace through faith apart from the works of the Law, and its concern to affirm the impact of the event of justification on the Christian life, in no sense entail a retreat from the basic Augustianian anthropology which underlies the Lutheran critique of Pelagianism. In all contexts, the Lutheran heritage insists on humanity's slavery to sin, on the idea that the human will is not really free with regard to matters spiritual, but is bound to sin.[33] So pervasive is the impact of sin that even the Christian, justified and baptized, is still totally a sinner. This is what Lutherans mean when they speak of the Christian as *simul iustus et peccator* (simultaneously saint and sinner). Such a conception helps portray the element of struggle, the struggle with evil, which Lutherans believe to be an inescapable dimension of the Christian life.[34]

These conceptions are given a new context, however, when deployed in relation to the Pauline-Lutheran conception of justification as union with Christ. The notions of humanity's unfree will and of the Christian as *simul iustus et peccator*, while they describe the "old identity" of Christians (Eph. 4:22; Rom. 6:6) and so accurately describe who Christians are, do not constitute the final word about Christian identity. Christians still live in the world of sin, and their nature reflects the impact of that environment, much as the scars of war or mistreatment in childhood indelibly leave their mark on a person's identity, never really going away. But, given this Lutheran view of justification, the primary influence on Christians, what ultimately determines their identities, is the family relation they have with Christ and his Body, given first in the event of justification and baptism. And like any good family relationship, the one with Christ, given in justification and baptism, cannot but leave its mark on the believer's identity and nature. On such grounds, the justification event clearly has existential, not merely forensic consequences.

The Lutheran emphasis on justification, coupled with its Augustinian anthropology, quite sharply poses the question of why Lutherans do not seem to fit in the evangelical coalition. If the Augustinian view of human persons and its emphasis on the primacy of grace (what Richard Hughes has termed *reformatio*) characterized American evangelicalism, one would think that Lutherans would find themselves quite at home in the coalition. But in fact, as we have suggested, only Lutherans influenced by a certain kind of pietism (neopietism) seem to locate themselves in the international evangelical coalition. Given the Lutheran pietist preoccupation with regeneration (whose end, it is insisted, can only be personal holiness or sanctification), could the openness to the evangelical coalition on the part of certain breeds of Lutheran pietism suggest that the evangelical coalition is basically characterized by a common emphasis on holiness or sanctification, that this common stress constitutes one of its primary limits?[35]

At any rate, the Confessional Lutheran emphasis on the centrality of justification by grace through faith is not all that keeps Lutheranism as a whole out of the evangelical coalition. There are other factors. Exploring these factors may lead us to more insights about the limits of evangelicalism.

Lutheranism: A Protestant or a Catholic Movement?

The answer to the question posed by this section's title is "neither." Lutheranism is neither entirely Protestant nor unambiguously Catholic. Its emphasis on justification by grace through faith does not entail that Lutheranism is sectarian in its intentions, preoccupied only with particular aspects of the Christian heritage. Various documents of the Lutheran *Book of Concord* quite clearly affirm the belief that the reformers have taken positions in accord with the church fathers and the Catholic faith. Such statements seem to confirm the contention of some Lutherans with ecumenical concerns that Lutheranism is a "reform movement inside the catholic Church."[36]

Indeed, the Catholic propensities of Lutheranism are evident in its very origins. Unlike other major sixteenth-century reformers, Luther did not aim to start a new church. Rather, he was asked to leave the Roman Catholic church. He did not leave of his own volition.

The Catholic heritage of Lutheranism is evident not only in the statements we have noted in *The Book of Concord*, which claim not to have departed from the teachings of the ancient church and the Catholic church. Nor is this Catholic heritage evident only in Lutheran Sacramentology and the other points of doctrinal convergence with the Roman Catholic tradition previously noted. This heritage also is seen in Lutheran worship (its use of the historic liturgy) and in the role tradition plays in Lutheran theological reflection.

With regard to the latter point, of course it is true that the Lutheran tradition endorses the Reformation *sola scriptura*.[37] But tradition (specifically the ecumenical creeds and the Lutheran confessions) functions for Lutheranism in much the way it does for the Roman Catholic church. It is acknowledged as playing a legitimate role as a hermeneutical guide for ruling out inappropriate interpretations.[38]

This Lutheran concern to do theology in dialogue with the Church's heritage is one aspect of what Lutherans mean when they identify themselves as a confessional tradition. Such a theological style is reflected in the continuing Lutheran fidelity to the documents of the Lutheran confessions. Insofar as these documents continue to function authoritatively among Lutherans in identifying the Lutheran heritage, insofar as Lutheran theology is always done in dialogue with them, Lutherans do a "confessional theology" in dialogue with their own and the Catholic church's heritage.

These considerations raise the question whether a similar "Confessional consciousness" is emerging today in American evangelicalism, not just among the Presbyterian-Reformed branches but, most interestingly, within traditions usually seen as anticreedal, experiential, or biblicistic. Is the attempt of such traditions—for example, the pentecostal and Wesleyan/holiness traditions—to reappropriate their heritage and to use that heritage as a partner in doing theology, akin to what Lutherans mean in calling themselves a "Confessional tradition?"

Certainly, this sort of Confessional consciousness (an appeal to the Church's historic traditions as a primary resource for theology) is indicative of a Catholic heritage in Lutheranism, no less than in other dimensions we noted, such as worship and sacramentology. Such considerations raise anew the main agenda item of this article. What is it about the

Lutheran heritage that accounts for its ambivalence toward American evangelicalism? Of course it is true that there is room for Anglicanism and its Catholic perspective in the present-day postfundamentalist evangelical coalition. But are Lutheranism's Catholic elements a factor which largely keep it out of the coalition? This raises the question of whether Lutheranism's ambivalence toward evangelicalism could imply that the inclination of the evangelical coalition runs more in the direction of sectarianism, that it is less a reformed movement *inside* the Catholic church than it is one which perceives itself as a restorationist, biblicist movement.

Diversity in Lutheranism: Other Clues to the Limits of Evangelicalism?

In a sense, the preceding representation of Lutheranism has been idiosyncratic, not sufficiently representative. For although it comes as a surprise to many non-Lutherans, if ten Lutherans are asked to describe Lutheranism, ten distinct answers likely will emerge. Of course, within this diversity certain commonalities will surface. All theologians in the debate about the nature of Lutheranism will agree on the importance of fidelity to the Lutheran Confessions, on an emphasis on justification by grace through faith apart from works of the Law, and on most of the doctrinal commitments already described in this chapter. (It must be granted, though, that due to a certain anti-Catholicism which characterizes most Protestant churches, as well as because of certain hermeneutical moves, described below, made by some Lutherans with regard to the authority of the Luteran Confessions, not all segments of Lutheranism would give the Catholic elements of the Lutheran heritage as much emphasis as I have.)

The clearest differences will begin to emerge in such an intra-Lutheran conversation, however, with regard to the precise authority of the Lutheran Confessions (*The Book of Concord*). Some will argue that *The Book of Concord* is authoritative *because* [*quia*] it agrees with the Gospel. Others will take a more critical stance and maintain that the confessions are authoritative only *insofar as* [*quatenus*] they agree with the Gospel.

Of the two alternatives, the former tends to be more influenced by Lutheran orthodox theology. Such Lutherans tend to endorse the authority of the whole *Book of Concord*, all of its documents. Those more inclined to subscribe to the confessions only insofar as they are in agreement with the Gospel are today the larger segment in American and international Lutheranism. For this group of Lutherans, there tend to be only two absolutely essential authoritative documents in *The Book of Concord*, specifically The Augsburg Confession and, to a lesser extent, The Small

Catechism (a prioritization which *The Book of Concord* itself seems to grant).³⁹

Within these two general families of Lutheran perspectives, several distinct theological streams may be identified. For purposes of a concise summary, four distinct theological movements within Lutheranism may be identified. To some extent they have analogs in other historic Protestant churches. (It is interesting to note that all four movements have their origins in Germany. This fact and the perduring influence of these movements on Lutheranism in America help to explain why Lutherans have not been able to develop a truly American Lutheran theology.)

The first of the distinct Lutheran theological movements we shall note is *Lutheran orthodoxy,* which emerged in the period just after Luther's death. It was and is principally a theological movement dedicated to codifying and systematizing the insights of Luther. But it undertook this task largely by means of the Aristotelian philosophical categories that the Reformer had rejected. Inasmuch as orthodoxy was responsible for the final formulation of *The Book of Concord*, it tends to subscribe to the authority of all the documents of the Lutheran Confessions.

The second Lutheran theological stream to emerge was *Lutheran pietism*. Its origins are primarily in the social and ethical turmoil imposed on Europe during the Thirty Years War. It also represented a reaction against the heavily structured character of life in the Protestant *Landeskirche* and its vigorous observance of class distinctions. But no less was pietism a reaction to the rationalizing tendencies of orthodoxy. In all cases, the pietist reaction has been to emphasize spiritual renewal and sanctification. In so doing, although the early pietists strongly subscribed to the Lutheran Confessions, they tended to display a certain critical perspective toward them, deferring to the believer's conscience for determining the extent of the confessions' authority.⁴⁰

Not long after its development, pietism was confronted with the liberal and moralistic tendencies of Enlightenment theology. When this confrontation reached its height in the second half of the eighteenth century, pietism altered its face and developed into *neopietism* (a coalition of pietism with certain concerns of orthodoxy, specifically orthodoxy's polemical concerns and its preoccupation with theories concerning biblical authority). This movement, under which the Lutheran charismatic renewal may be characterized, tends to be the segment of Lutheranism that today is most inclined to identify with the evangelical movement. It is also worth noting that this stream, as well as classical pietism, tend to be the segments of Lutheranism most critical of the Roman Catholic tradition and least inclined to appropriate Lutheranism's Catholic heritage.⁴¹

Another distinct reaction to the trends of Enlightenment theology is evident in the third major Lutheran theological stream, the *Lutheran renewal* (also sometimes called *neo-Lutheranism*). A self-conscious effort to return to the heritage of the Lutheran Confessions, this movement has largely reflected the approach of orthodoxy. In fact, most modern representatives of Lutheran orthodoxy, such as The Lutheran Church–Missouri Synod, in its theological style, tend to be indebted to this Lutheran stream.

In this century, largely influenced by the Luther renaissance (the renewal of scholarly study of Martin Luther, begun in the nineteenth century) and the rise of neo-orthodox theology, a fourth distinct Lutheran theological stream emerged. Sometimes this movement too is referred to as *neo-Lutheranism*. However, with its largely neo-orthodox view of Scripture and its critical perspective on the Lutheran Confessions (they are deemed authoritative only insofar as they bear witness to the Gospel), it differs quite radically from the revival of Protestant orthodoxy which also has been identified as neo-Lutheranism. At present, this more recent movement is predominant in the academic communities of most of the mainline Lutheran churches of North America and Europe (at the practical, denominational level, its impact is perhaps not as decisive as the "theology of management techniques" and "political theology" which set the agenda for the most mainline denominations). But with the demise of neo-orthodoxy in the broader theological community, new models for Lutheran theology, not least of all the attempt to formulate Lutheran theology with paradigms drawn from Anglo-American models of narrative hermeneutics, have begun to emerge.

The diversity within Lutheranism, and the different levels of engagement with the evangelical movement which characterize the proponents of these different Lutheran theological streams, offer some helpful insights about the character of the evangelical coalition and its limits. For example, it is interesting to observe that classical pietists are not as inclined to identify with the evangelical movement as are neopietists.[42] One way of distinguishing these two subgroups of the same family pertains to their relative interest in theories of biblical inspiration. Classical pietists do not share with Lutheran orthodoxy a concern about such theories.[43] By contrast, neopietists (like orthodoxy) and many evangelicals reflect at least a dialogue with the concepts of bibical inerrancy or infallibility. In view of these factors, an intriguing question about the limits of evangelicalism is raised by the neopietist affinities with the evangelical movement, affinities not shared by the classical pietists. Could neopietism harmonize more readily with the evangelical coalition than the classical pietists because it shares with the movement a common interest in theories of biblical inspiration? (It is interesting to note that in the United States, Lutheran charismatics, whose dependence on pietism reflects more the neopietist strand, largely identify with the evangelical movement. And they also tend to share the view of Scripture characteristic of Protestant orthodoxy.[44]) Is such a concern with biblical inspiration—at least some dialogue with the concepts of biblical inerrancy or infallibility—a limit of evangelicalism, at least distinguishing the postfundamentalist evangelical movement from the mainline ecumenical establishment which is no longer in dialogue with these concepts?

There are additional data relating to Lutheranism's ambiguous relationship to the evangelical movement which lend more credence to defining the movement's limits in terms of a preoccupation or concern with biblical inerrancy or infallibility. The point is made quite strikingly when it is recognized that even some Lutherans who affirm biblical infallibility do not readily identify themselves with the evangelical movement. In Amererica, the ambiguous relationship to the movement maintained by The Lutheran Church–Missouri Synod illustrates this point. Similar examples in German Lutheranism can be identified.[45]

The argument of these proponents of Lutheran orthodoxy is that, although the evangelical movement is to be commended for its endeavor to take biblical authority seriously, the postfundamentalist evangelical view is markedly different and seriously deficient in comparison to the orthodox Lutheran view of biblical inerrancy. Evangelicals are said to reflect an essentially Reformed-propositional view of Scripture. These theologically conservative Lutherans fear that evangelicals are placing so much stress on an intellectual understanding of the biblical propositions that they have overlooked the transforming power of the Gospel. Because they are thought to be focusing attention unduly on teachings *about* God in Scripture, evangelicals are said to be neglecting God's revelation of himself.[46]

This theologically conservative Lutheran concern to affirm that God is present in his Word, that spiritual experience is always related to, not independent of, the external Word, and to prioritize the transforming power of the Gospel over the Scripture and theories of biblical authority, is deeply rooted in the Lutheran heritage. One always must remember that, unlike other Reformation Confessional statements and unlike the statements of faith of most churches and organizations related to the evangelical movement, the Lutheran Confessions contain no article about Scripture or theories of its inspiration. Also, one must take into account that Luther's commitment to the centrality of justification by grace through faith alone could also function for him in certain contexts as a principle for criticizing Scripture, as, for example, in the famous instances when he proposed that the Book of James be removed from the canon because it fails to give adequate testimony to justification by grace through faith apart from works of the Law.[47]

At any rate, these theologically conservative, orthodox Lutherans do not find these affirmations of the transforming power of the Word stated as clearly in the evangelical coalition as they would like them to be. Much more clearly do they identify *theories* about Scripture and its inerrancy in evangelical circles. And so the question arises: Why do these Lutherans sense such a Reformed orthodox view of Scripture in the evangelical movement, finding such a Reformed view not just in the movement's presbyterian wing but also in its pietist, free-church, holiness, pentecostal, baptist, and restorationist segments? Could this perception by Lutherans who otherwise are genuinely in sympathy with the evangelical movement suggest that it is a common concern with questions of biblical authority and infallibility, or at least a common dialogue with conceptions compatible with the views of Princeton Theology and consequently with Scottish Common Sense Realism, which helps hold the evangelical coalition together?[48] In the final analysis, is one of the limits of evangelicalism the Princeton hermeneutic and the philosophical suppositions it draws from Common Sense Realism?

Of course, objections are likely to be raised in some segments of the evangelical coalition, notably by the evangelical left and by certain holiness and pentecostal theologians. But a careful study of contemporary statements of faith of most evangelical churches and organizations readily indicates that, if biblical inerrancy/infallibility and Common Sense Realism are not endorsed, they at least serve as interpretive tools or dialogue partners for all of these groups.[49] By contrast, for most Lutherans and theologians of other mainline churches, these issues no longer are or never were agenda items. At any rate, the ambivalence of theologically conservative, orthodox Lutherans toward the evangelical movement poses a challenge to those unwilling to identify biblical inerrancy and Common Sense Realism as two of the limits of evangelicalism (what helps hold the coalition together). At least it is necessary for such critics to account for why even Lutherans with affinities towards the evangelical movement perceive it the way they do. What keeps Lutherans out of the coalition says much about what the coalition's limits may be.

Summary Reflections

What factors account for Lutheranism's ambivalent relationship to evangelicalism? To this juncture we have examined only theological factors. This focus might be challenged by some, since it has been argued that to a large extent sociology sets the evangelical coalition apart from the mainline establishment. The argument is made that, at least since the fundamentalist-modernist controversy, evangelicals have felt themselves to be a cognitive minority, not really part of the American religious establishment.[50] But if that be a distinguishing factor of the movement, it does not distinguish it from Lutheranism. For, at least in America, Lutherans have never been part of the establishment, but (except perhaps in the Midwest) instead have been more of a ghetto church. Thus it cannot be sociology which accounts for their ambivalent relationship to the evangelical movement.

Of course, in one sense, cultural differences between American evangelicals and Lutherans could be noted. Evangelicalism tends to be an Anglo-Saxon phenomenon, while Lutheranism has its roots in Germany and Scandinavia. However, when one considers how certain free-church movements from these two nations—churches such as The Evangelical Free Church of America and The Brethren Church (Ashland, Ohio)—have successfully integrated into the evangelical movement, then these ethnic differences seem not to be decisive in accounting for Lutheranism's ambivalence towards the evangelical coalition. Indeed, in view of the American "melting-pot" experience, it is not clear how these differences could be decisive.

After our sojourn in sociology, it is possible to summarize our answer concerning what theological factors keep Lutheranism out of the evangelical coalition. My contention has been that the complex relationship of Lutheranism to evangelicalism suggests several characteristics or limits of the evangelical movement.

Lutheranism is kept out of the evangelical coalition, first of all, insofar as the Lutheran agenda does not include the mandate to dialogue with something like the Princeton version of inerrancy, shaped by Common Sense Realism. Nor does the Lutheran agenda include a critique in principle of the Catholic tradition (especially its sacramentology and ecclesiology). And finally, Lutherans seem to sense that the evangelical coalition is not endorsing the Augustinian soteriological framework, at least not affirming the centrality of justification by grace through faith apart from works of the Law with the kind of vigor Lutherans desire. Evangelical priorities seem to be elsewhere, with holiness or the character of the Christian life.

Given these limits (barriers to more complete fellowship), it is all the more significant that only Lutherans who are compatible with neopietist convictions—sharing the pietist emphasis on sanctification and critical perspective towards Roman Catholicism, as well as the orthodox concern with theories of biblical inspiration and polemics—are at home in the evangelical coalition.[51] Do the Lutheran reaction to the evangelical coalition, the factors which keep Lutherans out, and the commitments which facilitate neopietist/charismatic identification with the coalition give convincing clues to the limits or core commitments of the evangelical movement? Do these theological commitments help explain why groups on the fringe of the evangelical movement (the holiness, pentecostal, and restorationist traditions) find themselves more at home in the movement than does the Lutheran, Catholic heritage?

ABBREVIATIONS

Apology *Apology of the Augsburg Confession* (1531). Part of *The Book of Concord* (1580).

CA *The Augsburg Confession* (1530). Part of *The Book of Concord* (1580).

FC *Formula of Concord* (1577). Part of *The Book of Concord* (1580). The *Formula* is divided into two sections — the Epitome and the Solid Declaration (abbreviated as SD).

GK Martin Luther, *The Large Catechism* (1529). Part of *The Book of Concord* (1580).

LW Martin Luther, *Luther's Works*, ed. Jaroslav Pelikan and Helmut Lehmann, vols. 1–30 (St. Louis, Mo.: Concordia Publishing House, 1955–76); vols. 32, 33, 35–44, 46–55 (Philadelphia: Fortress Press, 1955–86); vols. 31, 34, 45 (Philadelphia: Muhlenberg Press, 1957–62). American edition of the English translation. Citations include volume and page numbers.

SA Martin Luther, *The Smalcald Articles* (1537). Part of *The Book of Concord* (1580).

SD Solid Declaration, *Formula of Concord* (1577). Citations include article number within the declaration.

TPPP Martin Luther, *Treatise on the Power and Primacy of the Pope* (1537). Part of *The Book of Concord* (1580).

WA Martin Luther, *D. Martin Luther's Werke*, Kritische Gesamtausgabe (Weimarer Ausgabe), 56 vols. (Weimar, GDR: Hermann Bohlaus Nachfolger, 1833ff.). Citations include volume, page number (following colon), and line number which immediately follows the preceding page number.

REFERENCES

1. This point has been made by the director on the Commission of Theology and Church Relations of the Lutheran Church–Missouri Synod, Samuel Nafzger, quoted in Darrell Turner, "Ecumenical Institute Seeks to Define 'Evangelical'," *Religious News Service*, 12 Mar. 1985, p. 3. Likewise, voices in another theologically conservative American Lutheran denomination, the Wisconsin Evangelical Lutheran Synod, have argued that their church should not be identified with the evangelical movement; see David Valleskey, "Evangelical Lutheranism and Today's Evangelicals and Fundamentalists," *Wisconsin Lutheran Quarterly* 80 (Summer 1983):216. Similar hesitation among certain theologically conservative Lutheran groups in Europe about identifying with the evangelical movement has been voiced by presiding bishop of the Lutheran Church–Missouri Synod–related Selbständige Evangelisch-Lutherische Kirche: see Gerhard Rost, "Die Selbständige Evangelisch-Lutherische Kirche," in *Weg und Zeugnis*, ed. Rudolf

Bäumer, Peter Beyerhaus, and Fritz Grünweig, 2d ed. (Bad Liebenzell, West Germany: Verlag der Liebenzeller Mission, 1981), 89; Joachim Heubach, chairman of the Kirchliche Sammlung um Bibel und Bekenntnis, personal to Mark Ellingsen, 8 Feb. 1985; and Gunnleik Seierstad, general secretary of the Lausanne Committee-related Santalmisjonen, private interview by Ellingsen during Lutheran World Federation Assembly, Budapest, Hungary, 28 July 1984.

2. This intention in the use of the term "evangelical" has been noted by one of the men who claim to have coined the term, Peter Schneider, general secretary of the Deutsche Evangelische Allianz, private interview, Strasbourg, France, 17 May 1985.

3. Martin Luther Apology, IV.2; FC, SD, III.6. Cf. Luther, *Lectures on Galatians* (1535), WA 40I:48/LW 26:9.

4. Martin Luther, *Ninety-Five Theses* (1517), esp. articles 6, 28, 37, in WAI: 233-35/LW 31:26, 28, 29. Also see Martin Luther, *Lectures on Romans* (1515-16), WA 56:417, 17/LW 25:409.; and Luther, SA, III/III.24ff.

5. Martin Luther, TPPP, 45-48. Martin Luther, SA, II/I.5. Martin Luther, *Proceedings at Augsburg* (1518), WA 2:13, 6ff./LW 31:270.

6. That a kind of Pelagianism is a general human condition, insofar as such a reaction often is stimulated by encounter with God's Law, is affirmed in Luther, SA, III/II.3. Also see FC, SD, V.10. Another document of *The Book of Concord*, perhaps its most influential one, *The Augsburg Confession* (CA, XX.17), regards justification by grace through faith as only intelligible in the context of the terrified conscience (which could be deemed as the existential consequence of the failure of the innate Pelagianism of sinful humanity).

7. Geoffrey Wainwright, "Ekklesiologische Ansätze bei Luther und bei Wesley," in *Ökumenische Erschliessung Martin Luthers*, ed. Peter Manns and Harding Meyer (Frankfurt: Verlag Otto Lembeck, and Paderborn: Verlag Bonifatius-Druckerei,/ 1983), 175-76. English trans. is *Luther's Ecumenical Significance*, ed. Peter Manns and Harding Meyer, in collaboration with Carter Lindberg and Harry McSorley (Philadelphia: Fortress Press, 1984), 142.

8. Martin Luther, *Lectures on Galatians* (1535), WA 40I:229, 22/LW 26:130. Cf. FC, Epitome III.5; Luther, GK, IV.53.

9. Luther SA, II/I.1.

10. FC, SD III.6; Martin Luther, *Commentary on Psalm* 117 (1530), WA 31I:254-55, 27ff./LW 14:36-37; Martin Luther, *Commentary on the Sermon on the Mount* (1532), WA 32:348, 4/LW 21:59; Martin Luther, *Die Promotionsdisputation von Palladius und Tilemann* (1537), WA 39I:205, 1.

11. For the Law-Gospel distinction, see FC, SD V.1; Luther, *Lectures on Galatians* (1535), WA 40I:207, 17ff./LW 26:115;Ibid., WA 40I:209, 16/LW 26:117. Among other places, the Christian's freedom from the Law is asserted by Lutherans in CA, XXVIII.51; Martin Luther, *Preface to the Epistle of St. Paul to the Romans* (1546), in Luther, *D. Martin Luthers Werke: Deutsche Bibel*, Kritische Gesamtausgabe, 15 vols. (Weimar, East Germany: Hermann Böhlaus Nachfolger, 1906-61), 7:21 (English translation: LW 35:376). The primary, most elaborated statement of the Two-Kingdom Ethic is found in Martin Luther, *Temporal Authority: To What Extent It Should Be Obeyed* (1523), WA 11:245-80/LW 45:81-129.

12. CA, VII.1: cf. SA, III/VIII.3; FC, Epitome II.13; FC, SD XI.76.

13. CA, V.

14. For the Lutheran desire to maintain the office of bishop, see Apology, XIV.1; Luther, SA, III/X.1. On an openness to a reformed papacy, see Melanchthon's note in subscribing to SA. (But see Luther's more negative assessment of the utility of the

office in SA II/IV.5-9.) For one of Lutheranism's strongest affirmations of the priest-hood of all believers, see Martin Luther, *The Freedom of a Christian* (1520), WA 7:56-57, 35ff./LW 31:354-55. The role of the universal priesthood as the instrument of God's call to the ordained ministry, insofar as congregations may elect pastors, is affirmed, among other places, in *The Book of Concord*, TPPP, 69-72.

15. Apology, XIII.17, 2. Ordination is said to be appropriately considered as a sacrament in ibid., XIII.11 and likewise, in ibid., XIII.4, 14-15, sacramental status is conferred upon confession and marriage. Also see Martin Luther, *Against the Thirty-Two Articles of the Louvain Theologists* (1545), WA 54:427, 26/LW 34:356; and Luther, *On the Councils and the Church* (1539), WA 50:628-43/LW 41:148-66.

16. CA, VII.1.

17. Second Vatican Council, *Lumen Gentium* (1964), 1; Martin Luther, *Sermo de virtute excommunicationis* (1518), WA 1:639, 2; and Luther, *A Sermon on the Blessed Sacrament of the Holy and True Body of Christ and the Brotherhoods* (1519), WA 2:747, 7/LW 35:50. For a fuller discussion of this dimension of Luther's thought, see Vilmos Vajta, "Die Kirche als geistlich-sakramentale Communio mit Christus und seinen Heiligen in der Theologie Luthers," in Manns and Meyer, *Ökumenische Erschliessung Martin Luthers*, 141-53 (in the English translation: 111-21). Compatibility of these themes with Roman Catholic thought was highlighted by Paul-Werner Scheele, "Eyn volck der gnaden." In "Ekklesiologische Implikationen der sakraments-bezogenen Sermones Martin Luther aus dem Jahre 1519," in Manns and Meyer, *Ökumenische Erschliessung Martin Luthers*, 154-68. (in the English translation: 123-35).

18. Luther, GK, IV.10, 27, 35, 52-55. Cf. CA, II.2; Apology, II.35; GK, II.54.

19. FC, SD VII.35; FC, Epitome VII.2.

20. Luther, SA, III/VI.1; GK, V.69; FC, Epitome, VII.16; FC, SD, VII.123. For the classic statement of the Reformed position, see John Calvin, *Institutes of the Christian Religion* (1559), IV/XVII.33, 34, 40.

21. Martin Luther, *The Babylonian Captivity of the Church* (1520), WA 6:511, 34ff./LW 36:35. Cf. FC, SD VII.35-37.

22. Martin Luther, *That These Words of Christ, "This is My Body," Still Stand Firm Against the Fanatics* (1527), WA 23:138-47, 4ff./LW 37:60-67; cf. Martin Luther, *Die Disputation de divinitate et humanitate Christi* (1540), WA 39II:93, 4; Martin Luther, *Die Promotionsdisputation von Theodor Frabricius und Stanislaus Rapagelanus* (1544), WA 39II:380, 16; FC, SD VIII.20, 31, 35, 36. For Reformed critiques, see Ulrich Zwingli, *A Clear Instruction about Christ's Supper* (1526), 2, in *Corpus Reformatorum* (Berlin and Leipzig, 1834-), 91:818-19; Johannes Oecolampadius, *De Genuina verborum Domini, "Hoc est corpus meum"* . . . *Expositio* (1525), D6v.

23. Martin Luther, Predigten des Jahres (1523), WA 37:41, 2ff; Martin Luther, *Lectures on Genesis* (1535-36), WA 42; 44, 8/LW 1:58-59.

24. Martin Luther, *The Bondage of the Will* (1525), WA 18:689f., 32ff./LW 33:146; ibid., WA 18:686, 8/LW 33:140. Cf. ibid., WA 18:664, 14/LW 33:107: Luther, *Lectures on Romans* (1515-16), WA 56:429, V11/LW 25:421; ibid., WA 56:502, 4/LW 25:496-97. For a thorough discussion of this subject, see Mark Ellingsen, "Luther in Context: A Critique of and Counter-Proposal to the Systematic Employment of Luther's Doctrine of God in Werner Elert, Gustaf Aulén, and Regin Prenter" (Ph.D. diss., Yale Univ., 1980).

25. FC, SD XI.75, 78.

26. Note Luther's numerous warnings in *The Bondage of the Will* (1525), WA 18:685 1ff./LW 33:139-40; ibid., WA 18:689, 18ff./LW 33:145-46; and ibid., WA 18:784, 1ff./LW 33:289-90, against speculation about the hidden will of God.

27. Philip Jacob Spencer, *Pia Desideria*, trans. and ed. Theodore G. Tappert

(Philadelphia: Fortress Press, 1964), 76–77, 125; Friedrich Adolf Lampe, *Geheimnis des Gnadenbunds dem grossen Gott zu Ehren* (1712–19), 5:819f. Johann Albrecht Bengel is another well-known pietist who engaged in eschatological speculation; see F. Ernest Stoeffler, *German Pietism During the Eighteenth Century* (Leiden: Brill, 1973), 96, 101–102.

28. CA, XVII.5.

29. For examples, see Apology, IV.252, 305–307; Martin Luther, *The Disputation Concerning Justification* (1536), WA 39I:97, 16/LW 34:166; ibid., WA 39I.:83: 35/LW 34:153; Luther, *Lectures on Galatians* (1535), WA 40I:229, 18/LW 26:130.

30. FC, Epitome III.8, 11; FC, SD III.18–24; The Lutheran Church–Missouri Synod, *Brief Statement of the Doctrinal Position of the Missouri Synod* (1932), 17.

31. For examples, see Wesleyan Church, *Articles of Religion* (1968), XI, XIV; Church of the Nazarene, *Articles of Faith* (n.d.), X; Church of God (Cleveland, Tenn.), *Declaration of Faith* (n.d.), articles 6, 8; Baptist Bible Fellowship, *Articles of Faith* (n.d.), X–XII; Southern Baptist Convention, *The Baptist Faith and Message* (1963), IV; *The Westminister Confession of Faith* (1646), XI.

32. Luther, GK, IV.65, 71–86; Luther, SA III/XIII.1; Martin Luther, *The Babylonian Captivity of the Church* (1520), WA 6:528, 10/LW 36:59. For references to Luther's use of the image of marriage to describe justification, see Martin Luther, *The Freedom of a Christian* (1520), WA 7:25, 34/LW 31:351–52; Martin Luther, *Treatise on Good Works* (1520), WA 6:207, 15/LW 44:26–27.

33. FC, Epitome I.8; FC, SD I.11; CA, II, XVIII; Apology, II, XVIII. Perhaps the classic Lutheran statement of this anthropology appears in Luther, *The Bondage of the Will* (1525), WA 18:600–787/LW 33:15–295. Cf. Augustine, *De Libero Arbitrio* (396), III.xviii.51–52.

34. Luther, *Lectures on Galatians* (1535), WA 40I:368f., 26ff./LW 26:232–33; Martin Luther, *Die dritte Disputation gegen die Antinomer* (1538–39), WA 39I:564, 3ff.; Martin Luther, *Against Latomus* (1521), WA 8:57–96/LW 32:157–213. Cf. Luther SA, III/III.40; Luther, GK, IV.65ff.

35. For indications of such emphases on regeneration and sanctification in Lutheran pietism, see Philip Jacob Spener, *Von der Wiederguburt*, ed. Hans-Georg Feller (Stuttgart, West Germany: J.F. Steinkopf, 1963), 13; Spener, *Pia Desideria*, 44–45, 64. Stoeffler, *German Pietism*, 16, finds a similar emphasis in August Hermann Francke.

36. CA, Preface, 2, 10; CA, XX.12; CA XXI.1; Apology, Preface 11, Apology, IV.325; FC, *Epitome*, Rule and Norm. 3. Sentiments favoring the contention that Lutheranism is a reform movement *inside* the Catholic Church have been expressed by Eric W. Gritsch and Robert W. Jenson, *Lutheranism* (Philadelphia: Fortress Press, 1976), 6; George Lindbeck, "Lutheran Churches," in *Ministry in America*, ed. David S. Schuller, Merton P. Strommen, and Milo L. Brekke (San Francisco: Harper & Row, 1980), 442.

37. FC, SD, Rule and Norm. 3; Martin Luther, *Defense and Explanation of All the Articles Which Were Rejected by the Roman Bull* (1521), WA 7:317, 1ff./LW 32:11–12; Luther, *The Babylonian Captivity of the Church* (1520), WA 6:508, 19/LW 36:29.

38. FC, Epitome, Rule and Norm. 6; FC, SD, Rule and Norm. 10. Luther made use of "Tradition" in this way to argue for the validity of infant baptism; see his GK, IV.50–51; and *Concerning Rebaptism* (1528), WA 26:167–68, 36ff./LW 40:256. For documentation of the Roman Catholic view of Tradition, see Council of Trent, *Decree Concerning the Canonical Scriptures*, 4th Sess., Apr. 1546. At the Second Vatican Council, *Dei Verbum* (1965), 8, there is a clear suggestion of the subordination of Tradition to Scripture.

LUTHERANISM 243

39. FC, SD, 10; FC SD, Rule and Norm. 5, 7, 8.

40. For references pertaining to pietism's overall emphasis, see note 35 above. For an indication of the pietist's attitudes towards the Lutheran Confessions, see Philip Jacob Spener, *Aufrichtige Ubereinstimmung mit der Augsburgischen Confession* (Frankfurt: 1695), pp. 91–92.

41. A good example of this critical perspective towards Roman Catholicism by Lutherans who are largely influenced by neopietism is evident in a pamphlet, "Die Bekennender Gemeinschafter" (1979), p. 4, issued by a large German evangelical, neopietist organization of the same name. For anti-Catholicism in classical Lutheran pietism, see Spener, *Pia Desideria*, pp. 39ff., 70, 77.

42. This dynamic is expressed almost classically in the Lutheran church perhaps most thoroughly influenced by pietism, the Evangelische Landeskirche in Württemberg. The church is in the midst of painful controversies concerning the evangelical movement in Germany and the appropriate degree of cooperation with the movement. The classical pietists, as well as those influenced more by neoorthodoxy, are critics of the evangelicals. Only those in the church whose theology has been influenced by neopietism tend to identify themselves with the evangelical movement.

43. A good example of this orientation in classical pietism is evident in Spener, *Pia Desideria*, pp. 56–57, 67.

44. American Lutheran identification with the evangelical movement has been affirmed by the director of the Charismatics' International Lutheran Renewal Center in a letter by Larry Christenson to Ellingsen 22 June 1985. Likewise, Christenson reportedly has endorsed the infallibility of Scripture (at least in the sense of "limited inerrancy"; Larry Christenson, ed., *Welcome, Holy Spirit: A Study of Charismatic Renewal in the Church* (Minneapolis, Minn.: Augsburg Publishing House, 1987), 216.

45. See note 1 above for references.

46. Samuel Nafzger to Ellingsen 2 Apr. 1984; Robert Preus to Ellingsen 20 Feb. 1984. The Reformed influence on the evangelical movement also has been noted by Valleskey, "Evangelical Lutheranism," 183, 204, 218.

47. Luther, *D. Martin Luthers Werke: Tischreden*, Kritische Gesamatausgabe, 6 vols. (Weimar, East Germany: Hermann Böhlaus Nachfolger, 1912–1921), 5:157 (English trans.: LW 54:424–25); Luther, *D. Martin Luthers Werke: Deutsche Bibel*, 6:10 (English trans.: LW 35:362). Cf. Luther, *Lectures on Galatians* (1535), WA 40I:458, 13ff./LW 26:294–95; Luther, *Adventpostille* (1522), WA 10½:48, 5.

For Luther's appreciation of the transforming power of the Word, see GK, Preface 11 and I.91. The Lutheran insistence that grace and spiritual experience are given only in conjunction with the Word is especially evident in the Lutheran Reformers' polemics against the Enthusiasts; Luther, SA, III/VIII.3; FC, SD XI.76; FC, *Epitome* II.13; Martin Luther, *Commentary on Psalm* 118) (1529–30). WA 31I:99–100, 16ff./LW 14:62.

48. For documentation of Princeton Theology's dependence on Common Sense Realism, see Charles Hodge, *Systematic Theology* (New York: Charles Scribner's Sons, 1871), 1:9; Archibald Alexander, handwritten ms. for lecture, "Nature and Evidence of Truth," in *The Princeton Theology, 1812–1921*, ed. Mark A. Noll (Grand Rapids, Mich.: Baker, 1983), 318.

49. Detailed analysis of the various evangelical statements of faith is provided in Mark Ellingsen, *The Evangelical Movement: Growth, Impact, Controversy, Dialog* (Minneapolis, Minn.: Augsburg Publishing House, 1988). For a more detailed discussion of the influence of Common Sense Realism on the development of several segments of the evangelical movement, see Mark Ellingsen, "Common Sense Realism: The Cutting Edge of Evangelical Identity," *Dialog* 24 (Summer 1985):197–205.

50. For examples of such an argument, see Donald Bloesch, *The Future of Evangelical Christianity* (Garden City, N.Y.: Doubleday, 1983), viii; and Donald W. Dayton, "Two Christianities: The American Church Divided" (paper presented at Hyde Park Ecumenical Project, Chicago, 18 Apr. 1986), 14–16.

51. For references to substantiate a number of these observations, see notes 35, 41, 44 above.

CHAPTER 14

Some Doubts about the Usefulness
of the Category "Evangelical"
Donald W. Dayton

As the author of one of the contributions to this volume (that on pente-costalism), I have anticipated much of the perspective that I now bring to the broader editorial task of reflecting on the meaning of the range of essays collected in this volume. In this concluding comment, I would like to reiterate and expand on my earlier analysis — arguing that the category "evangelical" has lost whatever usefulness it once might have had and suggesting that we can very well do without it.

A fundamental reason for taking this position has to do with the word "evangelical" itself, which is equivocal and obscures fundamental differences that are made clearer in languages such as German, where greater precision of description is possible. The issue is that, if the three separate meanings of the word "evangelical" (the sixteenth-century Reformational, the eighteenth-century pietist and conversionist, and the twentieth-century fundamentalist) are isolated and used as descriptors for establishing subsets of Christian traditions, they establish differing subsets. For this reason, the category "evangelical" remains an "essentially contested concept," and any effort to obscure these lines of difference implicitly resolves the conflict in favor of one or another basic sets of connotations of the word.

The essays in this volume amply document this point — even when allowance is made for the fact that my essay (with this analysis included) was used as a model by the contributors. Tim Weber's types of "evangelicalism" are similar to mine, although he adds a fourth category, "progressive." The difficulties in reconciling the first two of these types are at the root of the conflict between *refomatio* and *restitutio* in Richard Hughes' essay and between classical Lutheranism and "evangelicalism" (centering in the contrasting roles of justification and sanctification as organizing principles of theology and practice), that Mark Ellingsen identifies. The difficulties in reconciling the second and third types are at the core of George Marsden's struggle to relate nineteenth- and twentieth-century uses of the term *evangelical* — the contrast between "prefundamentalist" and "postfundamentalist" uses of the label. Similar issues are at the root of the difficulties of assimilating either pietism (John Weborg) or the holiness movement (Paul Bassett) into either the first or the third types. The black church is a paradigmatic case for revealing the equivocal character of the label *evangelical*—as Milton Sernett's essay amply demonstrates. And even more complex are the problems of encompassing Adventism, anabaptism, or confessional orthodoxy (whether Lutheran or Reformed) in any usual understanding of "evangelical."

The issue is not just one of gaining more precision in an academic exercise of classification and description. In addition to being equivocal, the label *evangelical* is inaccurate in some of its fundamental connotations and misleads our attempts to understand the phenomenon that we are observing. It blocks efforts to find a bridge of understanding between groups separated by the label. This is particularly true when the term *evangelical* is understood in the third sense of my typology and is then applied indiscriminately to the range of traditions and movements described in the essays in this volume. The use of the word *evangelical* derived from the fundamentalist/modernist controversy has conditioned us to understand the label primarily in terms of a conservative/liberal spectrum, in which an "evangelical" is more "conservative" than a "liberal," but not so "conservative" as a "fundamentalist." Even so careful an analyst as George Marsden, who has largely moved beyond the more narrow "presbyterian" construct of a Bernard Ramm (as analyzed above in my essay), still uses *fundamentalist* and *evangelical* as roughly synonymous with *conservative* or *traditional*.

The most powerful illustration of the problems with this "conservative/liberal" construct has to do with the ministry of women. If this construct were valid, then we would expect that the churches of the National Association of Evangelicals would be the ones that have resisted the ministry of women and that the churches of the National Council of Churches would have pioneered the practice and be its major champions. Indeed, the "conservative/liberal" construction of *evangelical* is so ingrained in our thinking that even informed persons will insist that this is actually the case, when the opposite is more nearly true. It has been the churches of the NAE that pioneered the ordination of women, that did so in many cases a hundred years before the churches of the NCC, and that have achieved a percentage of women ministers as yet undreamed of in the NCC. This is partly because of the predominance of holiness and pentecostal churches in the NAE, but once the pattern is noticed, it will be discerned in other centers of "normative evangelicalism"—as in the Evangelical Free Church or the "evangelical" currents in New England set in motion by the work of A.J. Gordon.

The more I work with groups and movements often called "evangelical" (precisely those described in this book), the more I am convinced that they are the newer and innovative edge of Christianity, and that they are characterized in many ways by their distance from "classical" or "traditional" Christianity. We would hardly think of calling "pentecostalism" a traditional form of Christianity; it is rather a modern form that has taken shape in the twentieth century, in such a way as to break the patterns of classical Protestant thought and force new questions. The nineteenth century was exceedingly productive of these new currents — Adventism, the holiness revival, the black church, restorationism, dispensationalism, as well as even more radical and nontraditional movements such as the Mormons and the Jehovah's Witnesses. These are the currents and issues that have dominated the life and theology of the groups described in this volume — most of which are far from being "conservative" or "traditional" in character.

It is true that these movements sometimes have certain features which may appear to be "traditional" and "antimodern," but careful analysis will reveal that the situation is easily oversimplified. In my essay above, I warned against the danger of confusing the "precritical" with the "anticritical" ethos of "fundamentalism." Thus pentecostalism often is accused of being "fundamentalist" in its use of Scripture; it would be better to describe it as "precritical." The movement is still young, and it is too early to tell if this is a permanent feature of pentecostalism. Indeed, evidence is accumulating that it is not. I have met many pentecostals in this country and abroad who have found ways to express their pentecostal faith in the context of critical biblical and theological reflection. Aspects of the charismatic movement also have managed to wed an essentially pentecostal piety and theology with a more critical outlook and reading of the Scriptures. Similarly, one can find both uncritical and more critical manifestations of anabaptism, restorationism, Adventism, pietism, the holiness tradition, and so forth.

Many of the movements described in this book are still in the early stages of developing a historical and critical consciousness (as evidenced by the recent establishment of historical archives, the founding of theological seminaries, and the cultivation of critical traditions of theology). We should not be comparing traditions dating from the sixteenth century with the modern movements; we should be making comparisons with the development of Methodism in the mid-nineteenth century or finding some other comparable developmental anaylsis before drawing conclusions about the character and future of these movements. When we do so, the construction of *conservative* as opposed to *liberal* will appear increasingly counterproductive and even quaint.

An early suggestion for the title of this book was "charting the uncharted." Many of the movements analyzed in this book are just now being studied as they ought — in part because critical study often is initiated by insiders only as they begin to move into a broader cultural context. Because these movements have grown up on the edge of society and outside the mainstream, they have not been well understood even in the academic centers of that mainstream. It has thus been easy to lump them under some such label as *evangelical* and dismiss them as fundamentalist, rather than taking them seriously as locations of theological and cultural innovation (the ministry of women, creative social experimentation and commitments) and even as sources of renewal and theological insight in the mainstream, as has clearly been the case with pentecostalism. A large part of my intention in working on this book has been to display the complexity of these movements, in the hope that we can move beyond easy generalizations to nuanced understanding of these movements and their diversity — a diversity that is compromised from the beginning by any effort to find a common label.

One could posit that these movements share little more than a common alienation from the so-called "mainstream" of American church life, though the reasons for this alienation may be diverse, including fundamental theological or ecclesiological dissent (baptists, anabaptism, and probably restorationism), racism (the black church), classism (pentecostalism, the black church, the holiness movement), dissenting eschatology (Adventism and premillennialism), traditionalism (fundamentalism, confessional Protestantism), and other such factors. Yet obviously there is a great deal of interplay among these traditions. Is it not possible to find a more positive delineation of the category "evangelical" than the negative one presupposed by a common alienation from a supposed "mainstream"?

There are some commonlities. There must be some experiential and historical grounding to the fact that a certain cluster of churches have come together in, for example, the National Association of Evangelicals. If this common ground is not to be found in a common "conservativism" (as is generally assumed), or in a common commitment to the "inerrancy of Scripture" (most pentecostal and holiness churches in the NAE are not committed by articles of faith to this doctrine, and most of those that are have moved in that direction only under the influence of the neo-evangelicals who have been the dominant force in the NAE), or in resistance to such innovations of modernity as the ministry of women (patently false, as indicated above), where are such commonalities to be found? One might make several proposals.

One might argue, for example, that the majority of the churches of the NAE are essentially "low-church" and revivalistic in orientation. Indeed, when the theological commission of the World Evangelical Fellowship (WEF, the international counterpart of the NAE, as the World Council of Churches [WCC] is the international arm of the ecumenical movement that includes the National Council of Churches [NCC] responded to the major ecumenical consensus document of the twentieth century, *Baptism, Eucharist, and Ministry*, it noticed the sacramentalism of that document and suggested that many WEF members would be resistant to such an orientation. This "sacramental" descriptor has a certain value, and since it is the sacramental churches that have been most resistant to the ministry of women, this characteristic helps explain how the ministry of women would appear first in the NAE churches rather than in the NCC. It also supports my point above, that what separates the NAE churches from the NCC churches is not their defense of "traditionalism," but their distance from the traditional churches.

Such a description does indicate some of the evangelical churches' continuities with the baptists and other "low-church" movements. But the situation gets more complicated as one moves further in analysis. Some of the movements sometimes labeled "evangelical" are decidedly more "sacramental" in orientation (traditional Protestant churches such as the Missouri Synod Lutherans, with their closed communion), while others are highly committed to particular understandings of baptism (certain restorationists and baptists, for example), still others are committed to a different set of sacraments (the foot-washing tradition in certain anabaptist groups is defended as more clearly taught by Jesus than the traditional sacraments), still others by a sacramental indifference or flexibility that allows a diversity of practice (certain holiness groups allow both infant and believers baptism, as does the supposedly more "liturgically oriented" Evangelical Covenant Church), while still others are strongly antisacramental (the Quakers and the Salvation Army). While there may be (I think there is) a predominance of "low-church" orientations within the traditions represented in this volume, the situation is so complex that one is reluctant to assert such a discriminator in any definitive way.

Instead, one might observe the importance of the rise of dispensational premillennialism in determining the theological and ecclesiastical ethos that has drawn the NAE together. This is perhaps the theological feature that is most common to the range of churches that have joined the NAE. The role of dispositional premillennialism in shaping the whole discussion has not been appreciated as it should. In his essay above, George Marsden has criticised Ernest Sandeen's view that dispensational premillennialism is the defining feature of fundamentalism. I am much more taken by Sandeen's proposal and find that this eschatology often lurks behind the ecclesiological struggles, the battles over the social gospel and missiology, the anti-cultural bias, and other features of the fundamentalism that lies behind "neo-evangelicalism." In a similar way, the biblical literalism required to make the prophetic constructs of dispensationalism work may be akin to fundamentalist traditionalism, but it is quite different and rooted in different motives.

In many ways, the NAE may be understood as a cluster of churches and traditions that have a common history with dispensational premillennialism. But this will not work entirely even within the NAE subculture, and utterly fails when one moves beyond. As Richard Hughes indicates, only a small part of the restorationists are premillennial. Similarly, though deeply influenced by dispensationalism, the holiness movement has significant segments that have resisted this tradition (such churches as the Church of the Nazarene and, even more, the Church of God, Anderson, Indiana, and the Salvation Army—both of which have stayed outside the NAE). The black church stands largely outside this influence and the confessional churches perhaps even more.

By such descriptors (low-church revivalistic conversionism; a common history with dispensationalism) one can pull out certain subclusters of churches that can be grouped together as "families" of churches that share certain characteristics. But can one, as my co-editor will suggest in the concluding chapter, establish a set of descriptors that allow one to argue that there is a "family resemblance" that holds together all the movements described in this book? I think not.

Many American Christian traditions share much, by virtue of a common history and context, and thus demonstrate a certain "family resemblance." To sustain their "family resemblance" argument, defenders of this position seem committed to arguing that some descriptor(s) exist that set apart the movements described in this book in ways that are more important and sharper than the ways in which divergent elements in this book may be related to other churches and movements not included. But is this so? Is there, for example, a line that binds "holiness churches" closer to "Orthodox Presbyterians" than to mainstream Methodists? If so, I fail to see it. What sense does it make to put Missouri Synod Lutherans and pentecostals in the same category? In what way does the black church belong to a family of restorationists—that is different from the sort of primitivism that one finds in Eastern Orthodoxy or the appeal of many Anglicans to the Patristic era? Do Adventists and anabaptists belong to the same family? Traditional Catholics and certain fundamentalists share some concerns—as do the variety of persons clustered together in the Institute for Religion and Democracy, but we do not argue that there is a family resemblance of comparable importance here.

I am inclined to think that the demand for the label *evangelical* has its roots not in the commonalities of a certain subcluster of churches, but more in the power politics of the neo-evangelicals after World War II. Those in this movement wanted to claim as large a power base as possible for the ecclesiastical struggles in which they were engaged. This led to the forging of certain alliances that had varying degrees of historical and theological justification. Whatever justification such coalitions may have had at the time (and one must be skeptical about the grounding at that point), trajectories that may have converged for a moment now have diverged sufficiently to reveal that such associations are not viable. We are living through the dissolution of such coalitions, in a way that calls into question the continuing usefulness of the label *evangelical* as a historical and theological category.

One knows what pentecostalism is. One can understand the holiness revival and its complex currents and subcurrents that have produced a bewildering variety of churches and institutions. One can describe the Church of God, Anderson, Indiana, as an attempt to synthesize a Campbellite ecclesiology and a holiness soteriology, and have some idea what one means by that. One can describe the difference between the nonconversionist orientation of the classical orthodoxies of Reformed and Lutheran varieties and the conversionist-oriented pieties of various forms of pietists and revivalism. One can understand the emergence of the black churches from the largely Methodist and baptist subcultures of nineteenth-century America and understand why they do not relate easily to the "postfundamentalist neo-evangelicals." For these and other similar questions, one can pursue and find illuminating answers. But I find myself unable to make a common label "evangelical" describe the range of movements covered in this volume. I, therefore, avoid the word wherever possible and even regret that it must be used in the title of this book. I would rather call for a moratorium on the use of the term, in the hope that we would be forced to more appropriate and useful categories of analysis.

CHAPTER 15

American Evangelicalism:
An Extended Family
Robert K. Johnston

> *There are three indisputable facts about the evangelical*
> *tradition in America. First, it is important. Second, it is*
> *understudied. Third, it is diverse.*
> Leonard I. Sweet[1]

Whether one speaks of an evangelical kaleidescope, an evangelical mosaic, an evangelical umbrella, or, less metaphorically, an evangelical movement, scholars of American evangelicalism struggle to express its present diversity and scope. Cullen Murphy is more colorful than most when he speaks of the "vast tent of evangelical faith," viewing it as a twelve-ring circus with acts performed by "peace-church" conservatives, Arminian conservatives, Wesleyans, baptists, conservative Calvinists, immigrant churches, pietist churches, Adventists, black pentecostals, white pentecostals, black evangelicals, and fundamentalists.[2]

   Such listings have been variously provided and are of use as one attempts a sociological mapping of American evangelicalism. Robert Webber, in his book *Common Roots,* finds fourteen subgroupings;[3] the present volume presents twelve theological traditions (although they constitute a "twelve-ring circus" different from Murphy's). The Roman Catholic missiologist Thomas Stransky finds American evangelicalism "a confusing conglomeration":

> What a wide variety of traditions! They come from within the mainline churches (Episcopalian, Presbyterian, Methodist); those Reformation churches with strict interpretations of their confessions (Missouri Synod, Lutherans, Christian Reformed); the "peace" churches (Brethern, Mennonite, Friends); the more conservative wing of the Restoration movement (Campbellites); the "Holiness" tradition (Wesleyan Methodists); Baptists, the fundamentalist groups . . . Pentecostals, most black churches. . . . No wonder it is difficult to reach a description in which all of the above would recognize themselves![4]

In an effort to co-opt the tradition, fundamentalists at times have tried to equate the limits of evangelicalism with the limits of their own movement (commentators with a jaundiced eye toward evangelicalism also at times have opted for such a false limitation). But the data will not support the equation. Black evangelicals have as little to do with fundamentalism as do the holiness denominations. Pentecostals still are scorned by many fundamentalists (cf. Jerry Falwell's problems with his constituency when he assumed control of the PTL Club). Mennonites and Lutherans, as the chapters in this volume reflect, want to distance themselves from fundamentalists, and the list could be continued. As Joel Carpenter points out, "Fundamentalists are evangelicals, but not all evangelicals (are) fundamentalists."[5] Others attempt to give definitions of the American evangelical that are similarly narrow. Some would limit the term *evangelical* to those who are descendants of American revivalism. (But what then of the Christian Reformed Church?) Others would stress human faith and active obedience. (But what of the Lutherans?) Or, conversely, God's initiating grace. (But what of the Restoration churches?) Many would equate evangelicalism with a commitment to biblical inerrancy or Baconian epistemology. Others would center on premillennialism and dispensationalism. Some would limit the category of evangelicals to those who oppose modern thought. Others would define evangelicalism according to a Reformed perspective. (The most frequently quoted example of this latter stance is John Gerstner's summary concerning the supposed "Pelagianism" of Charles Finney: "To this extent Finney, the greatest of nineteenth-century evangelists, became the greatest of nineteenth century foes of evangelicalism."[6]) All who would fall prey to such reductive definitions need to hear the warning of a former president of the University of Wisconsin, quoted by Robert T. Handy: "The mind lingers with pleasure upon the facts that fall happily into the embrace of the theory, and feels a natural coldness toward those that assume a refractory attitude."[7]

In seeking to move beyond such imperialistic and/or reductive definitions, William Abraham calls into question the very function of labels themselves. Rather than viewing labels as referential or descriptive, he would have us recognize their prescriptive character.[8] Thus understood, the term *evangelical* should be judged "an essentially contested concept" (the phrase is W.B. Gallie's, who writes in the British analytical tradition).[9] That is, Abraham believes there are alternate, competing specifications of those qualities central to the definition of evangelicalism itself. When a concept is "essentially contested," one finds various groups using it in different ways with no common standard. Even though the contestants recognize competing definitions, they continue to maintain the correctness of their own version, believing themselves to have convincing arguments.

The only hope, thinks Abraham, is to seek an appreciation of the *history* of the contested concept. But will this work?

Abraham would have us understand the Wesleyan roots of American evangelicalism, over against those who would emphasize its Reformed heritage. Abraham is, indeed, rightly sensitive to the present dominance of Reformed practitioners of evangelical historiography (e.g., Noll, Marsden, Hatch, Carpenter). Yet a focus on American evangelicalism's primary debt to pietist, rather than Puritan, traditions in America is reductive, not simply a necessary part of the "contest." By the nineteenth century, almost all American Protestants were evangelical. But this coalition reflected a "merger of Pietist and Reformed heritages."[10]

In a series of helpful essays, Donald Dayton has drawn attention to three periods in the history of Protestantism when the term *evangelical* came to be used.[11] During the *Reformation*, evangelicals gave a biblical, Christocentric expression to the Christian faith. (Here is Dayton's "type one": Protestant/Lutheran Evangelicalism.) During the *Great Awakenings* and the evangelical revivals in eighteenth- and nineteenth-century America, emphasis was on conversion and the process of personal appropriation of grace. (Here is "type two": Revivalistic Evangelicalism.) And during the *fundamentalist/modernist controversy* of the twentieth century, evangelicals have stressed orthodoxy and conservative values, whether political, social, or theological. (Here is "type three": Fundamentalist Evangelicalism.) Although Dayton recognizes that such a historical typology tends to ignore what is often "blurred and intermingled both historically and in contemporary usage," he nevertheless would side with Abraham, wanting "to preserve the label [*evangelical*] for those expressing the ethos of the awakenings and revivals and continue to use the word 'fundamentalist' to designate the descendants of the more recent conservative party."[12]

Dayton himself recognizes how difficult it is to "swim against the stream." It is not only the presbyterian hegemony which is a deterrent; history's multiple witness is not easily ignored. As Max Stackhouse observed, "The American evangelical heritage includes three periods: puritan Evangelicalism, pietistic Evangelicalism and fundamentalist Evangelicalism."[13] All three must find their place within the constellation of American evangelicalism.

A Family Resemblance

What can be said? Bloesch suggests that the term *evangelical* remains "fluid."[14] Hubbard admits that the term is presently "shrouded in controversy."[15] Sweet believes it "eludes definition."[16] In the preceeding chapters,

Weber considers the definition of evangelicalism "one of the biggest problems in American religious historiography."[17] Dayton understands there to be no "univocal definition of evangelicalism," leaning as we have seen above to the notion of "an essentially contested concept."[18] And Kraus believes "the movement defies a precise theological definition."[19]

Such a definitional impasse suggests the need of a new model for describing American evangelicalism. In the 1981 *Annual Review of Psychology*, Carolyn Mervis and Eleanor Rosch summarize contemporary research in the field of categorization. As they define it, a "category" exists whenever two or more items are made equivalent. Such categorization can be done poorly, but it is "one of the most basic functions of living creatures," allowing an organism to interact profitably with "the infinitely distinguishable objects and events it experiences." Traditionally, categories have consisted of "a specification of those qualities that a thing must have to be a member of the class" (intension) and a listing of "things that have those qualities" (extension). Categories are, thus, "seen as determinately established by necessary and sufficient criteria for membership." And "the role of rationality is to abstract out what is essential to a situation while ignoring what is inessential."[20]

One might say that categories traditionally have been viewed as more or less *black or white*. While recognizing the tidiness of such a definitional approach, Mervis and Rosch, with their colleagues, have begun to understand the limitations of such exactitude as well. They have become increasingly aware that categorization deals only *more* or *less* with black and white.

There is, for example, growing empirical evidence to support the conclusion that, within a category, all members need not be, nor are they equally representative, as has often been assumed. Whether one is considering "colors," or "dogs," or "furniture," it turns out that test subjects are able to agree on certain exemplars which are "more representative than others." Moreover, our language helps us code these gradients of representativeness through the use of qualifying terms or "hedges." We might say, for example, that "a penguin is technically a bird," even though we would not say, "a sparrow is technically a bird." In the latter case, the word *technically* is redundant, while in the former it recognizes that not all birds are equally birdlike. Researchers recognize that "category members differ in the extent to which they share attributes with other category members. They call this variable family resemblance (after Wittgenstein 1953 [*Philosophical Investigations*]). Items which have the highest family resemblance scores are those with the most shared attributes."[21]

The notion of family resemblance helps explain a variety of phenomena. As in any family, category boundaries are not always well defined. The poorer members (i.e., less representative) of categories often contain attributes from other categories which cause lines to be blurred and decisions to remain probabilistic. (For example, is a daughter-in-law a member of the family, or not?) On the other hand, the most representative members of a family are recognized rapidly and easily, even if the family is not named. Thirdly, although the recognition of family members can occur without the subject being told the rules of family membership ("where telling a subject the rule may retard performance"), the human mind does tend to categorize and classify in ways that involve abstraction, i.e., creatively sorting out "which elements of a situation are 'essential' and which irrelevant."[22]

The notion of family resemblance, as Mervis and Rosch describe the term, is a helpful one in coming to understand American evangelicalism. Rather than seek exclusive categories, it is useful to recognize the familial nature of American evangelicalism. Just as with other categorization, so with the term "evangelical" we must allow category boundaries a certain open-endedness. One observes this fluidity with regard to the term "evangelical," as we often and rightly use qualifying terms: "basically evangelical," "generally evangelical," "strict evangelical," "progressive evangelical," "conservative evangelical," "mainline evangelical," "establishment evangelical," and so on.[23]

Several of the essayists in this volume have adopted suggestive language similar to that of family resemblance. Ellingsen makes casual mention of the "evangelical family."[24] Dayton writes of "a family relationship of sorts."[25] Marsden at one point sees "particularly close relatives within an extended family."[26] Weber likes "to compare evangelicalism to a large extended family, some of whose members feel close and others estranged from time to time."[27] Yet, although the metaphor of family membership is used by commentators on American evangelicalism, its implications and significance with regard to categorization have not been recognized.

Several examples are useful in helping one to understand the importance of evangelicalism's family resemblance. In his book *The Coming Great Revival*, William Abraham points out that the term *evangelical* has meant different things in different ages. One only need consider the distinctives of Luther, Calvin, and Wesley to sense profoundly different accounts of the Christian tradition. Yet Abraham admits:

> What holds the various expressions together as one tradition is not one agreed set of doctrines; rather unity resides in family resemblance. Despite differences of emphasis and expression, there is sufficient common appearance for both outsiders and insiders to identify a single evangelical tradition within the Christian tradition as a whole.

Abraham opts methodologically not to follow through with the notion of family resemblance, choosing to develop, as we have seen above, the model of an "essentially contested concept." Reacting against those within neo-fundamentalism who have attempted doctrinally to "suitably can" what he believes is in reality "a complex vision of the Christian tradition," Abraham choses his own "suitable can," an alternate, Wesleyan model, one clear-cut and identifiable.[28]

Abraham does not want Wesley to be "tamed by placing him in the categories of the fundamentalist paradigm."[29] And he is right to resist. But if what is under consideration is not fundamentalism, one of evangelicalism's multiple expressions, but the broader familial category of evangelicalism itself, then such a fear is ungrounded. Although American evangelicalism historically has been influenced by fundamentalism, it is not synonymous with the movement. One need only observe, as Marsden points out in his essay in this volume, the irony of some who shun the use of the term *evangelical* because of its association with fundamentalism, while "with most who would call themselves fundamentalist in the 1980s, the designation evangelical is still anathema." Marsden, as usual, is perceptive at this point: "Is there one evangelicalism or many? The answer, of course, is both. This means that no one part can be equated with the whole. On the other hand, it affirms that there *is* a whole, even if sometimes it is difficult to define precisely."[30]

If Abraham stumbles over the concept of evangelicalism when defined more out of the Princeton tradition than the Finney tradition, David Wells, one strongly identified with the Reformed tradition within evangelicalism, has no less serious a dilemma.[31] Wanting a theological definition of evangelicalism rooted in a "simple enumeration of doctrinal points to which evangelicals agree," Wells nonetheless recognizes that such an approach "only deals with part of the reality." Wells would understand evangelicals as essentially "a doctrinal people," something Abraham, as well as many of the essayists in this volume, would dispute. But even Wells recognizes certain cultural and sociological factors within evangelicalism that must be taken into account doctrinally:

> It is true that a *rough* doctrinal agenda has been consistently maintained from the time of the Protestant Reformation to the present, but in every age that doctrine has been formulated in relation to, and sometimes as a result of, a confusion with the expectations, norms, and events that shaped that age's cognitive horizon. For this reason, it is true to say that evangelicalism has meant something different in every age.[32]

Wells thus bemoans the diversity of the evangelical family, even while allowing for its necessity.

A more integrated understanding of evangelicalism's "family resemblance" is offered by Samuel S. Hill, Jr., in his article, "The Shape and

Shapes of Popular Southern Piety." Hill outlines four particular versions of evangelicalism in the American South. Those who are "truth-oriented" he labels "fundamentalists." There are also those who are "conversion-oriented," the "evangelistic"; those who are "spiritually-oriented," the "devotional"; and those evangelical Protestants who are "service-oriented," the "ethical." Hill finds many independent baptist churches as well as the Churches of Christ (in their considerable variety) to be "truth-oriented." The Southern Baptists are largely "conversion-oriented," while the black churches and Southern Methodism are "spiritually-oriented." Hill finds individuals such as Clarence Jordan and Will D. Campbell representatives of "service-oriented" evangelical Protestantism. Despite the considerable differences these traditions represent, Hill believes they are nevertheless "four distinct versions of one family of Protestant Christianity." The emphases vary from what you "believe," to what you "get," to who you "are," to what you "do." Moreover, while these variant forms are identifiable, they are far from discrete. (One need only consider the current "truth-oriented" battle for the Bible going on in the "evangelistic" Southern Baptist Convention.) "Yet," writes Hill, "one [orientation] is likely to be dominant, standing as the animating principle, with the others recessive."[33] (Could we understand the current battle within the Southern Baptist churches as a fight over which of evangelicalism's possible "animating principles" will dominate?)

Turning to the present essays in this volume, one finds the notion of family resemblance useful and illuminating. Although the focus of C. Norman Kraus' chapter is a Mennonite critique of evangelicalism, he recognizes that, broadly speaking, anabaptist-Mennonites have always been within the evangelical tradition. They are part of the "family." The anabaptist dream has been more of "discovery" than of "recovery." Mennonites have been more "prophetic" than "evangelistic," less apologetic and rationalistic with regard to Scripture than hermeneutical; and more concrete and communal with regard to the church than is typical of wider evangelicalism. Moreover, to the degree that evangelicalism is defined by the "Calvinist faction, especially in its dispensationalist guise," Mennonites have shunned too close an identification. In Kraus' words, "The traditional Mennonite understanding of what is primary and what is secondary in the gospel differs from the American evangelical consensus." Yet, *despite such tensions*, Kraus admits that "a number of evangelical authors have attempted to include the anabaptist-Mennonites within evangelicalism."[34] One such writer, Ronald J. Sider, in a volume that Kraus himself edited, goes so far as to say, "If Evangelicals were consistent, they would be Anabaptists and Anabaptists here would be Evangelicals."[35] (Again we see the propensity to define the "family" simply in terms of oneself.) An emphasis on personal religious experience, an insistence upon witness and mission, a loyalty to biblical authority, an understanding of salvation by grace through faith — such family resemblances within most of evangelicalism are identified by Kraus and are enough to define anabaptists within evangelicalism's orb.[36] This is true, even as differences regarding scriptural interpretation, church, and society cause the Mennonites to be viewed by Kraus as less representative exemplars of evangelicalism in America.

Richard Hughes, in his provocative essay, "Are Restorationists Evangelicals?", similarly struggles with the typical understanding of the Churches of Christ as evangelical (e.g., Smith, Marsden, Harrell, Flynt). Have not evangelicals historically stressed a *reformatio* posture, relying solely on the power of God, while the Churches of Christ have opted for a *restitutio* sentiment, one stressing human initiative? Did not Alexander Campbell himself distance himself from the Evangelical Alliance which met in London in 1846? The answer on both counts is "yes." Campbellites have resisted any claim to "justification by faith *alone*," recognizing with James that faith *alone* is deficient. Within the Churches of Christ, the gospel itself has been viewed as a rational "system of facts." The Spirit has played a relatively minor role. And dispensational premillennialism has been consistenly opposed. And yet, as Hughes admits, "Measured by most contemporary understandings of evangelicalism, Churches of Christ throughout their history have appeared evangelical indeed."[37] That is, despite their central allegiance to the *restitutio* sentiment, those in the Churches of Christ also have expressed sufficient allegiance to the *reformatio* heritage to be recognizable "family" members.

In his conclusion, Hughes extends his *reformatio* argument to other relatives within the evangelical family. Pentecostals share a family resemblance, he believes, because of their reliance on spiritual empowerment. Premillennialists, similarly, because of their openness to the sovereignty of God in human affairs. Hughes is uncomfortable with any who limit evangelicalism to a "presbyterian," rationalistic model, but he also senses that a "pentecostal" model is too narrow. The family is more diverse and, for Hughes, ultimately rooted in the sixteenth-century Reformation itself. One might question the adequacy of Hughes' historical model. As both Dayton and Weber point out, the Reformation is but one of the historical analogues current within evangelicalism. Furthermore, can the core of the Reformation (and, thus, for Hughes, the center of evangelicalism) be reduced to the sovereignty of God? Surely it is more complex. But Hughes *is* correct to note, within the restoration churches, not only a distinctiveness from evangelicalism, but also a strong family resemblance.

Definitions or Descriptions?

The present contest over the definition of American evangelicalism has caused frustration, hostility, and, increasingly, boredom. Incessant argument over what constitutes the pure core of doctrine has turned evangelicals inward and threatens to undercut their effective evangelism and mission. The latest evidence of this sad but oft-repeated phenomenon is the decade of controversy in the Southern Baptist Convention, which now is slowing church growth.

Seeking to avoid such peril, some have attempted to posit evangelism as the *only* valid trademark of American evangelicalism. In a speech to the 1977 Consultation of Future Evangelical Concerns, evangelist Leighton Ford argued that evangelicals might become unified, if not by theological agreement, then by a commitment to a common mission. This in turn led Carl F.H. Henry to question in his rejoinder, "How much pragmatism can evangelical Christianity accommodate without jeopardizing its own evangelical ingredient?" Henry's own creedal propensity caused him to be particularly sensitive to a coalition built simply on evangelistic utility. He cynically proposed a tagline which the evangelical movement one day might be forced to use: "Doctrinal views professed by those involved are not necessarily those of the New Testament."[38]

But while Henry would opt for creedalism over pragmatism, neither will suffice as the key to an understanding of American evangelicalism. Rather, there are common understandings both of faith and mission that knit an otherwise disparate group of Christian subcultures together. What these common evangelical ingredients are, however, and how they are to be combined and/or valued relative to each other needs delineation.

In his essay in this volume, John Weborg provides a helpful "perspective for moving beyond the present definitional impasse" by viewing the term *evangelical* as a description, not a definition. It is more connotative, he thinks, than denotative. (One is reminded of the warning by Mervis and Rosch that being told the "rules" of family membership when dealing with categorization sometimes actually retards recognition of family members. It is often better to remain intuitive.) For Weborg, what is minimally connoted by the term *evangelical* is

> a confession that persons are redeemed solely by God's grace in Jesus Christ, the fully divine and human person, for no reason other than God's sovereign will to do so; that the hope of the world lies in God's redemptive deed at the end of history; that the Scripture contains all that is needed for life and salvation; and that persons need to be reborn by the power of the gospel.[39]

Some will think Weborg's listing "doctrinal" and potentially exclusionary, but it is meant to be inclusionary, describing the center of the evangelical faith.

A similar approach is observed in Thomas Askew's caution regarding a usable definition of evangelicalism. He says:

> It is well to keep in mind that evangelical Christianity has never been a religious organization, nor primarily a theological system, nor even a containable movement. It is a mood, a perspective, an approach rounded in biblical theology, but reaching into motifs of religious experience. The evangelical impulse reverberates across the denominational mosaic of American church life.

Turning to those characteristics, or descriptions, which "*most* evangelicals affirm" (note Askew's use of a qualifying term, something typical, as we have seen, of recent categorization theory), Askew mentions four. *The Bible* is the sole authority for belief and practice, and salvation comes through belief in the gospel. *Conversion* is a personal experience necessary for beginning a deliberate Christian life. The self-conscious *nurture* of spirituality and holiness is to be sought, releasing lay energies. And *mission*, both evangelism and social reform, is a Christian obligation.[40]

And to give yet a third example, in his book *The Future of Evangelical Christianity: A Call for Unity and Diversity*, Donald Bloesch argues that

> although there are centrifugal forces pulling evangelicals apart, there is also a unifying power bringing them back together. The key to evangelical unity lies in a common commitment to Jesus Christ as the divine Savior from sin, a common purpose to fulfill the great commission and a common acknowledgement of the absolute normativeness of Holy Scripture. Evangelicals of all stripes confess to an underlying affinity with their fellow believers no matter what their ethnic, denominational or confessional background. Evangelicalism may indeed be the ecumenical movement of the future because of this capacity to transcend age-old denominational and creedal barriers.[41]

Such a listing does not exactly match that of Weborg or Askew, but it need not, for the family resemblance is clear. For all of their variety and particularity, descriptions of contemporary American evangelicalism have a commonality centered on a threefold commitment: a dedication to the gospel that is expressed in a personal faith in Christ as Lord, an understanding of the gospel as defined authoritatively by Scripture, and a desire to communicate the gospel both in evangelism and social reform. Evangelicals are those who believe the gospel is to be experienced personally, defined biblically, and communicated passionately.

For some years now, historian Timothy Smith and his students at Johns Hopkins University have been at work on an analysis of twelve North American evangelical "movements." Smith's work is to be published in a forthcoming book, *The American Evangelical Mosaic.* In an essay already published, Smith delineates the descriptive parameters of his project. He sees four historical evangelical movements in America — Methodist Arminianism, Puritan Calvinism, pietism, and the "peace churches." All four had a "thoroughgoing commitment to the authority of the Old and New Testaments." All were "permeated with the promise of a personal experience of salvation from sin, received in a moment of living faith, which Jesus called being 'born again.' . . . Finally, all four of these inwardly diverse movements found that both the Scriptures and this inward experience of love for God and one's neighbor impelled them to missionary evangelism." Smith summarizes his preliminary findings: "These three charateristics — commitment to Scriptural authority, the experience of regeneration or 'new life in Christ,' and the passion for evangelism — have marked evangelicals ever since."[42]

Gabriel Fackre, in his entry on "Evangelicalism" in *The Westminster Dictionary of Christian Theology*, argues similarly, although his referent is the classical evangelicalism of the Reformation. He notes that the term came into use during the Reformation to identify Protestants as they held "to the belief in justification by grace through faith and the supreme authority of Scripture (often considered the material and formal principles of Reformation teaching)." Fackre then observes a subsequent "interiorization and intensification" of the meaning, as evangelicalism came to refer to those who emphasized "personal conversion and a rigorous moral life," who concentrated "attention on the Bible as a guide to conviction and behavior," and who sought to disseminate the Christian faith so conceived with a special zeal. Here, again, are the same three descriptions.[43]

Yet a third corroboration for this basic three-fold description of evangelicalism is that definition offered by George Marsden in his article, "Evangelical and Fundamental Christianity," for the *Encyclopedia of Religion, volume 5*: "The term *evangelicalism* usually refers to a largely Protestant movement that emphasizes (1) the Bible as authoritative and reliable; (2) eternal salvation as possible only by regeneration, being 'born again,' involving personal trust in Christ and in his atoning work; and (3) a spiritually transformed life marked by moral conduct, personal devotion such as Bible reading, and missions."[44]

In seeking to describe this core, or center, of evangelicalism, several of the essayists in this volume recognize evangelicals to be linked by both *a common theology* and *a basic ethos*, shared central commitments and a common way of life. Timothy Weber is, perhaps, most helpful at this point:

> The temptation is to define evangelicalism in either theological or existential/spiritual terms. Some want to force a kind of theological uniformity on

evangelicalism which historically it never had, while others want to speak almost exclusively of an evangelical spirit without specifying any theological boundaries. As is often the case, the truth lies somewhere in between these two extremes. From my perspective, evangelicalism is both a set of theological convictions and an ethos.[45]

For Weber (see chapter 2), the evangelical "family" is recognizable by both its dynamic bent on spiritual renewal and by its commitment to a core of basic Christian orthodoxy. For Ohlmann (see chapter 8), evangelicals are drawn together into an identifiable fellowship by a group of "underlying principles and dynamics." Among these commonalities are an aspiration for holy living, an emphasis on personal religion, a concern for religious freedom, a stress on religious experience, and a commitment to biblical authority. For Staples (see chapter 6), what seems to be common to the evangelical family is a deep commitment to mission and evangelism, to a biblically-based gospel, and to Christian moral values. In this broad sense, he believes, "evangelicalism is an identity-conferring community. Persons are self-consciously aware that they are evangelicals even though they may have cross-cutting religious affiliations."[46]

"Word" or "Spirit"?

In his article on "evangelicalism" for the *Dictionary of Christian Theology,* Gabriel Fackre focuses on two formative principles, justification and scriptural authority (what is often considered the material and the formal principles of Reformation teaching).[47] Fackre understands the controversy which often surfaces among evangelicals to be related to the focus on one or the other of these emphases. Surely this is at times the case, as Ellingsen points out in his essay on Lutheranism in this volume. Lutherans "prioritize the transforming power of the Gospel over Scripture and theories of biblical authority." They sense that the evangelical coalition does not affirm "the centrality of justification by grace through faith apart from works of the Law with the kind of vigor Lutherans desire. "Evangelical priorities," writes Ellingsen, "seem to be elsewhere, with holiness or the character of the Christian life."[48] Perhaps this is the reason why even the more theologically-conservative Lutheran denominations, such as The Lutheran Church — Missouri Synod, have avoided formal identification with the National Association of Evangelicals. It might also explain why Robert Preuss, president of Concordia Seminary in Fort Wayne, Indiana, was the only Lutheran involved in the leadership of the International Conference on Biblical Inerrancy.

Such a differentiation, however, speaks only to a partial listing of the evangelical family. As Ellingsen himself suggests, evangelical priorities are often elsewhere, on holiness and the character of the Christian life. Rather than stress the differences between those who speak of the Gospel of Scripture and those who focus on the Scripture of the Gospel, it is better to differentiate, on the one hand, both of these groups as subsets of *a theology of the Word* from, on the other hand, those other expressions of American evangelicalism which have emphasized a personal experience with Christ through his Spirit and which are oriented toward *a theology of the Spirit*. While one branch of the evangelical family has understood its informing center to be the Christ of Scripture, the other branch has stressed new life in Christ. To use Samuel Hill's language, what we have in contemporary evangelicalism is differing "animating principles."

Examples are easily multiplied. In his short personal statement in *Who's Who in America*, Carl F.H. Henry comments: "The Bible remains the world's most indispensable reading, and a personal walk with God remains man's unsurpassable privilege."[49] It is not accidental that Henry chooses to begin with our knowledge of God through Scripture and only then turns to the experiential dimensions of the faith. Although the importance of both Word and Spirit are recognized, and although the two are in fact conjoined, a clear priority is evident here, as in other of Henry's writings.[50]

In one of his albums of Christian rock music, Michael Card sings, "Jesus loves me, this I know; *it's not just the Bible that tells me so.* I can feel it within my soul; Jesus loves me, this I know."[51] Card goes on in the several stanzas to talk of Jesus' death for us, of Card's desire to "shout the news" to the world, of the wonder of the atonement, and of the glory of the Christian life. His theology is classical, biblical Christianity. Yet it also is distinct in emphasis from what most evangelicals learned from the cradle on: "Jesus loves me! This I know, *for* the Bible tells me so."

Timothy Weber provides a historical context for understanding this basic division within American evangelicalism (what Donald Dayton, Richard Hughes, and others have labeled the "presbyterian" versus the "pentecostal" paradigms).[52] He speaks of "four main branches in the family tree," two understanding the basic description of Christianity to move from Word to Spirit, and two who would opt for a Christian understanding that develops from Spirit to Word. *Classical evangelicals* tend to be "creedalists," downplaying the role of religious experience in the "doing" of theology, and looking to the Protestant Reformation for their orientation to the Word. *Pietistic evangelicals* are, in Weber's typology, "basically religious pragmatists" who stress the Spirit's transforming power to make new. *Fundamentalist evangelicals* focus on a recovery of a few "fundamentals" of the Word, in opposition to those critics who would challenge its authority. And *progressive evangelicals* seek to maintain their hold on traditional orthodox Christianity but do so with a conscious sense of "modernity," of the contribution the wider religious and secular contexts provide.[53] Each of the four branches of contemporary American evangelicalism arose in a particular historical era, but all are present and interactive today. Moreover, it is the propensity of each to narrow evangelicalism's definition to but one of its basic branches—to either a theology of the Word or a theology of the Spirit. This propensity has caused incessant argument and threatens to engender apathy.

Reviewing the descriptions offered in this volume, one finds that the anabaptists, the holiness churches, the pentecostals, the black churches, the pietists, and the baptists are oriented toward a theology of experience, one explicitly or implicitly grounded in the Spirit. Kraus would have us understand the informing vision of the *Mennonites* to emphasize conversion, discipleship, gospel witness, and gospel service. Mennonites are suspicious of "too exclusive an emphasis on orthodox doctrine," even while generally agreeing with such doctrine.[54] The *holiness churches*, according to Bassett, are "composed of those who hold to what they call the doctrine and experience of entire sanctification."[55] Donald Dayton's description of *pentecostalism's* "foursquare gospel"—salvation, healing, the baptism in the Holy Spirit, and the Second Coming of Christ—is centered in the Spirit's powerful activity. Milton Sernett recognizes that *black theology* "appeals to the experience of a people of long memory rather than to dogma or textbook theology."[56] For this reason, black Christians have been attracted more to evangelical convertive piety, where the message of freedom is decisive. John Weborg, in his chapter on *pietism*, begins his discussion with this straightforward distinction: "Pietism sought the life and liveliness of faith; evangelicalism, more the truth of faith."[57] Pietists would have us reform life, not doctrine, believing an inner and personal relationship with God to be foundational. Finally, Eric Ohlman's decription of *baptist* dynamics is also more experiential than doctrinal, more oriented to the Christian life in and through the Spirit than to the Word. Thus, for example, baptists are observed as emphasizing the human role in salvation and the Christian's life. Again, it should be pointed out that a focus on human experience as empowered by the Spirit in creation and redemption does not imply a denial of the Word. With baptists, as with other experience-oriented evangelicals, the Word remains authoritative and fundamental.

Turning to the other central branch of evangelicalism's family tree, that oriented around a theology of the Word, we mention again *Lutheran orthodoxy's* focus on the Gospel of Scripture. More typical, however, are those traditions which have centered on the Scripture of the Gospel—the self-consciously Reformed, fundamentalism, and premillennialism. Adventism and restorationism present their own special dynamics, but they, too, are best included in this list. Noll and Niemczyk see *the self-consciously Reformed* as set over against "intellectually slovenly, heart-on-the sleeve American Revivalism," emphasizing the centrality of the church and the maintenance of traditional doctrine.[58] From its inception, *fundamentalism* has centered on a vigorous defense of orthodox doctrine. Moreover, in George Marsden's words, "Fundamentalists universally see the war as primarily a war over the Bible."[59] The inerrancy of the Bible, the premillennial return of Christ, the denial of biological evolution, the opposition to speaking in tongues—such positions suggest fundamentalism's focus as a defender of the faith. *Premillennialism,* at its most elemental, is, according to Timothy Weber, that segment of the Christian church which teaches "an earthly reign of Christ which will be preceded by his Second Coming." This doctrine, writes Weber, is based on a "rather literalistic reading of a few key biblical passages."[60] It also rejects any notion of human instrumentality. What is emphasized is God's action in regard to humankind.

Adventism writes Russell Staples, has sought to avoid speculation, eschewing "any form of inner enlightenment or appeal to subjective mysticism." It stresses the importance of doctrine and is concerned with the truth about God and his dealings with human beings. At the same time, Adventism is distinct from most Word-oriented evangelicalism, being thoroughly Arminian in thought. Perhaps for this reason, Adventism is viewed by Staples as being "as much a way of life as a system of belief."[61] Lastly, Richard Hughes argues cogently that *restorationist churches* have as their starting point human initiative and activity. Yet the Campbellites have also a theology of the Word. While Word and Spirit are always united, the Spirit now operates through and in the Word. Moreover, like other more rationalistic evangelicals, restorationists often root their hermeneutics in Scottish Common Sense Realism. The Bible ultimately is a book of facts, the gospel, fundamentally propositional.

What one finds, then, within American evangelicalism are two classic approaches to theology.[62] The one begins with *God*'s action in regard to humankind. The other, with *humankind*'s experience of God in his creation and redemption. I have labeled the former a "theology of the Word." It tends toward creedal definition and is prone at its worst to a literalism in biblical interpretation and a legalism in regard to experience. The second approach I have called a "theology of the Spirit." It tends toward the intuitive and interpersonal and is prone at its worst to a mysticism or a psychologism. One would focus upon formal doctrine; the other, on Christian experience. Yet both belong to the family of American evangelicalism, for one can move from Spirit to Word or Word to Spirit without friction or reduction. Ultimately, within evangelicalism, Word and Spirit must be conjoined. The Word cannot take the place of the Spirit, but neither can it be ignored. Hans Küng is correct in recognizing that we "demonstrate to the world the good news of the gospel both with authority and love."[63]

Accommodation and Americanization

In a speech given to a joint meeting of the Evangelical Press Association and the Associated Church Press in May 1988, Mark Noll commented on the importance of "the passage of time in America" for recent religious history. He referred to (1) the increasing distantiation from the fundamentalist-modernist debate, (2) the shift in the center of American economic and political life to the South and Southwest, and (3) "the accelerating Americanization of the ethnic churches."[64] Noll's comments are provocative. Looking at the restrictive Immigration Act of 1924, he sees the general result to be a domino effect. With the flow of immigrants reduced, ethnic churches no longer could recruit their immigrant kin and so were forced into an Americanization. There was a push toward inculturation.

I understand other forces besides the Immigration Act to have been equally powerful, although I do not doubt its impetus. Immigrants often sent their children to public schools, where they quickly became acculturated. If the church was to speak to its youth, inculturation was a necessity. Similarly, if the immigrant church was to remain a church in mission, if it was to be able to reach out to address social needs and to speak the gospel with power, it needed to be rooted in its present soil. Thus, there were multiple factors at work on many of the members of what is now recognized as the family of evangelicalism. In short, there was a push toward Americanization.

Not all shared this pattern of accommodation, to be sure. Family resemblance is never univocal. Ellingsen, for example, believes that "Lutherans have not been able to develop a truly American Lutheran theology."[65] Here, perhaps, is a more important reason than its unique theological perspective within evangelicalism for Lutheranism remaining largely isolated and tangential within evangelicalism, even today. Anabaptist-Mennonites, with their twin doctrines of nonconformity and nonresistance, similarly have found themselves distanced from the center of American life and thought. A zeal for cultural differentiation and biblical pacifism often has pitted Mennonites against evangelicals, who have been prone to accept materialism and to identify God and country. The black churches often have stood outside the Americanization process for another reason, the larger white culture being too often guilty of racism.

But for other evangelical groups, Americanization was a necessary ingredient for effective mission strategy. The dispensational premillennialists, as Weber notes, were not traditionally a part of nineteenth-century evangelical America. But dispensationalism, when it came to America, "always sided with conservatives by maintaining traditional evangelicalism's high view of Scripture, its commitment to evangelism and foreign missions, and its belief that Christianity was rooted in the supernatural. In the Protestant holy wars of the late nineteenth century, no-one ever doubted where the new premillennialists stood."[66] In a similar way, Adventists, restorationists, pentecostals, and the holiness churches all sided with fundamentalists in the modernist-fundamenatlist controversy, as did the Scandinavian pietistic tradition embodied in the Evangelical Free Church, the Baptist General Conference, and the Evangelical Covenant Church. (Note how these pietists even took the American name "evangelical" into their title.) Often these traditions found much that was foreign if not outright objectionable in American fundamentalism, but the social reality left no other choice. Given only two viable American expressions of Protestant Christiantity — fundamentalism or modernism — the greater family resemblance with fundamentalism was all too readily apparent. These groups recognized themselves to be kin, however distant.

This perceived sense of kinship between fundamentalism and much of the rest of American evangelicalism has puzzled Martin Marty. He writes:

> In short, while fundamentalism and evangelicalism both defer to each other and show some respect for the way each retains at least nominal assent to the old nineteenth-century Protestant symbols, their behavior patterns show such divergences that we must be alerted to the possibility of needing to say that their similarities have "died the death of a thousand qualifications."[67]

Marty recognizes that most evangelicals have more similarities with and affinities to ecumenical Protestantism than to fundamentalism. Moreover, evangelicals largely resent the label fundamentalist, and vice-versa. Again, there are so many doctrinal disputes; why is it that family resemblance is maintained? The question is genuine for Marty and the issue real. But the answer is also straightforward. Those within the evangelical family identify primarily with those who believe the gospel is to be experienced personally, defined biblically, and communicated passionately.

A more recent example of the ongoing Americanization of evangelical subgroups is provided in this volume by Noll and Niemczyk in their essay on the self-consciously Reformed. The authors outline the history of the Orthodox Presbyterian Church, which seceded from the Presbyterian Church in the U.S.A. in 1936 over doctrinal matters. The OPC rejected as an alternate name for their new denomination the Evangelical Presbyterian Church, believing that real fellowship could exist only with other Reformed groups. Yet, despite the un-Reformed heresies of Arminianism and dispensationalism, the early leaders of the OPC initially stood with the fundamentalists against the modernists. Some within their midst even pushed for Americanization too quickly. Gordon Clark thought the OPC "too sectarian, too European, and too narrow in its doctrinal disputation." He wanted the OPC to adopt a general evangelical line. When the hardliners prevailed, he left the denomination. And yet his view prevailed within a scant twenty years. Now, in the 1980s, there is, according to Noll and Niemczyk, "a clear movement on the part of the OPC toward non-Reformed American evangelicals." They conclude: "The larger significance of the OPC's history of discussion about evangelicals must certainly be that it is very difficult to remain a strictly Reformed *American* denomination."[68]

Noll and Niemczyk see a pattern within several of the self-consciously Reformed churches in America, according to which "taking time to criticize American evangelicals may be the most direct road to becoming one of them."[69] But could it not be rather that opting to become one of them is the motivation for criticizing them? It is the desire for authentic American outreach and involvement, not the desire to engage critically, that has brought churches together under the evangelical family umbrella. Those more theologically conservative or classically orthodox Christian subcultures in America that have wanted to become effective in the larger culture have been forced to choose between limited, *viable,* available options. Put most simply, though they might have wished for a third contemporary option within American Protestantism which has "force and vitality, Protestantism in America has had since the turn of the century only two major expressions — evangelicalism or ecumenism."[70] The labels are unfortunate and not altogether descriptive. Some have wanted to be ecumenical in their evangelicalism; others, the reverse. But it remains possible to speak of these two central traditions. Even the more recent charismatic movement is best understood as a variant of evangelicalism.

Seen in this sociological light, those churches that have wanted effective, biblically-based evangelistic and social outreach in America have been drawn into the evangelical orb. They have come to affirm their family membership. Although nonevangelicals might veiw the evangelical tradition as reactionary, sentimental, or restrictive, those who have gravitated toward it have found in it a means both of expressing and of extending the *evangelion*, the gospel — the good news of Jesus Christ.

NOTES

1. Leonard I. Sweet, "The Evangelical Tradition in America," in *The Evangelical Tradition in America,* ed. Leonard I. Sweet (Macon, Ga.: Mercer Univ. Press, 1984), 1.
2. Cullen Murphy, "Protestantism and the Evangelicals," *Wilson Quarterly* 5 (Aug. 1981):105–116.
3. Robert Webber, *Common Roots* (Grand Rapids, Mich.: Zondervan, 1976), 32.
4. Thomas Stransky, "A Look at Evangelical Protestantism," *Theology, News and Notes* 35 (Mar. 1988):24.
5. Joel Carpenter, "The Fundamentalist Leaven and the Rise of an Evangelical United Front," in Sweet, *Evangelical Tradition in America,* 260. Cf. George M. Marsden, "Evangelical and Fundamental Christianity," in *The Encyclopedia of Religion,* ed. Mircea Eliade (New York: Macmillan, 1987), 5:195.
6. John H. Gerstner, "Theological Boundaries: The Reformed Perspective," in *The Evangelicals,* ed. David F. Wells and John D. Woodbridge (Nashville, Tenn.: Abingdon, 1975), 27.
7. Robert T. Handy, quoted in Sweet, "Evangelical Tradition in America," 66.
8. William J. Abraham, "E Pluribus Unim: Towards a Definitive Definition of Evangelicalism," (typewritten), 4.
9. William J. Abraham, *The Coming Great Revival: Recovering the Full Evangelical Tradition* (San Francisco: Harper & Row, 1984), 72.
10. George M. Marsden, "Fundamentalism and American Evangelicalism," ch. 3, this volume. Cf. William G. McLoughlin, "The American Evangelicals: 1800–1900," in *The American Evangelicals, 1800–1900,* ed. William G. McLoughlin (New York: Harper & Row, 1968), 5; C. Norman Kraus, "Evangelicalism: The Great Coalition," in *Evangelicalism and Anabaptism,* ed. C. Norman Kraus (Scottdale, Penn.: Herald Press, 1979), 43–59; Carpenter, "The Fundamenatlist Leaven," 267.
11. Donald W. Dayton, "Whither Evangelicalism?", in *Sanctification and Liberation,* ed. Theodore Runyon (Nashville, Tenn.: Abingdon, 1981), 143–47; Donald W. Dayton, "The Use of Scripture in the Wesleyan Tradition," in *The Use of the Bible in Theology: Evangelical Options,* ed. Robert K. Johnston (Atlanta, Ga.: John Knox, 1985), 121–26; Donald W. Dayton, "The Social and Political Conservatism of Modern American Evangelicalism: A Preliminary Search for the Reasons," *Union Seminary Quarterly Review* 32 (Winter 1977), 72–74.
12. Dayton, "Social and Political Conservatism," 74.
13. Max L. Stackhouse, "Religious Right: New? Right?," *Commonweal* 29 (Jan. 1982):52–56.
14. Donald G. Bloesch, *The Future of Evangelical Christianity: A Call for Unity and Diversity* (Garden City, N.J.: Doubleday, 1983), 9.
15. David Allan Hubbard, *What We Evangelicals Believe* (Pasadena, Calif.: Fuller Theological Seminary, 1979), 7.
16. Leonard I. Sweet, "Nineteenth-Century Evangelicalism," in *Encyclopedia of the American Religious Experience,* ed. Charles Lippy and Peter Williams (New York: Charles Scribner's Sons, 1988), 2:875.
17. Timothy P. Weber, "Premillennialism and the Branches of Evangelicalism," ch. 2, this volume.
18. Donald W. Dayton, "The Limits of Evangelicalism: The Pentecostal Tradition," ch. 4, this volume.
19. C. Norman Kraus, "Evangelicalism: A Mennonite Critique," ch. 11, this volume.

20. Carolyn B. Mervis and Eleanor Rosch, "Categorization of Natural Objects," *Annual Review of Psychology* 32 (1981):89, 94, 90, 95.

21. Ibid., 96, 99.

22. Ibid., 103.

23. Cf. Kenneth S. Kantzer, "The Future of the Church and Evangelicalism," in *Evangelicals Face the Future*, ed. Donald E. Hoke (South Pasadena, Calif.: William Carey Library, 1978), 132.

24. Mark Ellingsen, "Lutheranism," ch. 13, this volume.

25. Dayton, "Limits of Evangelicalism."

26. Marsden, "Fundamentalism and American Evangelicalism."

27. Weber, "Premillennialism and the Branches of Evangelicalism."

28. Abraham, *Coming Great Revival*, 9.

29. Ibid., 67.

30. Marsden, "Fundamentalism and American Evangelicalism."

31. Wells, a professor at Gordon-Conwell Theological Seminary; Mark Noll of Wheaton College; and Cornelius Plantinga, Jr., of Calvin Seminary recently were awarded a $400,000 grant for a four-year project to strengthen evangelical theology out of a Reformed perspective.

32. David F. Wells, "'No Offense: I Am an Evangelical': A Search for Self-Definition," in *A Time to Speak: The Evangelical-Jewish Encounter*, ed. A. James Rudin and Marvin R. Wilson (Grand Rapids, Mich.: Eerdmans, 1987), 32, 30.

33. Samuel S. Hill, Jr., "The Shape and Shapes of Popular Southern Piety," in *Varieties of Southern Evangelicalism*, ed. David Edwin Harrell, Jr. (Macon, Ga.: Mercer Univ. Press, 1981), 99–103.

34. Kraus, "Evangelicalism: A Mennonite Critique."

35. Ronald J. Sider, "Evangelicalism and the Mennonite Tradition," in Kraus, *Evangelicalism and Anabaptism*, 149.

36. Cf. C. Norman Kraus, "Anabaptism and Evangelicalism," in Kraus, *Evangelicalism and Anabaptism*, 175, 177.

37. Richard T. Hughes, "Are Restorationists Evangelicals?", in ch. 7, this volume.

38. Carl F.H. Henry, "Response to Conference Findings," in Hoke, *Evangelicals Face the Future*, 164.

39. C. John Weborg, "Pietism: Theology in Service of Living Toward God," ch. 10, this volume.

40. Thomas A. Askew, "A Response to David Wells," in Rudin and Wilson, *A Time to Speak*, 41–42.

41. Bloesch, *Future of Evangelical Christianity*, 5–6, 17–18.

42. Timothy Smith, "Evangelical Christianity and American Culture," in Rudin and Wilson, *A Time to Speak*, 58–75. Quote, 60.

43. Gabriel Fackre, "Evangelicalism," *Westminster Dictionary of Christian Theology*, ed. Alan Richardson and John Bowden (Philadelphia: Westminster, 1983), 191.

44. Marsden, "Evangelical and Fundamental Christianity," 5:190–197, 190. For similar descriptions, see C. Norman Kraus, "What Is Evangelicalism?", in Kraus, *Evangelicalism and Anabaptism*, 21–22; Martin E. Marty, "The Revival of Evangelicalism and Southern Religion," in *Varieties of Southern Evangelicalism,* ed. David Edwin Harrell, Jr., (Macon, Ga.: Mercer Univ. Press, 1981), 9–10; James Davison Hunter, *American Evangelicalism* (New Brunswick, N.J.: Rutgers Univ. Press, 1983, 7; Lars Lindberg, *Ny Skapelse* (Älvsjo, Sweden: Vebrum, 1986), 11.

45. Weber, "Premillennialism and the Branches of Evangelicalism."

46. Russell Staples, "Adventism," ch. 5, this volume.

47. Gabriel Fackre, "Evangelical, Evangelicalism," in *The Westminster Dictionary of Christian Theology,* rev. ed., ed. Alan Richardson and John Bowden (Philadelphia: Westminster, 1983), 191.

48. Ellingsen, "Lutheranism."

49. Carl F.H. Henry, quoted by Carl F.H. Henry and Kenneth S. Kantzer in their letter of July 1988 for the executive committee of Evangelical Affirmations, a conference held at Trinity Evangelical Divinity School, Deerfield, Ill., 14–17 May 1989.

50. Cf. Carl F.H. Henry, "Who Are the Evangelicals?", *Christianity Today* 16 (4 Feb. 1972):23–24

51. Michael Card, "Jesus Loves Me (This I Know)," *The Best of Michael Card,* Milk and Honey Records (Grand Rapids, Mich.: Zondervan, Singspiration Music, 1985).

52. Cf. Dayton, "Whither Evangelicalism?", 162–63: "The purpose of this chapter has been to demonstrate the debt of contemporary evangelicalism to the holiness movements of the last century, and to point to the impoverishment that has occurred as evangelicals have lost contact with that Arminian heritage and have been coopted by fundamentalism, premillennialism, and biblical literalism. The creative alternative to reactionary versions of Calvinism is to be found, I believe, in those Wesleyan sources. And the challenge to Methodist theologians of an evangelical persuasion today is to make the evangelical world aware of that alternative."

53. Weber, "Premillennialism and the Branches of Evangelicalism."

54. Kraus, "Evangelicalism: A Mennonite Critique."

55. Paul Merritt Bassett, "The Theological Identity of the North American Holiness Movement," ch. 6, this volume.

56. Milton C. Sernett, "Black Religion and the Question of Evangelical Identity," ch. 8, this volume.

57. Weborg, "Pietism."

58. Mark A. Noll and Cassandra Niemczyk, "Evangelicals and the Self-Consciously Reformed," ch. 12, this volume, quoting Marlin Van Elderen with "self-conscious overstatement."

59. Marsden, "Fundamentalism and American Evangelicalism."

60. Weber, "Premillennialism and the Branches of Evangelicalism."

61. Staples, "Adventism."

62. Cf., Robert K. Johnston, "Of Tidy Doctrine and Truncated Experience," *Christian Today* 21 (18 Feb. 1977):10–14.

63. Hans Küng, *The Church* (New York: Sheed and Ward, 1967), 149, quoted in Weborg, "Pietism."

64. Mark A. Noll, "Learning the Language of Heaven?", *The Reformed Journal* 38 (June 1988):16.

65. Ellingsen, "Lutheranism."

66. Weber, "Premillennialism and the Branches of Evangelicalism."

67. Martin E. Marty, "Tensions within Contemporary Evangelicalism: A Critical Appraisal," in Wells and Woodbridge, *The Evangelicals,* 178.

68. Noll and Niemczyk, "Evangelicals and the Self-consciously Reformed."

69. Ibid.

70. Ibid.

Contributors

PAUL MERRITT BASSETT

Bassett is professor of the history of Christianity at Nazarene Theological Seminary, Kansas City, Missouri. He is a past president of the Wesleyan Theological Society and is editor of the *Wesleyan Theological Journal*. A minister of the Church of the Nazarene, he has published:

(Co-author) *Exploring Christian Holiness, Volume 2: Historical Development*, Beacon Hill of Kansas City, 1985.

"History of Western Ecclesiology to about 1700," in *Wesleyan Perspectives, Volume 4: The Church*, Warner Press, 1985.

"The Fundamentalist Leavening of the Holiness Movement," *Wesleyan Theological Journal* (1979).

"The Holiness Movement and the Protestant Principle," *Wesleyan Theological Journal* (1983).

DONALD W. DAYTON

Dayton is professor of theology and ethics at Northern Baptist Theological Seminary, Lombard, Illinois; president of the Society for Pentecostal Studies (1988–89); president of the Wesleyan Theological Society (1989–90); and co-chair and former chair of the evangelical theology group of the American Academy of Religion. A layman in the Wesleyan Church of America, he has published:

Theological Roots of Pentecostalism, Scarecrow Press and Francis Asbury Press, 1987.

Discovering an Evangelical Heritage, Harper and Row, 1976; second edition, Hendrickson, 1988.

(Editor) 48-volume facsimile reprint series, *The Higher Christian Life: Sources for the Study of the Holiness, Pentecostal and Keswick Movements*, Garland, 1983–85.

(Co-editor) *Studies in Evangelicalism Monograph Series*, Scarecrow Press, 1980 on.

MARK ELLINGSEN

Ellingsen is pastor of the Haven Lutheran Church, Salisbury, North Carolina. Having previously served on the faculties of the Institute for Ecumenical Research (Strasbourg, France) and Luther-Northwestern Theological Seminary (St. Paul, Minnesota), he was commissioned by the Lutheran World Federation to a six-year study of the evangelical movement and its relationship to the Lutheran tradition. He has published:

Doctrine and Word: Theology in the Pulpit, John Knox Press, 1983.
The Evangelical Movement: Growth, Impact, Controversy, Dialog, Augsburg Press, 1988.
Narration and Biblical Reality, Fortress Press, forthcoming.
Cutting-Edge Issues in Global Society, World Council of Churches, forthcoming.

RICHARD T. HUGHES

Hughes is professor of religion, Pepperdine University, Malibu, California, and a member of the Church of Christ. Formerly a professor of history at Abilene Christian University and a member of the executive steering group of the American religion working group of the American Academy of Religion, he has published:

(Co-author) *Illusions of Innocence: Protestant Primitivism in America, 1630–1875*, University of Chicago Press, 1988.
(Edited) *The American Quest for the Primitive Church*, University of Illinois Press, 1988.
(Co-author) *Discovering our Roots: The Ancestry of Churches of Christ*, Abilene Christian University Press, 1988.
"Primitivism as Perfectionism: From Anabaptists to Pentecostals," in Stanley Burgess, ed., *Reaching Beyond: Chapters in the History of Perfectionism*, Hendrickson, 1986.

ROBERT K. JOHNSTON

Johnston is provost and dean of the seminary, and professor of theology and culture at North Park College and Theological Seminary, Chicago, Illinois. A co-chair of the evangelical theology group of the American Academy of Religion and an ordained minister in The Evangelical Covenant Church, he has published:

Evangelicals at an Impasse: Biblical Authority in Practice, John Knox Press, 1979.
(Editor) *The Use of the Bible in Theology: Evangelical Options*, John Knox Press, 1985.
"How We Interpret the Bible: Biblical Interpretation and Literary Criticism" and "Biblical Interpretation and Theology: Bringing the Bible to Life," in *The Proceedings of the Conference on Biblical Interpretation, 1988*, Broadman Press, 1988.
"Acculturation or Inculturation? A Contemporary Evangelical Theology of the Atonement" in Philip J. Anderson, ed., *Amicus Dei: Essays on Faith and Friendship*, Covenant Publications, 1988.

C. NORMAN KRAUS

Kraus is professor emeritus of religion at Goshen College, Goshen, Indiana, having also taught in India, Australia, and Japan. A Mennonite, he has served as director of the Center for Discipleship at Goshen College, book-review editor of *Mennonite Quarterly Review*, and board member of the Mennonite Central Committee. He has published:

Dispensationalism in America: Its Rise and Development, John Knox Press, 1958.
(Editor) *Evangelicalism and Anabaptism*, Herald Press, 1979.
Jesus Christ Our Lord, Christology from a Disciple's Perspective, Herald Press, 1987.
"American Mennonites and the Bible," *Mennonite Quarterly Review* (1967).

GEORGE M. MARSDEN

Marsden is professor of the history of Christianity in America at The Divinity School, Duke University, Durham, North Carolina. A member of the Christian Reformed Church, he taught for over twenty years at Calvin College. He has published:

Fundamentalism and American Culture: The Shaping of American Evangelicalism, 1870–1925, Oxford University Press, 1980.
Reforming Fundamentalism: Fuller Seminary and the New Evangelicalism, Eerdmans, 1987.
(Editor) *Evangelicalism and Modern America*, Eerdmans, 1984.
The Evangelical Mind and the New School Presbyterian Experience, Yale University Press, 1970.

CASSANDRA NIEMCZYK

Niemczyk is a graduate student in church history at the Wheaton College Graduate School, Wheaton, Illinois.

MARK A. NOLL

Noll is professor of history and senior advisor of the Institute for the Study of American Evangelicals at Wheaton College, Wheaton, Illinois. A member of the Orthodox Presbyterian Church, he serves on the editorial committee of *The Reformed Journal*. He has published:

Princeton and the Republic, 1768–1822, Princeton University Press, 1989.
Between Faith and Criticism: Evangelicals, Scholarship, and the Bible in America, Harper & Row, 1986.
(Editor) *The Princeton Theology, 1812–1921*, Baker Books, 1983.
"Evangelicals and the Reformed: Two Streams, One Source," *The Reformed Journal* (1981).

ERIC H. OHLMANN

Ohlmann is professor of Christian heritage and associate dean of Northern Baptist Theological Seminary, Lombard, Illinois. A member of the American Baptist Churches, USA, he belongs to the American Baptist Historical Society. He has published:

"The Essence of the Baptists: A Reexamination," *Perspectives in Religious Studies* (1986).
"An Ulterior Motive for Baptist Home Missions," *Foundations*, (1979).

MILTON C. SERNETT

Sernett is associate professor in the department of African American studies at Syracuse University, Syracuse, New York; a research associate at the W.E.B. DuBois Institute, Harvard University (1988– 89); and co-chair of the Afro-American religious history group of the American Academy of Religion. A member of the Evangelical Lutheran Church in America, he has published:

Black Religion and American Evangelicalism: White Protestants, Plantation Missions, and the Flowering of Negro Christianity, 1787–1865, Scarecrow Press, 1975.
Afro-American Religious History: A Documentary Witness, Duke University Press, 1985.
Abolition's Axe: Beriah Green, Oneida Institute, and the Black Freedom Struggle, Syracuse University Press, 1986.
"The Efficacy of Religious Participation in the National Debates Over Abolitionism and Abortion," *Journal of Religion* (1984).

RUSSELL L. STAPLES

Staples is chairman of the department of world mission and professor of world mission at Seventh-Day Adventist Theological Seminary, Andrews University, Berrien Springs, Michigan. A past president of the Association of Professors of Mission and an ordained minister in the Seventh-Day Adventist Church, he has taught and pastored in South Africa and Zimbabwe. In 1986, he gave the John Osborn Lecture at Loma Linda University, "The Role and Meaning of Adventism in the '80s: Doctrine, Morals, Experience, These Three: But the Greatest of These is Experience." He has published:

"Seventh-Day Adventist Mission in the '80's," in *Servants for Christ: The Adventist Church Facing the '80's*, Andrews University Press, 1980.
"Must Polygamists Divorce?" *Spectrum* (1982).
The Face of the Church to Come," *Adventist Review* (1986).

TIMOTHY P. WEBER

Weber is professor of church history at Denver Seminary, Denver, Colorado. An ordained Baptist minister, he currently serves as well as associate pastor of Heritage Church, Aurora, Colorado. He has published:

Living in the Shadow of the Second Coming: American Premillennialism, 1875–1982, enlarged edition, University of Chicago Press, 1987.

"The Two-Edged Sword: The Fundamentalist Use of the Bible," in Mark Noll and Nathan Hatch, eds., *The Bible in America: Essays in Culture History*, Oxford University Press, 1982.

"The Baptist Tradition," in Ronald Numbers and Darrel Amundsen, eds., *Caring and Curing: Health and Medicine in the Western Religious Tradition*, Macmillan, 1986.

"Divide and Prosper: An Institutional History of Baptist Fundamentalism," in Charles Chancy and William Hooper, eds., *The Baptist Contribution to Twentieth-Century American Culture*, Mercer University Press, forthcoming.

C. JOHN WEBORG

Weborg is professor of theology at North Park Theological Seminary, Chicago, Illinois; secretary-treasurer of the American Theological Society, Midwest Section; and a theological consultant to the Center for Parish Development in Chicago. An ordained minister in the Evangelical Covenant Church, he has published:

Alive in Christ, Alert to Life, Covenant Press, 1985.

"Pietism: The Fire of God Which Flames in the Heart of Germany," in Frank Senn, ed., *Protestant Spiritual Traditions*, Paulist Press, 1986.

"Lutherans in Their Theology: Luther and the Evangelical Covenant Church," *explor* (1986).

"Piety: The Convergence of Living Faith and Faith Lived," *Covenant Quarterly* (1986).

Index

Abraham, William, 253-54, 256-57
accommodation to American Experience, 214
—theological accommodation, 214
Adventism, 3, 57-71, 247-48, 265, 268
Alexander, Archibald, 207
Allen, Richard, 136
American Council of Christian Churches (ACCC), 29, 211
Americanization, a push toward, 267-68
—individualism, 198, 207, 216-18
—materialism, capitalism, 197, 217, 228, 267
—nationalism, patriotism, 197-98, 217
—positivism, 217
—racism, 267
Ames, William, 161
amillennialism. See eschatology
anabaptism, anabaptist-mennonite tradition, 3, 50, 112, 155, 157, 162, 169, 184, 187-90, 192-93, 196, 247-48, 258-59, 265, 267
anabaptist hermeneutics. See hermeneutics
Andreae, Jacob, 162
Anglicanism, 138, 233
anti-creedal. See creeds
apologetics, defense of faith, 190, 199
Arminianism, 63-66, 68, 71, 75, 162, 193, 195, 207, 210, 212, 217, 252, 266, 269
Arminius, Jacobus, 162
Askew, Thomas, 1, 261
atonement. See Jesus Christ

Bacon, Francis. See hermeneutics
Baconianism. See hermeneutics
baptism in the Holy Spirit. See Holy Spirit

baptists, 2-3, 13, 23, 28-29, 50, 109, 112, 114, 119, 121, 125, 129, 140, 148-60, 187, 195, 211, 237, 248, 252, 258, 265
—Baptist General Conference, 268
—black baptist churches, 138-39, 251
—Southern Baptist Convention, 29, 31, 260
Bassett, Paul, 2, 246, 265
Bavinck, Herman, 184
Bengel, Johann Albrecht, 169, 173, 178, 191
Bentley, William H., 144
biblical criticism, 13, 92; anti-. See polemics
biblical literalism. See Scripture, interpretation of
biblical theology. See Scripture, interpretation of
Binney, Amos, 108
black Christianity, 2-3, 29, 135-45, 247-48, 252-53, 265
Bloesch, Donald, 255, 261
Boll, R.H., 126
Brethren Church (Ashland, Ohio), The, 238
Brumbeck, Carl, 37
Brunk, George R., 194
Bucer, Martin, 112
Bullinger, Heinrich, 110, 112

Calvin, John, 82, 112-13, 119-20, 150, 209, 256
Calvinism. See reformed theology
Campbell, Alexander, 113-14, 119-20, 126, 251, 259, 266
Canadian Holiness Federation (CHF), 73
capitalism. See Americanization
Christian Church, Christianites, 60, 63

Christian Church (*cont.*)
—Churches of Christ, 113-14, 119,
   123-24, 127-28, 258
—Disciples, 113-14
Christian Holiness Association (CHA),
   73
Christian Reformed Church, 210, 214,
   253
Christianity Today, 1, 30, 204, 215
church, ecclesiology, 9-10, 46, 91, 127,
   149, 151, 153, 163-66, 169, 189-93,
   196, 198-99, 202, 205, 207, 213-14,
   216, 218-19, 225-26, 228, 249,
   258-59, 266
—an atomistic view, 217
—believers' church, 149, 155, 159
—a community, 114, 116, 163, 167,
   196, 206, 215
—a pure church, 46, 191
—a renewed church, 165, 168
—a worshipping community, 77, 82,
   84, 87
Church of God, Anderson, Indiana,
   251
Clark, Gordon H., 211-12, 269
Cocceius, Johannes, 162
common sense. *See* hermeneutics
Concordia Seminary, Ft. Wayne, Indiana, 263
confessionalism, a confessional consciousness, 208, 232-33, 248
conversion. *See* salvation, personal
creeds, 114, 119, 121, 167, 206, 215,
   232, 260, 264
—anti-creedal, 62, 216, 232
Criswell, W.A., 31

Daane, James, 216, 218
Dallas Theological Seminary, 31, 204
Darby, John Nelson, 8-9
Davis, John Jefferson, 175
Dayton, Donald, 2-3, 141, 254, 256,
   265
Denck, Hans, 184
Disappointment, The Great, 8, 60
discipleship, 178, 193, 195-96, 265
disciplined obedience. *See* sanctification
dispensationalism, 8-12, 14-15, 26-28,
   30-32, 39, 62, 64, 68, 109, 199, 210,
   247, 249, 253, 259, 268-69

Dobson, Ed, 32
Dollar, George W., 24, 27, 31-32
Douglass, Frederick, 140

ecclesiology. *See* church
ecumenism, ecumenical, 113, 210-13,
   231, 261
—Christian union, 114, 116
—cooperation, 211
Edwards, Jonathan, 6, 157, 179
electronic church, 5
Ellingsen, Mark, 245, 256, 263
Episcopalians, 109, 122, 129
eschatology, the Second Coming, 6-8,
   10, 12, 15, 27, 40-41, 55, 58-60, 63,
   67-68, 122, 142, 169, 175, 227,
   265-66
—amillennialism, 228
—millennialism, 57, 59, 114, 117, 139,
   169, 179, 191, 228
—postmillennialism, 6, 11, 58, 115,
   118, 126, 169, 174-75
—premillennialism, 2, 5-22, 26-27,
   29-30, 34, 41, 58, 62, 65, 68, 109,
   111, 122-23, 126-28, 199, 201, 209,
   214, 248-49, 253, 259, 265-66, 268
ethics, individual, 145, 153, 155, 204
—Christian discipline, 67, 149, 156,
   263
—legalism, 59, 64, 266
—personal ethics, 149, 155, 191
—separation from the world, 155, 174
—strict moral code, 23, 30, 67, 150,
   262
ethics, social, 145, 218
—peace witness, 192, 196, 252
—social gospel, 249
—social justice, 218
—social reform, 261
Evangelical Covenant Church, 178, 268
Evangelical Free Church of America,
   238, 246, 268
Evangelical Theological Society (ETS),
   48, 223
Evangelical Women's Caucus (EWC),
   175
evangelicalism, 33, 127, 140, 145
—"a family," 12, 33, 36, 218, 250,
   252-69
—definition of, 12-13, 255

— disdain for, 119, 128
— "essentially contested concept," 47, 245, 253
— neo-evangelicals, 30, 32–33, 48–50, 142, 188–89, 204, 214–18, 249–50
— paradigms, versions, traditions within, 12–15, 48, 50, 245, 257–58
Evangelicals for Social Action (ESA), 189
evangelism and mission, 11, 14, 16, 33, 45, 48, 67, 89, 159, 172, 179, 190–91, 197–98, 249, 258, 260–63
— soul winning, 22–23, 25–26
Evans, Anthony C., 144
evolution, anti-. See polemics
experience, religious. See salvation, personal

Fackre, Gabriel, 118, 262–63
Falwell, Jerry, 22, 32–33, 192, 203, 253
Faupel, David W., 39
Finney, Charles G., 6, 16, 51, 74–75, 141, 175, 179, 203, 206, 253, 257
Ford, Leighton, 260
Forsyth, P.T., 185
Francke, August Hermann, 170, 174, 177–78, 196
Fransen, Fredrik, 51
freedom, religious, 149
Fuller, Charles, 51
Fuller Theological Seminary, 15, 30, 51, 186, 197–98, 204, 218
fundamentalism, 1–3, 13, 15, 22–35, 48–50, 62, 68, 76, 82–83, 89–90, 92–93, 109, 119, 129, 142, 161, 174–75, 185, 187–88, 190, 193–96, 199–200, 204, 207, 209–11, 215–16, 238, 246–49, 252–54, 265–66, 268–69

glossolalia. See Holy Spirit
Gordon, A.J., 51, 54, 246
Gordon College and Seminary (Gordon-Conwell Theological Seminary), 204
Grace Theological Seminary, 31
Graham, Billy, 22, 28–30, 189, 203–4, 215, 218
— crusades, 1, 30
Green, Beriah, 140–41
Griffiths, H. McAllister, 208

Hardeman, N.B., 119, 121, 123–24, 126–27
Hargis, Billy James, 32
Haynes, B.F., 89
healing. See Holy Spirit
Henry, Carl F.H., 1, 30, 34, 195, 197, 217, 260, 264
hermeneutics, 42–43, 88, 90, 135, 144, 171, 184, 186, 189, 191, 193, 199, 232, 258, 266
— Anabaptist, 184, 187, 190
— Baconianism, Francis Bacon, 11, 115, 117–18, 122, 124–25, 129, 152, 253
— common sense, 7–8, 128, 237–38, 243
— Princeton theology, 14, 44, 49, 174–75, 177–78, 207, 237–38, 243, 257
— rationalism, reason, 58, 62, 80, 91–93, 115–17, 122, 127, 151, 185, 187, 190, 195, 200, 202, 258–59
— Scottish common sense realism, 11, 85, 93, 105–6, 115, 174, 177, 237, 266
Hershberger, Guy F., 195
Hill, Samuel S., 141, 257–58
Hindson, Ed, 32
history, 6, 8, 14, 17, 39, 57–58, 217
Hodge, A.A., 14
Hodge, Charles, 49, 184, 207
holiness. See sanctification
holiness movement, 2, 14, 25, 29, 42, 49, 71–108, 205, 247–48, 265, 268
— black holiness churches, 138
Hollenweger, W.J., 42
Holy Spirit, 117, 122–23, 128, 164–65, 167, 170
— baptism in the Holy Spirit, 39–43, 74, 224, 265
— gifts of the Spirit, 117
— glossolalia, speaking in tongues, 23, 37–39, 41, 43, 45–46, 70, 224, 266
— healing, 39–41, 44–46, 54, 63, 265
— prophetic guidance, 61, 65
— transformation of life, new life, 117, 168, 177
Hubbard, David, 254
Hughes, Richard, 2–3, 245, 259, 266

immortality, conditional, 65–66
individualism. *See* Americanization
Interdenominational Holiness Convention (IHC), 73
International Council on Biblical Inerrancy (ICBI), 186, 263
Israel, 9

Jesus Christ, 13, 39, 63, 82, 93, 116,
149, 184–85, 187, 194, 261
— His atonement, 23, 63, 175–76
— His priestly work in the heavenly
sanctuary, 65–67
Johnston, Robert K., 2
Jones, Bob, III, 31, 33
Jones, Bob, Sr., 22
justification, 41–42, 68, 75, 88, 111,
118, 121–24, 128, 138, 142, 145, 164,
169, 172, 223–24, 227–29, 233, 238,
245, 259, 263
— union with Christ, 229, 230

Kantzer, Kenneth, 186
Karlstadt, Andreas, 110, 121
Keswick Movement. *See* sanctification
Knox, John, 120, 209
Kraft, Charles, 198
Kraus, C. Norman, 3, 258, 265

Ladd, George, 15
Lard, Moses, 122
law, the, 64, 225
Lee, Mother Ann, 7
Lee, Robert G., 31
legalism. *See* ethics, individual
liberalism, 17, 23, 30, 32, 48, 89, 161,
174, 200, 208; anti-. *See* polemics
liberation, 135
Lightner, Robert, 32
Lindsell, Harold, 31, 72, 91, 94, 186
Lindsey, Hal, 5, 19
literalism, Biblical. *See* Scripture, interpretation of
liturgy, 83
Luther, Martin, 110, 112–13, 119–21,
124, 150, 173, 228, 232, 234, 256, 267
Lutheranism, 3, 14, 120–22, 138, 162,
169, 211, 222–44, 253, 263
— Lutheran orthodoxy, 81, 176, 222–39,
251, 265

— Lutheran pietism, 234
— Lutheran renewal (neo-Lutheranism),
235
— Lutheran theology, 64, 81, 161, 172,
178, 233
— Missouri Synod, 29, 222, 235

McDonnell, Kilian, 37
Machen, J. Gresham, 14, 49–50, 207,
209
McIntire, Carl, 29, 32, 211
McPherson, Aimee Semple, 48
Marsden, George, 2–3, 11, 19–20, 34,
245–46, 256, 262, 266
materialism. *See* Americanization
Mather, Cotton, 6
Mattox, F.W., 121
Mencken, H.L., 5
Mennonites, 3, 29, 184–200, 253, 265,
193–94
— General Conference Mennonite
Church, 193
— Mennonite Brethren Church, 193
— Mennonite Church, 193
Menzies, William, 43
Methodism, Methodist Church, 50, 60,
65, 75, 82–84, 89, 112, 114, 122, 140,
204, 211, 217, 247
— Black Methodism, 136, 138, 251, 258
Michaelson, Wesley, 175
Miley, 90–91
millenarian groups, 7
millenialism. *See* eschatology
Miller, William, 7–8, 58, 126
— Millerites, Millerite Movement, 7, 10,
57, 59, 60–61, 65
Mitchell, Henry, 144
modernism, anti-. *See* polemics
Moody, D.L., 16, 51, 89
— Moody Bible Institute, 29, 31, 204
— Moody Press, 15
moral code, strict. *See* ethics,
individual
Moral Majority, The, 32, 189, 192
Mormons, 7, 32, 37, 57, 109, 111, 129,
247
Moser, K.C., 124
Mouw, Richard, 218
Mullins, E.Y., 184–85
Murray, Andrew, 44, 54

Myland, D. Wesley, 45
mysticism, 7, 266

National Association of Evangelicals
(NAE), 1, 22, 29, 34, 39, 47, 50, 96,
143, 185, 197, 212, 215, 222–23, 246,
248–50, 263
National Black Evangelical Association
(NBEA), 143
nationalism. *See* Americanization
neo-evangelicalism. *See* evangelicalism
Nevin, John Williamson, 204–5
Niagara Bible Conference, 11
Nichol, John, 47–48
Nida, Eugene, 198
Niemczyk, Cassandra, 3, 266
Noll, Mark, 3, 109, 266–67
North American Presbyterian and Re-
formed Council, 211
Noyes, John Humphrey, 7

Ockenga, Harold John, 29–30
Odeneal, W. Clyde, 123
Ohlmann, Eric, 2–3, 265
Olbricht, Thomas H., 125
Oneida, 7
Orr, James, 184–85
Orthodox Presbyterian Church, 207–8,
210, 229, 268
orthodoxy, historic, 13–14, 22, 50, 81,
195, 208, 235, 251
— classical Christianity, 247, 264
— conservative Christianity, 32, 48, 161,
176, 263

pacifism, 194
Packer, J.I., 186
Palmer, Phoebe, 83–89, 92–93
Parham, Charles F., 37, 40, 42, 44, 53
Patton, Francis, 14
peace witness. *See* ethics, social
Pelagianism, 224, 228, 230
Pentecostal Fellowship of North America (PFNA), 40, 47
pentecostalism, 2–3, 13, 15, 25, 29–30,
32, 36–51, 111, 128–29, 142, 156,
205, 223, 229, 232, 237, 239, 247–48,
251, 253, 265, 268
— black pentecostalism, 136, 138,
142–43, 252

perfectionism. *See* sanctification
pietism, 3, 13, 23, 48, 50, 81, 152, 155,
157–58, 161–83, 191–93, 196, 231,
234, 237, 247, 254, 265, 268
piety, 48, 51, 157, 161, 205
Plymouth Brethren, 191
polemics, militancy, 24, 33, 162, 234
— anti-evolution, 10, 13, 22, 26, 119,
266
— anti-higher criticism of Bible, 10, 13,
24, 30–31
— anti-liberalism, 10–11, 13–14, 28,
30–31, 89, 91, 188, 193, 209–10, 218
— anti-modernism, 15, 25–26, 30, 48,
62, 76, 119, 127–29, 142, 210, 212,
217, 238, 246–47, 253, 269
— anti-Roman Catholicism, 238
— anti-secularization, 188
Pontoppidan, Eric, 177
Pope, William Burt, 90–91, 107
postmillennialism. *See* eschatology
practical theology, 161
premillennialism. *See* eschatology
Presbyterian, 114, 122, 129, 208–9,
211, 237
primitivism, Christian, 117–18, 149,
164
Princeton theology. *See* hermeneutics
prophetic guidance. *See* Holy Spirit
Puritans, Puritanism, 6, 13, 48, 50, 65,
112, 149–50, 152, 155, 157–58, 161,
172, 204–6, 224, 254

racial superiority, 141
racism. *See* Americanization
Ramm, Bernard, 49, 70, 246
rationalism. *See* hermeneutics
Rauschenbusch, Walter, 152
Reagan, Ronald, 5
reason. *See* hermeneutics
Reformed, 138, 252; self-consciously,
204–19, 265, 268
— Reformed theology, 14, 64, 68, 81,
83, 112, 121, 161–62, 195, 205, 207,
210, 212, 214, 216, 227, 258
— Reformed orthodoxy, 23, 68, 81, 176,
185, 187, 219, 226, 232, 237, 251,
254
Reformed Ecumenical Synod, 211
regeneration. *See* salvation, personal

restorationism, 2–3, 73, 109–29, 164,
233, 237, 239, 247–48, 253, 259, 266,
268
revivalism, renewal, 14, 16, 23, 25, 30,
48, 74–75, 84, 89, 143, 152, 156, 158,
178–79, 185, 188, 193, 204, 206, 248,
251, 253, 265
Rice, John R., 22, 27, 30–31
Riley, William B., 27–28
Robertson, Pat, 17, 192, 203
Roman Catholic, 120, 122, 138, 206,
224, 226, 232, 238
— anti-Roman Catholic. *See* polemics
Rowe, John F., 119–20, 123

Sabbatarianism, 65
— seventh day Sabbath, 61, 65, 67
salvation, personal; regeneration, 13,
23, 31, 41–42, 78–80, 87, 90, 93, 95,
116, 143, 152, 156, 172, 175, 185,
230–31, 262, 265
— conversion, 13–14, 48, 67, 74, 88,
117–18, 139–40, 151, 156–57, 164,
166, 173, 178, 190, 195, 198, 206,
218, 261–62, 265
— individual salvation, 87, 151, 156,
167, 193, 261–63, 265
— new life in Christ, 174, 193, 262
— religious experience, 149, 152, 157
sanctification, 40–41, 63, 68, 74–75,
118, 145, 150, 155–57, 178, 206, 218,
228–31, 234, 238, 245, 263
— disciplined obedience, 149, 168, 190,
194, 261
— entire sanctification, 72–74, 84–85,
88, 90–91, 95, 265
— holy living, holiness, 13–14, 17, 23,
30, 39–40, 64, 74, 111, 143, 156, 164,
166, 173, 193, 223, 230–32, 237–39,
247, 251, 253, 261, 263
— Keswick "higher life," 30, 51
— perfectionism, 50, 76, 155, 224
Sandeen, Ernest, 26, 34
Schaff, Philip, 205
Schowalter, G.H.P., 125
Scofield, C.I., 8
— Scofield Reference Bible, notes, 11,
15
Scottish common sense realism. *See*
hermeneutics

Scripture, authority of, 12–13, 23, 58,
65, 77, 78, 81–83, 90–91, 93, 109,
117–18, 127, 142, 144, 149, 158, 170,
175–76, 185–87, 190, 199, 234, 238,
261–63, 265
— Bible-believing, 26, 137, 143
— high view of, 11, 62, 68, 110, 118,
154, 158, 175, 189, 199, 232, 261
Scripture, inerrancy of, 13, 22, 24–25,
27, 29, 30–32, 48–50, 62, 68, 72, 94,
127, 129, 135, 142, 162, 175–77, 182,
186, 189–90, 199, 201, 235–38, 248,
253, 266
Scripture, interpretation of, 15, 65, 74,
88–89, 123, 177, 259
— Biblical "facts," an intellectual understanding, 115–16, 236, 266
— Biblical literalism, 14, 24–26, 30, 62,
119, 128, 143, 184, 195, 232–33, 266
— Biblical theology, 95, 125
— private interpretation, 171, 217
— Scripture of Christ, The
— Word of God obeyed, The, 67, 123,
176
Scripture, sufficiency of, 78–81, 90, 93,
95, 118
Second Coming. *See* eschatology
sectarians, 149
secularization, 17; anti-. *See* polemics
self-reliance, 111, 113, 116–18, 124, 127
separation from the world. *See* ethics,
individual
separatism (from other churches), 13,
15, 28, 30–33, 164, 170, 191, 212
— alienation from mainstream
churches, 28, 31–32, 215, 248
— antipluralistic, 210
— particularism, 62
— sectarianism, 150, 193, 206, 212, 231,
233
Sernett, Milton, 2–3, 246, 265
Seymour, William J., 142
Shakers, 7, 37, 57, 60
Shepherd, J.W., 120
Sider, Ronald, 175, 258
Simons, Menno, 184, 188, 191
Simpson, A.B., 42, 51, 54
Sine, Thomas, 175
Smedes, Lewis B., 218
Smith, Joseph, 7

Smith, Timothy, 12, 261–62
social gospel, social justice, social
  reform. *See* ethics, social
soul sleep, 61
Spener, Philip Jakob, 161, 164, 166,
  168–70, 173, 177–78, 228
Staples, Russell, 266
Stone, Barton W., 113–14
Stonehouse, Ned B., 215
Strong, A.H., 184
Strong, James, 186
Sweet, Leonard, 109, 254
Sword of the Lord, The, 22
Synan, Vinson, 49

Talbot Theological Seminary, 31
Torrey, Reuben A., 54, 89

Van Til, Cornelius, 211, 215

Warfield, Benjamin B., 14, 44, 47, 49,
  50, 184–85, 190, 207
Watson, Richard, 90–91, 107
Webber, Robert, 175

Weber, Timothy, 1–3, 109, 245, 256,
  262, 264, 266
Weborg, John, 246, 265
Wells, David, 1, 257
Wenger, John C., 195
Wesley, John, 50, 74–76, 78–90, 120,
  179, 217, 256–57
Wesleyan theology, 39, 49, 63–64, 73,
  76, 79, 89–90, 155, 157–58, 178, 195,
  204, 232, 252, 254
— Wesleyan Methodists, 29, 123
Westminster Theological Seminary, 50,
  208–10, 212
Wheaton College, 51, 204
White, Ellen Harmon, 57, 60–61, 65–66
Wiley, H. Orton, 83, 91, 93
Witherspoon, John, 209
Woodworth-Etter, Mary B., 46
World Evangelical Fellowship (WEF),
  248

Youth for Christ, 28, 215

Zwingli, Huldreich, 110, 119–21